CLINICAL SPORT PSYCHOLOGY

Frank Gardner, PhD, ABPP

La Salle University

Zella Moore, PsyD

Manhattan College

Human Kinetics

Library of Congress Cataloging-in-Publication Data

Gardner, Frank L., 1953-
    Clinical sport psychology / Frank L. Gardner, Zella E. Moore.
        p. cm.
    Includes bibliographical references and index.
    ISBN 0-7360-5305-0 (hard cover)
    1. Sports--Psychological aspects. 2. Athletes--Counseling of. I. Moore, Zella E., 1975- II. Title.
    GV706.4.G35 2005
    796.01—dc22
                                        2005005750

ISBN: 0-7360-5305-0

The Web addresses cited in this text were current as of June 3, 2005, unless otherwise noted.

Acquisitions Editors: Amy N. Clocksin and Myles Schrag; **Developmental Editors:** R. Chris Johns and Renee Thomas Pyrtel; **Assistant Editors:** Michelle M. Rivera and Kevin Matz; **Copyeditor:** Jocelyn Engman; **Proofreader:** Anne Rogers; **Indexer:** Betty Frizzéll; **Permission Manager:** Dalene Reeder; **Graphic Designer:** Fred Starbird; **Graphic Artist:** Dawn Sills; **Photo Managers:** Kelly J. Huff, Jody Roginson, and Sarah Ritz; **Cover Designer:** Robert Reuther; **Photographer (interior):** © Human Kinetics, unless otherwise noted; **Art Manager:** Kelly Hendren; **Illustrator:** Al Wilborn; **Printer:** Edwards Brothers

Printed in the United States of America   10   9   8   7   6   5   4   3   2   1

Human Kinetics
Web site: www.HumanKinetics.com

United States: Human Kinetics
P.O. Box 5076
Champaign, IL 61825-5076
800-747-4457
e-mail: humank@hkusa.com

Canada: Human Kinetics
475 Devonshire Road Unit 100
Windsor, ON N8Y 2L5
800-465-7301 (in Canada only)
e-mail: orders@hkcanada.com

Europe: Human Kinetics
107 Bradford Road
Stanningley
Leeds LS28 6AT, United Kingdom
+44 (0) 113 255 5665
e-mail: hk@hkeurope.com

Australia: Human Kinetics
57A Price Avenue
Lower Mitcham, South Australia 5062
08 8277 1555
e-mail: liaw@hkaustralia.com

New Zealand: Human Kinetics
Division of Sports Distributors NZ Ltd.
P.O. Box 300 226 Albany
North Shore City
Auckland
0064 9 448 1207
e-mail: info@humankinetics.co.nz

This book is dedicated to those who are no longer with me to see this accomplishment: To my grandparents who could only dream 100 years ago when they stood on Ellis Island; to my father who instilled the dream in me; and to Dr. Julia Vane from Hofstra University, my first and most long-standing professional role model, who made me believe that I could attain the dream for myself.

Frank

With my deepest respect, I dedicate this work to those I love so deeply, both living and those who have passed. To my unbelievable parents and brothers, and to my truest friends who will never be far from my heart. Thank you all for teaching me to be the person I am today.

Zella

Contents

Preface

This text addresses the task of developing an empirically informed and integrated approach to sport psychology. We hope that it promotes discussion, provides guidelines for effective practice, spurs future research, and creates a buzz of excitement. It is our fervent wish that this text helps cultivate clinical sport psychology as a defined practice emphasis in professional psychology and fills an important need for the sport psychologist, the clinical psychologist, and students of both disciplines. Many sport psychology books narrowly subdivide assessment and intervention, research and practice, and interventions for performance enhancement and for psychological well-being. However, such texts do not integrate the clinical and sport sciences to combine their theory, research, and practice information into a coherent theoretical model.

The practice of sport psychology is not based upon a single issue, problem area, or observation, but requires the practitioner to use a wide lens when viewing the athlete and the issues that culminate in consultation. The practitioner and student are often left to their own devices to integrate theory, research, and practice into clear principles to guide interventions for the full range of athlete issues. Unfortunately, practice decisions often evolve from anecdotal reports and an oral tradition based on presentations from those assumed to be masters. This is not the case in this text.

Like the authors of many textbooks, we began this book because we believed there was something missing in the texts available to practitioners and students. This void became clearest to us during our teaching of graduate courses in both clinical psychology and sport psychology, and while supervising new practitioners. Because current texts typically focus on one problem area (such as performance enhancement or career termination), one modality of intervention (such as psychological skills training), or one aspect of professional practice (such as assessment), most of the textbooks currently available do not suit the reality and complexity of real-world practice.

In undertaking this book, we also considered the needs of practicing psychologists engaging or interested in the new APA practice emphasis in sport psychology. Many psychologists feel trapped by the constraints of managed care within traditional practice settings and are seeking new horizons to utilize their skills and knowledge in non-health-care settings. In addition, seasoned sport psychologists have discussed for many years how texts and professional presentations reinforce a pseudoscientific and bisected approach to sport psychology. Thus, in this text we have attempted to step out of the classroom and address the practitioners on the front line who need guidelines in assessment, classification, case conceptualization, and intervention planning and implementation. We believe that our long history in the trenches of professional practice in sport psychology allows us to target the complex issues confronting practitioners, and hopefully allows us to present a more focused, efficient, and empirically informed means of providing professional services.

A primary value guiding this text is that the effective and ethical practice of any psychological specialty, including clinical sport psychology, must remain sensitive to the demands of different referral contexts and populations. We have long held that intervention decisions in any scientific and professional discipline cannot be based solely on the education, training, and philosophy of the practitioner, but must be based on the referral question and context. In writing this text, we kept in mind the caution of (FG) the first author's grandfather: "If all you have is a hammer, everything begins to look like a nail." In this regard, we have attempted to present the reality that our athletes have many needs, are of many personalities, and are embedded in organizations and settings of varying complexities. Thus, intervention efforts must address many factors, and practitioners must engage in the appropriate intervention to best meet the complex needs of each athlete.

We strove to address the wide range of athlete concerns in a manner consistent with the integration of science and practice for which the profession of psychology has long been known. In addition, we organized our text to reflect how theory and research direct proper assessment, and how effective assessment directs the utilization of empirically informed interventions specific for differing athlete needs.

Another core value behind this text is the critical notion that psychological interventions cannot *directly* affect outcomes. That is, the intervention must target the *process* that is involved in the development of the problem or issue to *indirectly* lead to desired outcomes. As such, understanding the mechanism of action (also referred to as the mechanism of change) inherent in an intervention approach is critical to correctly utilizing the associated strategies. For example, the physician does not treat pneumonia, or even the signs and symptoms of pneumonia. Rather, the physician treats the underlying infection that causes the illness. The mechanism of action of the prescribed medication is the elimination of the bacterial infection, unlike the palliative care of over-the-counter medications. Whether the athlete presents with severe emotional disturbance or preperformance jitters, practitioners must understand the associated underlying psychological processes in order to increase the well-being and behavioral functioning of our athletes.

Finally, our own professional journeys have shaped this text. In our 30 years of combined experience in all aspects of clinical sport psychology, with a full range of individual and organizational clients, we have developed a strong belief in the need for an integrated, holistic approach that goes well beyond the traditional models in the field of sport psychology. Our professional experiences working with professional teams, collegiate athletes, Olympic athletes, and recreational participants have taught us over and over that a narrow focus on performance enhancement is inappropriate, is ultimately not valued by the majority of athletes, and often does not provide the services truly required to assist our athletes. One of (FG) the first author's first consultations in professional sports involved an athlete referred by management for lethargic performance and practice effort, poor work habits as evidenced by being out of shape, and a negative, uncaring attitude. In his excitement to provide performance enhancement, FG ignored his foundational training in clinical psychology, unquestioningly accepted the referral presentation of others, and immediately (without thorough assessment) developed a psychological skills training package that included positive imagery, goal setting, arousal control, and self-talk modification. After a seemingly brilliant presentation of the rationale of this intervention protocol, the athlete, who listened intently, said, "That sounds great, but when can we talk about my wife who is threatening to leave me and the shortness of breath, intense anxiety, racing heart, and overwhelming feelings that make me think I am going crazy?" It very quickly became apparent that the athlete's symptoms were consistent with a diagnosis of panic disorder (thus explaining all of the management referral concerns). True efforts at performance enhancement in this circumstance required both the amelioration of the panic disorder and marital counseling, which ultimately helped the athlete return to premorbid all-star status. This event was FG's first major learning experience in clinical sport psychology and was in many respects the genesis of this text.

The previous example reflects the need for a text that respects the complex psychological needs of the athlete while also considering the sport context. Indeed, to our excitement, we have frequently been approached by our students as well as by sport psychology conference attendees requesting guidance in developing an integrated approach to practice that puts the *psychology* back into *sport psychology*. We hope that our text significantly contributes to this obvious need.

We have written this text for practitioners and students from all related educational backgrounds, including sport psychology, clinical and counseling psychology, and the sport sciences. The chapters are organized to systematically approach the relevant theory, research, and practice that make up *clinical sport psychology*. In part I, Theoretical and Scientific Foundations, we integrate relevant knowledge in both clinical and sport science to provide a foundation for practice in clinical sport psychology. In part II, Assessment and Classification, we provide an overview of assessment in clinical sport psychology and emphasize systematically collecting the data necessary to classify athlete issues in a new and exciting way. In part III, Interventions in Clinical Sport Psychology, we present treatment guidelines for the full range of issues confronting the practicing clinical sport psychologist, offer both innovative and empirically informed interventions for a variety of client problem areas, and discuss how to organize information into a cohesive case formulation. Finally, in part IV, Special Considerations, we discuss issues such as professional ethics, and supervision and professional development. We are proud of each and every chapter, and fully believe that both practitioners and students alike will greatly benefit from the expanded scope of discussion.

Acknowledgments

This book is the result of years of hard work on both of our parts. As we have each been students, practitioners, and teachers in both clinical and sport psychology, our efforts have been to consider, organize, and finally construct a text that can help practitioners and students in a multitude of ways. The book is most clearly the product of what we have learned from our athletes and our students. We have certainly learned from all of you, and we offer our heartfelt thanks. We have also developed together and have greatly enjoyed writing with and learning from each other. We are both better professionals and people for the experience.

Many others deserve our thanks. We must first send an overwhelming thanks to our families and friends for their sacrifice, support, and unconditional love. Second, we thank our friend and colleague Andrew Wolanin, whose passion for the science of psychology, inquisitive nature, and undying curiosity are a true inspiration. You have been a catalyst for our thinking and an unmatched friend. We also thank our professional family of students, faculty, and administration at La Salle University, especially within the departments of psychology and athletics, and Zella's new professional family at Manhattan College. We also thank the dedicated staff at Human Kinetics, especially Amy Clocksin, Myles Schrag, Chris Johns, Michelle Rivera, and Renee Thomas Pyrtel, for their guidance, unwavering support and encouragement, and also for their patience during the myriad of requests for one more deadline extension.

Lastly, we thank each and every one of our professional colleagues for making this exciting project possible and available to the next generation of sport psychologists. We can only hope that your journey in clinical sport psychology is as rewarding as ours has been.

Theoretical and Scientific Foundations

We believe that this text is markedly different than other texts on sport psychology research and practice. As such, prior to an in-depth discussion of assessment, intervention, case formulation, and special topics, part I of this text first provides a context for what *clinical sport psychology* actually is and how it is different than more traditional sport psychology practice. Chapter 1 provides an overview of the history of sport psychology, discusses the historical development of traditional theory and practice, and presents how clinical sport psychology differs.

Chapter 2 is critical to understanding clinical sport psychology. This chapter introduces the Integrative Model of Athletic Performance (IMAP), which is a new way of thinking about the psychological processes that go into attaining and maintaining sport expertise. Bridging the gap between clinical and sport science, this model connects athletic performance, basic psychological processes, and relevant empirical findings in exciting new ways. Far from traditional explanations of sport processes, the IMAP is based on cutting-edge theory and lays the foundation for the discussion of assessment, intervention, and case formulation in clinical sport psychology.

CHAPTER 1

Introduction to Clinical Sport Psychology

Why another book on sport psychology? Numerous available texts discuss practice issues and opportunities (Van Raalte & Brewer, 2002), summarize current theory and research (Singer, Hausenblas, & Janelle, 2001), provide specific suggestions for athletic performance enhancement (Hardy, Jones, & Gould, 1996), discuss implications of sport psychology for sports medicine (Nostofsky & Zaichkowsky, 2001), and provide specialty information regarding assessment (Nideffer & Sagal, 2001). Upon reviewing the available texts on sport psychology, we reached several conclusions that ultimately drove us to write this text for a professional audience. While we could glean a holistic approach to sport psychology from select chapters and articles across several sources, we found that the field was missing a single comprehensive text that could provide an integrative approach to sport psychology.

We hope that this text challenges the reader to view the athlete seeking or needing psychological services somewhat differently than typically presented. In addition, rather than adopting a narrow focus on the relationship between mental skills and performance, this text affords the contemporary clinical sport psychologist an opportunity to approach the athlete in a broad, integrative manner that relates psychological processes, psychological functions, and behavioral outcomes in the sport milieu. Further, we hope that this text spurs the sport practitioner to adopt an evidence-based methodology that leads to a healthy skepticism regarding current professional models and results in thoughtful consideration of alternative models based on empirically informed data.

The broad field of sport psychology is missing a contemporary text providing evidence-driven models for understanding, conceptualizing, assessing, and intervening with athletes that pres-

ent an array of personal, clinical, and performance concerns. In response to this absence, this book intends to provide a model of sport psychology that

- understands athletic performance in the context of recent empirical research in both athletic and nonathletic domains of human performance,

- adopts a holistic and comprehensive practice involving not only the enhancement of athletic performance but also the personal development and psychological well-being of the athlete, and

- adopts a style of practice consistent with the methodology most closely associated with evidence-based approaches to clinical and counseling psychology. This methodology supports the belief that appropriate professional practice is directly informed by empirical research and follows a logical sequence of thorough, evidence-based assessment, case conceptualization, and empirically informed intervention (when available).

Thus, this text presents a contemporary approach to sport psychology, which we call *clinical sport psychology,* which adopts a new scope, style, and model of practice (see figure 1.1). We hope this book is of value to clinical and counseling psychologists considering expanding their practice to include sport psychology and performance enhancement, and to sport psychology professionals who wish to consider an alternative model of conceptualizing and intervening with athletic clientele. However, before introducing the approach we call *clinical sport psychology,* let's consider how traditional sport psychology has evolved so that it now requires such a holistic and comprehensive model.

Context of practice	Scope of practice	Style of practice
• Based on an integration of research in both clinical and sport psychology	• Includes performance enhancement and personal psychological well-being	• Based on a foundation of empirical research informing practice

Figure 1.1   Description of the clinical sport psychology model.

History of Sport Psychology

Beginning with Norman Triplett's work with competitive cyclists in the 1890s and continuing with Coleman Griffith's work in the 1920s and '30s on the psychology of coaching, the study of sport psychology has a long and rich history (Anshel, 1990). During the 1950s and '60s, sport psychology as a discipline was primarily found in departments of physical education and exercise science, and issues relating to motor learning and development dominated sport psychology research. From this research perspective and professional interest, the North American Society for the Psychology of Sport and Physical Activity (NASPSPA) was founded in 1967 to promote and disseminate basic research on the psychology of sport and physical activity (Wiggins, 1984). As both the theory and practice of social-cognitive theory took hold in professional psychology (Bandura, 1977), interest grew regarding the cognitive, affective, and behavioral strategies athletes utilize to optimize competitive performance. This interest led to an increasing focus on the direct application of sport psychology services, and began the evolutionary process of bringing sport psychology into the mainstream of professional psychology. As an applied profession providing a specialized service, sport psychology has gained both professional and consumer recognition and acceptance over the past 25 to 30 years. We refer readers interested in a comprehensive history of sport psychology to an excellent chapter by Williams and Straub (1998).

Traditional Definitions and Scope of Practice

Sport psychology can be defined by its overarching concern with the psychosocial factors that influence both participation and performance in sport and exercise and that derive or emanate from such participation and performance (Williams & Straub, 1998). Basic research in sport psychology includes diverse topic areas such as achievement motivation; group dynamics and team cohesion; coaching education, style, and methods; children's sport; parent involvement; fan experience; sport violence; leadership; exercise and psychological well-being; issues and benefits of physical activity; and characteristics of peak athletic performance (Cox, 2002). In addition, numerous scientific and popular books and professional journals focusing exclusively on sport and exercise issues have appeared over the past two decades.

Applied sport psychology is a phrase that has evolved over the last two decades to differentiate the application of sport psychology principles from the science of developing and refining such principles (Cox, 2002). In 1985, the Association for the Advancement of Applied Sport Psychology (AAASP) was founded to bring together professionals from both psychology and sport science to promote the study of applied sport psychology (Williams & Straub, 1998). In 1988, the United States Olympic Committee (USOC) established a registry of sport psychology professionals that differentiated sport psychologists by educational background and professional activities. The registry categorized sport psychologists as educational, clinical, or research sport psychologists (Murphy, 1995) in order to provide information on who was trained to provide a given service.

Educational sport psychologist identified practitioners with education, training, and experience in providing psychoeducation for performance enhancement. *Clinical sport psychologist* identified practitioners whose professional backgrounds allowed them to counsel athletes using clinical methodology to enhance psychological well-being (such as ameliorating clinical issues). *Research sport psychologist* identified sport psychologists whose educational background directed them toward research and evaluation in sport psychology. While professionals were encouraged to apply for more than one designation if appropriate, this categorization initiated the tendency to both oversimplify and artificially compartmentalize sport psychology into educational (enhancing performance) and clinical (treating serious psychological disorders).

As a result of these categories, two unfortunate misconceptions evolved that are still largely in place. The first is that an athlete's performance concerns can be readily differentiated as those due to major psychopathology and those due to insufficient mental skills. Following directly from the first, the second misconception is that sport psychology professionals trained in clinical or counseling psychology are suited to *treat* the former while those trained in exercise science are trained to *consult* with the latter. This overly simplistic dichotomy has resulted in intense debates regarding the educational background and practice competencies required for the ethical (and even legal) practice of sport psychology (Gardner, 1991; Silva, 1989).

Certification and New Standards

The 1990s saw an upsurge in research, professional interest, and consumer acceptance of sport psychology. In 1991, AAASP implemented guidelines for recognizing individuals (AAASP-certified consultants) who achieved minimum standards of education and training in applied sport psychology (Zaichkowsky & Perna, 1992). In theory, this certification ensured that individuals practicing applied sport psychology possessed the basic education, training, and experience necessary to provide such services. While some have hailed these standards as a major step in the professionalization of sport psychology (Zaichkowsky & Perna, 1992), AAASP certification has not been without its detractors, who have questioned the fairness and appropriateness of applying those standards to professionals educated and trained in the sport sciences (Anshel, 1992), the utility of AAASP certification for professionals seeking employment in sport psychology, and the relevance of certification for the consumer seeking qualified practitioners of sport psychology (Gardner, Taylor, Zinnser, & Ravizza, 2000, October). As a direct consequence of AAASP certification, the USOC abandoned its previous registry standards and instead required AAASP certification and American Psychological Association (APA) membership for inclusion in its registry. As a result of requiring APA membership, the USOC thus accepted and required adherence to APA's Ethics Code (American Psychological Association [APA], 1992, 2002).

The debate regarding AAASP certification and its purpose, utility, and function may be best understood by addressing the definition of applied sport psychology most often adopted and utilized by its proponents. It has been suggested that the primary mission of applied sport psychology is to identify and understand theories and techniques that can be applied to sport and exercise to enhance athletic performance and promote physical activity (Williams & Straub, 1998). In fact, supervised practice hours involving nonperformance issues relating to athletes and sport participation (such as psychotherapy with athletes suffering from eating disorders) are not acceptable hours toward AAASP certification. Thus, in practice, *applied sport psychology* has become synonymous with *performance enhancement,* or what was formerly known as educational sport psychology described earlier. Further, performance enhancement has itself become synonymous with the cognitive-behavioral self-control strategies commonly referred to as psychological skills training (PST), which are theorized by many to improve competitive performance (Weinberg & Williams, 1998). These intervention strategies typically include goal setting, imagery, self-talk, arousal regulation, or some combination of these interventions.

In 2000, the Division of Exercise and Sport Psychology (Division 47) of APA petitioned the APA Committee on Recognition of Specialties and Proficiencies in Professional Psychology (CRSPPP) to recognize and designate sport psychology as a proficiency (also referred to as a practice emphasis) (APA, 2003). This petition had two main purposes. First, developing uniform standards for this proficiency would ensure the public that licensed psychologists practicing sport psychology (and thus legally referring to themselves as sport psychologists) would be properly educated and trained. Second, licensed psychologists (or those in training) desiring to practice in this proficiency would have clear guidance as to necessary standards for education and training. In fact, this petition recommended that the proficiency in sport psychology be measured by both examination and completion of 500 h of supervised practice.

In January of 2003, the APA Council of Representatives accepted the recommendation of CRSPPP and officially designated sport psychology as a proficiency (practice emphasis) within professional psychology (APA, 2003). Possibly the most important feature of this proficiency is its definition of sport psychology. The Division 47 proficiency petition defined sport psychology as a discipline "concerned with 1) Enhancing performance and satisfaction through the systematic development of psychological skills, 2) Optimizing the well-being of athletes, 3) Dealing with organizational and systemic issues in sport settings, and 4) Understanding the social and developmental issues related to sport participation." As can be seen, the implications of the proposed proficiency fundamentally differ from the implications of AAASP certification, in that the proficiency broadens the definition of the practice of sport psychology.

The definition of sport psychology utilized in the proficiency goes well beyond the definition most often attached to applied sport psychology. In fact, the sport psychologist practicing within the proficiency's definition has a much broader scope than when practicing within the boundaries of the AAASP definition. The proficiency's comprehensive approach clearly includes helping athletes enhance performance *as well as* helping athletes enhance their psychosocial health, development, and well-being.

Due to applied sport psychology's roots in both exercise science and psychology, tensions have understandably developed regarding which practitioner is qualified to provide which service to which client (Gardner, 1991; Silva, 1989). While this debate has often focused on educational background (exercise science versus clinical and counseling psychology), the issue is really how practitioners conceptualize both the *purpose* and *scope* of the discipline as well as the *manner* or *style* in which to apply the scientific body of

knowledge (Gardner, Taylor, Zinnser, & Ravizza, 2000, October). In many respects, the definition of sport psychology in the APA proficiency merges the old USOC designations of educational and clinical sport psychology into a more encompassing description of the direct service application of sport psychology.

Development of Theory and Practice

The acceptable definition of applied sport psychology has in many ways been the unspoken center of ongoing interdisciplinary tension. While the professional discourse has often focused on practitioner training and competence, the issue often lost in the debate is finding the best way to help the athletes. From this perspective, it is necessary to expand the discussion from narrowly considering the purpose or scope of practice to considering the style of practice.

As noted earlier, traditionally applied sport psychology has adopted a scope of practice defined by its focus on performance enhancement. It has also promoted a practice style that is essentially an educational endeavor to teach athletes psychological skills that, in addition to physical and technical skills, are believed to be effective and necessary for optimal athletic performance (Hardy, Jones, & Gould, 1996).

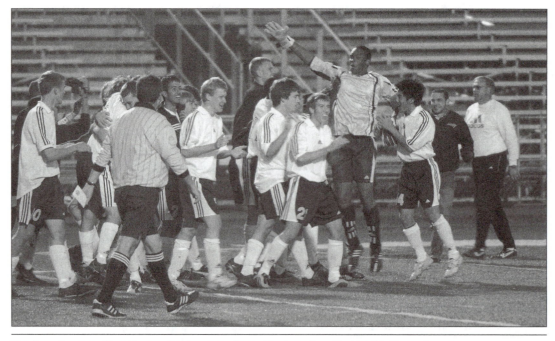

Hard work pays off as these athletes experience the joy of optimal athletic performance.

From this perspective, the practitioner of applied sport psychology does not practice as a psychologist, rather primarily practices as a mental coach or performance consultant. Let's review the historical development of both the scope and style of the practice of sport psychology as currently embodied in AAASP certification criteria. Sport psychology grew dramatically in the '60s and '70s as part of the social-cognitive revolution in professional psychology (Bandura, 1977), which was part of the second wave in behavioral psychology. The first wave, with two distinct wings, developed in the 1950s and '60s. One wing, represented by the traditions of John B. Watson (Watson & Rayner, 1920) and B.F. Skinner (1953), focused on laboratory studies of classical and operant processes. The second wing emphasized the same empiricism, but sought to develop stimulus-response (S-R) psychology into structured, empirically grounded procedures to be used with clinical problems. This wing is best associated with Eysenk, Wolpe, Rachman, and Lazarus (Dougher & Hayes, 2000).

The second wave of behavioral psychology was marked by the social-cognitive revolution in psychology as embodied by Bandura (1977), Mahoney (1974), and Meichenbaum (1977). During this time, the field of sport psychology was beginning to define itself, and adopted the social-cognitive perspective. During this time, many of the techniques of applied sport psychology developed from the early skills-based formulations of cognitive-behavioral interventions, as most clearly articulated by Donald Meichenbaum in his formulation of self-instructional training and stress inoculation training (1977). In this model, psychological intervention was a psychoeducational process aimed at the development of specific behaviors that could enhance an individual's ability to cope with particular life stressors and to ultimately enhance daily functioning. Human difficulties were conceptualized as the result of behavioral excesses, behavioral deficits, or interfering behaviors. Coping behaviors, described as skills, were thought to increase functional behavior and limit dysfunctional behavior and its associated negative affective responses. These early skills-based cognitive-behavioral interventions were delivered in a structured, psychoeducational format (which included rationale, skill-learning, and practice phases) and demonstrated some early empirical support in areas such as test and public-speaking anxiety (DiGiuseppe, McGowan, Sutton-Simon, & Gardner, 1990; Gardner, 1980), pain control (Turk, Meichenbaum, & Genest, 1983), and anger management (Novaco, 1976). Sport psychology's focus on psychological skills training came from the skills-based perspective most notably linked to Meichenbaum (1977). Early sport psychologists slightly tailored Meichenbaum's interventions to make them more specific for athletic performance enhancement. Yet, despite vast development and evolution within behavioral psychology, these interventions have continued as the dominant theoretical and applied models for enhancing athletic performance. Although other areas of professional psychology have evolved beyond these early principles, sport psychology has resisted this change. This resistance is at least partially because such approaches at least intuitively seem logical, especially when considering correlational research that suggests that athletes preparing for competition naturally use techniques such as goal setting, imagery, self-talk, and arousal regulation (Hardy et al., 1996).

In the intervening years, the second wave of behavioral psychology evolved rapidly. In the later stages of this second wave, considerations of schematic content and pathological aspects of cognitive processes (Beck, 1976) predominated and largely replaced the idea of cognitive activity (i.e., self-talk) as nonverbal behavior to be simply unlearned and relearned. Recently, a third wave of behavioral psychology has emerged, often referred to as clinical behavior analysis, neobehaviorism, or contextual behaviorism. During this wave, alternative views of cognitive-affective processes (including aspects of the previous waves) have been presented and innovative interventions have emerged (see figure 1.2).

First wave	Second wave	Third wave
• Operant and classical models	• Cognitive models	• Neo-behavioral contextual models (acceptance and mindfulness theories)

Figure 1.2 Three waves of behavioral psychology.

Such third-wave interventions include acceptance and commitment therapy (ACT) (Hayes, Strosahl, & Wilson, 1999), mindfulness-based cognitive therapy (MBCT) (Segal, Williams, & Teasdale, 2002), dialectical behavior therapy (DBT) (Linehan, Cochran, & Kehrer, 2001), integrative behavioral couples therapy (Doss, Jones, & Christensen, 2002), functional analytic psychotherapy (FAP) (Kohlenberg & Tsai, 1995), and cognitive-behavioral analysis system of psychotherapy (CBASP) (McCullough, 2000). In essence, the third wave of behavioral psychology "emphasizes such issues as acceptance, mindfulness, cognitive defusion, dialectics, values, spirituality, and relationship" (Hayes, Masuda, & De May, 2003, p. 70).

It appears that the field of sport psychology has simply not noticed the recent advances in behavioral psychology, beginning with the second-wave developments of Beck (1976) and continuing with the present third-wave enhancements in behavioral interventions. The literature in applied sport psychology has remained largely fixed on the early second-wave skills-based conceptualizations of human performance and its dysfunction; performance enhancement interventions have gone practically unchanged.

Making this more problematic, as detailed in chapter 5, the assumptions made throughout the years about the efficacy of skills-based (self-control) interventions for enhancing athletic performance appear to have significant shortcomings (Moore, 2003b; Moore & Gardner, 2005). Sport psychology has somewhat stagnated by limiting its intervention strategies to early cognitive-behavioral interventions, while other professional psychology domains have evolved well beyond these early models to incorporate an expanding number of problem-specific methodologies (Hayes et al., 1999; Nathan & Gorman, 2002).

Perusal of the numerous articles, chapters, and books on the goals, strategies, and techniques for enhancing athletic performance using the skills-based approach (Hardy et al., 1996) suggests that the following core components and suppositions make up this traditional style of practice:

- **Entrance.** The practitioner presenting herself as a sport psychology consultant (or possibly as a mental coach, a performance consultant, or as another nonpsychology term) attempts to differentiate her work from that of the traditional clinical or counseling psychologist and explains the nature, importance, and relationship of psychological skills in performance excellence. Some

(but certainly not all) practitioners suggest that using the term *psychologist* is inappropriate, contributes to a negative (and counterproductive) view of sport psychology (Halliwell, 1990; Rotella, 1990), and creates barriers to effective consultation (Ravizza, 1988; Gordon, 1990).

- **Service Delivery.** The consultant typically works with either individuals or groups in either contract-defined time limits or extended open-ended agreements. The consultant identifies performance goals, uses interviews (and possibly sport-specific questionnaires) to ascertain knowledge of psychological skills and personal strengths and weaknesses, and then teaches the necessary mental skills in a reasonably sequential manner. Typically, as described by Meichenbaum in his early clinical work (1977), psychological skills training for performance enhancement involves phases of didactic presentation, skill development, and finally practice and application of specific cognitive-behavioral self-control strategies. There is often an ongoing or end-point evaluation of service effectiveness measured by client satisfaction or performance improvement.

- **Suppositions.** It is typically assumed that most athletes are reasonably well-functioning individuals who are more or less homogeneous, as defined by their desire or need to enhance athletic performance (Vealey, 1994a). It is also generally assumed that the athlete will voluntarily bring forward any relevant personal and psychological issues relating to transitional concerns, developmental issues, personality (i.e., enduring behavioral characteristics), and affective-behavioral symptomatology. Conversely, if the athlete does not disclose such issues, it is often assumed such issues do not exist (or that their presence would not affect successful skills-based performance enhancement). Similarly, it is often presumed that a consultant who focuses on more personal issues risks being seen as a shrink, and thus such issues should be avoided, especially at the beginning of service delivery. Further, it is commonly believed that the skills-based (self-control) approach to performance enhancement is the only substantive and logical means of enhancing performance and that more therapeutic-based approaches are for severe psychopathology only (Silva, 1989). Finally, some practitioners often incorrectly assume that the evidence accumulated to date empirically supports each of the fundamental psychological skills as efficacious tools for performance enhancement (Hardy et al., 1996). These unfortunate suppositions are further discussed throughout this text.

Clinical Sport Psychology

What this book presents is a very different model for the practice of sport psychology: *clinical sport psychology*. In contrast to the common suppositions of traditional sport psychology, this new model suggests a comprehensive approach to practice that is similar to that seen in other disciplines of professional psychology. This new approach is driven by empirical findings in the clinical and sport sciences and follows the methodological traditions of behavioral psychology.

In the sport psychology literature, it has been incorrectly stated that clinical and counseling psychology are best defined by and limit themselves to providing service to the mentally disordered (Silva, 1989). In actual practice, clinical and counseling psychology professionally apply scientific knowledge and techniques from all domains of psychological science to the assessment and intervention of individuals desiring to enhance their daily functioning in numerous life domains (such as work, school, family, and recreation). Clinical and counseling psychology from this perspective are not simply content areas, but a professional attitude and style that improve human behavior by applying scientific principles and methods derived from the cognitive-affective, learning, social, and developmental content areas. This tradition in clinical and counseling psychology may best be seen in the historical development of cognitive behavioral therapy (CBT), with its empirical foundation and applied focus on specific behaviors in need of development or modification. If we overlap the content fields of clinical and sport science with the traditional focus and professional attitudes of clinical and counseling psychology, we will have constructed a subspecialty that can best be described as *clinical sport psychology*. Encompassing both psychosocial and performance concerns in its purview, we conceptualize *clinical sport psychology* by our following definition:

> The application of knowledge and methods from the various substantive fields of psychology for the promotion and maintenance of psychological and physical health and well-being; the optimization of athletic performance for individuals, families, and organizations involved in sport; and the prevention, assessment, and amelioration of personal or performance difficulties which psychological influences either contribute to or relieve.

It is important to note that although we are using the old USOC term, we are not using the USOC definition. In this text, *clinical sport psychology* suggests an approach to sport psychology that includes a comprehensive and holistic *scope* of practice and a *style* of practice that is standard in professional psychology. The use of *clinical sport psychology* is not intended to suggest that only sport psychology professionals trained in clinical or counseling psychology should practice this model of sport psychology. Rather, the term is a new definition of practice that includes a distinctive style and an expanded scope.

The style of practice we advocate is essentially the standard approach to practice in contemporary clinical and counseling psychology, in which assessment, case conceptualization, and intervention are interconnected and informed by an evolving empirical base. The core of this model requires carefully conceptualizing client issues within a complete psychosocial context and comprehensively assessing the client before initiating an empirically supported intervention (when available). This model rejects the idea that athlete concerns can be neatly and dichotomously categorized as performance related or clinical in nature. In reality, in the majority of cases presented to the sport psychologist, situational variables and dispositional characteristics affect the athlete's ability to maximize competitive performance. In these circumstances, while enhancing athletic performance may be the primary objective stated by the client, understanding and ameliorating subclinical psychological barriers is often the essential mechanism of change.

As described later in the text, the practice of clinical sport psychology is logically focused on

© Sport The Library

Both of these athletes bring a set of personal characteristics that contribute to their ability to perform well.

the development of a comprehensive and holistic understanding of the psychosocial reality of the athlete, as opposed to simplistically focusing on performance as often seen in applied sport psychology. The clinical sport psychologist may treat clinical disorders (such as eating disorders), provide psychological counseling for transitional reactions (such as affective reactions to life circumstances), or provide athletic performance enhancement (such as enhancing concentration and poise). A professional practicing clinical sport psychology does not have to be able to *treat* all clinical disorders, transitional and developmental issues, and enduring interpersonal and intrapersonal characteristics. However, the clinical sport psychologist must be able to accurately assess their presence and know when to refer clients to other professionals when necessary. Unfortunately, some of the basic suppositions noted earlier often guide the prevailing method of practice and may actually prevent the sport psychologist from recognizing critical issues that must be addressed. Over the course of this text, we discuss these suppositions and present a comprehensive and holistic framework for the assessment, conceptualization, and treatment of a vast array of athletes' needs. In the remainder of this chapter, we briefly discuss the changes in both scope and style of practice suggested by our clinical sport psychology model.

Clinical Sport Psychologists

The expansion of sport psychology promoted both in this text and by the new APA proficiency does not use educational background to reflexively exclude any professionals from practice. In any profession, there are defined practitioners who are trained and experienced in working with a particular type of client, and who are also comfortable referring to another professional when necessary. Clinical and counseling psychologists are expected to recognize the need or benefit of psychotropic medication for certain clients and are expected to refer to medical colleagues as indicated. Both of these professions share in the mental health field and engage in overlapping activities (i.e., psychotherapy), but both respect the inherent differences and have clear professional areas of expertise. Recognizing practice limitations is fully expected and is addressed in the APA Code of Ethics (APA, 2002). Thus, we do not seek to artificially dichotomize the clinically trained practitioner from the sport scientist, and suggest that all members of the field can practice clinical

sport psychology as long as each practitioner respects the natural limitations to their training and areas of competence. Clinical sport psychology includes a broad spectrum of issues such as emotional or behavioral disturbance, performance development or dysfunction, career termination, psychological response to injury, perfectionism, fear of failure, anxiety, depression, and all other areas of interpersonal and intrapersonal functioning. What follows in this text is a model by which practitioners of all educational backgrounds can effectively practice across the broad scope of clinical sport psychology.

Scope of Practice

Basic to our clinical sport psychology model is an expanded scope of professional practice. The scope we advocate clearly implies that the sport psychologist must be prepared to address the multitude of issues presented by the athlete. Furthermore, all athlete issues cannot be reduced to and defined by simple performance concerns. Our scope suggests that personal and psychological issues, whether diagnosable psychological disorders or more developmental, transitional or interpersonal concerns, are clearly within the bounds of practice and need to be adequately addressed in order to provide thorough psychological services. Further, this broadened scope of practice suggests that organizational issues beyond team cohesion, leadership development, and coaching effectiveness are within the purview of the clinical sport psychologist.

Larger systems-based issues are also within the domain of clinical sport psychology, as

To fully understand this athlete, the sport psychologist should broadly consider the individual, organizational, and situational factors that contribute to his performance and overall life functioning.

group, team, and organizational concerns can require as much attention as individual performance difficulties. Additionally, psychological assessment in player selection, as well as the impact of organizational culture on staff and player development are examples of reasonable practice domains.

Style of Practice

Equally important to the scope of practice is the style of practice used to provide ethical and effective service. *Style* of practice denotes two critical elements inherent within the professional practice of sport psychology. The first is the fundamental need for an evidence-based approach in which theory guides research efforts, which then informs practice with empirically informed assessment and intervention strategies. The importance and history of an empirically supported approach to the practice of psychology is highlighted in chapter 5.

The second critical element is a model by which performance concerns are not automatically viewed in the narrow terms initially presented by an athlete, rather in terms of the entire context of the athlete's life. From this perspective, clinical sport psychologists carefully assess the possibility that transitional, developmental, interpersonal, intrapersonal, and more serious psychological issues are involved in performance concerns; they incorporate those issues that are linked to the presenting problem, and they reject unsupported hypotheses. They then, while considering the outcome goals implied by the specific issues noted by the client, conceptualize the case and use the most recent empirical evidence to select an intervention.

Final Thoughts

We wrote this text to offer a systematic model for the practice of clinical sport psychology and hope that when fully introduced, formalized, and operationalized, the text will effectively guide the practitioner and help advance professional practice. This, in turn shall provide an impetus for both the applied researcher and practitioner to engage in a more comprehensive and meaningful approach to working with such a unique, fascinating, and complex clientele.

CHAPTER 2

Integrating Clinical and Sport Science

A number of factors, both internal and external, are intricately tied into understanding, predicting, and enhancing athletic performance. In this chapter, we describe a model for understanding the issues most often brought to the clinical sport psychologist. With this model, evidence-based interventions can be rationally applied. This chapter utilizes scientific evidence in both sport and clinical psychology to integrate internal processes with external demands in an adapted model of athletic self-regulation—the Integrative Model of Athletic Performance (IMAP) (Gardner & Moore, 2005a; Moore & Gardner, 2001, October).

Understanding Athletic Performance

No one activity, mechanism, or variable is responsible for all the internal and external concerns that impede performance or psychologically distress the athlete. As with all types of human performance, athletic performance is a complex activity that involves a number of highly interconnected components:

- **Instrumental competencies** include the athlete's specific physical and sensorimotor skills and abilities.

- **Environmental stimuli and performance demands** include the competitive, interpersonal, situational, and organizational circumstances, issues, and challenges that the athlete experiences.

- **Dispositional characteristics** include intrapersonal variables such as coping styles, and cognitive-affective schemas, that are the psychological templates by which athletes per-

ceive, interpret, and respond to explicit and implicit performance stimuli and demands.

- **Behavioral self-regulation** includes cognitive, affective, physiological, and behavioral processes that are the foundation of goal-directed behavior (such as performance).

When these four components align (see figure 2.1), it is assumed that the result is the ideal performance state (Hardy et al., 1996). Several authors have discussed the ideal performance state using somewhat different terminology. Csikszentmihalyi (1975) described this state as "flow," while Gould and Udry (1994), in their description of necessary factors for creating an ideal performance state, described it as a required "recipe of emotions." Hanin (1980) utilized the phrase "zone of optimal functioning" to describe the idiographic arousal

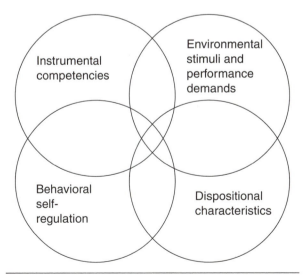

Figure 2.1 Interacting variables affecting athletic performance.

state necessary for optimal athletic performance. All of these terms suggest that underlying peak athletic performance is an optimal biopsychosocial state that promotes and sustains automated, goal-directed behavior. We, and the others mentioned, believe, in essence, that the right combination of cognitive, affective, and physiological conditions allows well-learned physical (behavioral) skills to occur in a seemingly effortless and automatic manner. This chapter focuses on how this state occurs and on what processes promote or interfere with optimal performance.

The extant literature on sport psychology tends to view the elements of performance as segregated and disconnected. In fact, texts commonly discuss self-efficacy, motivation, arousal, physical skill development, and self-regulatory processes as separate and discreet elements of sport participation and performance (Singer et al., 2001). With the notable exceptions of the models proposed by Hardy et al. (1996) and Vealey and Garner-Holman (1998), there have been few models of athletic performance that carefully integrate and consider all of the individual components necessary for high-level athletic performance.

The multidomain assessment framework for applied sport psychology by Vealey and Garner-Holman (1998) suggests that athlete characteristics, organizational culture characteristics, contextual characteristics, and consultant characteristics must be considered in the assessment process, the intervention process, and during the evaluation of intervention effectiveness. The model by Hardy et al. (1996) suggests that at the base of peak performance are core "personality, motivational, and philosophical foundations" (p. 240). Adding the requisite physical skills, psychological skills, and adversity coping strategies to this core foundation results in task-specific ideal performance states. While Hardy and colleagues state that all aspects of this model need to be considered for a complete understanding of athletic performance, they provide little direction as to how this integrated consideration should occur. In spite of these fairly comprehensive approaches, these authors suggest strategies for enhancing athletic performance that focus almost exclusively on cognitive-behavioral techniques (traditional psychological skills training), which as discussed in chapter 5, may not always be the most efficacious strategies to optimize performance (Gardner & Moore, 2004a; Moore, 2003b; Moore & Gardner, 2005). These strategies focus on modifying and controlling internal cognitive-affective processes and external behaviors in the hopes of creating the ideal performance state (Hardy et al., 1996). Likewise, much of the current literature in sport psychology emphasizes these self-control skills (Van Raalte & Brewer, 2002), yet often neglects other significant psychological mechanisms, dispositional variables, and alternative methods for performance enhancement such as cognitive defusion and behavioral refocusing (Gardner & Moore, 2004a). Only rarely have more holistic perspectives of athletes and athletic performance been suggested (Andersen, 2002a; Bond, 2001; Leahy, 2001). As such, sport psychologists have not had the benefit of comprehensive and integrated models by which to conceptualize, study, understand, and ultimately modify athletic performance.

Since the field of sport psychology was certainly not the first to study human performance, sport psychology may benefit by looking to the vast literature in other domains of professional psychology to better understand functional and dysfunctional performance. Significant advances in nonathletic performance domains over the last decade could add much to the understanding of athletic performance. Human performance, be it athletic, academic, social, or sexual, involves the coordinated activation of core personality variables, learned skill sets specific to the performance domain, situational demands, and coping strategies. As such, the similarities of human performance domains appear far greater than the specific differences. It would be incomprehensible to ignore these theoretical and empirical advances.

We hypothesize that incorporating theoretical and empirical developments from the various human performance domains will catalyze future research on athletic performance enhancement and will help develop evidence-based intervention practices in sport psychology, which are not yet available (see chapter 5).

For several decades, clinical scientists have worked to better understand performance issues and develop effective interventions to treat or enhance sexual, academic, occupational, and social performance (Bach, Brown, & Barlow, 1999; Barlow, 2001, 2002; Heimberg, Hope, Dodge, & Becker, 1990; Hofmann & Barlow, 2002; Rapee & Lim, 1992). Perusal of the current literature indicates that sport psychology has given scant attention to this empirical database and has therefore failed to benefit from these relevant findings.

Integrative Model of Athletic Performance (IMAP)

The Integrative Model of Athletic Performance (IMAP) integrates empirical findings in both the clinical and sport sciences. This model has been adapted from a general model of behavioral self-regulation (Carver & Scheier, 1988) and from empirically supported models of human sexual performance (Sbrocco & Barlow, 1996) and general social performance (Turk, Heimberg, & Hope, 2001). The IMAP integrates additional empirical findings in sport psychology, self-regulation, and nonathletic human performance into a comprehensive understanding of functional and dysfunctional athletic performance. The model (shown in figure 2.2) involves three broad yet interactive phases. The *preparatory phase* involves internal and external demands and processes that direct readiness for competitive behavior. The *performance phase* involves the interaction of cognitive, affective, and behavioral processes in actual athletic performance and skill execution. The *postperformance response phase* involves responses to external consequences and internal processes associated with athletic performance.

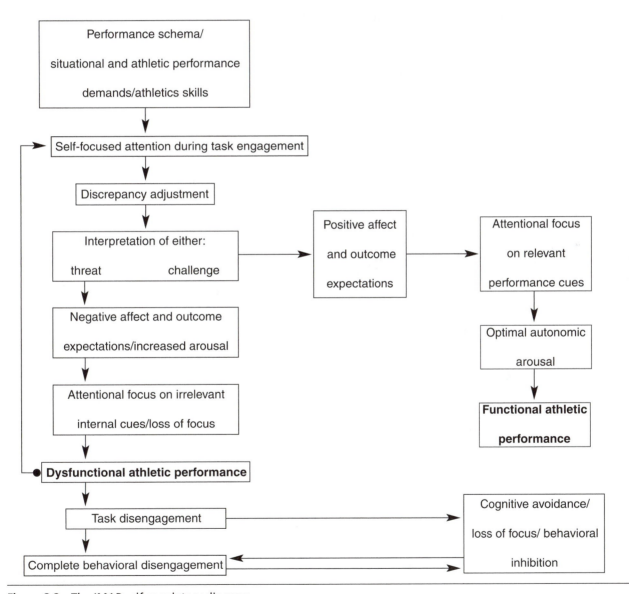

Figure 2.2 The IMAP self-regulatory diagram.

Adapted from Carver and Scheier 1988 and Sborro and Barlow 1996.

Preparatory Phase

We must consider a variety of internal and external variables to fully understand athletic performance. Most basic to athletic performance are the sensorimotor, general athletic, and sport-specific abilities that an athlete develops over time. While a complete discussion of athletic skill development is beyond the scope of this chapter, the professional literature in motor learning has elucidated the processes of developing and maintaining physical skills (Starkes, Helsen, & Jack, 2001; Wrisberg, 2001). As with all human behavior, biological and genetic realities (in this case physical skills and abilities) limit the overall impact of psychosocial variables and, to a large extent, predict athletic performance beyond mental processes. Instrumental competencies are the result of well-practiced, highly developed physical skills that become increasingly automatic over time (Wrisberg, 2001). To a large extent, psychological skills training in sport aims to enhance underdeveloped athletic skills and to sustain existing physical skills.

In addition to basic athletic skills and abilities, athletes as human beings bring dispositional

The athlete must possess sound sensorimotor abilities and both general and sport-specific athletic skills to be successful.

characteristics that are the template for the assimilation and accommodation of environmental stimuli. Clinical and cognitive psychology literature both suggest that individuals develop an interactive pattern of self and other mental schemas (internal rule systems) as cognitive representations of the self and its relation to the world based on repeated experiences (Safran & Segal, 1990). These representations are implicit cognitive structures that influence the allocation of attention to stimuli that are perceived as dangerous within the context of the specific schema. The attentional biases associated with schemas are a function of misclassifying innocuous stimuli as somehow dangerous based upon previous learning histories (Teachman & Woody, 2004). Schemas serve as a basis for understanding the world, controlling affective responses, and maintaining interpersonal relatedness. As such, schemas serve as personal radars that allow an individual to scan for possible (psychological) threats, and they result in learned patterns of cognitive, affective, and behavioral responses to the world. Self-defeating response patterns often result, as the psychological self-protective function of these schemas often occur at the expense of more functional behavior (such as goal-directed athletic behavior). In the athletic domain, the personal meaning and importance the athlete places on performance help form an organizing system by which the athlete evaluates, interprets, and responds to his competitive world.

Schemas tend to be self-perpetuating and highly resistant to change efforts. They generally develop from a pattern of early events in childhood (contingency-shaped behavior) and form the core of an individual's self-concept, interpersonal functioning, and overall view and expectations of the world, including performance needs, expectations, and standards (Young, Klosko, & Weishaar, 2003). These schemas and their resultant coping styles can be viewed as trait functions that organize the individual's world (including competitive performance). Environmental stimuli tend to be distorted to maintain the validity of these schemas.

There has been controversy between psychologists who suggest human behavior can be best understood as a compilation of traits and psychologists who view behavior as primarily situation-specific learning of individual responses (states) (Auweele, Nys, Rzewnicki, & Van Mele, 2001). Nonetheless, trait-like dispositional characteristics (schemas) can be understood from a social-cognitive (state) perspective by conceptualizing them as overgeneralized responses to a variety of environmental stimuli that are (at times inappropriately) grouped into stimulus classes (stimulus generalization). As such, schemas often result in affective and behavioral inflexibility. This inflexibility protects against negative affective states, yet does not promote the individual's long-term self-interest in achieving valued personal goals. These concepts are likely familiar to psychologists trained in the cognitive-behavioral, family systems, or dynamic-interpersonal models of clinical and counseling psychology, in which similar conceptualizations are at the foundation of understanding personality development. Theorists have described schema-like conceptualizations as internal working models (Bowlby, 1982), early maladaptive schemas (Young, 1999), core beliefs (Beck, Rush, Shaw, & Emery, 1979), irrational beliefs (Ellis, 1962), core conflictual relationship themes (Luborsky, 1984), and cognitive-affective person systems (Mischel & Shoda, 1995). Despite the long-standing integration of these concepts into the understanding of nonathletic behavior, mainstream sport psychology has insufficiently considered them.

While several models of schema development and their relationship to human behavior have been empirically evaluated, one recent model particularly relates to athletic performance. Blatt and colleagues (Blatt & Blass, 1990; Blatt, Zohar, Quinlan, Luthar, & Hart, 1996) have proposed a model of personality development suggesting that functional and dysfunctional human behavior develops across two distinct yet interacting dimensions. The first is a relatedness, or anaclitic, dimension that involves the capacity to establish and maintain effective interpersonal relationships. The second is a self-definitional, or introjective, dimension that involves establishing a positive and realistic self-identity. These dimensions interact and inevitably affect each other. The model suggests that self and self-other (interpersonal) schemas, while developing separately, reciprocally affect each other. This is similar to Safran and Segal's (1990) view of schema development, in which interpersonal schemas are inextricably tied to the development of both self-concept and interpersonal relatedness. Thus, from the perspective of Blatt and colleagues (1990; 1996), an individual's behavioral style (and behavioral difficulties) results from these interacting dimensions. Specifically, an individual's difficulties arise from the exaggeration of, or overemphasis on, one of these dimensions, and from the resulting negative impact on, or avoid-

ance of, the other. Anaclitic (interpersonal) difficulties result in issues of relatedness, including problems with trust, response to real or perceived interpersonal loss, and overdependence on others. Such difficulties affect an athlete's relationships with coaches, teammates, parents, and so on, and can have clear performance ramifications. Introjective (self-definitional) difficulties result in issues of sense of self and include problems such as anger and aggression, unrelenting standards (perfectionism), concerns about autonomy and control, and extreme responses to real or perceived loss of status (such as athletic career). Introjective difficulties affect an athlete's ability to cope with adversity or respond to injury, performance progress, parental pressures, and coaching styles and decisions.

Of the numerous schemas, certain classes particularly relate to performance (which we call performance schemas). It is important to clarify that the presence of these schemas in an individual does not necessarily reflect serious concerns or clinical disorders. Rather, schemas are characteristic ways of interpreting and responding to the world (including performance cues and stimuli) (Young et al., 2003) that affect the athlete's ability to respond to the competitive environment. The following are examples (described in a sport context) of some of the particular schema domains likely to be triggered by competitive performance situations:

- **Dependency schema.** These athletes frequently feel unable to handle responsibilities without help from others. They tend to avoid taking on new challenges due to excessive reliance on others and frequently need the help and support of others. They may need help making decisions and are likely to respond poorly to changes in their environment or life circumstance. For example, an athlete with a dependency schema may frequently call his father after the coach asks something of him or attempts to assist him in his development.

- **Failure schema.** These athletes have a fundamental belief that they will fail, and typically do not feel successful even in the face of conflicting evidence. When successful, they often believe the success is too little or fleeting. They tend to ceaselessly strive (the overachiever) only to become defeated and give up easily in response to perceived failure, or they characteristically procrastinate, avoid challenges, and make numerous excuses.

- **Entitlement schema.** Athletes holding this schema often feel superior to others and entitled to special privileges. These athletes focus on their own success (and power) and are unlikely to readily accept rules and structure imposed by others. They can be demanding without sufficient empathy for others. These athletes often brag about accomplishments and at the same time may display minimal task-related effort unless success is guaranteed. In addition, they frequently avoid situations in which average performance is likely.

- **Low frustration tolerance schema.** These athletes typically cannot or will not exercise sufficient self-control and frustration tolerance to achieve personal goals. They often have difficulty consistently regulating emotion or behavior and attempt to completely avoid discomfort. As such, they are likely to give up easily on tasks, avoid prolonged work effort, and refuse personal responsibility for negative outcomes.

- **Extreme standards schema.** These athletes must meet very high, internalized standards in order to feel adequate. They tend to feel constant internal pressure and are hypercritical of themselves and their performance. They are likely to present with rigid personal rules, inordinate attention to detail and general perfectionism, and constant preoccupation with time and efficiency. They often believe that they should be harshly punished for errors and may avoid or put off tasks in which performance is judged.

- **Approval and recognition-seeking schema.** These athletes appear to value recognition and approval from others over more adaptive valued goals. They base their self-esteem excessively on the reactions and beliefs of others rather than on a rational assessment of themselves. They may appear self-absorbed and possibly ingratiating. They typically find the possibility of negative evaluation and disapproval from important others highly threatening.

- **Negativity schema.** These athletes tend to focus exclusively on the negative aspects of their performance, of themselves, and of others. They often go to great lengths to avoid negative outcomes and tend to worry excessively and constantly. They frequently feel stress and utilize overt avoidance to reduce personal distress.

- **Self-punishing schema.** These athletes often treat themselves (and others) in an excessively harsh manner. They beat themselves up for the smallest of mistakes and often become sullen and noncommunicative when confronted with their failings.

- **Vulnerability schema.** These athletes often scan for possible misfortune and fear that medical, emotional, and external catastrophes are imminent and that they will not be adequately prepared or able to defend themselves from harm. They frequently assume they will be emotionally hurt by others, and therefore typically hold enmeshment and abandonment schemas as well.

- **Enmeshment schema.** These athletes have excessive emotional ties with those close to them and typically do not reach full individuation or become self-sufficient. They often believe that they cannot survive on their own or lead enjoyable lives without ongoing support.

- **Abandonment schema.** These athletes perceive that others close to them will not provide emotional support when needed, will be unreliable and eventually replace them with someone more favorable, or will abandon them through death.

- **Mistrust schema.** These athletes typically distrust those around them and question the motives of others. They believe that others will harm, manipulate, or take advantage of them, and therefore scan the environment for signs of maltreatment. Distrust of authority figures (often including coaches and staff) is common and can lead to significant interpersonal difficulties.

- **Defectiveness and inadequacy schema.** These athletes believe that they are inherently inadequate and inferior to others, and will not be cared for if others uncover this perceived defectiveness. They are self-conscious, insecure, and extremely sensitive to real or perceived criticism.

The conceptualization of schemas suggests a mechanism that directly influences the information-encoding process and cognitive-affective mediation of situational context and ultimate behavioral responses. When existing cognitive schemas are triggered, worry is often utilized to prepare for and cope with real or perceived threats in a particular domain. A mental activity common to most human beings, nonpathological worry, can facilitate an athlete's readiness for engagement and can promote effective problem solving. Low levels of worry can promote proactive behavior or corrective action as needed. However, as worry intensifies, exaggerated mobilization and hypervigilance to threat cues begins. Worry is a related yet separate phenomenon from anxiety, and it becomes increasingly associated with anxiety in more intense and chronic states (Borkovec, Alcaine, & Behar, 2004). The relationship between worry, as recently conceptualized by Borkovec and colleagues (2004), and the concept of cognitive anxiety proposed by some sport psychologists (Hardy et al., 1996) is discussed later in this chapter.

The role of dispositional characteristics in understanding functional and dysfunctional athletic performance is central to the IMAP. However, IMAP's discussion of these variables does not follow the typical discussion in the traditional sport psychology literature (Cox, 1998; Van Raalte & Brewer, 2002), which views dispositional constructs as encapsulated functions (e.g., achievement motivation, competitive state anxiety, and so on) disconnected from each other in their respective roles in functional and dysfunctional athletic performance.

Dispositional characteristics largely determine how an individual interprets and responds to external demands and environmental stimuli. Environmental stimuli are the external factors that the athlete confronts both in and out of competition. Personal and professional relationships, organizational realities and demands, physical and psychological aspects of training and competition (travel, time commitments, and so on), financial pressures, physical strain and injury, nonsport experiences, and developmental transitions all have stimulus properties that an athlete may respond to based upon her personal learning history. These are but some of the factors that athletes must successfully confront in order to perform at optimal levels. The IMAP defines performance demands as specific cues and general requirements to perform under conditions in which the athlete is challenged to achieve at or above an established standard. While the established standard varies depending on the athletic level (i.e., recreational, collegiate, Olympic, professional), all levels of athletic engagement explicitly or implicitly establish some performance standard.

Athletic skill, environmental stimuli and performance demands, and dispositional characteristics are the precursors for engagement in athletic performance and the context for behavioral self-regulation. Furthermore, as schemas are generalized responses to overgeneralized stimulus classes, environmental stimuli and performance demands can trigger schematic content for predisposed athletes, setting the stage for dysfunctional athletic performance through disrupted self-regulation. For example, the athlete who holds an interpersonal schema that self-acceptance can only come from approval by significant others and who plays for a coach who is emotionally distant and nonreinforcing, may approach athletic competition with a different cognitive-affective response than the athlete without such a schema. Another example is the athlete whose schema suggests that successful performance exclusively defines personal worth. This athlete approaches competition believing that mistakes are inexcusable, poor performances should not happen to someone who works as hard as she does, and mistakes reflect personal inadequacy. Such inadequacy schemas lead the athlete to establish unrealistic and unrelenting personal expectations and performance standards, which result in metacognitive scanning in which actual or perceived performance errors are misinterpreted or overinterpreted. There is also a corresponding affective and behavioral response to these threatening stimuli, such as frustration, anxiety, dysfunctional performance, and premature athletic termination.

Using empirical data collected in a variety of human performance domains (Barlow, 2002), we can reasonably conclude that, like all human beings, athletes develop performance schemas around issues relating to performance and the resultant implications for the self. These performance schemas influence thoughts, affect, and behavior and directly influence the athlete's ability to effectively self-regulate during competition. The content of performance schemas typically differs in individuals whose performances are functional or dysfunctional, in that the performance schemas associated with dysfunctional performance

During competition, unforeseen events may trigger thoughts, feelings, and behaviors that can negatively affect an athlete's performance.

include exaggerated and unrealistic standards, expectations, and self-implications. As noted earlier, these schemas are rigid and not amenable to new, accurate information. Athletes who do not hold rigid performance schemas and who function well in competition may also posses some exaggeration about performance. However, schema-driven cognitive content is characterized and most easily recognized by its rigidity, intensity, and relevance to the self. These characteristics contrast with the cognitive content of individuals *not* holding maladaptive performance schemas, which is more amenable to logical analysis, less affect producing, and less related to self-concept.

Adopting a stress-diathesis model (Chorpita & Barlow, 1998) may help us further understand the role of dispositional variables in athletic performance dysfunction. From this perspective, performance schemas interact with real or perceived skill deficits and idiographically relevant environmental events and performance cues to sensitize athletes to performance dysfunction. Similarly, nonperformance schemas can indirectly affect athletic performance by affecting the athlete's overall psychological state. A collegiate athlete with problematic interpersonal schemas may respond to the breakup of a significant relationship with an affective and behavioral intensity that decreases performance secondary to his general psychological state. Conversely, the same environmental and performance demands confronted by an individual with different dispositional characteristics (i.e., no significant interpersonal schemas) make her substantially less susceptible to dysfunction and allow for more typical self-regulated performance (see figure 2.3)

Performance Phase

Understanding athletic performance requires a fundamental understanding of self-regulatory processes. A foundation of IMAP is that athletic

behavior (as with all human behavior) is regulated by a system of feedback control. In the feedback control process, individuals metacognitively attend to relevant aspects of their own behavior and systematically utilize reference points to evaluate and adjust their behavior to meet their own established standards (Carver & Scheier, 1988; Wells, 2000). The individual's standards, either appropriate or inappropriate, play a significant role in the development of functional or dysfunctional performance.

As individuals engage in performance tasks, including athletic tasks, they self-monitor (attend to) their behavior to determine how it conforms to preset standards. In all areas of human performance, an adjustment process occurs, which is a metacognitive and automated function in which relevant behavior is adjusted to conform to these preset standards (Carver & Scheier, 1988; Sbrocco & Barlow, 1996). The metacognitive process of self-monitoring, self-evaluation, and corrective action is central to effective behavioral self-regulation. This process occurs naturally and operates smoothly and automatically for individuals with functional performance. However, many times performance schemas or environmental disruptions confound this process by creating unreasonable standards or altering existing skill sets. The perfectionistic athlete with unrelenting performance standards compares his real or perceived performance with unrealistic and possibly unattainable standards and is thus unable to functionally engage in discrepancy adjustment. In addition, due to rigid preexisting schemas, the athlete is unlikely to be amenable to logical analysis of his exaggerated standards. Similarly, the recently injured athlete whose skill level has temporarily (or sometimes permanently) been altered may be unable to make necessary corrective adjustments and may respond with a dysfunctional spiral. In each of these examples, as in all self-regulatory disruptions (Sbrocco & Barlow, 1996), there is a deleterious shift from effective behavioral self-regulation (based upon subtle metacognitive and automatic processes) to a greater utilization of self-focused, verbal-linguistic cognitive processes.

Of particular importance is the degree to which the self-focus inherent in this discrepancy adjustment process is task-relevant. In order to engage in the self-monitoring or discrepancy adjustment process, one *must* focus on the self to some degree. However, the athlete exhibiting functional performance experiences a nonjudging, metacognitive, mindful absorption in the task, whereas an athlete

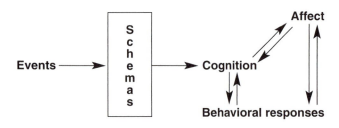

Figure 2.3 The relationship between schemas, internal states, and behavioral responses.

experiencing dysfunctional performance typically focuses on inflexible rule systems, perceived deficits, self-doubts, efforts to control affect and cognition, and ramifications of failure. The concept of *metacognition* we use is congruent with the definition of mindfulness as "paying attention in a particular way: on purpose, in the present moment, and non-judgmentally" (Kabat-Zinn, 1994, p. 4). In addition, the concept (presented here) of mindful (present-moment, nonjudging) task absorption as a foundation of functional athletic performance is an extension of similar descriptions of flow or peak experiences in sport (Csikszentmihalyi, 1990; Gardner & Moore, 2004a). Although several sport psychologists have touched on mindfulness concepts in the sport context, mindfulness has been around for thousands of years and is not new to sport psychology. Mindfulness is covered in greater detail in chapter 6.

The accumulated empirical evidence has led to similar findings in studies on other related forms of human performance (Barlow, 2002). For example, research on academic test performance suggests that most individuals experience similar physiological arousal before completing an academic test. However, when equating for academic preparation, only those with self-doubts and an attentional focus on task-irrelevant cues during the exam perform poorly (Rich & Woolever, 1988). This finding is similar to past research on athletic performance which suggested that athletes who interpreted somatic arousal as facilitative maintained task-relevant focus and performed adequately, while those interpreting arousal as debilitative focused more on internal processes, which interfered with competitive performance (Jones, Hanton, & Swain, 1994; Jones, Swain, & Hardy, 1993; Swain & Jones, 1996). The literature on human sexual performance has similar findings. Individuals who engage in functional sexual performance focus on erotic cues, while those experiencing sexual dysfunction focus on self-doubts, sexual inadequacies, and exaggerated self-implications regarding performance failures (Jones, Bruce, & Barlow, 1986, November).

In athletic performance, as in other areas of human performance, individuals enter into athletic situations with markedly different expectations about their performance. David Barlow's (1986) work on sexual performance clearly demonstrated differential outcome expectations between functional and dysfunctional performers. Similarly, Vealey's (1986) model of sport confidence suggests that outcome expectancies mediate objective sport situations, ultimate behavioral responses, and actual performance outcomes.

In essence, due to a combination of dispositional characteristics and personal performance history, functional performers expect a positive outcome and dysfunctional performers expect a negative outcome. Once established, these expectancies are often difficult to change, and they affect how the athlete interprets challenge or threat in performance situations (Sbrocco & Barlow, 1996). For example, in studies comparing sexually dysfunctional and functional individuals, sexually functional participants, told that they were ingesting a pill that would negatively affect sexual arousal, responded to this experimental condition as a challenge and demonstrated greater sexual arousal. Conversely, sexually dysfunctional individuals responded to this same condition as a threat and with lower levels of sexual arousal (Cranston-Cuebas, Barlow, Mitchell, & Athanasiou, 1993). Similarly, sexually functional individuals demonstrated no increase in arousal when presented with a performance enhancement placebo pill, whereas sexually dysfunctional individuals responded with greater arousal (Cranston-Cuebas & Barlow, 1995). In each of these studies, outcome expectancies mediated performance demands and actual performance outcomes. These results are consistent with the findings of Gould, Weiss, and Weinberg (1981), that confidence was the most stable and consistent factor differentiating highly successful from less successful athletes. Thus, athletes who believe that their skills and abilities match performance demands are likely to perform better, and athletes who question their skills and experience and are overly concerned with outcome are likely to perform more poorly.

What makes outcome expectancies difficult to change? Part of the answer lies in a combination of automated cognitive-affective behavioral chains learned over repeated trials, and performance schemas that orient those with functional or dysfunctional performance to view their affective and behavioral responses in a way that verifies their expectations. That is, dysfunctional performers often overrespond to performance decrements, while functional performers minimally attend to these decrements. Functional individuals develop an illusion of control that allows them to overlook or minimally respond to small decrements in performance (Mitchell, Marten, Williams, & Barlow, 1990, November). These individuals are less vulnerable to exaggerated negative self-judgments and resulting performance dysfunction. Similarly, recent studies on chronic depression suggest that multiple relapses of clinical depression often occur because over time, the individual begins to respond strongly even to triggers that are less and less extreme. Thus, over time, minor environmental stressors trigger the same cognitive-affective chains as (previously) more significant events (Segal et al., 2002). Applied to the sport domain, it can be hypothesized that with chronic performance difficulties, an athlete may notice and respond to smaller and smaller performance decrements and thus may become particularly vulnerable to chronic performance dysfunction.

Positive or negative outcome expectancies and associated threat or challenge interpretations also involve an accompanying affective response (Sbrocco & Barlow, 1996). Negative outcome expectancies and associated beliefs about the uncontrollability of salient events increase hypervigilance to threat, negative affect, and increased arousal (Barlow, 1986). The attentional bias associated with this intensified hypervigilance can (at least in part) explain the tendency for dysfunctional performers to note minor performance decrements and engage in excessive self-focus at the expense of task-focused attention and behavior. Attentional narrowing to real or perceived threats exacerbates the dysfunctional performer's tendency to interpret cues negatively. The self-judging, future-oriented focus characteristic of performance dysfunction markedly contrasts to the mindful, in-the-moment task-focus characteristic of functional performance. In addition, increases in negative affect and somatic arousal may further disrupt task-relevant concentration and athletic performance, as arousal levels may rise beyond the optimal requirements of a specific sport.

Using the extant scientific literature from a variety of human performance domains, we can summarize the following sequence in functional athletic performance: Functional athletic performance involves a metacognitive (automated) process of self-monitoring, self-evaluation, and corrective action as needed, and does not involve cognitive processes to control or modify internal experiences. This functional process of effective discrepancy adjustment feeds into the athlete's positive performance expectations (self-efficacy) and the athlete interprets performance demands as challenging. This further results in mindful task focus, appropriate levels of arousal and affect, automated motor skills, and, ultimately, in functional athletic performance. Conversely, ineffective discrepancy adjustment in concert with nega-

tive outcome expectations leads to interpretations of performance cues and demands as threatening, and thus often results in a task-irrelevant, self-judging, threat-scanning self-focus. This can lead to excessive negative affect, heightened arousal, reduced concentration, disruption of automated motor skills, and, ultimately, to dysfunctional athletic performance (see figure 2.2).

Disruptions in self-regulated athletic performance may occur in acute episodes or become a habitual (learned) pattern resulting in chronic performance dysfunction. It seems logical that preexisting performance schemas and characteristic behavioral coping responses can strongly influence whether episodes of dysfunctional performance become chronic or remain situational. These coping responses form the foundation of the next phase of the self-regulatory process.

Postperformance Response Phase

The postperformance response phase typically follows one of three paths. The athlete either sustains involvement in athletic activity or competitive performance, reengages in athletics following some brief dysfunctional period, or disengages from athletics covertly (through worry, distraction, experiential avoidance) or overtly (terminating involvement).

When performance is relatively functional, the athlete's ongoing and future performance behavior remains committed, approach-oriented, and directly linked to valued athletic goals. That is, the athlete tolerates short-term discomfort related to poor performance and continues to approach performance cues and demands with committed training, practice, and preparation. Approach behavior can be additional practice time, additional work with coaches on technical or tactical development, additional conditioning, and so on. Motivation remains strong (as goal-directed behavior is reinforced at a relatively high rate) and positive outcome expectations evolve and strengthen. Focus on performance cues intensifies and promotes ongoing physical skill development. Positive performance outcomes then feed back to the earlier components of the self-regulatory process (such as appropriate discrepancy adjustment) and increase the likelihood of future successful behavior. Even when faced with performance adversity, the athlete with a positive learning history of performance who does not hold maladaptive performance schemas and who has maintained a reasonably positive outcome expectation is not likely to overinterpret the personal meaning or future ramifications of the specific negative performance. This athlete thus reengages in the performance task as the cues and demands of the competitive situation dictate. In this situation, the negative performance is viewed as an isolated episode, does not become chronic or problematic, and does not interfere with adaptive coping (approach) behaviors. The athlete effectively problem solves and focuses on skill development or enhancing technical and tactical aspects of performance with a minimum of negative affect.

Some athletes, however, respond quite differently to negative performance events, and chronic or debilitating problems may occur. Previously, we described both the functional and the dysfunctional performance sequence. In some athletes, discrepancy adjustment difficulties can negatively affect performance, but the athletes quickly recover due to adaptive dispositional characteristics or positive outcome expectancies that isolate the temporary dysfunction as situational and nonthreatening. Other athletes, however, due to new or changing external circumstances (such as a higher level of competition), the triggering of preexisting performance schemas, or athletic skill disruption (such as recent injury), experience persistent performance dysfunction that may be time-limited (slump) or chronic and pervasive. A study by Klinger and colleagues (Klinger, Barta, & Glas, 1981) provides some support for this conceptualization. This study, utilizing thought sampling with college basketball players, suggests that in response to decrements in team performance or a strong challenge from the opposing team, athletes often shift attention from game-related contextual (external) cues and demands to excessive self-focus on both behavior and internal experiences. Based on social-cognitive theory (Bandura, 1977), it can be hypothesized that athletes who do not hold negative schemas maintain a committed, approach-oriented coping style when faced with performance adversity, continue to engage in the athletic task, and eventually find their way back to functional performance through effective problem solving or coaching.

However, when chronic performance dysfunction occurs due to negative schemas, the athlete is likely to utilize an avoidant coping style. This style may be overlearned from childhood or develop gradually in response to the repeated failure of more adaptive efforts toward successful athletic reengagement. Negative outcome expectancies

This athlete is ready to enter the game and is focused on the athletic tasks ahead.

develop and strengthen over repeated dysfunctional experiences. Consistent with social-cognitive models of motivation and goal-seeking behavior (Carver & Scheier, 1988), athletes remain task-engaged as long as they reasonably believe that positive outcomes are likely, and they disengage when negative outcomes are consistently anticipated. From this perspective, the athlete experiencing chronic or persistent performance dysfunction is likely to respond with either covert or overt avoidance or task disengagement.

To fully understand avoidance and task disengagement, we must first understand their function. Inherent in our conceptualization of performance dysfunction and consistent with recent research on behavior disorders (Hayes, Wilson, Gifford, Follette, & Strosahl, 1996) is the idea that experiential avoidance provides the individual experiencing heightened negative affect a means of short-term emotion regulation. While experiential avoidance does not fulfill long-term valued (performance) goals, it does immediately reduce affect, and as such is strongly (negatively) reinforced. The individual often learns and generalizes this reinforced pattern across life situations prior to athletic involvement, but the pattern can also develop specifically in the competitive performance context. Avoidance-based task-disengagement can be covert and less obvious, such as worry and associated task-distraction, or can be obvious and overt, such as termination of athletic involvement.

Previously, we discussed that worry is a naturally occurring process and that at nonpathological levels it adaptively prepares individuals to confront challenge or threat. In excess, worry is linked to anxiety and its performance ramifications. Borkovec (1994) presented a theoretical formulation describing the process and function of both extreme (clinical) and nonpathological worry. In his formulation, worry is a covert verbal-linguistic (also known as verbal-semantic) activity that allows individuals to avoid the complete experience of negative affect or affect-provoking stimuli. Driven by initial signs of arousal, the verbal-linguistic process of worry occupies attentional focus and effectively suppresses the full experience of anxiety (Barlow, 2002) or other affective responses such as sadness (in response to loss associated with injury), anger (in response to hurt over demotion to the second unit), or guilt (associated with performance deficits). Worry blocks the stimuli, affective-behavioral responses, and schematic meanings of the negative affect and the cues triggering the affect. Importantly, Borkovec (1994) noted that unlike anxiety, which is associated with increased arousal, worry has a distinctive physiological process of sympathetic arousal *restriction*, which has been viewed as evidence of the inability of individuals engaged in worry to fully experience the physiological components of anxiety. Essentially, worry inhibits the affective-physiological arousal components of anxiety and is thus negatively reinforced. As such, worry, which is a coping strategy that at nonpathological levels can aid problem solving, in more pathological situations is an avoidance strategy that subsequently disengages the athlete from necessary task-focus and effective behavioral response.

Some of the studies supporting Borkovec's formulation are particularly relevant to sport and performance psychology. Studies of both pathological and nonpathological worry suggest that individuals who worry report more thoughts than images during the worry process (Borkovec, 1994; Borkovec & Inz, 1990; Freeston, Dugas, & Ladouceur, 1996). Rapee (1993) noted the verbal-linguistic nature of worry in a study in which subjects were instructed to worry while engaging in tasks that were primarily either verbal or visuo-spatial. Only the verbal tasks interfered with worry, demonstrating its verbal-linguistic nature. Similarly, a study by Bergman and Craske (1994, November) found that individuals preparing for public speaking shifted from visualizing a neutral scene to verbal-linguistic activity as they began to worry about the imminent task. In addition, Carter, Johnson, and Borkovec (1986) found that individuals engaged in a worry task demonstrated increased frontal cortical activation in the left hemisphere, which indicates verbal-linguistic activation. In an important study specifically related to the sport environment, Crews and Landers (1993) found that highly skilled golfers engaging in a competitive putting task demonstrated a significant increase in left hemispheric alpha activity, which indicates *reduced* verbal-linguistic processes. To clarify, the golfers who performed better experienced less cognitive disruption (thought less) than those who performed more poorly. This study provides some evidence for an inverse relationship between internal verbal processes and successful athletic performance. Similar results have been found in other studies utilizing elite marksmen and archers (Hatfield, Landers, & Ray, 1984; Janelle, Hillman, Apparies, et al., 2000; Janelle, Hillman, & Hatfield, 2000; Salazar, Landers, Petruzzello, & Han, 1990). When we view all these studies together, it appears that worry, a process of enhanced verbal-linguistic activity, may particularly impede optimal athletic performance, as optimal performance seems to require *reduced* cognitive activity (i.e., quiet mind).

Borkovec's (1994) empirically based conceptualization of worry may also explain the conflicting and inconsistent findings in the sport psychology literature examining the relationship between competitive anxiety and athletic performance (McNally, 2002). The multidimensional theory of competitive trait anxiety (Martens, Burton, Vealey, Bump, & Smith, 1990) and the newer cusp-catastrophe model of the anxiety–performance relationship both utilize the concept of cognitive anxiety, defining it as fear of failure and negative expectations about performance (Hardy et al., 1996). Woodman and Hardy (2001) recently referred to cognitive anxiety and worry as synonymous terms. At present, the sport psychology literature does not clearly distinguish worry and anxiety, despite clear distinctions expressed in other psychology domains. While worry is a fundamental component of all types of anxiety (Barlow, 2002), recent evidence convincingly suggests that worry is a functional process that is more than just a *symptom* of anxiety. The inconsistencies in the sport science research relating to the relative impact of cognitive or somatic anxiety on competitive performance (McNally, 2002) may be explained by the fact that current theoretical models do not consider and incorporate the construct of worry and its effects on performance independently of its contribution to the negative affective state of anxiety. In fact, clinical scientists have recently suggested that worry and anxiety are partially independent constructs (Craske, 1999; Davey, Hampton, Farrell, & Davidson, 1992).

In its nonpathological form, worry functions to plan for possible negative events and can reduce the seemingly unpredictable and uncontrollable nature of these events. However, worry in its subclinical or clinical forms as defined by Borkovec (1994) and others (Barlow, 2002) is a maladaptive effort at emotion regulation through avoidance. As noted, this effort at experiential avoidance does not serve the individual's valued long-term goals, but serves to immediately reduce discomfort. Worry may successfully remove immediate discomfort, but it does *not* help develop necessary skills and achieve valued life goals. Over time, worry can become highly automated and resistant to change. The athlete utilizing worry as covert experiential avoidance in response to performance dysfunction therefore tends to sustain his performance difficulties

- by disrupting the automated execution of motor skills as worry loops back and negatively influences self-regulation in both the preperformance and performance stages, or
- by engaging in task-avoidant worry, which does not allow for effective problem solving (including increased practice, training intensity, and self-care considerations) or for skill modification and development in response to performance difficulties.

Another consequence of worry (based on dysfunctional performance) is task disengagement, which can be episodic or chronic. We previously noted that athletes experiencing performance dysfunction demonstrate reduced task-focus and concentration. In essence, such athletes are distracted from the task at hand by competing (verbal-linguistic) internal processes. Current clinical literature has defined this type of distraction as attentional processes diverted from more appropriate task-focus (Sbrocco & Barlow, 1996). For such athletes, performance cues may trigger

this self-focused attention, and negative performance concerns thus increase self-judging at the expense of functional attention to external cues and demands.

Distraction is likely to occur when the athlete compares himself to preset standards and tries to make adjustments (discrepancy adjustment), or during threat interpretation. The athlete will then respond to competitive cues, reengage in the task at hand, and continue performance efforts, or he will disengage through increased self-focused attention. From this perspective, distraction is synonymous to covert task disengagement, as mental processes become increasingly task irrelevant.

When performance dysfunction becomes chronic, task disengagement may become overt and complete. Repeated failure to perform at expected standards can eradicate approach behaviors and negatively reinforce avoidant behaviors such as withdrawal. As Smith (1986) suggested, the balance between reinforcement and aversive consequences of continued athletic involvement becomes such that dissatisfaction and negative affect predominate. The cost–benefit analysis of continued athletic participation often leads to complete disengagement from active sport participation. Smith (1986) and others (Hardy et al., 1996) have termed this phenomenon *burnout*.

A somewhat less dramatic, but no less problematic form of avoidant task disengagement is occasionally seen when athletes avoid athletic participation by using vague or inconsistent reasons for time away from practice and competitive performance. Lingering injuries with no clear pathophysiology, motivation loss, and similar presentations may indicate avoidant mechanisms for escaping athletic activities that are under aversive control. As these presentations can also describe real phenomena (undiagnosed injury, depression, and so on), extreme care must be taken in concluding that task avoidance is the most likely explanation.

While self-regulation of athletic performance has been discussed in the sport science literature (Crews, Lochbaum, & Karoly, 2001), what differentiates the IMAP from these previous discussions is its empirical foundation of work in allied areas of human performance and its equal and fully integrated emphasis on physical skills, environmental events, and dispositional variables such as performance schemas, self-regulatory mechanisms, and coping behaviors. In addition, the IMAP presents these components as an integrated process, as opposed to the classic methodology of applied sport psychology, which often presents them as discreet, seemingly orthogonal components (Cox, 1998).

IMAP Practice Implications

While Hardy and colleagues (1996) suggest a practice model of sport psychology adapted from Thomas (1990) in which dispositional variables, mental skills, coping skills, and physical skills are believed necessary for optimal athletic performance, their model does not theoretically integrate these variables. Similarly, few intervention strategies match client needs and issues beyond those strategies normally involving psychological skills training, the predominant intervention methodology in applied sport psychology. Similarly, while Andersen (2002a) calls for "comprehensive sport psychology services," he then asserts that "there is no formula for comprehensive care of athletes" (p. 22). He further states that "continued thought, research and discussion are warranted to create comprehensive sport psychology interventions that best serve the needs of athletes and coaches" (p. 22). Bond (2001), in a thoughtful discussion, suggests that sport psychological services should focus on a holistic or "multifaceted psychology program not simply directed towards traditional performance enhancement skills training models promoted in the past" (p. 218). He further suggests that a sport psychology program should recognize "the complexity of personal, lifestyle, and sport-related issues that face the aspiring elite athlete" (p. 218). Others, such as Trisha Leahy (2001) and Gershon Tenenbaum (2001), advocate for the holistic care of the athlete, and suggest that comprehensive care considers the multiple performance, educational, and therapeutic needs of the athlete.

Numerous authors have noted the extreme pressures and environmental demands that athletes must confront (Andersen, 2002b; Baillie & Ogilvie, 2002). Competitive athletics are more likely to tax an individual's personal and social resources than many other human endeavors. Psychological issues and behavioral styles that do not overtly impair function must still be carefully addressed in a truly comprehensive practice of sport psychology. The IMAP suggests that it is not reasonable to artificially separate performance demands, physical skills, dispositional variables, and self-regulatory skills in understanding athletic performance.

Perusing the theoretical and empirical studies on the traditional performance enhancement strategies, it is often suggested that general psychological functioning related to transitional or developmental issues and personality variables (i.e., dispositional characteristics) is a relatively unnecessary focus for enhancing athletic performance (Rotella, 1990). Yet in the IMAP, addressing the skill, dispositional, environmental, and self-regulatory issues confronting the athlete is both central and critical to promoting the athlete's well-being and performance. At its most fundamental level, the IMAP suggests a completely integrated relationship between these factors and athletic performance. The suggestion that performance can be enhanced apart from this holistic understanding contradicts both theory and empirical data across numerous areas of human performance.

We hypothesize that interventions using traditional psychological skills training to enhance athletic performance are unlikely to succeed when significant dispositional variables (performance schemas) and other environmental or transitional demands (such as injury or interpersonal conflict) are present, and when performance difficulties are moderate to severe or more chronic. For individuals experiencing inconsistent performance or who are slow in developing skills but have few, if any, significant external or internal issues, skills training may be more likely to enhance athletic performance. However, as when treating clinical phenomena (such as clinical depression and anxiety) in which dispositional factors (such as perfectionism) appear to predict poor response to otherwise empirically supported psychosocial treatments (Blatt & Zuroff, 2002), dispositional factors undoubtedly negatively impact the effectiveness of interventions that directly target psychological skills.

In addition, alternative cognitive-behavioral interventions, such as mindfulness and metacognitive procedures for enhancing task-focused attention, acceptance and commitment procedures for behavioral activation and valued goal attainment, schema-focused interventions, and interventions focusing on exposure and response prevention for anxiety or anger-related concerns, are indicated for a large number of athletes presenting performance concerns. These therapeutic interventions would, in and of themselves, be performance enhancement interventions. We certainly believe that the term *performance enhancement* is more appropriate as a statement of *outcome* rather than a definition of a particular intervention technique. Others have also suggested the performance effects of more therapeutic interventions, as Giges (2000) stated that the removal of psychological barriers (described in chapter 7) is "an effective method in helping athletes improve their performance" (p. 18).

The IMAP suggests that efforts at performance enhancement require behavioral interventions that to be optimally effective must be individually tailored following careful assessment of self-regulatory disruption. For example, recent studies indicate that thought suppression, when confronted with persistent and repetitive maladaptive thought processes, is generally ineffectual and often increases targeted thoughts, emotions, and autonomic arousal (Clark, Ball, & Pape, 1991; Wegner, Ansfield, & Pilloff, 1998; Wegner, Shortt, Blake, & Page, 1990; Wegner & Zanakos, 1994; Wenzlaff, Wegner, & Klein, 1991). There is growing evidence that in situations in which negative cognitive processes emerge and spiral quickly and chronically, interventions targeting mindfulness and acceptance of negative thoughts and emotions are superior to standard self-talk (change-based) procedures (Segal et al., 2002). As such, the IMAP suggests that before modifying, restructuring, or otherwise controlling the negative self-talk that occurs at various points of self-regulatory disruption (e.g., threat interpretation, negative outcome expectancy), the practitioner should carefully address the schematic and chronic nature of the cognitive content. Since current evidence suggests that more enduring characteristics best respond to metacognitive, acceptance-based behavioral approaches rather than to traditional cognitive change-based interventions (Hayes et al., 1999; Segal et al., 2002; Wells, 2000), fully assessing dispositional factors becomes a necessity.

Final Thoughts

The IMAP was developed by carefully integrating the current literature in clinical and sport science to provide a theoretical understanding of the internal and external components of functional and dysfunctional athletic performance. This theoretical framework ultimately drives the assessment and intervention process, which are intended to promote the psychosocial well-being and competitive performance of the athlete. We hope this discussion provides you with an understanding of how interpersonal, intrapersonal, environmental, and self-regulatory processes affect both the athletic performance and psychosocial functioning of individual athletes. Certainly, athletes do not function solely in an athletic domain, but function in many life domains that also require attention and occasional assistance. With the IMAP in mind, we now introduce a way of understanding and classifying athletes' needs that will bridge the theoretical framework presented in this chapter with an understanding of the particular interventions most helpful in ameliorating the vast array of athlete issues.

PART II

Assessment and Classification

Working on the front line with athletes is both enjoyable and rewarding for the practitioner. As such, each year numerous practitioners and students fill symposia presentations and read journal articles that discuss the interventions we use with athletes. Although many conference presentations discuss athlete assessment, such presentations draw far fewer conference attendees. Yet, the appropriate assessment and classification of athletes is equally as important as the interventions we utilize, as intervention decisions cannot justifiably be made without a clear understanding of the athlete's needs.

In this section, we take a dimensional view of normal and abnormal human behavior and provide the reader with an appreciation for the holistic assessment of the athlete. Chapter 3 introduces the Multilevel Classification System for Sport Psychology (MCS-SP),

which is a classification system designed to help the practitioner clarify what information is needed to understand the athlete and his individual needs, the type of case (nonclinical, subclinical, or clinical), and the primary issues to be addressed. Chapter 4 highlights the types, purposes, goals, and strategies of assessment in clinical sport psychology, and describes the MCS-SP assessment process. The assessment approach and classification system we provide go well beyond a simplistic consideration of performance needs and goals, and instead consider the athlete in all life contexts. By truly understanding the athlete in all major life domains and effectively classifying the athlete's needs, the practitioner can determine the appropriate empirically informed intervention to best meet those needs, and the athlete can trust that the practitioner has her overall best interest in mind.

CHAPTER 3

Multilevel Classification System for Sport Psychology (MCS-SP)

Professionals within sport psychology have proposed many instruments for assessment and evaluation, most of which provide specific information on one variable related to performance. These measures, focusing on understanding a specific variable, are necessary tools and assist practitioners in gathering specific data relating to the athlete's needs. On the other hand, most of these measures do not (and do not claim to) evaluate the *whole* athlete, including performance, intrapersonal, interpersonal, developmental, transitional, and clinical concerns. While these measures can be excellent in and of themselves, one of the greatest challenges applied sport psychology faces is developing a systematic approach to professional practice in which thorough assessment leads to sound case conceptualization and to rational intervention goals, strategies, and techniques. Such is the topic of this chapter.

As noted, applied sport psychology has most often been defined by its focus on athletic performance enhancement (Hardy et al., 1996; Ravizza, 2001; Williams & Straub, 1998), although some have argued for a more comprehensive definition that considers the overall psychological well-being and development of athletes (Bond, 2001; Danish, Petitpas, & Hale 1995; Gardner, 2001). While much has been written about both performance enhancement and personal counseling for athletes (Van Raalte & Brewer, 1996), there has been no formal system by which sport psychologists can rationally differentiate issues and problems presented in day-to-day practice.

In day-to-day practice, practitioners make judgments on the scope of a client's presenting problems and the primary, secondary, and tertiary issues, the outcome goals, and the strategies to employ. In psychology, as in most professions, these judgments are based on information derived from four primary sources (Kanfer & Schefft, 1988):

- Specific client characteristics and information
- Scientific database
- Professional folklore (cumulative experiences and skills passed on from professional to professional)
- The professional's personal experience

When using a model of practice informed by scientific data (rather than pseudoscientific approaches), the practitioner integrates client information and characteristics, professional knowledge and experience, and theoretical frameworks in order to understand the client's concerns. With this integrated knowledge, the practitioner then refers to the scientific database of empirically supported treatments to formulate sound intervention plans and provide informed, ethical, and efficacious interventions.

Unfortunately, while provided with numerous intervention techniques purported to enhance athletic performance, sport psychologists largely lack a clear classification system by which to consistently conceptualize and classify the wide variety of issues brought forth by their athletes. Since the reader may wonder, "What is a classification system, and why use such a system?", let's address this topic in further detail.

Classification Systems

A classification system is a means of "delineating the major categories or dimensions of [psychological and behavioral characteristics], as well as the boundaries and interrelations among these categories" (Waldman & Lilienfeld, 1995, p. 21). Despite limitations and criticisms (Waldman & Lilienfeld, 1995), classification systems in medicine and psychology, such as the *Diagnostic and Statistical Manual of Mental Disorders, fourth edition, text revision* (*DSM-IV-TR*) (American Psychiatric Association [APA], 2000) and the *International Classification of Diseases* (*ICD-10*) (World Health Organization [WHO], 1992), provide both researchers and practitioners a model by which to describe and categorize the symptoms, behaviors, and overall life issues clients present. As a further benefit, diagnostic clarity from such systems allows for the identification of specific empirically supported treatments (see chapter 5) for particular diagnostic categories, and therefore promotes an evidence-based approach to the treatment of a wide variety of concerns (Chambless & Hollon, 1998; Chambless & Ollendick, 2001; Kendall & Chambless, 1998).

Criticisms of classification systems typically follow two related lines of reasoning. The first posits that classification systems are simply a means of pigeonholing individuals. The second suggests that standard intervention practices should be abandoned and interventions should instead be designed for each client's unique concerns and characteristics.

However, such criticisms not only oversimplify, but also fail to reflect the reality of professional practice. Disregarding commonalities among athletes and solely viewing athletes as unique individuals with distinct difficulties essentially preclude necessary scientific study and prevent the development of empirically supported interventions for common athlete concerns. In addition, classification systems utilize a nomothetic model for understanding human behavior, focusing on the commonalities among clients manifesting similar psychological characteristics and difficulties (Waldman & Lilienfeld, 1995). Although understanding specific client characteristics and needs is crucial for successful and holistic treatment, nomothetic approaches inherently guide both the education and application of any applied scientific discipline.

Classification systems, therefore, are tools for systematic research, comprehensive assessment, evidence-based intervention, and ethical decision making. We believe classification systems are necessary to meet these essential goals and to guide researchers and practitioners in the study and application of sound intervention procedures. For these reasons, such systems can also help the practitioner determine if she has the training and experience to consult or intervene with a specific case and when referrals to other professionals are required.

Further, research in applied sport psychology has typically addressed performance enhancement intervention efficacy with the underlying assumption that athletes seeking to improve performance are inherently psychosocially well functioning and possess essentially homogeneous personal characteristics and intervention needs (Vealey, 1994a). Since athletes are rarely differentiated by psychological and behavioral factors beyond their most obvious performance needs, the sport psychologist is often left with no systematic way of determining which type of intervention is appropriate for which athlete.

In responding to the absence of a clear, systematic, and comprehensive classification system within sport psychology, we have two primary purposes for this chapter. First, we present a system for assessing, conceptualizing, and classifying issues frequently seen by practicing sport psychologists. We call this system the Multilevel Classification System for Sport Psychology (MCS-SP) (Gardner & Moore, 2004b), which suggests a clear and logical decision-making process for client assessment and intervention planning. Second, we provide the needed structure and impetus for future efficacy research in sport psychology that can help us better understand which interventions are effective (and necessary) for different clients and situations. The MCS-SP has garnered excitement among practitioners and researchers at professional conferences (Gardner & Moore, 2001, October; Gardner, Moore, & Wolanin, 2003, October), and we hope that its recently published conceptualization attracts further attention and utilization, guides practitioners in their decision making, and promotes the evidence-based practices described throughout this text.

Developing a Conceptual Consensus

As mentioned in chapter 1, applied sport psychology has a long history of classifying consultants into broad categories such as educational and clinical sport psychologists (Heyman & Andersen, 1998; United States Olympic Committee [USOC], 1983). As a result, sport psychologists often consider educationally based psychological skills training for performance enhancement appropriate for athletes not suffering from serious mental disorders. This consideration has led to two unfortunate suppositions. The first is that sport psychologists trained in clinical or counseling psychology should restrict their practices to athletes with severe diagnosable disorders and allow others trained in the exercise and sport sciences to intervene with all other performance issues (Gardner, 1991; Silva, 1989). From this perspective, it is assumed that only those interventions directly aimed at developing psychological skills (psychological skills training) are performance enhancement interventions. Based on this way of thinking, interventions that enhance performance *without* the use of psychological skills training are somehow not considered performance enhancement interventions.

Following from the first, the second incorrect supposition is that interventions that ameliorate developmental, transitional, interpersonal, or intrapersonal issues negatively affecting athletic performance (such as counseling and psychological treatment) are not, in their own right, effective forms of performance enhancement (Heyman & Andersen, 1998; Weinberg & Williams, 1998). We certainly disagree with such suppositions, as they infer a simplistic and unrealistic dichotomy. According to the above suppositions, a consultant providing overlapping services or working with individuals whose issues do not neatly allow for dichotomization (such as purely performance or clinical issues) risks being accused of practicing outside his professional boundaries. Such beliefs limit the growth of the professional field and also hinder the athlete who is more concerned with efficacious treatment than with the intraprofession disagreements over service provision.

The significant problem does not lie in the education or training of sport psychologists. Instead, it is both an antecedent and consequence of inconsistent conceptualization of athlete issues. In essence, discrepancies in our conceptualization (and thus intervention) of athlete needs are likely the primary reason for dichotomous thinking and practice. To synchronize our conceptualization, we will introduce and encourage practitioners to use a system for describing and categorizing the full range of athlete issues confronting the real world of applied sport psychology. Thus, the goal of the Multilevel Classification System for Sport Psychology (MCS-SP) is to clearly differentiate athlete issues and problems into functional categories that

- suggest which areas and issues to carefully assess for a comprehensive and holistic understanding of the athlete;
- help practitioners conceptualize cases, develop appropriate assessment and intervention strategies, determine when to refer athletes to outside sources, and determine where to refer athletes; and
- guide future research aimed at developing empirically supported interventions for specific athlete issues.

Multilevel Classification System for Sport Psychology (MCS-SP)

Sport psychology could greatly benefit from new perspectives that challenge the current scope and style of professional practice, renegotiate traditional practice standards, and facilitate the development of evidence-based practice. In addition, the appropriate levels and types of care for given athletes remain in question. The answer should not depend on individual education, training, competency areas, and personal bias, but should logically follow from the needs and life circumstances of the athlete. As seen in figure 3.1, efficacious and ethical interventions should focus on the athlete's environmental, interpersonal, intrapersonal, behavioral, and performance history and demands, and not simply focus on performance goals. Thus, the MCS-SP categorizes athlete issues and problems into four classifications using the above critical factors. These classifications include Performance Development, Performance Dysfunction, Performance Impairment, and Performance Termination.

Performance Development (PD)

This category encompasses athlete issues brought to clinical sport psychologists in which

- a desire to improve athletic performance is clearly stated as a primary goal of intervention;
- there is an *absence* of significant developmental, transitional, behavioral, interpersonal, or intrapersonal psychological factors affecting performance or requiring practitioner attention;

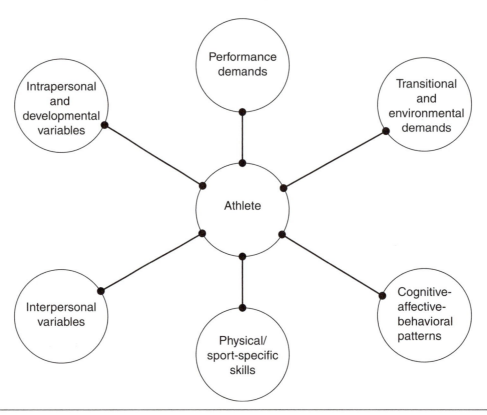

Figure 3.1   A combination of factors affect the athlete.

• developing or refining psychological (mental) skills is likely to enhance athlete or team performance; and

• enhanced performance is the primary intervention goal.

Within the PD category, there are two subtypes, PD-I and PD-II. PD-I refers to cases in which mental skills are considered necessary or helpful in the ongoing development of physical skills, as well as in the enhancement of competitive performance. For this type of athlete, athletic skill development is under way but not complete. PD-II refers to cases in which physical skills have already been highly developed and the development of mental skills is considered necessary for attaining optimal and consistent athletic performance.

Performance development in general subsumes issues traditionally thought of as requiring psychological skills training to enhance performance. In this category of athlete issues, the clinical sport psychologist must first determine that the athlete's psychological functioning is adequate and that the athlete desires a realistic level of performance (or performance consistency) that she has yet to attain or demonstrates inconsistently. In addition, the practitioner must carefully

determine that there are *no* significant developmental, transitional, intrapersonal, interpersonal, or clinical issues affecting the athlete. This must be determined using sound methods and with careful consideration. Practitioners should guard against seeing only those athlete characteristics that are within their competency areas, such as the sport psychology consultant who only focuses on performance enhancement when more significant issues are present, or the clinical psychologist who overpathologizes the athlete when performance enhancement is sufficient.

The typical athlete in the PD category is a reasonably well-functioning individual who desires to further develop his physical skills and performance consistency to attain a high level of performance within realistic limits. The athlete wants to learn to more effectively utilize his psychological and behavioral processes to aid those pursuits. Examples of performance issues falling within the PD domain include attaining consistent quality practice, improving mental preparation and concentration, regulating affective responses and cognitive processes, maintaining perspective, and setting appropriate goals. PD also includes cases in which athletes exhibit inconsistent performance or experience a relatively short-term

This young athlete is beginning to gain basic physical and mental skills that will take years to fully develop.

yet persistent decrement (slump) not explained by intrapersonal, interpersonal, developmental, transitional, or clinical factors.

The PD issues and interventions are most frequently thought of as performance enhancement. As such, PD athlete issues suggest the need for developing or refining self-regulatory strategies for attaining optimal performance. These strategies have traditionally included goal setting, arousal regulation, cognitive self-control, stimulus control (such as precompetitive and preperformance routines), guided imagery and mental rehearsal, and attention control and refocusing (Gould, 1998; Gould & Krane, 1992; Hall, 2001; Hardy et al., 1996; Nideffer & Sagal, 1998; Zinsser, Bunker, & Williams, 1998). More contemporary approaches to performance enhancement have been developed, such as mindfulness-acceptance-commitment (MAC) based performance enhancement (Gardner & Moore, 2004a), which is presented in chapter 6. Although these strategies significantly differ, they are primarily self-regulatory and have been systematically developed in the cognitive-

behavioral framework of professional psychology (Meyers, Whelan, & Murphy, 1996). Counseling or psychological treatment is not indicated, and the interventions utilized are fundamentally educational and strategic.

Note that an absence of clinical, developmental, transitional, intrapersonal, and interpersonal factors is required for this classification. Although the athlete may not immediately mention these concerns when meeting with a sport psychologist, the practitioner cannot automatically assume these issues do not exist. A practitioner who focuses exclusively on the athlete's stated goals may miss critical psychological concerns, and then the athlete is unlikely to fully benefit from the efforts at performance enhancement. Failure to appropriately assess subclinical or clinical issues can harm the client and places the practitioner at risk for malpractice. This ethical and legal issue is further discussed in chapter 12. Therefore, a thorough, semistructured or structured assessment should be conducted prior to formulating hypotheses. The next chapter discusses assessment in detail, including semistructured and structured interviews.

Once the aforementioned issues are determined absent, the case can be classified as PD-I or PD-II. The following examples offer typical PD-I and PD-II cases the clinical sport psychologist will likely confront.

PD-I Example

Tina, an 11-year-old figure skater, and her parents and coach consulted with a sport psychologist to help her develop her physical skills and enhance her competitive performance. Her coach believed she had the raw ability to become an elite skater and wanted Tina to develop better practice focus and intensity, as well as better precompetitive preparation and the ability to cope with the inevitable errors that occur during skating. Tina was well adjusted in all life domains, was motivated to develop as a skater, enjoyed her skating experience, and had supportive and nonintrusive parents.

PD-II Example

Bob, a 32-year-old professional golfer, consulted with a sport psychologist to improve his current level of performance and reach his full potential as a golfer. He recognized that mental factors play a significant role in success on the PGA tour and believed that he needed help in maintaining concentration and in recovering rapidly from mishaps and errors made during tournament play. His performance history indicated that he had been at the same level of play for several years and had not yet attained the level of golf performance expected of and predicted for him years earlier. He presented with no clinical symptoms and no significant interpersonal or intrapersonal difficulties. His overall life situation was stable and he functioned well in family, social, and recreational domains.

These examples typify PD cases. Psychological and behavioral functioning are sound and the issue is an unfulfilled promise or a general desire to enhance skill or competitive performance. In these examples, as in most PD-I or PD-II cases, efforts to promote appropriate self-regulation are rational.

Performance Dysfunction (Pdy)

This category encompasses athlete issues brought to clinical sport psychologists in which

- the desire to improve athletic performance is clearly stated as a primary *or* secondary goal of intervention;
- athletic performance has been consistently greater than the athlete's current level, or performance progress has been slowed or delayed;
- the athlete is generally psychologically healthy, but identifiable psychological barriers, such as developmental, interpersonal, transitional, and schema-based issues (intrapersonal, personality, enduring behavioral characteristics) negatively affect the athlete;
- overall psychological and behavioral functioning are somewhat reduced (either chronic or situational); and
- the athlete may benefit from developing self-regulatory skills as a secondary intervention, but counseling and psychological treatment are the primary intervention options.

The two subtypes within the Pdy category are Pdy-I and Pdy-II. Pdy-I refers to cases in which developmental, transitional, interpersonal, or exogenous (external) life events lead to psychological reactions and result in dysfunctional performance. Pdy-II refers to cases in which performance cues and the competitive environment trigger underlying endogenous (internal) psychological factors such as core cognitive schemas or enduring behavioral characteristics, including unrelenting standards (extreme perfectionism), excessive fear of failure, irrational need for approval, and low frustration tolerance, thereby leading to performance disruption.

In most Pdy cases, athletes *initially* come to the practitioner due to their performance difficulties and not because of their psychological or personal issues. The chief complaint or request may seemingly have little to do with the intrapersonal, interpersonal, developmental, or transitional issues underlying the performance decrements because these athletes are generally psychologically healthy and have previously performed at a higher level. However, subclinical psychological issues are affecting the athlete in one of two ways. In Pdy-I, developmental issues, transitional issues, current life circumstances, or interpersonal psychological barriers have resulted in affective, physiological, or behavioral consequences that affect not only their ability to optimally perform but also their ability to navigate life's demands. In Pdy-II, the athlete already has underlying schemas, personality variables, and enduring behavioral characteristics that are typically not disruptive. However, when exacerbated by increased life stress, these endogenous psychological factors result in some form of dysfunction (such as athletic, academic, or social dysfunction). In the Pdy category, the clinical sport psychologist would not overly focus on the performance issues initially presented, but would carefully assess the athlete's enduring behavioral characteristics and current emotional and behavioral functioning, including intrapersonal, interpersonal, work and educational, and recreational domains.

Findings by Bauman (2000, October), Bond (2001), and Meyers et al. (1996) indicate that Pdy cases are frequent in the day-to-day practice of applied sport psychology. Although these researchers did not use the MCS-SP classification system (it had yet to be developed), they did find that a significant number of cases originally presenting as performance-based (which we classify as PD) were, after thorough assessment, actually cases in which performance decrements were mainly due to the athlete's personal or developmental circumstances (which we classify as Pdy).

The criteria for the Pdy category clearly indicate that developmental, transitional, intrapersonal, and interpersonal issues are the main focus of intervention. Pdy also includes cases in which athletes experience a persistent though possibly short-term performance decrement (slump) *primarily* explained by developmental, transitional, intrapersonal, or interpersonal factors. A key feature of Pdy is that these personal issues are largely responsible for the performance decrements reported by the athlete and concurrently affect overall psychological functioning and quality of life. In addition, these issues should be viewed as more significant than performance issues to the athlete's overall life and adjustment. Examples of Pdy issues include sport transitions, significant family or relationship disruption, psychological reactions to non-career-threatening injury, death and loss, and significant role changes. Also included are intrapersonal and interpersonal issues such as performance anxiety and minor behavioral dysregulation during competition, low frustration tolerance, avoidance, patterns of overinvolvement and underinvolvement, perfectionism, fear of failure and success, acute stress reactions not meeting the criteria for posttraumatic stress disorder, and poor coach and peer relationships.

Personal issues affecting the athlete can reduce concentration and impair sport performance.

The nature of Pdy cases suggests that despite the initial presentation of performance concerns, the athlete would benefit most from counseling or psychological treatment. In this regard, interventions provided during counseling and psychological treatment are very much performance enhancement tools (albeit not necessarily self-regulatory). In these cases, the practitioner's goal is to foster improvement in both psychosocial functioning *and* competitive performance. Although possibly helpful, traditional psychological skills training geared toward performance enhancement would clearly be secondary in the overall treatment for most Pdy athletes. This is because traditional PST procedures do not target the processes that are responsible for the Pdy athlete's difficulties.

The following examples offer typical Pdy-I and Pdy-II cases confronted by the clinical sport psychologist.

Pdy-I Example

Joan, an 18-year-old female swimmer attending an NCAA Division I program, was referred to a clinical sport psychologist when her race times fell well below her personal best and she began repeatedly missing or showing up late for practice. Her performance history indicated that she was a state champion while in high school and had the potential to be an NCAA champion. She had no history of psychological problems before attending college. She reported feeling increasingly lethargic and unhappy, and while she was still functioning adequately in her social, academic, and recreational domains, she was becoming increasingly isolated and losing interest in friendships, schoolwork, and swimming. A recent physical examination was negative. Joan described being homesick and was spending extended periods away from home for the first time in her life. She was the youngest of four siblings and described herself as the baby of the family.

Pdy-II Example

Ted, a 24-year-old professional soccer player, consulted with a clinical sport psychologist due to a recent and serious slump in which his performance was dramatically reduced during both practice and game situations. Ted described his coach, who was in his first year as a head coach for a professional team, as cold, harsh, and unforgiving. Further, Ted described his coach as resembling his own father in personality, and described his own play as tentative and unfocused. Ted was highly perfectionistic, often became highly anxious, was prone to excessive worry, and became easily distracted. He reported frequent sideline glances to gauge his coach's reactions and excessive thought about immediate decisions required on the field. While his overall interpersonal functioning was adequate, deciding about even the slightest life issue had become difficult, and he looked for an inordinate amount of reassurance and comfort from his girlfriend, whom he claimed was straining their relationship.

In these cases, as is typical in Pdy, the initial referral does not typically result from the athlete's life adjustment issues or subjective discomfort, but rather from decrements in competitive performance (swim times, slump) and sport-related behavior (practice truancy, tentative decision making). What are most pronounced in these examples are the developmental and transitional issues surrounding the adjustment to college in the Pdy-I example and the core cognitive schemas relating to approval and perfectionism in the Pdy-II example. In both cases, transitional and intrapersonal issues negatively affect psychological functioning and athletic performance suffers as a result. Counseling or psychological treatment is the clearly indicated intervention, with the possible secondary use of self-regulation training (which was initially requested). In order to maintain rapport and respect ethical considerations, the sport psychologist should both explain and rationalize the necessity for the selected psychological intervention so the athlete is fully aware of the nature of the intervention. Furthermore, the athlete must provide verbal and written informed consent, and the consent form should establish clear goals, any alternative solutions, and expected outcomes of any and all interventions (also see chapter 12).

Performance Impairment (PI)

This category encompasses athlete issues brought to clinical sport psychologists in which

- clinical issues clearly exist, causing the athlete extreme emotional distress or behavioral dysregulation, possibly resulting in reduced performance or a total inability to compete due to outside agency involvement (league suspension, judicial involvement, team action);
- clinical issues severely impair at least one (typically more) major domain of life, such as familial, social-interpersonal, self-care,

recreational, educational, and occupational (athletic performance could fall into this domain for professional and Olympic athletes);

- performance enhancement, while possibly desired, is clearly of secondary importance to the clinical issues affecting the athlete;
- the significance of the clinical issues makes it highly unlikely that developing or refining traditional sport-focused psychological skills will have a substantial effect on the performance issues or overall psychosocial functioning of the athlete; and
- intensive psychological treatment (possibly including psychotropic medication) is the intervention of choice.

The two subtypes within the PI category of the MCS-SP are PI-I and PI-II. PI-I refers to cases in which clinical disorders, such as affective, anxiety, eating, and posttraumatic stress disorders, severely impair overall life functioning and nearly or completely disable the athlete's performance. PI-II refers to cases in which behavioral dysregulation, such as in anger and impulse control disorders, drug and alcohol abuse, and personality disorders, both significantly impairs a major life domain (such as family) and results in an external decision to limit, in either the short term or long term, an individual's participation in athletic competition. External limitations include team suspension or dismissal, legal suspension, judicial actions, and jail time.

The overall PI category subsumes issues often thought to require formal psychiatric diagnoses and typically encapsulates athletes with clear clinical emotional distress or behavioral difficulty. While athletes experiencing PI will likely report (at least intermittently) significant difficulties in their competitive performance, the performance decrements are clearly secondary to the psychological distress and reduced functioning typically seen in these cases. In fact, such performance decrements usually directly result from the psychological distress or behavioral dysregulation the athlete experiences.

Clinical sport psychologists should carefully assess an athlete's psychological and behavioral functioning to either rule out or confirm a case of PI. When noted, such cases must be treated by or referred to practitioners trained to treat them. The voluminous examples of PI cases cover the entire range of psychological difficulties experienced by humans. Some of the more frequent examples sport psychologists encounter include addictive disorders, severe anxiety disorders, bipolar and major affective disorders, anger and impulse control disorders, eating disorders, attention deficit disorders, and severe stress and trauma-based disorders (to name a few).

The following examples illustrate typical PI-I and PI-II cases confronted by clinical sport psychologists.

PI-I Example

Caroline, a 23-year-old professional basketball player, was referred to a clinical sport psychologist after missing her third team practice in two weeks. Earlier in the season, Caroline behaved erratically on a road trip, missed a curfew check, and bought extravagant gifts on an extended shopping spree. She described times in which she felt "tremendous sadness and lack of energy" and other times in which she felt "wired," unable to relax, and as though her thoughts were racing. She felt unable to control these shifts in mood and was afraid that she might be "going crazy."

PI-II Example

Mike, a 28-year-old professional athlete, was referred to a clinical sport psychologist after being arrested on charges of assault and sexual battery. He was an all-star athlete and had a long history of aggressive behavior. He reported that his relationships with family and friends were severely impaired and that he was frequently angry, anxious, and depressed. In addition, Mike believed that the world was out to get him and that he was targeted unfairly because of his celebrity status. He also noted that at times he became so angry on the field that he lost focus and made dumb mistakes. At the time of consultation he was suspended indefinitely from the team and believed that he was in danger of both going to jail and being permanently cut.

In the previous PI-I example, Caroline recognized her inability to function as a professional athlete in her current psychological condition, and would probably not expect performance enhancement interventions. In this example, the primary intervention is mood stabilization, not performance enhancement. Since Mike's difficulties controlling his anger and behavior directly affect his performance, Mike may likely deny the need for psychological treatment and instead request performance enhancement. However, interventions in the second example must

focus on anger regulation and enhanced impulse control, and not performance enhancement. His affective and behavioral dysregulation and the resultant dangerous and inappropriate behaviors encompass impairments in multiple life domains, and thus they should be the central focus of any psychological intervention. Such efforts, if successful, will likely not only foster more adaptive emotional and behavioral functioning but also improve performance via greater emotion regulation and reduced psychological distress. Most psychological and behavioral disorders in PI cases can be treated effectively with empirically supported interventions that have long been used with clinical populations. Since PI athletes are experiencing clinical concerns, these well-established interventions should be employed (possibly including psychotropic medication). Psychological skills training, despite the connection between the athletes' difficulties and performance, would be inappropriate and potentially harmful (Heyman & Andersen, 1998).

Performance Termination (PT)

This category encompasses athlete issues brought to clinical sport psychologists in which

- the primary concerns relate to the multiple stressors and issues accompanying termination of athletic careers due either to serious injury or to voluntary or involuntary career completion, where there is little realistic prospect of reinstituting or preserving the career;

- psychological reactions reflecting either a normative or exceptional grieving process such as anger, depression, and anxiety may exist, and family and interpersonal issues are likely to require significant attention;

- career realities contraindicate performance enhancement; and

- counseling or psychological treatment is clearly the psychosocial intervention of choice, and referral for adjunctive career counseling and financial planning may be necessary.

The two subtypes within the PT category of the MCS-SP are PT-I and PT-II. PT-I refers to cases in which the athlete's competitive career ends expectedly (possibly voluntarily), typically due to free choice, age, or natural diminution of physical skills. The most likely psychological reaction is similar to the normative grieving following the expected death of a loved one and may include a slow, subclinical progression through stages such as shock, denial, anger, depression, and acceptance (Hopson & Adams, 1977; Kubler-Ross, 1969).

PT-II refers to cases in which the athlete's competitive career ends unexpectedly and involuntarily due to serious injury or sudden noninjury termination, with the athlete typically having few, if any, alternative options for the career to continue. In these cases, in addition to facing the unexpected reality of career termination and the need to plan a new lifestyle and career, the athlete may experience more severe psychological symptoms similar to those in individuals experiencing delayed or extreme grief reactions, acute stress reactions, or posttraumatic stress disorder. PT-II individuals also tend to progress through shock, denial, anger, depression, and acceptance (Hopson & Adams, 1977; Kubler-Ross, 1969), but usually this progression is significantly more severe than that of PT-I individuals. As such, the PT-II client likely requires greater treatment intensity.

This athlete is beginning to realize that years of injury are preventing her from maintaining her competitive edge.

The following examples are typical PT-I and PT-II cases that clinical sport psychologists confront.

PT-I Example

Kim was a 30-year-old competitive skier. Although she had experienced a long and enjoyable career, she had never been selected to her national Alpine ski team. Over the last several competitive seasons, her times and rankings steadily declined despite sound training, vigorous workout strategies, and a relative absence of injury. Consulting with family and coaches, she began to accept the degeneration of her physical abilities and to consider life after skiing. As Kim grieved the loss of her competitive career, she began to feel lost and uncertain about her future. She saw herself as having few skills or interests to fall back on and wondered if others close to her would find more exciting friends. It was at this point that Kim consulted a clinical sport psychologist for help in dealing with her situation.

PT-II Example

Carlos was a 26-year-old minor-league baseball player who had been a first-round draft choice and was previously viewed throughout professional baseball as a definite major-league pitching star. During the off-season two years earlier, Carlos suffered multiple injuries in a bar fight, including a serious tear of his rotator cuff. After surgery and a long period of rehabilitation, Carlos was once again approaching his presurgery level of performance, when during the first inning of a game he felt a pop in his pitching shoulder and left the game in pain. After medical testing, he was told that he had again torn his rotator cuff and that it was highly unlikely he would ever be able to pitch professionally. Carlos soon became angry, depressed, and socially withdrawn. He had recurrent flashbacks to the pitch that resulted in the tear and believed that he was useless and that his life was over. He had not completed college and saw no realistic possibility of future happiness. As Carlos became more despondent and angry, a family member referred him to a clinical sport psychologist.

In both of these cases, which typify PT-I and PT-II, the athletes confronted the end of their competitive careers, which led to varying psychological distress and discomfort. While Kim's termination was gradual and less intense, the end of her career triggered intrapersonal and interpersonal issues surrounding competence, identity (Baillie & Danish, 1992; Brewer, Van Raalte, & Linder, 1993), and social desirability. She needs to address these issues in order to move forward productively, happily, and with purpose and self-agency. For Carlos, the end came swiftly, was traumatic, and was accompanied by a multitude of psychological and behavioral symptoms reflecting traumatic stress reactions (Follette, Ruzek, & Abueg, 1998). Carlos needs to confront and habituate to the intense emotions associated with his traumatic injury and to modify the maladaptive assumptions relating to his self-worth and future possibilities (Follette et al., 1998). In both cases, the intervention of choice is counseling or psychological treatment with a clinical sport psychologist educated, trained, and licensed to treat such cases.

As table 3.1 shows, the MCS-SP provides a broad but useful means of classifying the most common issues encountered in applied sport psychology. The classification system is based on the primary issues and subsequent intervention needs of the athlete and is designed to guide both the assessment and intervention phases of the consultant's applied work.

MCS-SP Implications for Sport Psychology

We have discussed the theoretical rationale and the categories of the MCS-SP, and we believe the practice and research implications of the MCS-SP now warrant further description. The global purpose of the MCS-SP is to guide the thorough evaluation of athletes' needs, provide strategies for in-depth case conceptualization, and systematically formulate the most appropriate type and level of professional service. Yet comprehensive assessment should precede any intervention. The MCS-SP provides the framework for a thorough assessment and broad understanding of the athlete's presenting issues, mental status, developmental level and demands, intrapersonal and interpersonal functioning, and psychosocial history, as well as the competitive performance history and current athletic demands. This information is not just useful for determining the athlete's needs and tailoring interventions but is also "designed to enhance rapport building and client-practitioner regard" (Hays, 2000, p. 265). While some argue that comprehensively assessing athletes is often unnecessary or impractical, we suggest that failure to adequately determine intervention targets is unacceptable and can harm both the well-being of the athlete and the credibility of the professional and the field.

The MCS-SP clearly suggests that practitioners beware of prematurely beginning performance enhancement before clarifying the full psychosocial picture. Without fully assessing the athlete's world, how can the practitioner logically and ethically employ intervention strategies? How can he ensure that the intervention is the most helpful

Table 3.1 MCS-SP Intervention Guide

Classification	Primary therapeutic focus	Secondary therapeutic focus	Intervention
Performance development (PD)	Performance issues (athletic performance enhancement)	Psychosocial issues	Psychological skills training or mindfulness-acceptance-commitment performance enhancement (MAC)
Performance dysfunction (Pdy)	Developmental issues, transition, reaction, and adjustment to significant life events; psychological barriers	Performance issues	Psychological treatment or counseling (possibly with psychological skills training)
Performance impairment (PI)	Psychological and behavioral dysfunction	Performance issues	Psychological treatment or counseling (possibly with medication)
Performance termination (PT)	Psychological reactions to career termination	Future planning (such as career and financial)	Psychological treatment or counseling

Reprinted, by permission, from F.L. Gardner and Z.E. Moore, 2004 "The multi-level classification system for sport psychology (MCS-SP)," *The Sport Psychologist* 18:(1):89-109.

for the athlete? Completely understanding the athlete as the MCS-SP suggests leads to intervention strategies based on the overall psychosocial and performance needs of the athlete and suggests referrals to other professionals (physician, nutritionist) when necessary (Cogan, 2000).

Final Thoughts

The purpose of this chapter was to provide a classification system for categorizing and conceptualizing the array of issues athletes present to the clinical sport psychologist. While not unmindful of the criticisms of classification systems in the behavioral sciences (Beutler & Malik, 2002), we believe using this system will not create unnecessary pejorative labels, but will help sport psychology practitioners, students, and research scientists accurately assess, conceptualize, and intervene with the differing needs of athletes. As practitioners who enhance the psychological well-being and subsequent athletic performance of such a unique clientele, we must respect the individual differences of athletes and integrate sound intervention strategies with the athlete's specific characteristics and concerns.

Applying the MCS-SP "in no way implies the absence of important differences among these individuals" (Waldman & Lilienfeld, 1995, p. 24), and it incorporates both nomothetic and idiographic approaches to the assessment and treatment of athletes. Additionally, the MCS-SP potentiates more specific and appropriate efficacy research in sport psychology consistent with trends across other professional psychology domains. This system will hopefully assist focused empirical research that will advance an evidence-based approach to the practice of sport psychology. Now that we have discussed the MCS-SP and provided a rationale for a comprehensive preintervention assessment, the next chapter discusses traditional assessment approaches in sport psychology and recommends a comprehensive and holistic assessment based on the MCS-SP model.

CHAPTER 4

Assessment in Clinical Sport Psychology

In this chapter, we discuss the fundamental purposes and strategies of effective assessment in clinical sport psychology. This chapter does not intend to provide a compendium of instruments available to clinical sport psychologists, as both sport and clinical psychology resources are available from multiple sources (Antony, Orsillo, & Roemer, 2001; Duda, 1998; Groth-Marnat, 1999; Nideffer & Sagal, 2001). Rather, our task is to highlight the goals, strategies, and guidelines for comprehensively assessing athletes.

Assessment in clinical sport psychology, as in all areas of professional psychology, is conducted to answer specific questions and to guide relevant and meaningful decisions (most often regarding intervention but at times regarding personnel screening or selection). Assessment has four fundamental goals. The first three fall under the category of *understanding behavior,* while the fourth belongs to the category of *predicting behavior:*

1. **Classification or diagnosis of the presenting issue.** This is often referred to as *topographical assessment.* An example of this is using a semistructured interview to determine the correct MCS-SP classification (based on the identification of specific characteristics) or to identify a *DSM-IV-TR* disorder (based on the identification of specific clinical symptoms).

2. **Identification of the etiology of a particular issue or problem.** For example, a set of inventories and a structured interview may determine that harsh parenting that punished any slight error made by the child (athlete) has resulted in the child's overgeneralized fear of failure that now intensifies under the high stress associated with athletic competition.

3. **Functional (specific and detailed) understanding of both personal and sport issues or problems.** This understanding allows the practitioner to identify target behaviors, triggering stimuli, and behavioral consequences and to rationally select an intervention strategy and an objective means to monitor and evaluate the effectiveness of the intervention.

4. **Prognosis or prediction (with or without intervention).** An example of this goal is using inventories, behavioral observation, and a comprehensive interview to confirm panic disorder as the reason for the rapid fatigue, shortness of breath, lack of game intensity, and seemingly poor conditioning in a star athlete. This finding then suggests that a specific empirically supported cognitive behavioral intervention is likely to reduce such difficulties to manageable levels relatively quickly and similarly suggests that not intervening is likely to exacerbate the difficulties.

In many respects, all assessment questions seek information relating to goals 1, 2, and 3 in order to provide an appropriate prognosis to meet goal 4 (see figure 4.1).

Assessment Strategies

The three primary strategies of assessment in professional psychology are the interview, behavioral observation, and psychological testing. Combined, these elements are broadly referred to as *psychological assessment.* As we describe in this chapter, when performed correctly, these three strategies can be seamlessly integrated to determine prognosis, direct the selection and implementation of an

Obtain information relating to topographical assessment	Obtain information relating to functional assessment
Obtain information relating to problem/issue etiology	Obtain information relating to prognosis from other 3 quadrants

Figure 4.1 The four-quadrant interview guideline.

appropriate intervention strategy, and reasonably predict the outcome (goal 4).

Interview

The earliest form of assessment in professional psychology was the clinical interview (Groth-Marnat, 1999). Long before the development of psychological testing, the information required for understanding personal difficulties and dynamics was ascertained through unstructured interviews that allowed clients to freely discuss personal information that *they* deemed relevant, with little direction from the practitioner. Over the years, however, psychology increasingly became more scientific, and the natural subjectivity inherent in the unstructured interview and the desire for more objective and reliable means of collecting information led to a myriad of psychological tests (Groth-Marnat, 1999) and semistructured and structured interview formats (First, Spitzer, Gibbon, & Williams, 1997).

Over the years, many practitioners came to view the *un*structured interview as unreliable, as it is procedurally inconsistent, subject to clinician biases, and lacks empirical validation (Groth-Marnat, 1999). The subjective dangers inherent in the unstructured interview, which by definition relies on the interviewer's clinical judgment, are most clearly noted in a recent meta-analysis by Grove and colleagues (Grove, Zald, Lebow, Snitz, & Nelson, 2000). Their comprehensive review of the professional literature found that mechanical prediction of human behavior (using statistically derived scales and formulas) was consistently

more accurate than clinical judgment (predictions made by subjectively evaluating test or interview data) in nearly all of the 136 studies comparing the two approaches. Even more troubling is their finding that clinical interpretations of objective test data become *less* accurate when the clinician has interview data at his disposal (Grove et al., 2000). These findings indicate that the clinical sport psychologist engaging in unstructured interviews must take great care in drawing subjective conclusions about athletes' issues. The unstructured interview without goal-directed aims or psychometric data can quickly dissolve into a likeability contest in which the practitioner makes inferences based on the overall *feeling* she has about the athlete. Thus, variables such as the personal appearance, ethnicity, history, attitude, and belief system of the athlete can impact the practitioner's interpretation of the athlete's presenting issues, etiology, and likely intervention needs. The comprehensive review by Grove et al. (2000) reinforces the need for objective assessment, including both inventories (psychological tests) and semistructured or structured interviews. Objectifying the assessment process leads to more reliable and valid assessment in all areas of professional psychology (Segal, 1997).

Despite such findings and the limited use of unstructured interviews in other psychology domains, sport psychology practitioners have yet to unanimously embrace the importance of objectively collecting relevant client information. While numerous practitioners have called for inventories and other objective methods to be integrated into the work of the sport psychologist (Gardner, 1995; Gordin & Henschen, 1989; Nideffer & Sagal, 2001; Perna, Neyer, Murphy, Ogilvie, & Murphy, 1995), others have proposed that using inventories and other semistructured or structured assessment approaches is unnecessary or even detrimental to their work (Dorfman, 1990; Halliwell, 1990; Orlick, 1989; Ravizza, 1990; Rotella, 1990). From their perspective, informal interviews that are consistent with personal style and practice philosophies allow for information collection in an atmosphere that is nonthreatening and more accepted by the athlete. While this style does promote a comfortable atmosphere, there are clear dangers in making decisions based on personal style, beliefs, or philosophies. The proposition that experience and professional judgment are both necessary and *wholly* sufficient to make important professional decisions is inconsistent with the data and unacceptable to an evidence-based practice of sport psychology. The data regarding clinical judgment are clear, and a legitimate evidence-driven profession cannot ignore such findings based on anecdotal reports and personal opinion alone.

In response to the dangers of the unstructured interview, semistructured and structured interviews (First et al., 1997) have become popular among professional psychologists and have been shown to be both reliable and valid indicators of client concerns (Helzer, Robins, Croughan, & Welner, 1981; Robins, Helzer, Cottler, & Goldring, 1989). One particular interview, the Sport-Clinical Intake Protocol (SCIP), is an example of a structured interview for sport psychology (Taylor & Schneider, 1992). The SCIP focuses on both sport and nonsport issues and allows for comprehensive and consistent data collection with face-to-face collaborative client interaction not typically found in pencil-and-paper inventories. The SCIP interview clearly demonstrates that semistructured or structured interviews do not inherently create an artificial or noncollaborative atmosphere.

One particular form of semistructured interview, described later in this chapter, is the functional analysis of behavior. This type of interview does not suggest a specific, structured set of questions to ask the client in order. Instead, during the collaborative interchange with the client, the practitioner inquires about the who, what, when, where, why, how, and how much relating to the client's presenting issue or problem. With the goal of obtaining such a breadth and depth of information, it is no wonder that the functional analysis is at the heart of a comprehensive case formulation (see goal 3 of assessment). This interview process identifies the stimuli (both internal and external) that trigger problematic behaviors along with the obvious and subtle consequences (reinforcers) of those behaviors. In essence, functional analysis explicates relevant target behaviors, triggers, and factors that maintain specific behaviors needing reduction or augmentation. For example, if an athlete is missing practice, and thus the intervention target is responsible practice behavior, a functional analysis would seek to understand the prepractice stimuli, their relationship to attendance, and the consequences for the athlete. If this athlete has had a significant interpersonal conflict with a teammate over a girlfriend, the anger or anxiety at the thought of seeing that teammate may result in avoidance of the affective state (by avoiding practice). The consequence of immediately reducing the negative affect serves as a negative reinforcer, increasing the likelihood

of further avoidance. Although only briefly elucidated, this form of assessment represents the functional analysis.

Regardless of interview style, the interview process may also benefit from the active participation of family members, coaching personnel, and other relevant parties (with client approval and written consent). This participation is often essential to comprehensively understanding the problem context and typically ensures that the critical people in the athlete's life both support and understand the utilization of sport psychology services.

Behavioral Observation

The second primary strategy in the assessment process is directly observing client behavior, which can occur in several contexts. First, the clinical sport psychologist may have the opportunity to directly observe the athlete within the original context in which the issue (of treatment focus) arose. For example, the practitioner may witness a competitive event, a coach–athlete or parent–athlete interaction, or a meeting with teammates. While attending competition or practice, the practitioner can directly observe interpersonal interactions, verbal and nonverbal responses to both good and bad performances, body language in response to coach or referee decisions, and similar types of overt behavior along with antecedent events and consequent behavior. These observations allow the practitioner to create a real-life context for the words and descriptions the athlete provides in private meetings.

Second, behavioral observations are inherent to the interview itself. The clinical sport psychologist should note an athlete's response to frustrating questions or inventories, behavior when anxious or angry, and similar reactions. These reactions yield critical information about the athlete's internal and external experience. Whatever the context, directly observing behavior provides the clinical sport psychologist useful information to integrate into the assessment process. However, behavioral observations are most useful when described *objectively* and when the practitioner limits subjective interpretation of behaviors and responses until she has fully collected the relevant data. For example, the practitioner observing that the athlete rolled her eyes each time her coach criticized her is significantly more objective than the practitioner witnessing the action and subjectively concluding that the response represents oppositional and defiant behavior. The latter is clearly more judgmental and evaluative and may lead to data misinterpretation. Although the practitioner's interpretation may be true, early subjective interpretation can cloud the practitioner's judgment and lead to confirmatory bias. Thus, we recommend objective description of behavioral observations and suggest withholding interpretation of these data until sufficient data have been collected.

Behavioral observations are integrated into a problem formulation within the context of all the data collected. Certainly, the most important observations are those behaviors directly relating to the presenting issues. The professional literature refers to observed (in-session) behavior directly relevant to the presenting issue as "clinically relevant behavior" (Kohlenberg & Tsai, 1995), which is particularly important in the assessment process.

Psychological Testing

Psychological testing, often referred to as psychometric evaluation, is the third basic assessment strategy and is one of the most controversial topics in sport psychology (Vealey & Garner-Holman, 1998). As noted, some practitioners view testing as unnecessary or even negative, while others describe it as positive and helpful. Sport psychologists often base their decision to use or not use psychometric testing on educational background, training, and consulting philosophy (Vealey & Garner-Holman, 1998). We suggest, however, that practitioners should base the decision on the available tests' abilities to provide information needed for thoroughly understanding the athlete's needs and determining appropriate interventions. When effective measures exist, we believe it is in the athlete's best interest to integrate the knowledge gained from these assessment measures into the holistic understanding of the athlete.

There are basic recommendations for using psychometric instruments. To ethically and effectively utilize data from psychological inventories or tests, clinical sport psychologists should understand that individual scores derived from these instruments are not end products, but rather are additional data points in the assessment process that allow practitioners to generate or confirm hypotheses. The data obtained from assessment instruments should be integrated with information from other assessment strategies (such as the semistructured interview and behavioral observation) into a comprehensive whole. Considerable

evidence supports the use of psychological testing in organizational contexts for purposes not unlike those found in sport psychology (Hogan, Hogan, & Roberts, 1996). In organizational settings, as in sport settings, formal assessment material is intended to complement information derived from interview and observation and is rarely used as a sole source of data. For example, some of our work with professional sport organizations includes the use of psychometric instruments as a complementary source of information. Specifically, when interviewing athletes for draft selection, the information we obtain from semistructured interviews and psychological inventories does not specifically determine draft choices. In actuality, our data and the opinions derived from these data are considered along with scouting reports based on skill presentation and potential, and physical testing data.

With this in mind, to utilize psychological testing appropriately, the clinical sport psychologist should consider a variety of factors, including construct validity of the test in the context of the referral question, reliability, standardization, practical considerations, and data synthesis.

Construct Validity and Testing Context

When evaluating the validity of a given instrument, the primary issue is the degree to which the instrument measures what it purports to measure and the degree to which the construct the instrument measures relates to the issue under consideration (Kazdin, 1998). For example, when assessing an athlete referred for frequent verbal conflicts with

Data from formal testing should never stand alone and must be considered only within the context of interview data and behavioral observation.

staff, psychometric evaluation of state and trait anxiety likely relates very little to the problem context. Using this measure is thus inappropriate, regardless of how well a chosen instrument assesses this construct. Similarly, a measure of anger and hostility that has not been shown to have valid psychometric properties is inappropriate, as the degree to which the measure assesses the construct of anger or hostility is unknown. The construct the instrument measures and the construct we wish to evaluate must match. For example, the empirically based studies on the construct validity of the Beck Depression Inventory (Beck, Steer, & Brown, 1996) allow practitioners to confidently utilize this instrument to measure depression, yet do not indicate its success in measuring anxiety.

Reliability

Reliability reflects the stability, consistency, predictability, and accuracy of a given instrument (Kazdin, 1998). Reliability is the estimate of the random fluctuation that can be expected in an individual's score on a particular instrument, or the extent to which a score will be replicated by the same instrument on the same athlete at different times. If an individual scores 2 standard deviations above the mean on an anxiety measure that has low reliability, we cannot be sure if the score reflects the individual's level of anxiety or is an inherent inconsistency of the instrument. Obviously, an instrument with low reliability has minimal value and its professional use is inappropriate.

Standardization

Evaluating the appropriateness of a measure's standardization depends on the population on which the instrument was normed compared to the population on which it is being used. Sport psychology literature has often discussed this issue in terms of the relative merits of sport-specific measures versus general measures of psychological functioning (Nideffer & Segal, 2001; Vealey & Garner-Holman, 1998). The underlying question at all times must be the degree to which the individual being assessed is similar to the measure's standardization population. For example, for a clinical sport psychologist assessing worry in a college-aged athlete, it is critical to consider if the selected instrument was normed on a college-aged population, as opposed to only an adult clinical sample. The issue of athlete and nonathlete is likely of secondary importance. Of course, the

practitioner may feel even more comfortable if the collected data provide subgroup norming (such as on college athletes). However, subgroup norming is certainly not necessary, as the primary goal is to evaluate the individual with respect to a particular aspect of general psychological functioning (such as worry in the previous example).

On the other hand, if the issue is *competitive* worry (with the related assumption that it differs from noncompetitive worry), a sport-specific measure may be particularly helpful. It may be important for the instrument to be *sport-specific* if the issue is one that is exclusive to sport situations, such as competitive anxiety. Conversely, a more general instrument is more appropriate if the issue (or construct) is cross-situational, such as general anxiety or overall interpersonal functioning. The issue of standardization is not exclusive to sport psychology. It also occurs in clinical psychology, as measures of specific constructs such as social anxiety and posttraumatic stress clearly contrast to measures of more general constructs such as general (trait) anxiety and depression (see chapter 8 for further discussion of such measures). When considering standardization, no single recommendation can be made regarding the choice of sport-specific or generalized assessment measures. The choice should be based on the specific construct and the degree to which using a given measure can be justified by the normative sample reflecting this construct.

There may be times sport psychologists need a general measure of psychopathology, such as the Psychological Assessment Inventory (PAI) (Morey, 2003), as well as general measures of personality, such as the Test of Attentional and Interpersonal Style (TAIS) (Nideffer, 1976) or the Sixteen Personality Factor Questionnaire, Fifth Edition (16PF) (Russell & Karol, 1994). These instruments can confirm specific hypotheses or findings noted during the semistructured or structured interview or during behavioral observation. Likewise, these instruments can generate initial hypotheses when not enough time is available to fully complete a comprehensive assessment (including interview) or when minimal history is available. The semistructured or structured interview can then follow up on the collected information.

A full discussion of the uses and misuses of psychological testing is beyond the scope of this chapter, but interested readers can find a comprehensive discussion of the effective uses of such instruments in several articles and texts (Gardner, 1995, 2001; Nideffer & Sagal, 2001;

Vealey & Garner-Holman, 1998). In addition, we refer the reader interested in detailed study of psychometrics and measurement theory to Anastasi (1996).

Practical Considerations

The question considered here is the appropriateness of an instrument given the practical considerations inherent in specific testing circumstances. For example, does the reading level the instrument requires match that of the athlete? Is the time required to complete the selected instruments appropriate for the time allotted for assessment? Does the physical setting in which the instrument is administered allow for privacy and focus, and are the conditions of the setting relatively similar to the norming conditions? These practical considerations are important in constructing an assessment package that can effectively address the relevant referral questions. Reading level, time availability, and the degree of expertise and training the practitioner has in administering, scoring, and interpreting the instrument are all critical to ethically and effectively utilizing psychological inventories.

Synthesizing Data

So far, we have described the important uses of the three assessment strategies in answering specific referral questions. Yet a comprehensive assessment ultimately requires that the data collected are gathered, organized, and synthesized. Since the strategies briefly outlined above allow for data collection, we now turn to a separate yet related process, data synthesis.

When data collection is complete, the goal becomes synthesizing information into reasonable evidence-based hypotheses and beginning to conceptualize the case. Once again, empirical findings suggest that actuarial (often referred to as mechanical or statistical) prediction is superior to clinical judgment (Grove et al., 2000; Kleinmuntz, 1990; Meehl, 1954, 1965). It is not suggested, however, that there is no place for clinical judgment. Quite the contrary: the challenge for the practitioner is to use the evidence accumulated in nomothetic research studies to make empirically informed idiographic decisions based on the needs and special circumstances of the individual athlete. To clarify, individual (idiographic) plans are developed from the knowledge obtained from sound empirical research on larger samples (nomothetic data). Practitioners should understand relevant cutoff scores, individual

scale interpretations, and regression formulas and consider them within the specific context of the client, and they should correspondingly understand how the athlete and his particular life circumstances differ from the individuals in the nomothetic studies. When considering these factors, the athlete should not be viewed as distinct from the normative group simply because of his athletic involvement and related demands. There are no data to suggest that athletes differ from the general population in long-standing personality variables, dispositional factors, interpersonal styles, state characteristics, lifetime prevalence of psychopathology, and so on. Thus, the factors to consider when utilizing psychological instruments with athletes will typically be the same as in nonathlete populations (see figure 4.2).

Given the inherent dangers surrounding the accuracy of clinical judgment, here are some suggestions to increase the reliability and validity of judgments made in the assessment process:

• Clinical sport psychologists should develop expertise in the instruments utilized, the person or group they are evaluating, and the issues or problem areas with which they work. This knowledge base should not be static, but should be a dynamic base that requires active, ongoing, and lifelong learning. Extensive familiarity with both past and current professional literature and involvement in continuing professional education are essential to maintaining professional competence in this area.

• In the course of assessment, the clinical sport psychologist is encouraged to use comprehensive structured or semistructured interviews with athletes. Effective and ethical practice requires that the clinical sport psychologist determine the means of collecting important interview data, as

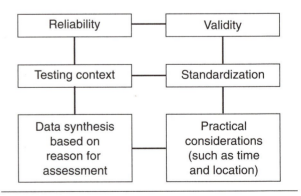

Figure 4.2 Factors to consider when utilizing psychological tests.

the sport environment often makes formal private conversation difficult (see chapter 12). The challenges of providing psychological service in an often inflexible environment do not free the practitioner from providing care that fulfills the ethical and professional standards dictated by the greater professional psychology community. Creativity and honesty regarding these requirements allow the practitioner to navigate the difficult realities that are inherent in sport psychology consulting (Moore, 2003a).

• We encourage the clinical sport psychologist to carefully record behavioral observation during the task (not afterward), as memory is a reconstructive process that is naturally biased and prone to error.

• When utilizing a psychometric instrument, clinical sport psychologists should understand its reliability, validity, and standardization, and they should select only instruments that will provide information directly relevant to the referral question or generated hypothesis.

• To reduce confirmatory bias, clinical sport psychologists should consider all accumulated data and should guard against excessively focusing on the data that support their preconceived notions or their practice philosophies.

• When classifying or diagnosing, clinical sport psychologists should carefully attend to the specific criteria contained in the MCS-SP (for sport-specific classifications), the *DSM-IV-TR* (for clinical classifications) (APA, 2000), or other current and relevant systems. In addition, when deciding on interventions after the assessment process, clinical sport psychologists should follow available data and empirical evidence and not simply their practice philosophies or professional training (see sidebar).

Recommendations to Enhance the Reliability and Validity of Psychological Assessment

• Develop instrument expertise

• Know the psychometric standardization, reliability, and validity of the instruments

• Develop expertise in the content areas that are the focus of assessment

• Engage in relevant, lifelong continuing education

• Utilize structured or semistructured interviews

• Carefully note and record observations

• Include all relevant data when generating hypotheses

• Carefully utilize nomothetic classification systems, comprehensively understanding their use

Steps in the Assessment Process

Assessment in clinical sport psychology is a sequential process and has several discreet steps. The first is thoroughly evaluating the referral question. In this initial step, the practitioner has two very clear goals. The first is to understand the issues, problems, and expectations inherent in the referral. Questions to consider include the following:

• Who is making the referral?

• What is the expectation of the person receiving the service as opposed to that of the person making the referral (if not self-referred)?

• What was the immediate trigger for the referral?

• Are there any unspoken or hidden agendas, needs, or purposes in the referral?

At times, these questions can be answered before beginning the assessment process (phone contact), while at other times this information is gathered during the first meeting between the athlete and the clinical sport psychologist. In either case, these questions must be considered and answered. Through careful consideration of these questions the practitioner gains preliminary insights and, maybe most importantly, can avoid legal or ethical dilemmas relating to service expectations, confidentiality, professional expertise, and boundaries. While considering these questions and refining the referral question, the practitioner can initially hypothesize what information is required and which relevant assessment strategies may be most useful. To provide an example that will be conceptually familiar to many readers, let's consider a phone referral for a high school swimmer experiencing competitive anxiety. At first, this referral may appear relatively simple. However, when considered more carefully, the practitioner may find that the athlete has long experienced anxiety across numerous domains when in the presence of a cold and often punitive father who has a great deal of personal investment in his child's success in swimming. In addition, the athlete has mixed feelings about her swimming and has no desire to consult a sport psychologist. This information suggests a more complex situation requiring a different interview strategy (including parent and possibly coach participation), possible psychometric evaluation beyond competitive anxiety (assessing for depression, anger and hostility, quality of life), and particular attention to the subtle consequences of her successes and failures in competitive swimming. While certainly not all referral questions demonstrate this level of complexity, quick efforts to enhance performance that do not consider these critical factors are likely to be unsuccessful. In addition, failing to consider or dismissing the more significant concerns will surely demonstrate that the practitioner does not understand the athlete and will likely result in a poor practitioner–athlete relationship. Thus, even if deeper concerns are not present, the practitioner is encouraged to gain a holistic understanding of the athlete before intervening.

The second goal of evaluating the referral question is to ascertain whether or not the clinical sport psychologist has adequate knowledge regarding the issue in question. Important questions to consider include the following:

- Does the practitioner have (current) empirically informed knowledge of the issue?
- Is the presenting issue within the practitioner's education, training, experience, and competence?
- Are the psychological instruments required for a comprehensive assessment available to the practitioner?
- Does the practitioner understand these instruments or need to review the manuals or other supporting literature?

Once again, these questions must be answered before an appropriate assessment can begin. Failure to answer them could result in intervention failure (a negative outcome) and possibly a negligence or malpractice claim against the professional. For example, again consider the high

school swimmer. In this case, the practitioner should gauge the degree to which he is equipped to both evaluate family dynamics and engage in a full assessment with a high school athlete whose issues are only secondarily related to competitive performance. After carefully considering the referral question and gathering the requisite knowledge relating to the referral question, the actual assessment process can begin.

The pragmatic issues of comprehensively assessing all athletes (or in some cases entire teams) are also important. The clinical sport psychologist must balance the time restraints inherent in sport psychology consulting and the need to properly assess individuals (or larger groups) to ensure appropriate interventions. While there is no simple balance, we prefer to emphasize to the athlete or team the necessity of holistic assessment before intervention. There are certainly times that the assessment process needs shortening, but abbreviating the process should not be random. Reducing components of the assessment process must be done carefully, with clear goals in mind.

MCS-SP Assessment

At its basic level, psychological assessment should follow a sequential model in which the referral question leads to systematic data collection. This allows for hypothesis generation based on the information collected and on a comprehensive understanding of situational context, physical skills, and personal characteristics, as outlined in the Integrative Model of Athletic Performance (IMAP) in chapter 2. The hypotheses both promote understanding of the current issues facing the athlete and allow for behavioral prediction (with and without intervention). Next we describe a comprehensive assessment process that integrates the three assessment strategies discussed at the beginning of this chapter. This approach to assessment in clinical sport psychology includes a topographical assessment for MCS-SP categorization as well as a functional assessment to detail the relationships among triggering events and stimuli, functional and dysfunctional behaviors, and outcomes and consequences.

As indicated in chapter 3, a comprehensive assessment in clinical sport psychology can be undertaken by using the MCS-SP, which rules out severe psychological issues before beginning performance enhancement or any other intervention. As noted, a best-practice assessment involves systematic personal data collection, which includes a semistructured interview and relevant psychometric tools as necessary. A brief measure utilized in our research laboratory and in field testing is the Performance Classification Questionnaire (PCQ) shown on this page (Gardner, Wolanin, & Moore, 2005). This tool, used as an adjunct to the semistructured interview process, has been shown to discriminate between PD and Pdy classifications, which are the hardest classifications to differentiate. This questionnaire does not evaluate more clinical concerns (PI) (there are sound clinical measures for this) and does not evaluate

termination issues (PT) (which are more easily identifiable). This brief self-report assessment tool contains 10 items in a Likert-scale format. To score the measure, add all scores (reverse score items 5 and 7). Scores less than 30 suggest a classification of PD, and scores 30 and above suggest a classification of Pdy. This measure can help initial hypothesis generation, but it is not intended to replace the semistructured interview.

The most important element in data collection is completing a semistructured or structured interview. A model semistructured interview for the MCS-SP is provided at the end of this

---

Performance Classification Questionnaire (PCQ)

Initials_____ Date_____ Age_____ Sport_____ Gender_____

Please read each of the following statements and indicate how typical each statement is of you in terms of why you are seeking consultation. Please rate your answer 1 through 5 according to how true or characteristic each statement is of you. Please fill in the bubble that contains the appropriate number.

	Not at all true - - - - - - - - - - Very true				
1. I have performed at a higher level or more consistently in the past, but my current performance or development has been slowed, reduced, or delayed.	①	②	③	④	⑤
2. My personal standards sometimes make it difficult for me to perform as well as I could.	①	②	③	④	⑤
3. I am unable to perform well because of conflicts with people or other issues with people in my life.	①	②	③	④	⑤
4. Feelings or emotions such as anxiety, sadness, frustration, or anger prevent me from performing as well as I would like.	①	②	③	④	⑤
5. I rarely have difficulty staying focused and concentrating during a performance task.	①	②	③	④	⑤
6. Negative beliefs about myself such as pessimism or lack of confidence prevent me from performing as well as I would like.	①	②	③	④	⑤
7. My physical or technical skills are developed near or at their potential.	①	②	③	④	⑤
8. I am unable to perform well because of conflicts with coaches (bosses) or teammates (coworkers).	①	②	③	④	⑤
9. My thoughts or feelings make it difficult for me to perform well.	①	②	③	④	⑤
10. Negative events that are occurring around me or in my life make it more difficult for me to perform well.	①	②	③	④	⑤

chapter (see pages 57-60). In this discussion, a semistructured interview is a process in which a number of critical domains are systematically assessed. The term *structure* in this context does not imply rigidity or inflexibility, but rather the need to be comprehensive and ensure that all necessary information is obtained before intervening. In addition to directly meeting with the athlete, the interview process may include meeting with individuals involved with the athlete, such as family, coaches, and trainers, depending on the referral question and its surrounding circumstances (and client consent). The goal of the interview is to collect relevant information about the presenting issues, personal and competitive history, and the history of the presenting issues. A sound semistructured interview should last 60 to 90 min, though some information can be ascertained (and time saved) before the first meeting by using questionnaires to collect some personal, social, and performance data. The clinical sport psychologist can review this data with the athlete during or immediately before the initial interview. During this first interview, initial hypotheses will likely guide the selection of focused psychometric inventories (when necessary) and the decision (if applicable) to directly observe the athlete out of session. In addition to gathering responses to interview questions, the clinical sport psychologist makes a number of behavioral observations during the interview itself. These observations are mostly interpersonal, but may also involve

Collecting necessary information allows the sport psychologist to make initial hypotheses and direct intervention decisions.

issues such as the athlete's openness to discussing issues, apparent readiness for change, insight and judgment regarding the current issues, and beliefs about the current issues.

Following are descriptions of the specific phases in the MCS-SP assessment process. These phases are sequentially described in order to impart a clear understanding of the information needing consideration. Please note that practitioners can approach topics in their own desired sequence, so they can build rapport with the client and establish the necessary trusting relationship. As long as the practitioner collects all of the recommended data, he can be flexible in his interview style, decision-making process, question sequencing, and choice of psychological instruments. The semistructured interview for the MCS-SP provided at the end of this chapter is devised to take the practitioner across each phase of the MCS-SP assessment process.

Clinical Assessment Phase

The first phase in MCS-SP assessment is the *clinical assessment phase*. Its primary goals are to rule out major psychological disorders that are either obvious (such as anger and impulse control disorders) or more subtle (such as bipolar or attention deficit disorders), and to rule out termination issues (with or without intense psychological reactions).

Accurately evaluating clinical conditions requires education, training, and experience with semistructured clinical interview formats such as the Structured Clinical Interview for *DSM-IV* Axis I Disorders (SCID-I) (First et al., 1997) and mental status examinations (Rogers, 1995). The entire SCID, which is quite lengthy, need not be utilized. Rather, SCID questions follow the format of *DSM* diagnostic groups, and a negative response to the first screening question in each diagnostic area (such as depression or anxiety) allows the practitioner to skip the remaining questions in the area and move to the next diagnostic possibility. Used in this way, the SCID functions as a structured screening tool that allows the practitioner to note possible diagnostic concerns for further examination. When the client's responses to the initial screening questions do not require further inquiry, using the SCID is quite brief. As noted earlier, instead of or in addition to the SCID, the Sport-Clinical Intake Protocol (SCIP) may also be a useful structured interview during the clinical assessment phase and subsequent MCS-SP assessment phases, as the SCIP generates information regarding both sport and nonsport issues (Taylor & Schneider, 1992).

When appropriate, the clinical assessment phase may include clinical psychometric instruments such as the Minnesota Multiphasic Personality Inventory-II (MMPI-II) (Butcher, Dahlstrom, Graham, Tellegen, & Kaemmer, 1989), the Millon Clinical Multiaxial Inventory-III (MCMI-III) (Millon, Millon, & Davis, 1994), the Symptom Checklist-90 (SCL-90-R) (Derogatis, 1983), and the Beck Depression Inventory (BDI) (Beck et al., 1996). We are certainly not suggesting that any or all of these psychometric instruments are needed for every athlete. In many cases, the clinical assessment phase can be conducted solely through a semi-structured or structured interview and thorough psychosocial history, with little (if any) psychometric evaluation. Other cases may require extensive clinical assessment including psychometric testing. Psychometric evaluation should be based on the need for additional data and the degree to which a psychometric instrument is likely to produce the needed information. We encourage the practitioner to be selective when choosing instruments for psychometric evaluation. Once again, this choice should be based on a clear rationale (hypotheses or questions to be answered) and a fundamental understanding of the psychometric properties of the instruments in question.

If the data collected in the clinical assessment phase supports a classification of performance impairment (PI) I or II (such as the diagnosis of a major psychological disorder) or performance termination (PT) I or II, the practitioner still collects the rest of the data necessary for a full understanding of the athlete. Following the interview process, the consultant's task with the PI or PT athlete is determined by her education, training, and experience. The practitioner who is trained, licensed, and certified to intervene with PI or PT cases can begin case formulation (see chapter 11) and intervention planning. The professional not trained, licensed, and certified in these areas should not intervene, but should instead refer the athlete to the appropriately licensed and certified professional. When the clinical assessment phase reveals negative PI or PT findings (indicating no clinical or career termination issues), the clinical sport psychologist has essentially ruled out PI or PT and can consider PD or Pdy classifications once further data have been collected. The next assessment phase is the personal development assessment phase.

Personal Development Assessment Phase

The primary goal of the *personal development assessment phase* is to fully understand the athlete's current life circumstances, overall developmental history, intrapersonal and interpersonal development, and transitional issues. During this phase, the clinical sport psychologist determines the impact of developmental and transitional issues on the athlete and develops an understanding of the interpersonal processes and intrapersonal characteristics that may affect or interfere with the athlete in her athletic pursuits. This information rules in or out a classification of performance dysfunction (Pdy) I or II. Techniques and measurements appropriate for this phase are comprehensive interviews, full psychosocial histories, and psychometric inventories developed for both clinical and nonclinical uses. Relevant inventories include the Profile of Mood States (POMS) (McNair, Lorr, & Dropplemen, 1971), the Test of Attentional and Interpersonal Style (TAIS) (Nideffer, 1976), the Competitive State Anxiety Inventory-2 (CSAI-2) (Vealey, 1990), the State-Trait Anxiety Inventory (STAI) (Spielberger, Gorsuch, Luschene, Vagg, & Jacobs, 1983), and the Sixteen Personality Factor Questionnaire, Fifth Edition (16-PF) (Russell & Karol, 1994).

If the data accumulated during the personal development assessment phase lead to positive Pdy findings, the practitioner still continues to collect necessary data in other domains. For Pdy cases, the sport psychologist trained and licensed in clinical or counseling psychology would begin case conceptualization and intervention planning. Those professionals without such training should refer the client to an appropriate practitioner. If the collected data are negative for Pdy, the practitioner can consider the presence of PD, which is determined during the performance assessment phase.

Performance Assessment Phase

The goal of the *performance assessment phase* is to completely understand the athlete's performance skills, history, expectations, and goals. This phase should include a thorough assessment of current skills, short-term and long-term athletic goals and expectations, self-efficacy relating to athletic performance, and knowledge and current or previous use of mental skills in both practice and competition. It is useful to know the athlete's past attempts to maximize performance, which techniques helped or did not help and why or under what conditions, how those techniques were learned, and so on. Clinical sport psychologists may commonly find that athletes have been taught mental skills techniques not matching their personal needs, have been incorrectly or insufficiently taught these techniques, have had a poor relationship with a previous sport psychologist, or have been unwillingly forced to work with the current practitioner by a coach or parent. These experiences are undeniably important for the current practitioner to know, as they may affect the current relationship or hinder intervention progress if not addressed.

Interviews with family and coaches may also be warranted during the performance assessment phase. A critical component of this phase is a complete functional analysis (introduced earlier) of the athlete's practice and competitive behaviors. The term *functional analysis* comes from the behavioral model in professional psychology and refers to a systematic assessment of the stimulus-response-reinforcement patterns and contingencies that maintain or diminish desired behavior (Kazdin, 2001). Contemporary approaches to

functional analysis assess external stimuli, cognitive processes, affective responses, physiological reactions, behavioral responses, and primary and secondary reinforcers. Understanding these factors leads to a sound understanding of human behavior (including athletic performance) and suggests appropriate cognitive-behavioral strategies (Kanfer & Schefft, 1988).

The performance assessment phase should lead to a classification of performance development (PD) I or II or to no classification at all, which suggests that the athlete would probably not benefit from mental skills development, counseling, or psychological treatment. Alternate referrals to a personal trainer, nutritionist, or coach may instead be appropriate. If efforts at performance enhancement appear warranted (based on a classification of PD-I or PD-II), the practitioner must have education, training, and experience in psychological approaches to performance enhancement in order to continue with intervention. Thus, clinical and counseling psychologists without such specialty training or experience should refer the athlete to an appropriate professional. If the clinical or counseling psychologist is looking to expand his practice area to include performance enhancement, he should get ongoing supervision on the case.

Direct observation can provide important information about the athlete's competitive behavior.

Once these assessment phases are complete and the necessary interview, behavioral observations, and applicable psychometric testing have been performed, hypotheses can be generated. The practitioner evaluates the data and determines the appropriate topographical (MCS-SP categorization) and functional explanation for the referral question. This directly leads to an evidence-driven intervention chosen according to the assessed needs of the athlete (see figure 4.3).

The assessment model we suggest seems to diametrically oppose sport psychology's more traditional assessment and intervention sequence and more closely resembles the assessment models utilized in clinical, counseling, and school psychology. While sport psychology assessment commonly focuses first on performance and moves to personal or clinical issues only if or when they emerge in the course of intervention (Andersen, 2000a; Heyman & Andersen, 1998; Ravizza, 2001), the traditional approach rarely includes sufficient preintervention assessment of more personal or serious concerns, and despite the empirical evidence suggesting otherwise, begins by assuming that most issues athletes present are fundamentally performance based. In contrast, the assessment model dictated by the MCS-SP requires a more complete preintervention assessment that rules out more serious concerns before *strictly* focusing on performance-related issues. Of course, assessing for clinical issues does not have to precede discussion of performance concerns during the initial interview. Both types of information can be gathered interchangeably throughout the interview process, and can certainly be done in a nonmechanical, natural, and conversational manner. In the end, all of the information needed for thorough case conceptualization and intervention planning should be gathered. Although here we presented these phases in a specific order to improve clarity, the specific order during the interview is flexible.

In essence, the traditional performance-focused assessment and our holistic approach of viewing the athlete as a complex being begin at opposite ends of the spectrum. As stated throughout the text, sport psychologists often assume that athletes presenting with performance concerns are free of more significant personal or psychological issues unless the athletes directly report them (Heyman & Andersen, 1998; Ravizza, 2001). Practitioners also frequently believe that athletes with deeper or more serious concerns will bring them up freely, without direction or inquiry (Andersen, 2000a). In such a model, practitioners inevitably restrict their focus to performance concerns unless more serious issues are directly endorsed by the athlete. As a result of this interview and intervention style, some practitioners work with an athlete as though the overt presenting issue is by definition the *actual* issue. As noted in the literature, however, the presenting concern may actually not be the problem at all (Henschen, 1998). Athletes (like clients in all domains of professional psychology) occasionally minimize or exaggerate initial goals and concerns, possibly due to personal anxiety related to early engagement in psychological counseling, to lack of an established rapport with the practitioner, to lack of self-awareness of their difficulties, to confidentiality concerns, to fear of being viewed as a head case, and so on. Another concern is the practitioner who fears that athletes will object to bringing up their more personal concerns and who therefore overlooks the possibility of more clinically significant issues (Heyman & Andersen, 1998). This is unacceptable professional practice for the clinical sport psychologist in two critical ways.

First, it implies that athletes cannot or will not accept appropriate interview questions regarding nonperformance issues in their lives. Yet many athletes not only accept these questions, but also feel relieved that the topics are open for discussion (Eyal, 2001; Gardner & Moore, 2001, October). Although some practitioners have proposed legitimate concerns that this particular approach enhances the shrink role (Singer, 1996; Van Raalte, Brewer, Brewer, & Linder, 1992; Weinberg & Williams, 1998), this is not our experience and is not endorsed by many others in the field. Regardless of title or training, we believe that a shrink is as a shrink does, and this role typically results from static and mechanistic efforts to obtain information without proper engagement between the practitioner and athlete. Hopefully, clinical sport psychologists do not and will not practice in such a way. If conducted in a holistic manner that seeks to clarify the entire psychosocial picture *and* relevant athletic concerns, discussion of more personal issues can empower the athletes we serve. Because each client is the ultimate expert of her life, making any assumption about significant concerns before or without accumulating necessary data is presumptive of the practitioner, possibly harmful to the therapeutic relationship, and both disrespectful and

Clinical assessment phase

Function/strategy	Assessment of mental status, psychological and behavioral functioning
Purpose	Rule out significant psychological and/or behavioral disorders, rule out PI-I/II, PT-I/II
Technique	Clinical interview, mental status exam, clinical and psychometric evaluation (as needed)
Outcome	If PI-I/II or PT-I/II are present, initiate psychological treatment plan; if not present, proceed to next level

Personal development assessment phase

Function/strategy	Assessment of intra/interpersonal, transitional, and developmental levels and coping behaviors
Purpose	Rule out Pdy-I and Pdy-II, rule out significant intra/interpersonal, and developmental issues impacting athletic performance
Technique	Comprehensive psychosocial history, psychometric assessment (as needed)
Outcome	If Pdy-I or Pdy-II are present, initiate appropriate psychological treatment plan; if Pdy-I or Pdy-II are not present, proceed to next level

Performance assessment phase

Function/strategy	Assessment of performance history, goals, skills, and demands (including physical and mental skills)
Purpose	Determine performance issues and expectations, physical and mental skill development, motivation, realistic nature of performance goals, confidence/self-efficacy
Technique	Personal interview, functional analysis of current athletic performance, use of questionnaires, and possible interviews with family and coach
Outcome	Determination of need for/benefit from psychological skills training for performance enhancement

Figure 4.3   The MCS-SP assessment sequence.

potentially detrimental to the athlete's well-being.

Secondly, there is a significant risk-management issue to be considered. Failing to ask necessary questions and therefore potentially overlooking or missing a more serious need for professional care can quickly place a practitioner at risk for professional liability, and it can also place the athlete at risk. Although not all sport psychologists are licensed psychologists and bound by a formal code of ethics, it can be argued that they are still responsible for identifying problems in need of greater attention. The athlete inherently presumes that all necessary assessment will occur before intervention (we are not referring to the use of outcome measures given throughout treatment), regardless of practitioner training. A comprehensive assessment (such as the MCS-SP) does *not* have to emphasize the search for serious psychopathology if conducted appropriately. This approach does, however, suggest that clinical sport psychologists need to fully understand and engage in comprehensive psychosocial assessment.

Readers may now be thinking that the recommended assessment process is too time-consuming and cannot be easily integrated into their time-limited practice. First, our experience has shown us that we often have more time than we believe and that we often feel rushed to intervene when careful assessment is quite possible. Second, the process is not as time-consuming as imagined. Our experience, even with clinical sport psychology trainees working at a university athletic department, suggests that sufficient information is easily obtained in approximately 1 h (additional time

for psychometric instruments can easily be organized around the athlete's schedule, if needed). We assume that those practitioners conducting traditional interviews and assessments spend the same initial amount of time with the athlete, so we doubt a 1 h session will be considered excessive. Third, if there are severe time limitations, we suggest that the practitioner remember that appropriate assessment is a professional responsibility, and as such, he should carefully consider time-limited screening for information (for example, regular use of the SCIP [Taylor & Schneider, 1992]), which he can follow up with more time-intensive approaches as indicated. We also recognize that there are circumstances in which sport psychology consultants are brought into a team setting to provide brief team-oriented educational presentations regarding the relationship between mental skills and performance. In such circumstances, there may be no opportunity or need for individual assessment. While we respect the reality of those situations, we caution the practitioner of the limits of these consultations. While some athletes may benefit from this educational information, athletes with more significant subclinical or clinical issues may find it at best unhelpful and at worst frustrating in its inability to help.

MCS-SP Semistructured Interview

In this final section, we provide a semistructured interview based on the MCS-SP (see table 4.2), which highlights the most important questions for determining MCS-SP classification.

Table 4.2 Semistructured Interview for the MCS-SP

Performance Development module		
1. Why have you decided to seek assistance at this time?	Performance enhancement is the primary goal: Y or N	If yes, continue through the remaining questions for PD and Pdy. If no, skip to PI module. If response suggests issues relating to career termination (recent, impending, or near future) proceed to PT module.
2. Tell me about the performance issues you wish to work on. (Note any performance strengths and weaknesses, inconsistent performance, brief or extended slumps, and so on.)		

(continued)

Table 4.2 *(continued)*

Performance Development module

3.	Tell me about any new, changing, or special circumstances in your life in and out of sports at this time.	Transitional issues: Y or N	
4.	Have there been any recent incidents or situations that got you into trouble or caused you any problems?	Behavioral issues: Y or N	
5.	Are there currently any intense feelings or emotions that you are having difficulty handling or seem overwhelming? If yes, what are they, and how have you tried to cope with them? (Carefully explore these emotions and behavioral coping strategies.)	Emotional or psychological distress: Y or N	If responses to 2-5 are all no, continue through the remainder of the PD module. If any of the responses to 2-5 are yes, move immediately to the Pdy module.
6.	Tell me about your present relationships (coach, teammates, staff, friends, family, significant others, and so on).	Interpersonal conflict: Y or N	
7.	How have you tried to work on your performance before? How has that worked for you? How would you describe your practice efforts and intensity?	For questions 7 to10, assess physical and mental skill development.	
8.	Explain your athletic goals. How likely are they? Has anyone suggested that these goals are reasonable or unreasonable? Who?		
9.	Tell me about your attention and concentration during practice and competition. How often do you get distracted? What are the thoughts, emotions, or situations that distract you? What do you do to reduce distraction and maintain concentration?		
10.	Tell me how you react when you become upset. What triggers this upset? What do you think about and feel during this upset? What do you do to deal or cope with this upset? How well does this work for you?		Use responses to questions 6-10 as a framework to determine the appropriateness of psychological intervention for performance enhancement. If psychological intervention (skills training) may help, consider a classification of PD.
11.	To what degree do you believe that you are still developing your physical and technical skills? Do you believe that you are still some distance away from your physical peak? (Obtaining this information may require consultation with parents or coaches.)	Positive responses suggest a classification of PD-I.	
12.	To what degree do you believe that you have attained a high level of skill, possibly reaching your peak, and need help attaining even greater performance or greater consistency?	Positive responses suggest a classification of PD-II.	Responses and discussions emanating from 11 and 12 determine a classification of PD-I or PD-II.

Performance Dysfunction module

13.	(Fully explore any yes responses to questions 2-5.)	The following questions help determine the specific developmental, transitional, interpersonal, intrapersonal, or behavioral causes of problematic performance.	

Performance Dysfunction module

14.	To what degree are the issues and problems you are experiencing away from sports more significant than your problems with athletic performance? (Explore this possibility carefully, using follow-up questions as needed.) Do you believe that we should focus on these issues first and deal with athletics afterward?	Performance issues: Y or N Personal issues: Y or N	If personal issues are the primary concern, continue with questions 15 and 16 and then move to the PI module.
15.	Tell me how these issues have affected other areas of your life. Have they made these other life areas significantly less satisfying? Are there major problems in these other areas of life that are causing significant disruption or difficulty for you at this time?	Positive responses suggest a classification of PI.	If responses are positive, move to PI module.
16.	Tell me about other times in your life when these or similar issues have been a major problem. (Fully explore data obtained from psychometric evaluation of schemas and personality.)		
17.	Do you believe that dealing with these issues would also improve your performance?		
18.	Has your competitive performance previously been better? Do you feel as though you have stopped improving your performance? Was your performance consistently better at some time in your past? Are there now significant peaks and valleys in your performance?		
19.	Do you believe that recent outside events or relationship stresses are most responsible for your performance issues? Do you think that internal factors such as worry, perfectionism, and concentration are the primary cause of the difficulties?	Responses to questions 18 and 19 determine a classification of Pdy-I (transitional or external factors) or Pdy-II (endogenous factors).	

Performance Impairment module

| 20. | Perform a clinical interview at this time (possibly including selected SCID modules) to establish appropriate topographical (diagnostic) and functional assessment. Integrate psychometric evaluation data as needed. | Difficulties affecting overall life functioning as well as athletic performance that are primarily internalized (anxiety, depression, eating disorders, and so on) indicate a classification of PI-I. Difficulties that are more externalized (anger and impulse control disorders, drug or alcohol abuse, personality disorders) indicate a classification of PI-II. | |

(continued)

Table 4.2 *(continued)*

Performance Termination module

21.	Describe your current situation to me. How long have you been competing? What has made you consider the end of your athletic career? Do you believe that it is the right time for you to end your competitive career? How would you compare your current skills to what you have come to expect from the past? (Focus on the reasons for consideration of career termination: injury, deselection, and so on.)	If career termination is voluntary or expected, consider a classification of PT-I. If career termination is rapid (due to injury or unexpected deselection), consider a classification of PT-II.
22.	What are your emotional reactions to career termination? Anger or irritability? Depression or sadness? Anxiety or fear? Hopelessness or pessimism? Feeling of loss? Feelings of life seeming unreal? Numbness? Relief? Excitement? Optimism or looking forward to new challenges?	
23.	What are your greatest fears and concerns about ending your athletic career? How do you see your life in the future? What do you see yourself doing with the rest of your life? Tell me how your family and closest friends are responding to this and how you are responding to them.	
24.	How have you been handling these termination issues? Have you been avoiding people or situations that remind you of athletic involvement? Are you doing things differently to escape the distress (drinking, drug use, gambling, and so on)? Have you changed the way you live life, the things you do, and the people you see?	
25.	If termination is based upon serious injury or unexpected deselection, are you having flashbacks, dreams, or thoughts and images that you can't control (intrusive) about the injury or moment that you were told that your career was (or would likely be) over? Are you having difficulty concentrating?	
26.	Is there any other information that you think I should know that I haven't asked about?	

This interview greatly assists the assessment process and clarifies presenting issues, which inevitably assists case formulation and intervention efforts. Again, while this interview can be utilized in a systematic manner, the format is in *no* way required to be static and sequential. We recommend that practitioners view the interview questions as a guide for sound data collection. Instead of asking rote and mechanical questions that challenge a sound therapeutic bond, practitioners can be conversational throughout the interview by collecting information during the natural ebb and flow of the practitioner–client interaction. When following any semistructured or structured format (including manual-based

treatment protocols), many nuances in the session can derail the therapeutic focus. Yet, if the practitioner knows the specific *goals* that should be achieved by the end of the session, she can meet these goals while responding to moment-to-moment situational demands, integrating her unique personality characteristics, and bonding with the athlete.

Final Thoughts

While the goal of this chapter was to highlight critical variables associated with assessment in clinical sport psychology, we are also pleased to provide a semistructured interview to assist the full assessment of athletes. Since the interview and assessment process is ultimately followed by choosing the best interventions to meet an athlete's personal needs, chapter 5 discusses the empirical support for the common performance enhancement intervention strategies utilized in sport psychology.

PART III

Interventions in Clinical Sport Psychology

Performance concerns and a desire for performance enhancement are not the only reasons athletes seek sport psychology services. As humans, athletes experience the same frequency and intensity of emotions as the rest of the population, and engage in the same behaviors in response to endogenous emotional processes and exogenous life challenges. However, over the years we have noticed that professional conferences and journal publications seldom discuss subclinical and clinical concerns among athletes, and often restrict discussions to perceived nonclinical issues. In addition, we have noticed that clinical psychologists working with athletes often clearly understand subclinical and clinical concerns, but rarely consider these concerns within the context of athletics. As such, Part III is the largest and most exciting section of this text, as it weaves previous discussions of basic psychological processes, the MCS-SP, and holistic assessment with cutting-edge interventions for the wide range of athlete issues and difficulties.

To begin this section, we discuss the empirical efficacy research on traditional performance enhancement interventions, such as goal setting, imagery, self-talk, arousal regulations, and multicomponent strategies. Following a detailed discussion of these research findings in chapter 5, chapters 6-10 are sequentially organized to follow the MCS-SP. As such, chapter 6 introduces the mindfulness-acceptance-commitment (MAC) approach to performance enhancement with nonclinical athletes (PD). Chapter 7 describes the effect of dispositional variables on athletic performance and highlights empirically informed interventions for athletes with subclinical issues (Pdy). Chapters 8 and 9 discuss interventions for the most common clinical disorders (PI-I and PI-II) found among athletes, and chapter 10 considers interventions for difficulties with the termination process (PT). Following the intervention chapters, chapter 11 describes our approach to case formulation. This approach utilizes the Integrative Model of Athletic Performance (IMAP) to organize assessment data into the appropriate MCS-SP classification, thereby leading to rational intervention planning to best meet the needs of the individual athlete.

From this section, we hope sport psychology consultants not trained in psychology will develop a greater sophistication in their understanding of the varying dimensions of subclinical and clinical phenomena and their effect on athletic performance. We also aspire for clinical psychologists working with athletes to gain a greater understanding of the particular demands of the athletic environment, and how aspects of athletic participation affect the athlete's overall life functioning. We believe that achieving these goals will truly lead to a more comprehensive and holistic approach to sport psychology.

CHAPTER 5

Evaluating the Efficacy of Traditional Performance Enhancement Interventions

Sport psychology literature has successfully described *what* we do and *how* we do it. However, *why* we do it and *if* it works have largely been unanswered. This chapter discusses the current state of efficacy research in sport psychology with the hope that these questions will be appropriately addressed.

The primary focus of sport psychology has long been to identify and understand theories and techniques that can be applied to sport and exercise to enhance the performance of athletes and participants in physical activity (Williams & Straub, 1998). Sport psychology is often considered primarily psychoeducational, seeking to teach athletes psychological skills that, in addition to physical and technical skills, are believed effective and necessary for attaining and maintaining optimal athletic performance (Hardy et al., 1996).

Using correlational studies, sport psychologists have long believed that successful performers are less anxious, more confident, and less prone to negative thoughts (Gould, Eklund, & Jackson, 1992; Gould et al., 1981; Orlick & Partington, 1988). Inferred causality from this research led early sport psychologists to adopt clinical self-regulatory approaches in order enhance performance among athletes. The fundamental self-regulatory psychological skills, based largely on cognitive-behavioral principles, continue to be abundantly utilized by athletes in an attempt to maximize highly valued peak performance (Whelan, Mahoney, & Meyers, 1991). Traditional performance enhancement techniques such as goal setting, imagery (also known as visualiza-tion and mental rehearsal), self-talk (also known as cognitive self-regulation), and arousal regulation (such as relaxation and psyching up) are believed to help athletes achieve consistently high performance and peak performance states (Andersen, 2000b; Hardy et al., 1996; Van Raalte & Brewer, 2002; Williams, 1998).

Traditional Performance Enhancement Interventions

To enhance performance, psychological skills (self-regulation strategies) have been utilized to create or enhance psychological states such as attentional focus, confidence, and optimal arousal, which are theorized to promote optimal performance and physical skill development (Gould et al., 1992; Gould et al., 1981; Orlick & Partington, 1988). The difference between athletes who achieve highly desired performance states and those who do not is often considered to be the use of self-regulatory techniques that theoretically enhance the specific internal mediating variables facilitating performance excellence (Gould et al., 1992; Hardy et al., 1996). Researchers and practitioners of sport psychology have thus both studied and utilized these cognitive-behavioral self-regulatory techniques with athletes of all ages and skill levels (Gould et al., 1981; Orlick & Partington, 1988). The most popular performance enhancement techniques include goal setting, imagery, self-talk, arousal regulation, and multicomponent interventions combining these techniques.

Evidence-Based Practice

A multitude of empirical studies have examined the common self-regulatory procedures known as performance enhancement interventions (goal setting, imagery, self-talk, arousal regulation, and multicomponent packages), and numerous meta-analyses and systematic literature reviews have attempted to compile and report the findings of these studies (Feltz & Landers, 1983; Gould & Udry, 1994; Greenspan & Feltz, 1989; Hinshaw, 1991; Jones & Stuth, 1997; Kyllo & Landers, 1995; Meyers et al., 1996; Murphy & Jowdy, 1992; Onestak, 1991; Vealey, 1994b; Weinberg, 1994; Weinberg & Comar, 1994; Whelan et al., 1991). Overall, the authors of these meta-analyses suggest some preliminary evidence (often equivocal) for performance enhancement interventions (small to large effect sizes), yet at the same time voice concerns of poor methodology among empirical studies and a lack of sufficient and consistent empirical validation for such procedures.

As discussed later in this chapter, interpreting meta-analytic findings requires care, as the collection of empirical data alone is insufficient for the productive development of an applied field such as sport psychology. The empirical research on common performance enhancement interventions must undergo and withstand careful scientific scrutiny, utilize sound statistical measures, and be replicable. In addition, the data must demonstrate positive follow-up results, clearly describe populations studied, utilize appropriate experimental design, be procedurally consistent, and demonstrate significant support for its utilization without substantial contradictory evidence (Chambless & Hollon, 1998).

When well-designed studies regularly produce empirical data that do not support the applied procedures, the theoretical basis upon which research is conducted should be evaluated, research efforts should be critically examined and possibly altered, and interventions that have not proved efficacious should be questioned, contemplated, and modified to better meet the recipients' needs. Likewise, if the empirical literature is not methodologically sound and data on intervention efficacy are skewed to represent success, both the state of the field and the needs of the client will suffer. Therefore, it becomes crucial for clinical and sport scientists to apply more rigorous scientific standards to their research in order to accurately represent the efficacy and effectiveness of interventions and reliably direct the advancement of the field.

Indeed, sport psychology professionals have long called for scientific and empirical accountability in response to questionable experimental standards and a lack of consistently supportive data for common performance enhancement interventions (Dishman, 1983; Greenspan & Feltz, 1989; Hill, 2001; Meyers et al., 1996; Smith, 1989; Strean & Roberts, 1992; Whelan et al., 1991). According to Hill (2001), "the inherent problems of conducting well-controlled empirical studies using competitive performance as a dependent variable continues to plague the sport psychology literature today" (p. 46). Additional difficulties include "lack of attention to the integrity of treatment delivery" (Meyers et al., 1996, p. 153) and "the general failure to assess the maintenance of treatment effects" (Meyers et al., 1996, p. 154). Researchers have also raised concerns over professionals applying interventions based on intuition rather than on empirical data (Dishman, 1983) and publishing studies that inflate the positive effects of performance enhancement interventions (Feltz & Landers, 1983; Greenspan & Feltz, 1989). These concerns highlight the need for greater professional accountability and more rigorous methodology to accurately obtain, interpret, and disseminate the research findings that guide the application of sport psychology interventions.

Although many sport psychology professionals have called for more rigorous methodological principles to facilitate the development of the field, some professionals have challenged the need for formal scientific accountability. For example, Martens (1987) has suggested that "practitioners' experience of treatment success and athletes' reports of treatment gains are the only meaningful data for judging clinically significant treatment effectiveness" (Meyers et al., 1996, p. 146). Such positions are the antithesis of the scientific method and are problematic in a field with increasing demand for accountability and ethical responsibility (Smith, 1989). Strean and Roberts (1992) assert that sport psychology interventions "have not been critically examined, and practitioners do not know the efficacy of many procedures they employ" (p. 62). They further contend that "to be taken seriously by other professionals, sport psychology consultants must begin to demonstrate empirically the effectiveness of their interventions . . . [and] must begin to evaluate critically what we do rather than assume what we do is automatically well founded"

(Strean & Roberts, 1992, p. 62). Authors reporting empirical findings must also take great care in accurately representing the data, thus allowing sport psychologists to make informed decisions regarding the most effective interventions to meet the needs of specific athletic clientele.

As it is generally accepted that rigorous, systematic, and empirical research is the fundamental catalyst for the advancement of any applied discipline (Fishman & Franks, 1997; Kazdin, 2000; O'Donohue & Krasner, 1995), sport psychologists look to the professional literature for cutting-edge information they can apply to their work. Thus, it is critical for studies to include sound methodological principles and for data to be represented accurately, so that professionals can appropriately integrate empirical findings into their practice. Within the broader professional psychology community, there has been a strong movement toward defining and utilizing empirically supported interventions as part of an evidence-based approach to practice for a wide range of psychological issues (Chambless & Ollendick, 2001). This practice approach provides standards for efficacious and ethical service provision and has been accepted in numerous traditional and specialty areas in psychology (Chambless & Hollon, 1998; Kendall & Chambless, 1998; Nathan & Gorman, 2002; Roth & Fonagy, 1996; Spirito, 1999). As an applied discipline in professional psychology, sport psychology also needs to adopt this approach.

The empirically supported treatment movement began in 1993 under the direction of the Society of Clinical Psychology (Division 12) of the American Psychological Association (APA). This division established the Task Force on Promotion and Dissemination of Psychological Procedures (now called the Committee on Science and Practice, referred to herein as the Committee). Its task was to define standard criteria to evaluate intervention efficacy, identify interventions meeting the criteria, disseminate these findings to professionals, and promote psychological interventions demonstrating efficacy in clinical trials. The Committee began by defining the parameters for evaluating the empirical literature base and then established the specific criteria to determine levels of empirical support for each intervention (Chambless et al., 1998; Chambless & Ollendick, 2001; Chambless et al., 1996). Since these initial developments, several other groups have adapted this approach to a variety of interventions and client populations (Chambless & Hollon, 1998;

Kendall & Chambless, 1998; Nathan & Gorman, 2002; Roth & Fonagy, 1996; Spirito, 1999). The established criteria (see sidebar on page 68) categorize interventions within three levels of empirical support: *well-established*, *probably efficacious*, or *experimental* (Chambless et al., 1998; Chambless & Ollendick, 2001). Using this approach and adaptations by other groups (Chambless & Hollon, 1998; Chambless & Ollendick, 2001; Kendall & Chambless, 1998; Nathan & Gorman, 2002; Roth & Fonagy, 1996; Spirito, 1999), a list of efficacious treatments has been constructed and is updated regularly so that psychology students and professionals can easily identify evidence-based interventions appropriate for their clientele and settings (Nathan & Gorman, 2002).

Only randomized controlled between-group designs and single-case design studies providing comparison to another intervention can be evaluated for empirical support, as they can "reasonably conclude that benefits observed are due to the effects of the treatment and not to chance or confounding variables" (Chambless & Hollon, 1998, p. 7). Research designs that do not meet these criteria, such as those not using random assignment or a control group, are not appropriate for the determination of intervention efficacy. These designs are certainly not considered useless, but they are simply not considered optimal for the research evaluation necessary to determine intervention efficacy (Chambless & Ollendick, 2001). Randomized controlled between-group designs and single-case designs with intervention comparison are evaluated for empirical support according to additional inclusion criteria. Depending on criteria fulfillment, each evaluated intervention demonstrates one of the three levels of empirical support.

Well-Established Interventions

The highest level of empirical support is *well-established* (Chambless et al., 1998; Chambless & Ollendick, 2001). Again, only randomized controlled between-group designs and single-case designs with intervention comparison are eligible for this designation. Well-established interventions must also meet additional criteria, depending on the experimental design. For studies that utilize a randomized controlled between-group design, "at least two good between-group design experiments must demonstrate efficacy (criterion I) in one or more of the following ways":

Criteria for the Determination of Empirically Supported Interventions

Well-Established Interventions

I. At least two good between-group design experiments must demonstrate efficacy in one or more of the following ways:
   A. Superiority to pill or psychotherapy placebo or to another treatment
   B. Equivalence to already established treatment with adequate sample sizes

or

II. A large series of single-case design experiments must demonstrate efficacy with the following:
   A. Use of good experimental design and
   B. Comparison of intervention to another treatment

Further criteria for both I and II:

III. Experiments must be conducted with treatment manuals.

IV. Characteristics of the client samples must be clearly specified.

V. Effects must have been demonstrated by at least two different investigators or investigating teams.

Probably Efficacious Interventions

I. Two experiments must show that the treatment is superior to waiting-list control group.

or

II. One or more experiments must meet well-established criteria IA or IB, III, and IV above but V is not met.

or

III. A small series of single-case design experiments must meet well-established treatment criteria.

Experimental Treatments

Treatment not yet tested in trials meeting task force criteria for methodology

Adapted, with permission, from the *Annual Review of Psychology,* Volume 52 © 2001 by Annual Reviews, www.annualreviews.org.

---

a) The intervention must demonstrate "superiority to pill or psychotherapy placebo or to other treatment" (criterion IA).

b) The intervention must demonstrate "equivalence to already established treatment with adequate sample sizes" (criterion IB) (Chambless & Ollendick, 2001, p. 689).

In addition, all studies must provide clear intervention descriptions (criterion III), which allow other researchers to replicate the studies, operationally define procedures, and enhance generalizability. Also, sample characteristics of study participants must be clear, specific, and thorough (criterion IV) in order to help applied professionals understand and apply the data to their practice. Finally, in order to reduce experimenter bias, intervention effects must be demonstrated by at least two independent investigators or investigation teams (criterion V).

For studies that utilize a single-case design, a large number of such experiments must dem-onstrate efficacy (criterion II) by utilizing sound experimental design (criterion IIA) and by comparing the intervention to another known treatment (criterion IIB) (Chambless & Ollendick, 2001). Like randomized controlled between-group design experiments, all single-case design studies must provide full intervention descriptions (criterion III) and include thorough sample characteristics of study participants (criterion IV), and the intervention effects must be demonstrated by at least two different investigators or teams (criterion V).

Probably Efficacious Interventions

The second level of empirical support is *probably efficacious* (Chambless et al., 1998; Chambless & Ollendick, 2001). Interventions are classified in this category when *only one* of three criteria has been fulfilled (among randomized controlled between-group designs or single-case designs with intervention comparison). Criterion I is that two randomized controlled between-group design experiments "must show that the treatment is superior to waiting-list control group" (Chambless & Ollendick, 2001, p. 689). If this criterion is not met, criterion II states that one or more randomized controlled between-group design experiments must show either "superiority to pill or psychotherapy placebo or to other treatment" (p. 689) or "equivalence to already established treatment with adequate sample sizes" (p. 689). Criterion II also requires the studies to provide full intervention descriptions and thorough sample characteristics of study participants. To fulfill criterion II, intervention effects do not need to be demonstrated by more than one investigator. If a study does not fulfill criteria I and II, it must meet criterion III to be categorized as probably efficacious. Criterion III is that "a small series of single-case design experiments must meet well-established treatment criteria" (Chambless & Ollendick, 2001, p. 689), which include sound experimental design, supportive results when compared to another intervention, clear intervention description or a manual, and thorough sample characteristics.

Experimental Interventions

The third and lowest level of empirical support is *experimental* (Chambless et al., 1998; Chambless & Ollendick, 2001). This designation includes interventions that have not been adequately tested in experimental trials meeting methodological standards established by the Committee. Interventions in this category, therefore, have yet to demonstrate efficacy, and therefore are not empirically supported.

It is important to state that the fulfillment of criteria and an adequate number of supportive studies do not automatically indicate efficacy status when opposed by a preponderance of contradictory evidence. It is crucial to critically assess the methodology of individual studies and to thoroughly evaluate contradictory research. In cases where a discrepancy exists, the relative number of contradictory studies and the results from the best-designed studies should be considered in the determination of empirical support (Chambless & Hollon, 1998). If all studies are designed well and methodological quality is not an issue, evaluators should remain conservative when designating empirical support until the factors causing the discrepancy are identified or future research resolves the controversy. However, the controversy should not open the door for researchers to explain away negative findings.

Regardless of the efficacy of an intervention, these categorizations are not meant to completely replace a practitioner's personal decision on the best intervention for a client, to strictly suggest the best intervention, or to negate nonspecific factors, relationship variables, and specific client and therapist variables. Instead, the categorizations indicate the scientific basis for specific interventions. Further, there may be current interventions or interventions in development that either demonstrate or will one day demonstrate efficacy but cannot be categorized at this time because they lack the supportive outcome data required for inclusion as a well-established or probably efficacious intervention. Certainly, if an intervention has not yet met the criteria as a well-established or probably efficacious intervention, it is not to be hastily assumed that the intervention is ineffective; rather it suggests that a sufficient number of methodologically sound empirical studies have not yet been conducted that show largely unequivocal support for the intervention (Chambless & Hollon, 1998; Kendall & Chambless, 1998).

Aware of the benefits for both practitioners and clients, numerous areas of professional psychology utilize the empirically supported treatment criteria to evaluate both past and current empirical data and to enhance the future scientific database of common interventions (Chambless & Ollendick, 2001). Until recently (Moore, 2003b), however, the field of sport psychology had yet to apply the empirically supported treatment criteria to the currently accepted sport psychology interventions in order to evaluate and report their empirical support.

For many years, applied sport psychology has utilized self-regulation techniques such as goal setting, imagery, self-talk, and arousal regulation to enhance athletic performance and has conducted numerous empirical studies on the efficacy and effectiveness of these individual and combined interventions. Yet, until recently, the empirical research had not been reviewed using the contemporary, structured approach to determining intervention efficacy. Such a review is predicated on both ethical standards and practical utility. The practitioner has an ethical responsibility to provide empirically supported interventions to clients (when available), and the client similarly has the right to fully understand intervention options, potential benefits, and risks. The busy practitioner cannot review hundreds of studies in order to gather quality research information. Rather, the scientific discipline is responsible for

Sport psychologists have an ethical and professional responsibility to use interventions that have gained sound scientific support.

reviewing the available data, evaluating these data with clear and consistent standards, and categorizing the data into levels of empirical support in order to help applied professionals ethically meet their professional responsibilities. Therefore, examining interventions based on the empirically supported treatment criteria may help sport psychologists choose interventions based on scientific standards, abide by ethical mandates regarding best-practice procedures, and honestly provide athletes with sufficient confidence in the interventions they receive.

Meta-Analyses, Case Studies, and Anecdotal Reports

Sport psychology has welcomed anecdotal reports, case studies and single-subject designs without a direct control comparison, and analogue studies, which have often been interpreted as support for self-regulatory performance enhancement procedures. Such purported support has catalyzed professional acceptance and consumer attention. Yet, although anecdotal reports, case studies, and analogue studies may seem to suggest support for procedures, a scientific discipline cannot justifiably trust these enticing demonstrations alone.

An example of the potential dangers of less methodologically rigorous approaches to research was clear at a recent sport psychology conference. During a symposium, the second author of this text (ZM) was discussing the limited empirical support for the use of imagery to enhance performance (discussed later in this chapter). After providing data suggesting the lack of positive efficacy findings among empirical studies on imagery with competitive athletes, a woman in the audience became clearly frustrated and interrupted the presentation to make a statement. The woman proceeded to state, "In Michael Jordan's book, he described how he used imagery throughout his career, and he ended up being the best basketball player in history, so this shows that imagery *must* work!" Surprised by the implication that imagery *caused* him to perform so well instead of there simply being a relationship between imagery use and his stellar skill, ZM could only reply, "Or, he could have just been the best basketball player of all time, regardless of whether he used imagery, ate Wheaties, or wore purple socks." Although probably not as sensitive as she intended to be, the purpose of ZM's reply was to make it clear how misinterpreted correlational data (and anecdotal reports) can lead to problematic conclusions, misguide the practitioner, and ultimately provide false hope to consumers.

According to Lilienfeld, Lynn, and Lohr (2003), although "testimonials and anecdotal evidence can be quite useful in the early stages of scientific investigation . . . such evidence is typically much more helpful in the context of discovery (i.e., hypothesis generation) than in the context of justification" (p. 8). Case studies and single-subject designs without a direct control comparison are also important in the early stages of scientific data collection, but "almost never provide sufficient evidence for a claim, although they often provide necessary evidence for this claim" (p. 8). With any intervention, a number of case studies will likely demonstrate supportive outcomes. However, they do not "provide adequate evidence that the improvement was attributable to the [intervention], because this improvement could have been produced by a host of other influences" (Lilienfeld et al., 2003, p. 8). For example, in three recent empirical studies (Johnson, Hrycaiko, Johnson, & Halas, 2004; Pates, Cummings, & Maynard, 2002; Thelwell & Greenlees, 2003), data suggested substantial performance improvements immediately following the initiation of a psychological skills training package. Yet at such an early point, skills could not possibly have been adequately taught or practiced. Psychological skills training models do not theoretically explain such results. Rather, these rapid gains are just as likely, if not more likely, associated with some relationship variable, client expectation, or enhanced hopefulness. These results are equivalent to a psychotherapy patient showing markedly decreased symptomatology following *one* therapy session, which is clearly improbable and calls into question the true mechanism of action.

Likewise, it is not optimal to evaluate the efficacy of an intervention using studies with analogue populations (such as undergraduate volunteers) and tasks (such as strength or endurance tasks) (Meyers et al., 1996; Murphy & Jowdy, 1992), which make up a large portion of the empirical research in the field. Although studies with analogue populations and tasks can be informative, they are not sufficient for a field dedicated to enhancing athletic performance among competitive athletes. Such studies do not generate generalizable data, as they are almost exclusively conducted on undergraduate volunteers who may not possess the knowledge, skill, attitude, and motivation of athletic competitors. Many of these studies use noncompetitive performance measures, such as grip strength, artificial endurance tasks, and novel motor skills, rather than directly measuring competitive performance.

However, it has recently been suggested that randomized controlled trials are inappropriate for use in applied sport psychology. The position that "...it is impractical to offer a service to one group of athletes and deliberately withhold the service from another group" (Anderson, Miles, Mahoney, & Robinson, 2002, p. 437) is wholly without merit and contributes to the stunted growth of the field. The utilization of methodologically sound randomized controlled trials is no more or less problematic in applied sport psychology as it has been in clinical psychology and psychopharmacology, yet scientist-practitioners in these fields have long been able to design appropriate and ethical randomized controlled trials (Nathan & Gorman, 2002). As such, these fields have achieved tremendous growth, respect, and consumer acceptance. Although case studies and single-case designs should certainly not be abandoned, randomized controlled trials are essential not only for the future of sport psychology, but also and more important, for the well-being of our athletic clientele.

Traditionally, long before the Committee's criteria for empirically supported treatments, the primary means for determining empirical support for psychological interventions, including performance enhancement procedures, was the meta-analysis, a primarily quantitative empirical review. Yet, meta-analyses and systematic literature reviews assessing the efficacy of performance enhancement interventions consistently demonstrated marginal support for the interventions. In addition, meta-analyses suggested caution when using these interventions, due to a lack of scientific sophistication among individual empirical studies. Most of these meta-analyses also compiled studies utilizing both competitive athletes and nonathletes, used very few studies to calculate overall effect sizes, and minimally discriminated among the methodological qualities of the studies they included.

Meta-analyses and systematic literature reviews for goal setting suggest that "the predicted impact of goal setting on physical performance has not been verified" (Meyers et al., 1996, p. 142) and that significant methodological flaws complicate the collection of clear intervention results (Meyers et al., 1996; Weinberg, 1994; Whelan et al., 1991). According to the meta-analyses, direct empirical support for goal setting remains tentative. However, there is some evidence of indirect performance benefits, as goal setting may enhance motivation, self-efficacy, and commitment, which are commonly believed to be indirectly related to valued performance achievements (Meyers et al., 1996; Weinberg, 1994). Meta-analyses evaluating goal setting included an effect size of .34, $p < .001$ (Kyllo & Landers, 1995) and .54, $p < .01$ (Meyers et al., 1996).

Meta-analytic support for imagery also remains equivocal. Although some authors have suggested that using imagery to aid performance is empirically validated (Jones & Stuth, 1997; Onestak, 1991), others have disagreed. Meta-analyses evaluating imagery included an effect size of .48, $p < .01$ (Feltz & Landers, 1983); .57, $p < .01$ (Meyers et al., 1996); and .68, $p < .01$ (Hinshaw, 1991). As Whelan, Mahoney, and Meyers (1991) noted, researchers have called for "cautious optimism that mental practice benefits motor skill acquisition and execution" (p. 310) (Feltz & Landers, 1983; Weinberg,

1982). Due to contradictory outcomes on the positive effects of imagery, numerous researchers agree that further empirical evaluation is required to understand the role of mediating variables and to determine overall efficacy (Meyers et al., 1996; Murphy, 1994; Murphy & Jowdy, 1992; Onestak, 1991; Whelan et al., 1991).

Similarly, meta-analyses and systematic literature reviews provide insufficient clear support for self-talk (Hardy et al., 1996; Meyers et al., 1996). While researchers typically agree that cognitive content can positively or negatively affect an individual's affective and behavioral states, the empirical literature has not verified the direct link between self-talk modification and successful performance. Although self-talk has received some support for its relationship to mediating variables such as effort (Rushall, 1984), anxiety management (Meichenbaum, 1977), attention control (Williams & Leffingwell, 2002), and self-confidence (Wilkes & Summers, 1984; Williams & Leffingwell, 2002), these variables have only an indirect and assumed relationship to performance enhancement. The one meta-analysis evaluating self-talk, which only included six studies, found an effect size of .76, $p > .05$, ns (nonsignificant) Meyers et al., 1996).

Arousal regulation strategies, such as relaxation and psyching up, fare no better in meta-analyses and systematic literature reviews. According to Gould and Udry (1994), although arousal interventions may facilitate performance, "caution is warranted in interpreting these results because of the failure to establish causal relationships between relaxation training and improved performance in much of the research" (p. 482). Other researchers with similar concerns have suggested that sufficient support for arousal regulation does not yet exist in the empirical literature (Meyers et al., 1996; Murphy & Jowdy, 1992; Onestak, 1991; Whelan et al., 1991). Thus, while arousal regulation has improved some mediating variables, such as cognitive and somatic anxiety (Gould & Udry, 1994; Onestak, 1991), empirical validation for arousal techniques is limited and plagued by methodological weaknesses and contradictory evidence. One meta-analysis evaluating relaxation procedures found an effect size of .73, $p < .01$ (Meyers et al., 1996). A separate meta-analysis on psyching up, which included only five studies, found an effect size of 1.23, $p < .01$ (Meyers et al., 1996).

Finally, like the individual interventions, multicomponent interventions, which combine two or more intervention strategies into one independent variable, receive limited support from meta-analyses. Only one meta-analysis has compiled and evaluated the empirical data on multicomponent interventions, thus making it difficult to draw formal conclusions. Using the one meta-analysis available (Meyers et al., 1996), the most detailed conclusions can be drawn from studies utilizing visuo-motor behavior rehearsal (VMBR), which is a multicomponent intervention essentially consisting of imagery and arousal regulation (in the form of relaxation) (Suinn, 1985). Authors of meta-analyses have suggested some preliminary support for VMBR, yet have largely excluded the evaluation of other multicomponent interventions (Meyers et al., 1996; Whelan et al., 1991). The only available meta-analysis found an effect size of 1.01, $p < .001$ (Meyers et al., 1996). However, this effect size is based on only nine studies, the majority of which evaluated VMBR.

Regardless of the conclusions drawn from the various meta-analyses, there are fundamental flaws with meta-analytic procedures that are rarely discussed in the sport psychology literature. First, the meta-analytic procedure inevitably involves significant biases and meta-analyses inescapably reflect biases within the primary research (Slavin, 1995). The meta-analytic procedure, like any review procedure, cannot wholly prevent the meta-analyst's personal biases from directly or indirectly affecting the review. Likewise, meta-analyses are susceptible to the post hoc bias intrinsic within any retrospective study (Geller & Proschan, 1996).

A second criticism of meta-analytic procedures is their tendency to attempt to substantiate cause-and-effect relationships or to test hypotheses. Although "individual well-designed trials can be used for hypothesis testing, meta-analyses [should not be used] for estimating treatment effects and for generating new hypotheses" (Yusuf, 1997, p. 596). Care must be taken when interpreting conclusions of efficacy from meta-analyses that yield low to moderate effect sizes, include studies using both analogue and competitive populations, and include studies with significant methodological weaknesses. In addition, both individual empirical studies and meta-analyses often poorly support intervention efficacy, yet the author's conclusions often misrepresent implications for the field and support the continued use of the interventions. For example, one author wrote, "of course a note of caution is called for due to the lack of any significant statistical findings, but these preliminary findings are certainly encouraging to practitioners who are interested in using goal setting" (Weinberg, Stitcher, & Richardson, 1994, p. 174). Another example demonstrating this concern in the statement that "although statistical tests indicated no significant performance differences, the magnitude, direction, and consistency of the differences in favor of the goal group offer some support for the effectiveness of specific goals across an athletic season" (Weinberg et al., 1994, p. 166). These statements reflect the tendency to favorably misrepresent findings and mislead consumers of the scientific literature, who may largely base their practices on such statements.

Finally, meta-analyses often include studies with significant methodological weaknesses and studies indirectly related to the research under investigation (Slavin, 1995). These trends likely skew the appraisal of treatment effects. Thus, "only when well-designed trials exist is a reliable meta-analysis possible" (Yusuf, 1997, p. 596), and importantly, "meta-analyses are only as good as the studies from which they are constructed" (Charlton, 1996, p. 398).

As can be gleaned from previous reviews of the existing empirical research in sport psychology, contradictory evidence and poor methodological standards among individual trials (Meyers et al., 1996; Murphy, 1990; Murphy & Jowdy, 1992; Suinn, 1997; Weinberg, 1994; Whelan et al., 1991) limit the capacity for meta-analyses to accurately reflect the efficacy of interventions for performance enhancement. Even when meta-analyses reflect *seemingly* supportive results, some authors assert that these results provide real evidence of intervention efficacy (Gould & Udry, 1994; Jones & Stuth, 1997; Kyllo & Landers, 1995). Meta-analyses, however, cannot provide such uncontroverted evidence because they typically include studies with a range of procedural, design, and statistical adequacies, and such statements of efficacy potentially mislead consumers of the scientific literature. On the other hand, researchers of both empirical studies and meta-analyses commonly explain away negative findings and continue to support procedures instead of acknowledging the relevance of the negative results. For example, "the nonsignificant main effect for goal groups was attributed to the spontaneous goal-setting behavior of the control group" (Boyce & Bingham, 1997, p. 312), and "the imagery condition was not successful as anticipated perhaps because the participants stated they simply thought too much about the actual movements they made when shooting the free-throws" (Lerner, Ostrow, Yura, & Etzel, 1996, p.

392). Although these statements may have merit, the authors cannot reject competing hypotheses (no effect) for the nonsignificant findings. Conclusions drawn from individual experimental trials and meta-analyses must accurately represent the findings and not immunize negative findings from criticism and refutation. According to Lilienfeld, Lynn, and Lohr (2003):

> *The repeated invocation of ad hoc hypotheses to explain away negative findings is a common tactic . . . [and they can be] simply "pasted on" to plug holes in the theory in question. When taken to an extreme, ad hoc hypotheses can provide an impenetrable barrier against potential refutation (p. 6).*

Misrepresenting results also misleads the consumer (athletes and hiring organizations) and perpetuates misrepresentation in future research and reviews. While the average practitioner is probably well aware of these concerns on a theoretical level, the fact that incorrect conclusions are often drawn in the professional literature suggests the need to alert the busy practitioner who may rapidly scan journal articles without paying particular attention to statistical analyses.

Applying the Empirically Supported Treatment (EST) Criteria to Psychological Skills Training Procedures

To respond to the current concerns and to evaluate empirical findings for the common performance enhancement interventions without including the difficulties of combining and averaging data from individual trials, sport psychology must again look to allied areas of professional psychology for cutting-edge efficacy evaluation. A recent study by Moore (2003b) embraced this task. This study collected the empirical research in sport psychology and analyzed it according to the empirically supported treatment criteria designed both to facilitate future empirical research and to help practitioners make ethical and informed decisions about which interventions to use. The study comprehensively reviewed outcome data across the varying performance enhancement interventions and utilized the criteria suggested by the Committee to determine the level of empirical support for the commonly utilized interventions (goal setting, imagery, self-talk, arousal regulation, multicomponent packages). After analyzing the traditional sport psychology interventions, the author considered the implications of the findings and provided suggestions for conducting future empirical research and implications for sport psychology practitioners. Since conducting the study in 2003, Moore (second author of this text) has updated the study to include the additional empirical studies (through October, 2004) published since (Moore & Gardner, 2005).

Method of Analysis

The study thoroughly searched for all peer-reviewed empirical research studies published in sport psychology since 1960 that focused on goal setting, imagery, self-talk, arousal regulation, and multicomponent interventions for directly enhancing athletic performance. Studies were collected regardless of population (competitive athletes or analogue populations) or methodology. However, in order to be included in Moore's study (according to the Committee's criteria), studies were required to empirically examine the *direct* enhancement of *competitive* athletic performance; to utilize clear, objective (athletic) performance-dependent variables; to utilize appropriate methodological designs (randomized controlled between-group designs or single-case designs with comparison to another intervention); and to utilize one (or a combination) of the major intervention techniques as the independent variable.

Each study was evaluated according to the general criteria established by the Committee for designation as an empirically supported intervention (p. 68) (Chambless & Ollendick, 2001). As the research sample must accurately represent the target population for the purpose of generalizability (Chambless & Ollendick, 2001), the empirical studies were required to utilize competitive performers as the defined population. In addition, the criteria require a methodological design including either a randomized controlled between-group design or single-case design with comparison to another intervention. The criteria also require that studies provide an intervention manual or thoroughly detailed description. However, the vast majority of sport psychology research has yet to use intervention manuals, and relatively few studies describe interventions in sufficient detail.

The established criteria also require studies to specify sample characteristics beyond simple inclusion and exclusion criteria. As sport psychology research typically does not detail subject information, Moore did not consider descriptive sample characteristics an absolute criterion when initially screening studies, but did consider them an absolute criterion when formally determining levels of empirical support.

Studies were grouped by intervention modality (goal setting, imagery, self-talk, arousal regulation, or multicomponent), and individual studies within each intervention modality were separately analyzed according to the established criteria for empirical support. For each study, analysis began by distinguishing the population as either competitive performers or analogue populations and tasks. Studies utilizing analogue populations were evaluated separately, as empirical support can be determined only for studies utilizing actual competitive performers. Second, the methodological design was evaluated, and studies were rejected if they did not utilize appropriate methodological design (randomized controlled between-group design or single-case design with comparison to another intervention), competitive performers, or dependent measures of actual competitive performance.

Within each intervention class, the studies meeting the design and population criteria were compiled to determine the level of empirical support for the given intervention. This process included determining the total number of supportive and nonsupportive outcomes within all studies representing the particular intervention. When contradictory evidence occurred among the studies on a given intervention, the relative numbers of contradictory studies and the results of the best-designed studies were considered. The number of independent investigators or investigation teams within a specific intervention modality was also evaluated, as supportive outcomes should be demonstrated by more than one independent investigator or team. After applying each relevant variable in the established criteria for empirically supported interventions, each intervention modality was categorized as a well-established intervention, probably efficacious intervention, or experimental intervention.

Although analogue studies could not be included in the determination of empirical support due to their lack of population and task specificity and generalizability, analogue studies make up a significant portion of the research on intervention strategies. As such, in order to thoroughly examine the sport psychology research on these common interventions and to report any related trends, the same evaluation procedure was conducted on analogue studies. However, findings from analogue research could not be included in the determination of level of empirical support.

Results of Analysis

A total of 104 empirical studies (n = 104) using objective measures of athletic performance were collected (see table 5.1 for a summary of all results). Of those, 46 included competitive performers, which were the target population, and 58 utilized analogue populations and tasks.

As mentioned, when specifically determining empirical support for athletic performance enhancement interventions, only those studies utilizing actual competitive performers as the target population were assessed according to the established criteria. However, analogue studies were also reviewed to fully reflect empirical trends among the research. Again, analogue studies, although informative, cannot be included in the determination of empirical support, but are nonetheless discussed for their relevance in the field.

Several studies compared more than one intervention to another intervention and control within the same experimental design, allowing for multiple independent variables and, thus, multiple comparisons. Although the formal number of reviewed studies is 104, the cumulative number of comparisons within the studies is 120, so that the number of comparisons exceeds the number of studies reviewed. Within the 104 studies, 27 comparisons included goal setting, 30 included imagery, 12 included self-talk, 13 included arousal regulation, and 38 included multicomponent interventions.

Of the 104 total studies (including both competitive and analogue populations), 44 studies were rejected from the evaluation of empirical support due to unacceptable experimental designs based on established criteria. Of those, 26 were discarded because they lacked random assignment or a control group, and 17 were discarded because they utilized single-case design studies without comparison to another intervention. One study was rejected due to a serious design confound preventing data interpretation.

Of the 104 total studies, 60 were accepted for further review due to adequate design and methodology. Of those, 19 utilized actual competitive performers (the target population), and 41 utilized analogue populations. Of the 60 accepted,

57 were randomized controlled between-group design experiments, and three were single-case design studies with comparison to another intervention.

Some of the criteria required for the determination of intervention efficacy highlight serious problems in sport psychology research that significantly challenge the development of empirically supported interventions. For example, only two studies included posttreatment follow-up (Crocker, Alderman, & Smith, 1988; Howard & Reardon, 1986), and only eight included sufficient intervention descriptions or a manual to facilitate replicability and to help ensure treatment integrity. Rarely did the studies describe samples beyond age, gender, and fundamental statements of team membership or sport involvement, such as personal inclusion and exclusion criteria. As a whole, the studies also did not describe the training of those delivering the intervention and did not monitor the delivery of the intervention (also referred to as treatment integrity).

The majority of the studies did not utilize a blind approach (controlling for investigator allegiance), an approach where the individuals delivering treatment are unaware of the research hypotheses. Further, none of the studies assessed nonspecific or relationship factors, their potential impact on intervention results, and the possibility that these factors may provide alternative explanations for intervention results, such as participants' expectations of success and participant and experimenter alliance.

Finally, some studies, although accepted for review, were considerably tainted by statistical and methodological weaknesses, which inevitably affect outcome results. Such weaknesses include excessive analyses (increasing Type I error) (Beauchamp, Halliwell, Fournier, & Koestner, 1996; Clark, 1960; Corbin, 1967b; Daw & Burton, 1994; Grouios, 1992; Lee & Hewitt, 1987; Short et al., 2002) and a large number of dependent variables with a low number of subjects (contributing to low power) (Burton, 1989b), and potential investigator allegiance concerns (Johnson et al., 2004). The following sections review the results for each intervention.

Goal Setting

The 104 studies yielded 27 comparisons utilizing goal setting for the direct enhancement of athletic performance. Of these 27, six utilized competitive performers and 21 utilized analogue populations or tasks.

As can be seen in table 5.1, of the six comparisons utilizing competitive performers (target population), two met basic design criteria and four were rejected for not meeting basic design criteria. Of those rejected, one was rejected for lacking random assignment or a suitable control group and three were rejected as single-case designs with no comparison to another intervention. Of the two accepted comparisons, both utilized randomized controlled between-group designs. Of the six comparisons utilizing competitive performers, three provided manuals or detailed intervention descriptions, three provided insufficient intervention descriptions, and none utilized follow-up procedures.

Neither of the two goal-setting comparisons utilizing competitive athletes and meeting basic design criteria demonstrated significant performance enhancing effects for goal setting beyond that of control conditions. When these results are evaluated using the established criteria for the determination of empirical support, goal setting must be categorized as an *experimental* intervention for competitive performance enhancement, as the criteria require at least two experiments demonstrating positive results for the intervention to receive formal empirical support.

Of the 21 comparisons on goal setting utilizing analogue populations or tasks, 17 met basic design criteria and four were rejected for lack of random assignment or a suitable control group. All 17 accepted comparisons utilized randomized controlled between-group designs. Of the 21 total comparisons utilizing analogue populations or tasks, seven provided manuals or detailed intervention descriptions, 14 insufficiently described interventions, and none utilized follow-up procedures.

Of the 17 analogue comparisons on goal setting that met basic design criteria, four demonstrated significant performance enhancing effects beyond that of control conditions and 13 found no performance enhancing effects beyond that of control conditions.

Imagery

The 104 total studies yielded 30 comparisons utilizing imagery as a performance enhancement intervention. Of these 30 comparisons, seven utilized competitive performers and 23 utilized analogue populations or tasks.

Six of the seven comparisons utilizing competitive performers met basic design criteria, while one was rejected as a single-case design with

no comparison to another intervention. All six accepted comparisons utilized randomized controlled between-group designs. Of the seven total comparisons utilizing competitive performers, two provided manuals or detailed intervention descriptions, five provided insufficient intervention descriptions, and one utilized follow-up procedures.

None of the six imagery comparisons utilizing competitive athletes and meeting basic design criteria demonstrated performance enhancing effects beyond that of control conditions. As the criteria for formal empirical support require that at least two experiments of sufficient design demonstrate positive results, imagery must be categorized as an *experimental* intervention for athletic performance enhancement.

There were 23 imagery comparisons utilizing analogue populations or tasks. Sixteen of these met the basic design criteria and utilized randomized controlled between-group designs. Seven were rejected for lack of random assignment or a suitable control group. Of the 23 total analogue comparisons, six provided manuals or detailed intervention descriptions, 17 provided insufficient intervention descriptions, and none utilized follow-up procedures.

Of the 16 analogue comparisons meeting basic design criteria, six demonstrated that imagery or imagery plus physical practice enhanced performance beyond that of control conditions. Ten demonstrated no performance enhancing effects for imagery or imagery plus physical practice beyond that of control conditions.

Self-Talk

Twelve comparisons out of the 104 total studies utilized self-talk as a performance enhancement intervention. Of these 12, seven utilized competitive performers and five utilized analogue populations or tasks.

Of the seven comparisons utilizing competitive performers, four met basic design criteria, and three did not. Of these three, one was rejected for lack of random assignment or a suitable control group and two were rejected as single-case designs with no comparison to another intervention. Of the four accepted comparisons, three utilized randomized controlled between-group designs and one utilized a single-case design with comparison to another intervention. Of the seven total comparisons, four provided manuals or detailed intervention descriptions, three provided insufficient intervention descriptions, and one utilized follow-up procedures.

None of the four accepted self-talk comparisons utilizing competitive athletes demonstrated significant performance enhancing effects beyond that of control conditions. Although one study suggested inconsistent performance enhancing effects (2 out of 3 individuals) among competitive athletes in a practice situation, it was unable to demonstrate enhancement during a competitive situation. Therefore, due to the lack of supportive findings, self-talk is also categorized as an *experimental* intervention for the enhancement of athletic performance.

Five self-talk comparisons utilized analogue populations or tasks. The four accepted as meeting basic design criteria utilized randomized controlled between-group designs. One study was rejected due to a significant design confound in which different coaches were utilized across groups, rendering results uninterpretable. Four of the five studies provided manuals or detailed intervention descriptions and none utilized follow-up procedures.

Four of the five analogue comparisons utilizing self-talk and meeting basic design criteria demonstrated significant performance enhancing effects beyond that of control conditions. In the other comparison, self-talk improved performance on 2 out of 3 performance measures.

Arousal Regulation

The 104 total studies yielded 13 comparisons utilizing arousal regulation as a performance enhancement intervention. Five of the studies utilized competitive performers and eight utilized analogue populations or tasks.

Four of the five comparisons utilizing competitive performers were accepted for meeting basic design criteria. All four utilized randomized controlled between-group designs. One comparison was rejected due to lack of random assignment. Of the five total comparisons utilizing competitive performers, two provided manuals or detailed intervention descriptions, three provided insufficient intervention descriptions, and none utilized follow-up procedures.

None of the four accepted comparisons utilizing arousal regulation with competitive athletes demonstrated significant performance enhancing effects beyond that of control conditions. Based on the studies' failure to demonstrate support, arousal regulation is categorized as an *experimen-*

tal intervention for the enhancement of competitive athletic performance.

Eight arousal regulation comparisons utilized analogue populations or tasks. Five were accepted for appropriate design, and all five utilized randomized controlled between-group designs. Three were rejected for lack of random assignment or a suitable control group. Of the eight total analogue comparisons, three provided manuals or detailed intervention descriptions while five did not, and none utilized follow-up procedures.

One of the five accepted analogue comparisons utilizing arousal regulation demonstrated significant performance enhancing effects beyond that of the control condition, and two demonstrated significant performance enhancing effects for arousal regulation beyond that of both imagery and the control condition. One demonstrated performance-enhancing effects equal to an imagery condition and greater than the control condition. Finally, one comparison demonstrated that arousal regulation strategies were equal to the control condition on tasks evaluating reaction time, and that arousal regulation strategies resulted in performance improvements beyond the control condition on a strength task.

Multicomponent Interventions

The 104 total studies yielded 38 comparisons utilizing a multicomponent (package) intervention to enhance athletic performance. Of these, 32 utilized competitive performers and six utilized analogue populations or tasks.

Of the 32 comparisons utilizing competitive performers, 12 were accepted for meeting basic design criteria. Eight were rejected for a lack of random assignment or a suitable control group and 12 were rejected as single-case designs with no comparison to another intervention. Of the 12 accepted comparisons, 10 utilized randomized controlled between-group designs and two utilized single-case designs with comparison to another intervention. Of the 32 total comparisons utilizing competitive performers, 19 provided manuals or detailed intervention descriptions, 13 provided insufficient intervention descriptions, and two utilized follow-up procedures.

The 12 accepted multicomponent comparisons utilizing competitive athletes produced a variety of results. Two single-case designs with comparison to another intervention demonstrated that a combination of goal setting, imagery, self-talk, and relaxation enhanced competitive performance.

Many interventions frequently used by sport psychologists have not demonstrated sufficient efficacy for performance enhancement.

Although this multicomponent intervention partially fulfills the criteria for a categorization of "probably efficacious," the two single-case design experiments do not fully meet established criteria. Specifically, the same general research team evaluated these comparisons, one study failed to provide a clear intervention description or manual, and both failed to thoroughly describe sample characteristics. Thus, the findings from these two single-case design experiments categorize this multicomponent intervention as *experimental*.

One comparison evaluating the combined use of self-talk and arousal regulation demonstrated no significant performance enhancing effects beyond that of control conditions. As such, multicomponent interventions combining self-talk and arousal regulation are categorized as *experimental*.

One randomized controlled between-group design comparison evaluating a combination of imagery and preparatory arousal demonstrated performance enhancing effects beyond that of control conditions with 10- to 12-year-old boys. According to the criteria, one study may be sufficient to categorize an intervention as probably efficacious *if* the study also provides a clear intervention description or manual and thoroughly describes sample characteristics. However, the comparison did neither. As such, the multicom-

ponent intervention consisting of imagery and preparatory arousal is categorized as an *experimental* intervention.

Among three comparisons evaluating a combination of relaxation, imagery, and self-talk, one found no significant performance enhancing effects beyond that of the control condition while two did enhance performance beyond controls. In one of the studies demonstrating improvement, performance gains were actually enhanced at follow-up. As these three comparisons provided contradictory and equivocal data and did not provide thorough sample characteristics, the combined use of relaxation, imagery, and self-talk is categorized as an *experimental* intervention.

Three comparisons utilized a multicomponent intervention known as visuo-motor behavior rehearsal (VMBR), which is a manualized intervention that consists of imagery and arousal regulation in the form of relaxation. The three studies gave contradictory and equivocal results, as two demonstrated marginal statistically significant performance enhancing effects beyond that of the control group, while one found no enhancement beyond that of the control condition. The contradictory findings and the studies' failure to thoroughly describe sample characteristics categorize VMBR as an *experimental* intervention.

One additional study utilized a combination of imagery and relaxation similar to VMBR but did not utilize the actual VMBR protocol. This comparison did not demonstrate performance enhancing effects beyond that of the control group, and thus the intervention is *experimental.*

Finally, one comparison evaluated a combination of goal setting, activation regulation, self-talk, mental imagery, and concentration. Although results found increased subjective performance ratings by the athletes' coaches (which cannot be included), they found nonsignificant *objective* performance effects, which were measured by actual achievement in each match (such as runs scored). Due to the lack of significant objective improvement on objective performance measures, this combination is considered an *experimental* intervention.

Six multicomponent comparisons utilized analogue populations or tasks. Of these, four were accepted, and all four utilized randomized controlled between-group designs. Two comparisons were rejected due to lack of random assignment or a suitable control group. Of the six multicomponent analogue comparisons, three provided manuals or detailed intervention descriptions, three provided insufficient intervention descriptions, and none utilized follow-up procedures.

Of the four analogue comparisons meeting basic design criteria, one found that a combination of relaxation, imagery, goal setting, and self-talk enhanced performance beyond the control condition. One demonstrated no performance enhancing effects for the combination of imagery, self-talk, and relaxation. Finally, two comparisons demonstrated performance enhancing effects beyond that of both placebo and control conditions for VMBR.

Why Are These Results So Important?

The greatest single focus of applied sport psychology has been to define psychosocial characteristics directly related to optimal athletic performance and to develop mechanisms for enhancing competitive athletic performance. The purpose of Moore's study was to systematically review the empirical studies on the common interventions for athletic performance enhancement and to determine the interventions' levels of empirical support according to the criteria established in allied domains of professional psychology (Chambless

et al., 1998; Chambless & Hollon, 1998; Chambless & Ollendick, 2001). Moore's study indicates insufficient empirical support among well-conducted research for the efficacy of goal setting, imagery, self-talk, arousal regulation, and multicomponent interventions with competitive athletes. Moore's results indicate that these procedures must at this time be categorized as experimental interventions. These conclusions have profound implications for the theory, research, and practice of sport psychology, and they should be meaningful for practitioners assisting athletes in performance endeavors.

Efficacy of Traditional Performance Enhancement Interventions

The systematic research evaluation demonstrated consistent findings across the goal setting, imagery, self-talk, arousal regulation, and multicomponent intervention modalities. Uniformly, the evaluation indicated insufficient empirical support for all of the procedures, regardless of the population utilized (competitive or analogue). For empirical studies utilizing competitive athletes, results were unequivocal for all single interventions, and contradictory findings only existed among the multicomponent packages.

For studies utilizing analogue populations and tasks, contradictory supportive and nonsupportive intervention results were common. However, analogue studies often inflate data on efficacy, as they do not employ the target group intended to receive performance enhancement services. Analogue participants are not likely to have the same attitudes, skills, external demands, and requirements of the target population (competitive performers), and also have the capacity for greater skill development, or more room to grow. In fact, analogue studies' tendency to inflate results has previously been discussed in meta-analytic research. Meyers and colleagues (1996) stated, "noncompetitive performance assessments, therefore, appear to overestimate the effectiveness of the treatment" (p. 156). As already noted, as Moore's study investigated the level of empirical support for performance enhancement interventions with competitive performers, studies utilizing nonathlete populations could not be formally considered. Even if these studies could be included, the equivocal findings would not be sufficient to determine intervention efficacy, as contradictory evidence must be carefully weighed, the relative numbers of contradictory studies and the direction of the best designed studies must be considered, and empirical categorization must be conservative (Chambless & Hollon, 1998).

In the event that Moore's review, though thorough, missed some studies, a few supportive studies would not alter the present findings of insufficient empirical support. Among the studies utilizing competitive performers, adding several supportive studies would simply add contradictory data and would not change the experimental classifications. Given the well-designed studies' general findings that the common interventions do not enhance performance among competitive athletes, a vast body of research supporting these interventions would be required to change the levels of efficacy. Regardless of type of research (competitive or analogue), goal setting, imagery, self-talk, arousal regulation, and multicomponent interventions significantly lack empirical support, and all of the evaluated intervention modalities are thus currently experimental procedures. Let's discuss the results for the specific interventions under investigation.

Goal Setting

It has been stated that "the predicted impact of goal setting on physical performance has not been verified" (Meyers et al., 1996, p. 142) and that "the efficacy of goal setting in sport remains, by and large, untested and unsupported" (Strean & Roberts, 1992, p. 59). However, researchers and practitioners in sport psychology highly value goal setting as an intervention strategy, and anecdotal, correlational, and case studies suggest that using it with athletic clientele is valid (Burton, Naylor, & Holliday, 2001; Kyllo & Landers, 1995; Meyers et al., 1996). Despite empirical inadequacy, some strongly support its applied use and oddly suggest clear empirical findings. For example, Burton, Naylor, and Holliday (2001) stated that their research review led to the "unmistakable conclusion" that "goal setting is an effective performance enhancement strategy" (p. 521).

Although goal setting is one of the most widely researched and practiced interventions in sport psychology, Moore's study suggests that this procedure has been advocated well beyond the level of empirical validation necessary to ethically and responsibly incorporate it into standard practice. In fact, in Moore's study, goal setting receives status only as an experimental intervention, given the complete absence of positive outcomes in

well-designed studies utilizing the target population. These findings remain consistent even when illegitimately applying the evaluation criteria to studies that utilize analogue populations (such as undergraduate volunteers) or tasks (such as strength and endurance tasks), which make up the majority of the empirical research. While four analogue studies suggested intervention efficacy, many more (13) studies of similar methodological quality demonstrated contradictory findings. Thus, even analogue studies suggest limited support for goal setting.

Imagery

The complete absence of positive performance enhancing effects among the studies reviewed by Moore strongly indicates that there is currently no empirical evidence to suggest that imagery is an efficacious intervention for athletic performance enhancement. This is not a novel finding, as Suinn (1997) has stated that "research on mental practice has been extensive, but leads to few conclusive findings, a number of trends, and a variety of inconsistent results" (p. 199). Applying the established criteria for empirical support to the studies collected on imagery with competitive athletes determined that imagery must be characterized as an experimental intervention. In studies utilizing analogue populations and tasks, the result of six studies demonstrating significant (positive) outcomes and 10 demonstrating nonsignificant outcomes certainly leads to the same conclusion.

Self-Talk

Compared to the other common interventions, few research studies have evaluated self-talk for the direct enhancement of athletic performance. However, the number of empirical studies reviewed by Moore was adequate to determine its level of empirical support. Although several literature reviews and correlational accounts (Gould et al., 1992; Orlick & Partington, 1988; Williams & Leffingwell, 2002) suggest support for this intervention, Moore's study suggests that the empirical data collected to date do not support the use of self-talk. In fact, based on the complete absence of positive outcomes when used with the target population, self-talk is also categorized as an experimental intervention. The positive results found among analogue studies were unable to alter this categorization. Yet despite the limited number of empirical studies and the lack of efficacy support, self-talk is often utilized and receives prominent attention in chapters and literature reviews on sport psychology.

Arousal Regulation

Although arousal regulation strategies such as psyching up and relaxation enjoy popularity and purported support from anecdotal reports, correlational literature, and systematic literature reviews (Anshel, 1992; Gould & Udry, 1994; Meyers et al., 1996; Murphy & Jowdy, 1992; Taylor & Wilson, 2002), some researchers are also concerned about the empirical research base for arousal regulation. According to Zaichkowsky and Baltzell (2001), "although coaches and sport psychologists teach arousal regulation techniques to athletes, little quality empirical research has been conducted supporting their efficacy and effectiveness" (p. 334). After evaluating this research base to determine empirical support, Moore suggests that arousal regulation must also be categorized as an experimental intervention, as quality empirical studies do not show performance enhancing effects. Yet while no empirical study utilizing competitive athletes and meeting basic design criteria demonstrated positive outcomes beyond that of control conditions, applied practitioners widely use arousal regulation strategies.

This lack of empirical support is not a novel assertion among sport psychology professionals, who have stated that "support for the possible instrumental role of increased arousal in performance improvement has remained tentative" (Meyers et al., 1996, p. 144) and that "caution is warranted in interpreting [experimental] results because of the failure to establish causal relationships between relaxation training and improved performance in much of the research" (Gould & Udry, 1994, p. 482). Moore reaffirms the need for caution, as there are currently no supportive data on the efficacy of arousal regulation strategies (Moore, 2003b; Moore & Gardner, 2005).

Multicomponent Interventions

As the use of individual performance enhancement interventions has grown, researchers have begun incorporating multiple interventions into combination packages in order to provide athletes with numerous techniques for improving performance. Although theoretical rationale for prescribed packages is typically absent, numerous combinations have been applied to athletes and research participants in order to foster performance excellence

and evaluate the efficacy and effectiveness of the combinations. Despite their widespread use, the multicomponent interventions reviewed by Moore did not fulfill the criteria for a formal determination of empirical support, and thus they are also categorized as experimental interventions. However, there are some interesting discrepancies and promising trends among the empirical literature.

First, three multicomponent studies (two competitive and one analogue) showed promise, finding that packages consisting of goal setting, imagery, self-talk, and relaxation enhanced competitive performance beyond that of control conditions. Together, the two studies utilizing competitive performers did not meet formal requirements for designation as an empirically supported intervention, as there were only two single-case designs, a common research partner investigated both, only one clearly described the intervention, and neither provided thorough sample characteristics. Although this multicomponent intervention is therefore categorized as experimental, the results warrant additional well-designed studies by *different* research teams using manuals and thorough sample characteristics. Further well-designed research with competitive athletes may help establish this combination of strategies as a probably efficacious or well-established intervention for the enhancement of athletic performance.

One randomized controlled between-group design comparison evaluating a multicomponent intervention consisting of imagery and preparatory arousal demonstrated performance enhancing effects with 10- to 12-year-old boys. As this study did not include a clear intervention description or manual and did not provide thorough sample characteristics, this intervention must also be classified as experimental. Although it is unclear if the performance enhancing effects demonstrated in this study will generalize to adult competitive athletes, it is certainly possible that additional research meeting the established criteria will provide more powerful efficacy support for the combined use of imagery and preparatory arousal.

Although visuo-motor behavior rehearsal (VMBR) is currently experimental, contradictory yet somewhat promising results with competitive athletes warrant further well-designed research. Interestingly, although VMBR includes a manual and is a clearly replicable protocol that may enhance performance with competitive athletes, empirical research utilizing either a randomized controlled between-group design or single-case design with comparison to another intervention has not been published on VMBR since the 1980s. Thus, what may be the most promising multicomponent intervention available in sport psychology has possibly been overlooked.

When examining each of these multicomponent interventions, it is clear that there may be promising trends. Yet, similar to the individual interventions, the data do not support the use of these procedures for enhancing competitive performance. At this time, outcome research on the individual and multicomponent interventions for athletic performance enhancement has not demonstrated sufficient intervention efficacy, and each of these interventions must currently be seen as experimental.

Moore's results, while not inconsistent with previous cautions (Dishman, 1983; Meyers et al., 1996; Smith, 1989; Strean & Roberts, 1992), are inconsistent with current use in actual practice. However, although formal empirical support is clearly lacking, the specific reasons for this lack of efficacy are currently unclear and may include a number of possibilities. First, support may lack because the interventions do not target the necessary elements or variables of optimal performance, are theoretically unsound, or are truly ineffective. Second, the interventions may not be delivered in an optimal manner or dose. Third, applying interventions to individuals or groups (teams) without considering individual needs and personal characteristics may mask the potential positive effects the intervention could have if delivered only to those that could truly benefit from the intervention. Fourth, small sample sizes, often a result of practical realities (such as finite team size), may not provide empirical studies with the statistical power necessary to obtain statistical significance. Fifth, the dependent variables utilized in intervention research are complex and therefore demonstrating improvement may be challenging. This does not suggest that objective performance measurements are unwarranted, rather that more thoughtful and carefully considered measurements for competitive performance should be undertaken (Thelwell & Maynard, 2003). Finally, the lack of empirical efficacy may result from failure to adhere to clear intervention protocols or to rigorous scientific and methodological standards.

Regardless of the specific reasons for Moore's results, the proposition that these interventions lack efficacy is not new, and numerous sport psychology practitioners have cautioned against insufficient efficacy support (Dishman, 1983; Meyers et al., 1996; Smith, 1989; Strean & Roberts, 1992). Despite such cautions, these procedures continue as standard practice and are typically

Intervention decisions should not be based simply on anecdotal reports, correlational research, and personal philosophy.

presented within professional literature in a manner that suggests strong empirical validation. In response to these noted yet often overlooked concerns, researchers and practitioners need to consider how these findings can enhance the future development of sport psychology.

Implications for Professional Practice

The ultimate purpose of the determination, development, and dissemination of empirically supported interventions is to help the practitioner provide appropriate professional services to the consumer. For over 30 years, sport psychology professionals from a number of disciplines have researched goal setting, imagery, self-talk, arousal regulation, and multicomponent interventions and have implemented these strategies in their practices.

The sport psychology literature is replete with strong encouragement to use these procedures for athletic performance enhancement, and the literature largely suggests that ample evidence backs this encouragement (Burton et al., 2001; Jones & Stuth, 1997). Yet Moore's analysis makes it difficult to justify the automatic use of traditional interventions that have not demonstrated efficacy, have been supported only by studies plagued by methodological weaknesses, or have been wrongfully and hastily assumed to generalize among populations regardless of age, physical skill, competition level, intra- and interpersonal factors, and developmental, transitional, or clinical issues. This clear but disconcerting conclusion must be carefully considered, and its implications for both the practitioner and consumer must be thoroughly weighed.

When considering Moore's findings and related cautions, the empirical research on these interventions provides little guidance for the practitioner interested in best-practice procedures. While it cannot be decisively stated that these procedures do not work, as the null hypothesis can never be proven, the evidence suggests that practitioners should use these procedures cautiously and inform clients of their efficacy in attaining performance excellence. The ethical imperative for the sport psychologist is to honestly and openly describe the potential risks and benefits of the proposed interventions. While there has been no evidence of negative effects from these procedures, investing time and money into an intervention not demonstrated to work as advertised carries some risk of loss, and the consumer has a right to know the current state of research on intervention efficacy and effectiveness.

Further, the experimental status of the common performance enhancement procedures has disconcerting implications for the future public support for sport psychology. If sport psychology has promoted the common interventions beyond their scientific support, the profession must acknowledge and resolve several critical issues. We have several recommendations for practitioners who wish to integrate these findings.

First, the sport psychologist should resist interpreting the experimental data in a manner that verifies preconceptions and beliefs, and he should instead allow the data to inform the style and substance of his practice. Second, the ethical practitioner will develop an appropriate informed consent clearly stating that the traditional interventions are experimental and cautioning that their efficacy for directly enhancing competitive performance cannot be ensured (refer to chapter 12 for more information on informed consent). Given the scarcity of nomothetic outcome data to guide practice, sport psychologists should use a more idiographic analysis of client needs to determine if an intervention may be more or less effective for a particular client.

Final Thoughts

With a greater emphasis on understanding contemporary theoretical and empirical findings in the area of self-regulation, we highly encourage practitioners and researchers to consider alternative intervention models for attaining athletic excellence. As no one intervention will meet the needs of every athlete or solve every psychological problem, we encourage practitioners to remain open to new developments, as new and alternative interventions may more effectively serve specific athlete populations. One new intervention we developed, mindfulness-acceptance-commitment (MAC)-based performance enhancement (Gardner & Moore, 2004a), is introduced in the next chapter. This innovative approach to performance enhancement is an adaptation of existing approaches in behavioral psychology and has demonstrated initial success in providing a subset of athletes the behavioral self-regulation needed to attain athletic success.

Table 5.1 Summary of Collected Empirical Studies by Intervention, Population, and Task

Study	Intervention	Research design	Manual	Results	Subjects	Accept or reject
Boyce (1994)	Goal setting	RCT		Goal setting = control on performance measure	30 high-level pistol shooters ages 31-45	Accept
Burton (1989b)	Goal setting	Single group, pretest and posttest design, no control		Goal setting > control with women goal setting = control with men	30 collegiate swimmers	Reject
Lerner, Ostrow, Yura, Etzel (1996)	Imagery alone, goal setting alone, combination of goal setting plus imagery	Case study, multiple baseline design, no comparison		Support for goal setting, minimal support for combination, negative support for imagery (negative imagery decreased performance)	12 female college basketball players	Reject
Swain, Jones (1995)	Goal setting	Case study, multiple baseline design, no comparison	X	3 of 4 subjects increased basketball performance	4 college basketball players	Reject
Ward, Carnes (2002)	Goal setting	Case study, multiple baseline design, no comparison	X	Goal setting plus performance feedback increased performance	5 collegiate football players	Reject
Weinberg, Stitcher, Richardson (1994)	Goal setting	RCT	X	Goal setting = control	24 male college lacrosse players	Accept

Goal Setting—Analogue

Study	Intervention	Research design	Manual	Results	Subjects	Accept or reject
Barnett, Stanicek (1979)	Goal setting	RCT	X	Goal setting > control	30 undergrads	Accept
Boyce, Bingham (1997)	Goal setting	RCT		Goal setting = control	288 undergrads	Accept
Boyce, Wayda, Johnston, Bunker, Eliot (2001)	Goal setting	RCT		Self-set goal setting = instructor goal setting > control on performance measure	156 undergrads	Accept
Burton (1989a)	Goal setting	Randomized pretest and posttest between-group design, no control		Specific goals > general goals	23 undergrads	Reject
Filby, Maynard, Graydon (1999)	Goal setting	RCT		Multiple-goal strategies > control > single-goal strategies	40 undergrads	Accept

		Goal Setting—Analogue				
Study	Intervention	Research design	Manual	Results	Subjects	Accept or reject
Giannini, Weinberg, Jackson (1988)	Goal setting	Nonrandomized, pretest and posttest between-group design with control		All goal-setting conditions equal to each other competitive goal setting > control	100 undergrads	Reject
Hall, Weinberg, Jackson (1987)	Goal setting	RCT		Goal setting > control	94 undergrads	Accept
Hollingsworth (1975)	Goal setting	RCT	X	Goal setting = control	90 junior high school students	Accept
Johnson, Ostrow, Perna, Etzel (1997)	Goal setting	RCT		Goal setting = control	36 undergrads	Accept
Lane, Streeter (2003)	Goal setting	RCT		Goal setting = control	72 male high school basketball club members	Accept
Lerner, Locke (1995)	Goal setting	RCT	X	Goal setting = control	60 undergrads	Accept
Miller, McAuley (1987)	Goal setting	RCT		Goal setting = control	18 undergrads	Accept
Smith, Lee (1992)	Goal setting	RCT		Goal setting = control	51 undergrads	Accept
Theodorakis (1995)	Goal setting	Nonrandomized, pretest and posttest single-group design, no control		Results uninterpretable	42 undergrads	Reject
Weinberg, Bruya, Garland, Jackson (1990) (two studies)	1. Goal setting 2. Goal setting	1. RCT 2. RCT	X X	1. Goal setting = control 2. goal setting = control	1. 87 undergrads 2. 120 undergrads	Accept Accept
Weinberg, Bruya, Jackson (1985)	Goal setting	RCT	X X	Goal setting = control	96 undergrads	Accept
Weinberg, Bruya, Jackson (1990)	Goal setting	RCT		Goal setting = control	85 undergrads	Accept
Weinberg, Bruya, Jackson, Garland (1987) (two studies)	1. Goal setting 2. Goal setting	1. Nonrandomized, pretest and posttest between-group design, no control 2. RCT	X X	1.All goal setting conditions equal 2. goal setting = control	1. 30 undergrads 2. 123 undergrads	Reject Accept
Wraith, Biddle (1989)	Goal setting	Nonrandomized, pretest and posttest between-group design, no control		No improvements for all groups from baseline to post-intervention	51 females ages 11-13	Reject

(continued)

Table 5.1   *(continued)*

Imagery—Competitive

Study	Intervention	Research design	Manual	Results	Subjects	Accept or reject
Grouios (1992)	Imagery	RCT	X	Physical practice > imagery > no practice	30 intermediate divers	Accept
Howard, Reardon (1986)	Imagery alone, self-talk alone, and combination (cognitive hypnotic imagery)	RCT	X	Combination > self-talk = imagery = control	32 male weight-lifter volunteers	Accept
Lerner, Ostrow, Yura, Etzel (1996)	Imagery alone, goal setting alone, and combination goal setting plus imagery	Case study, multiple baseline design, no comparison		Support for goal setting, minimal support for combination, negative support for imagery (negative imagery decreased performance)	12 female college basketball players	Reject
Mumford, Hall (1985)	Imagery	RCT		Imagery = control	59 high-level skaters	Accept
Rodgers, Hall, Buckolz (1991)	Imagery alone, self-talk alone	RCT		Imagery = self-talk = control	40 adolescent elite figure skaters	Accept
Weinberg, Seabourne, Jackson (1981)	Imagery alone, relaxation alone, and combination (VMBR)	RCT	X	VMBR > imagery = relaxation = control on 1 of 3 performance measures	32 undergrads in karate club	Accept
Wrisberg, Anshel (1989)	Imagery alone, arousal alone, and combination imagery plus arousal	RCT		Combination > imagery = arousal = control	40 males ages 10-12	Accept

Imagery—Analogue

Study	Intervention	Research design	Manual	Results	Subjects	Accept or reject
Andre, Means (1986)	Imagery	RCT		Imagery = control	66 undergrads	Reject
Burhans, Richman, Bergey (1988)	Imagery	RCT		Imagery = control	65 students in physical education class	Accept
Clark (1960)	Imagery	Nonrandomized, pretest and posttest between-group design with control		Results mixed	144 high school males	Reject
Corbin (1967a)	Imagery	RCT		Imagery = control	120 male undergrads	Accept
Corbin (1967b)	Imagery	RCT		Physical practice > imagery = control	30 high school males	Accept

Imagery—Analogue						
Study	Intervention	Research design	Manual	Results	Subjects	Accept or reject
Elko, Ostrow (1992)	Imagery alone, arousal alone	RCT	X	Imagery > control, imagery = arousal, arousal = control	60 undergrads	Accept
Epstein (1980)	Imagery	RCT	X	Imagery = control	45 undergrads	Accept
Gould, Weinberg, Jackson (1980)	Imagery alone, Arousal alone	RCT		Arousal > imagery = control	60 undergrads	Accept
Hird, Landers, Thomas, Horan (1991)	Imagery	RCT		Control > imagery	72 undergrads	Accept
Isaac (1992)	Imagery	Nonrandomized, pretest and posttest between-group design with control	X	Imagery > control	78 novice to experienced trampolinists	Reject
Minas (1978)	Imagery	RCT		Imagery = control	32 undergrads	Accept
Peynircioglu, Thompson, Tanielian (2000)	Imagery alone, arousal alone	Nonrandomized, pretest and posttest between-group design with control		Imagery > arousal = control for performance measure, arousal > imagery = control for strength measure	120 undergrads	Reject
Powell (1973)	Imagery	Pretest and posttest between-group design, no control		Positive imagery > negative imagery	18 graduate students	Reject
Rawlings, Rawlings, Chen, Yilk (1972)	Imagery	RCT	X	Imagery plus physical practice = physical practice > control	24 female undergrads	Accept
Ryan, Simons (1981)	Imagery	RCT		Physical practice > imagery = no practice	39 undergrads	Accept
Shick (1970)	Imagery	Nonrandomized, pretest and posttest between-group design with control		Imagery > control for serve measure, imagery < control for volley measure	10 undergrads	Reject
Short, Bruggeman, Engel, Marback, Wang, Willadsen, Short (2002)	Imagery	RCT	X	Positive imagery > control, negative imagery < control	83 undergrads	Accept
Start, Richardson (1964)	Imagery	Nonrandomized, pretest and posttest between-group design, no control		No motor task improvements	32 undergrads	Reject

(continued)

Table 5.1 *(continued)*

Imagery—Analogue

Study	Intervention	Research design	Manual	Results	Subjects	Accept or reject
Van Gyn, Wenger, Gaul (1990)	Imagery	RCT		Imagery plus physical training = physical training > control on power measure, imagery plus physical training > control on sprint measure	40 undergrads	Accept
Weinberg, Jackson, Seabourne (1985)	Imagery alone, arousal alone	RCT	X	Imagery = specific, arousal = non-specific, arousal > control	25 male undergrads	Accept
White, Ashton, Lewis (1979)	Imagery	RCT		Imagery plus physical practice > imagery = physical practice > control	24 undergrads	Accept
Wilkes, Summers (1984)	Imagery alone, arousal alone	RCT		Arousal > attentional focus = imagery = control	60 undergrads	Accept
Woolfolk, Murphy, Gottesfeld, Aitken (1985)	Imagery	RCT		Positive imagery = control, negative imagery = reduced performance	50 male undergrads	Accept

Self-talk—Competitive

Study	Intervention	Research design	Manual	Results	Subjects	Accept or reject
Barling, Bresgi (1982)	Self-talk alone, arousal alone, and combination of self-talk plus arousal	RCT		Self-talk plus arousal = self-talk = arousal = control	24 college swimmers	Accept
Howard, Reardon (1986)	Self-talk alone, imagery alone, and combination (cognitive hypnotic imagery)	RCT	X	Combination > self-talk = imagery = control	32 male weight lifter volunteers	Accept
Johnson, Hrycaiko, Johnson, Halas (2004)	Self-talk	Case study, multiple baseline design with comparison	X	2 of 3 participants improved performance in practice only	4 female adolescent soccer players	Accept
Landin, Hebert (1999)	Self-talk	Case study, multiple baseline design, no comparison	X	Inconsistent results, some positive results	5 collegiate tennis players	Reject

Self-talk—Competitive

Study	Intervention	Research design	Manual	Results	Subjects	Accept or reject
Maynard, Smith, Warwick-Evans (1995)	Self-talk	Nonrandomized, pretest and posttest between-group design with control		Self-talk = control	24 semipro soccer players	Reject
Ming, Martin (1996)	Self-talk	Case study, multiple baseline design, no comparison	X	Marginal support for intervention	4 figure skaters ages 11-13	Reject
Rodgers, Hall, Buckolz (1991)	Self-talk alone, imagery alone	RCT		Imagery = self-talk = control	40 adolescent elite figure skaters	Accept

Self-Talk—Analogue

Study	Intervention	Research design	Manual	Results	Subjects	Accept or reject
Hatzigeorgiadis, Theodorakis, Zourbanos (2004)	Self-talk (motivational), self-talk (instructional)	RCT		Self-talk (M) > control Self-talk (I) > control	60 swimming class volunteers	Accept
Perkos, Theordorakis, Chroni (2002)	Self-talk	RCT, serious design confound (different coaches across groups)	X	Self-talk improved performance in 2 of 3 performance measures	62 novice adolescent basketball participants	Reject
Theodorakis, Chroni, Laparidis, Bebetsos, Douma (2001)	Self-talk	RCT	X	Self-talk ("relax") > self-talk ("fast") = control	60 male undergrads	Accept
Van Raalte, Brewer, Lewis, Linder, Wildman, Kozimor (1995)	Self-talk	RCT	X	Positive self-talk > negative self-talk = control	60 undergrads	Accept
Weinberg, Smith, Jackson, Gould (1984)	Self-talk	RCT	X	Positive self-talk > control	130 undergrads	Accept

Arousal Regulation—Competitive

Study	Intervention	Research design	Manual	Results	Subjects	Accept or reject
Barling, Bresgi (1982)	Self-talk alone, arousal alone, and combination of self-talk plus arousal	RCT		Self-talk plus arousal = self-talk = arousal = control	24 college swimmers	Accept
Caudill, Weinberg, Jackson (1983)	Arousal	Within groups design		Arousal > control	16 college hurdlers and sprinters	Reject

(continued)

Table 5.1 *(continued)*

Arousal Regulation—Competitive

Study	Intervention	Research design	Manual	Results	Subjects	Accept or reject
Maynard, Hemmings, Warwick-Evans (1995)	Relaxation	RCT	X	Relaxation = control	17 semipro soccer players	Accept
Weinberg, Seabourne, Jackson (1981)	Relaxation alone, imagery alone, and combination (VMBR)	RCT	X	VMBR > imagery = relaxation = control on 1 of 3 performance measures	32 undergrads in karate club	Accept
Wrisberg, Anshel (1989)	Arousal alone, imagery alone, and combination of imagery plus arousal	RCT		Combination > imagery = arousal = control	40 males ages 10-12	Accept

Arousal Regulation—Analogue

Study	Intervention	Research design	Manual	Results	Subjects	Accept or reject
Elko, Ostrow (1992)	Arousal alone, imagery alone	RCT	X	Imagery > control, imagery = arousal, arousal = control	60 undergrads	Accept
Gould, Weinberg, Jackson (1980)	Arousal alone, imagery alone	RCT		Arousal > imagery = control	60 undergrads	Accept
Lee (1990)	Arousal	Nonrandomized, pretest and posttest between-group design with control		Arousal > control	52 undergrads	Reject
Peynircioglu, Thompson, Tanielian (2000)	Arousal alone, imagery alone	Nonrandomized, pretest and posttest between-group design with control		Imagery > arousal = control for performance measure, arousal > imagery = control for strength measure	120 undergrads	Reject
Weinberg, Gould, Jackson (1981)	Arousal	Randomized, pretest and posttest between-group design, no control		No difference between groups	80 undergrads	Reject
Weinberg, Jackson, Seabourne (1985)	Arousal alone, imagery alone	RCT	X	Imagery = specific preparatory arousal = nonspecific preparatory arousal > control	25 male undergrads	Accept

Arousal Regulation—Analogue

Study	Intervention	Research design	Manual	Results	Subjects	Accept or reject
Whelan, Epkins, Meyers (1990)	Arousal	RCT	X	Arousal > control for increasing strength performance, arousal = control for reaction time	86 undergrads	Accept
Wilkes, Summers (1984)	Arousal alone, imagery alone	RCT		Arousal > attentional focus = imagery = control	60 undergrads	Accept

Multicomponent—Competitive

Study	Intervention	Research design	Manual	Results	Subjects	Accept or reject
Annesi (1998)	Combination of relaxation plus self-talk	Case study, multiple baseline design, no comparison		Marginal performance improvements	3 elite adolescent tennis players	Reject
Barling, Bresgi (1982)	Self-talk alone, arousal alone, and combination of self-talk plus arousal	RCT		Self-talk plus arousal = self-talk = arousal = control	24 college swimmers	Accept
Crocker, Alderman, Smith (1988)	Combination of relaxation plus self-talk	Nonrandomized, pretest and posttest between-group design with control	X	Combination > control	31 elite volleyball players	Reject
Davis (1991)	Combination of imagery plus self-talk plus stimulus control	Case study, no multiple baseline design, no comparison		Combination improved performance on 3 of 4 performance measures	1 female tennis player	Reject
Daw, Burton (1994)	Combination of goal setting plus imagery plus arousal	Nonrandomized, pretest and posttest between-group design with control	X	Combination improved performance on 1 of 4 performance measures	24 college tennis players	Reject
De Witt (1980)	Combination of relaxation plus imagery plus self-talk	RCT	X	Combination > control	12 collegiate basketball players	Accept
Gravel, Lemieux, Ladouceur (1980)	Combination (VMBR)	RCT	X	VMBR > placebo on ski race times	12 high-level undergrad skiers (6 per group)	Accept

(continued)

Table 5.1 *(continued)*

				Multicomponent—Competitive		
Study	**Intervention**	**Research design**	**Manual**	**Results**	**Subjects**	**Accept or reject**
Hall, Erffmeyer (1983)	Combination of VMBR plus modeling	Randomized, pretest and posttest between-group design, no control	X	VMBR plus modeling > VMBR alone	10 skilled female college basketball players	Reject
Holm, Beckwith, Ehde, Tinius (1996)	Combination of relaxation plus imagery plus self-talk	RCT	X	Relaxation plus imagery plus self-talk = control	62 undergrads from football and swim teams	Accept
Howard, Reardon (1986)	Imagery alone, self-talk alone, and combination (cognitive hypnotic imagery)	RCT	X	Combination > self-talk = imagery = control	32 male weight lifter volunteers	Accept
Kendall, Hrycaiko, Martin, Kendall (1990)	Combination of imagery plus relaxation plus self-talk	Case study, multiple baseline design, no comparison		Marginal improvements	4 varsity intercollegiate basketball players	Reject
Kirschenbaum, Owens, O'Connor (1998)	Combination of self-monitoring plus imagery plus stimulus control	Case study, multiple baseline design, no comparison	X	Improvement in golf scores	5 golfers	Reject
Lee, Hewitt (1987)	Combination of imagery plus relaxation	Nonrandomized, pretest and posttest between-group design with control		Relaxation plus imagery in tank > relaxation plus imagery on mat = control	36 female gymnasts ages 9-17 (beginning to intermediate)	Reject
Lerner, Ostrow, Yura, Etzel (1996)	Imagery alone, goal setting alone, and combination of goal setting plus imagery	Case study, multiple baseline design, no comparison		Support for goal setting, minimal support for combination, negative support for imagery (negative imagery decreased performance)	12 female college basketball players	Reject
Li-Wei, Qi-Wei, Orlick, Zitzelsberger (1992)	Combination of relaxation plus imagery	Nonrandomized, pretest and posttest between-group design with control	X	Relaxation plus imagery > video observation > control	40 males ages 7-10, table tennis players	Reject

Study	Intervention	Research design	Manual	Results	Subjects	Accept or reject
Lohr, Scogin (1998)	Combination (VMBR)	Nonrandomized, pretest and posttest between-group design with control	X	VMBR > control	36 college athletes from 7 sports	Reject
Madden, McGown (1988)	Combination of relaxation plus imagery	RCT		Relaxation plus imagery = control	17 female volleyball players	Accept
Meyers, Schleser (1980)	Combination of relaxation plus imagery plus self-talk	Case study, no multiple baseline design, no comparison	X	Performance improved	1 collegiate basketball player	Reject
Meyers, Schleser, Okwumabua (1982)	Combination of imagery plus relaxation plus self-talk	Case study, multiple baseline design, no comparison	X	Intervention successful	2 collegiate basketball players	Reject
Noel (1980)	Combination (VMBR)	RCT	X	VMBR = control	14 collegiate tennis players	Accept
Palmer (1992)	Combination of self-talk plus imagery	Nonrandomized, pretest and posttest between-group design with control	X	Imagery > control	13 competitive figure skaters	Reject
Pates, Cummings Maynard (2002)	Combination of relaxation plus hypnotic induction plus hypnotic regression plus trigger control plus imagery	Case study, multiple baseline design, no control	X	5 participants improved immediately after intervention	5 collegiate basketball players	Reject
Patrick, Hrycaiko (1998)	Combination of goal setting plus relaxation plus imagery plus self-talk	Case study, multiple baseline design with comparison	X	2 of 3 subjects marginally improved	3 male triathletes	Accept
Prapavessis, Grove, McNair, Cable (1992)	Combination of relaxation plus self-talk	Case study, multiple baseline design, no comparison		Performance improved	1 male rifle shooter	Reject
Rogerson, Hrycaiko (2002)	Combination of relaxation plus self-talk	Case study, multiple baseline design, no comparison	X	Marginal performance improvements	5 male junior hockey goalies	Reject

(continued)

Table 5.1 *(continued)*

				Multicomponent—Competitive		
Study	**Intervention**	**Research design**	**Manual**	**Results**	**Subjects**	**Accept or reject**
Savoy (1993)	Combination of imagery plus attentional training plus arousal	Case study, multiple baseline design, no comparison		Increase in game performance and coach ratings	1 NCAA female basketball player	Reject
Thelwell, Greenlees (2001)	Combination of goal setting plus relaxation plus imagery plus self-talk	Case study, multiple baseline design, no comparison		Performance improved	5 triathletes	Reject
Thelwell, Maynard (2003)	Combination of goal setting plus activation regulation plus imagery plus self-talk plus concentration	RCT		Nonsignificant objective performance effects	16 semipro cricketers	Accept
Wanlin, Hrycaiko, Martin, Mahon (1997)	Combination goal setting plus imagery plus self-talk	Case study, multiple baseline design with comparison		Goal setting produced mild treatment effects	4 female elite skaters	Accept
Weinberg, Seabourne, Jackson (1981)	Imagery alone, relaxation alone, and combination (VMBR)	RCT	X	VMBR > imagery = relaxation = control on 1 of 3 performance measures	32 undergrads in karate club	Accept
Weinberg, Seabourne, Jackson (1982)	Combination (VMBR)	Nonrandomized pretest and posttest between-group design, no control	X	No performance increase for any VMBR intervention	32 undergrads in karate club	Reject
Wrisberg, Anshel (1989)	Imagery alone, arousal alone, and combination of imagery plus arousal	RCT		Combination > imagery = arousal = control	40 males ages 10-12	Accept

			Multicomponent—Analogue			
Study	**Intervention**	**Research design**	**Manual**	**Results**	**Subjects**	**Accept or reject**
Beauchamp, Halliwell, Fournier, Koestner (1996)	Combination of arousal plus self-talk plus imagery plus concentration plus goal setting plus performance routines plus energy control plus self-monitoring plus physical practice	RCT		Combination > control = physical practice	65 undergrads ages 17-28	Accept
Murphy, Woolfolk (1987)	Combination of imagery plus relaxation plus self-talk	RCT	X	Combination = control	61 undergrads	Accept
Seabourne, Weinberg, Jackson, Suinn (1985)	Combination (VMBR)	RCT	X	VMBR > placebo >no-contact control	43 undergrads	Accept
Straub (1989)	Combination of relaxation plus goal setting plus imagery	Nonrandomized, pretest and posttest between-group design, no control	X	No differences	75 undergrads	Reject
Thelwell, Greenlees (2003)	Combination of goal setting plus imagery plus relaxation plus self-talk	Case study, multiple baseline design, no control		3 of 4 participants improved	4 recreational gymnasium members	Reject
Weinberg, Seabourne, Jackson (1987)	Combination of VMBR vs. arousal plus imagery	RCT		VMBR > arousal plus imagery = control	42 students in self-defense class	Accept

RCT = Randomized controlled trial, denotes use of randomized controlled between-group design

Reprinted from Moore 2003.

CHAPTER 6

Mindfulness-Acceptance-Commitment (MAC) for Performance Development (PD)

The previous chapter elucidated how recent structured qualitative reviews have questioned the empirical support for traditional performance enhancement techniques predicated upon classic change-based cognitive-behavioral methods (Moore, 2003b; Moore & Gardner, 2002, August; Moore & Gardner, 2005). Despite these findings, psychological skills training (PST), with its focus on self-control of internal processes such as thoughts, feelings, and bodily sensations, continues to be the choice intervention for enhancing athletic performance (Van Raalte & Brewer, 2002).

Recently, within the broader field of psychology, however, evidence increasingly suggests that the change-based traditional cognitive-behavioral interventions may have limited effectiveness on some areas and clients (Roemer & Orsillo, 2002; Segal et al., 2002). In diverse areas such as substance abuse (Hayes et al., 1999), depression (Teasdale, Segal, & Williams, 1995), and relationship distress (Cordova & Jacobson, 1993), behavioral theorists are advocating for conceptual and practical changes. In fact, theorists have demonstrated empirical support for interventions that target *acceptance* rather than the direct control of cognitive and affective experiences.

This chapter discusses modern metacognitive and acceptance-based theories, research, and practice and carefully considers how the theoretical aspects of self-regulatory processes in athletic performance may benefit from the mindfulness-acceptance-commitment (MAC) approach to performance enhancement (Gardner & Moore, 2004a; Gardner et al., 2003, October; Gardner, Moore, & Wolanin, 2004, July). This approach markedly differs in both theoretical assumptions and intervention strategies from the traditional psychological skills training approach that has dominated applied sport psychology. The MAC approach was adapted from empirically informed clinical methodology (Hayes et al., 1999; Segal et al., 2002) and was developed specifically for athlete populations.

History of Psychological Skills Training

Historically, efforts to enhance athletic performance have been based on early skills-training models of cognitive-behavioral interventions (Meichenbaum, 1977) and social cognitive theory (Bandura, 1977). These skills-training interventions have been utilized for some time to help athletes develop psychological (mental) skills such as goal setting, imagery and mental rehearsal, arousal control, self-talk, and precompetitive routines. The fundamental goal of these procedures is to create the ideal performance state through self-control of internal processes such as confidence, attention, emotion, cognition, and bodily states (Hardy et al., 1996).

For decades, psychological skills training (PST) has been the primary approach to performance enhancement. Numerous authors describe and support traditional PST procedures while concurrently commenting on their inconsistent and inconclusive empirical support (Gould, Damarjian, & Greenleaf, 2002; Gould & Udry, 1994; Meyers et al., 1996; Weinberg, 1994; Weinberg, 2002; Williams & Leffingwell, 2002; Zaichkowsy & Baltzell, 2001).

Alternative Approaches to Performance Enhancement

In recent years, literature emerging across a range of psychology subdisciplines has questioned the assumption that negative internal experiences invariably lead to negative behavioral outcomes (Hayes et al., 1999). It is now believed that suppressing unwanted thoughts and emotions can have a paradoxical effect, triggering metacognitive scanning that actively searches for signs of negative or unwanted cognitive activity and brings it to awareness when detected (Purdon, 1999; Wegner & Zanakos, 1994). It has been hypothesized that both the scanning process and the resultant cognitive awareness lead to excessive self- and task-irrelevant focus, which is certainly not the athlete's goal during training and performance. As such, scanning can debilitate performance by heightening the athlete's cognitive activity and task-irrelevant focus instead of promoting enhanced performance through metacognitive, task-relevant attention and goal-directed behavior. Gould and colleagues (Gould et al., 1992) carefully examined qualitative studies and found that task-irrelevant thoughts, failure to follow competitive strategic plans, and poor competitive strategic choices strongly related to poor performance in elite athletes.

The scientific literature further suggests that suppressing thoughts and controlling negative thinking patterns can actually *increase* unwanted cognitive activity (Clark et al., 1991). These findings certainly contraindicate using self-talk procedures to alter negative cognitions. In addition, reactivation of previously suppressed thoughts has been found to increase corresponding affective states and autonomic activity (Wegner et al., 1990), which will negatively affect desired performance outcomes. These apparent consequences of thought suppression, referred to as "ironic processes of mental control" (Wegner & Zanakos, 1994), are particularly relevant to our work with athletes.

So if a careful examination of self-regulation in athletic performance suggests that on theoretical grounds, controlling, changing, or suppressing internal experiences (thoughts, emotions, bodily states) may in fact be counterproductive, where should we go from here? Recent models describing self-regulation across several human performance domains (Barlow, 2002), particularly the athletic performance domain (see chapter 2), suggest that consistent functional performance requires meta-cognitive attention to external cues, options, and contingencies involved in both immediate performance tasks and valued distal goals. At the same time, optimal self-regulation involves *minimal* self-judgment, *minimal* vigilance to external or internal threat, and *minimal* worry (i.e., scanning for threat) about possible performance consequences.

As noted earlier, the empirical data (Sbrocco & Barlow, 1996) obtained in studies on numerous performance concerns convincingly suggest that optimal performance requires directing attentional resources toward task-relevant, in-the-moment external contingencies and not toward self-judgment, threat-scanning, and future-oriented cognitive activities. In light of these developments,

This athlete is engaged in task-focused attention to external cues and demands rather than focusing on internal experiences such as self-evaluation or physical discomfort.

traditional PST techniques intended to control or change internal processes, such as self-talk (to change or control cognitive and affective processes), positive imagery (to control the content of internal images), and arousal regulation (to control bodily states), contradict the metacognitive, externally oriented task focus currently believed necessary for optimal performance. We want to stress that positive imagery and self-talk are not always intended to suppress negative thoughts or images. However, this is typically the primary aim. From an acceptance model, it is problematic to even label experiences as positive or negative and it is even more problematic to try to change or control them. Instead, the goal is to help the athlete recognize that internal experiences of all kinds naturally come and go and do not have to be labeled, judged, managed, or controlled. Efforts to control internal experiences may actually create a hypervigilance to internal processes, which is precisely the activity associated with dysfunctional performance according to contemporary, evidence-based models of self-regulation (Barlow 2002; Carver & Scheier, 1988; Gardner & Moore, 2003, August; Gardner & Moore, 2005a; Moore & Gardner, 2001, October).

Since traditional PST strategies for performance enhancement typically target control of internal processes, they may inadvertently trigger a task-irrelevant attentional focus and thus unintentionally *promote* rather than reduce self-regulatory disruption. These theoretical incongruities between traditional PST procedures and the self-regulatory requirements of athletic performance may help explain the disappointing empirical support for PST procedures as efficacious interventions, and the incongruities may suggest that the basic premise of control-based PST procedures is in fact faulty.

Additionally, the sport psychology literature rarely evaluates the mechanisms of change mediating traditional PST performance enhancement interventions and actual competitive performance. In those few studies directly or indirectly addressing change mechanisms, the results do not support the assumptions made about traditional PST procedures (Holm, Beckwith, Ehde, & Tinius, 1996).

For instance, Holm and colleagues (Holm et al., 1996) conducted a study in which they provided a PST package including self-talk, imagery, and goal setting to collegiate athletes. They compared the group to a randomly assigned wait-list control after matching for gender, athletic skill, and experience. Their results indicated that following the program,

competitive anxiety was significantly lower in the intervention group than in the control group, and ongoing utilization of psychological skills was quite high for the intervention group. However, they noted *no* significant differences in athletic performance between groups. This well-controlled and well-designed study successfully taught the psychological skills assumed necessary for enhanced performance, and it reduced competitive anxiety—an assumed primary mediating variable for enhanced performance. Yet, performance was not significantly enhanced *despite* reduced competitive anxiety.

Similarly, a study providing goal setting to competitive collegiate swimmers (Burton, 1989b) and a study providing a multicomponent PST intervention of self-talk, imagery, and goal setting to competitive collegiate tennis players (Daw & Burton, 1994) indicated inconsistent and minimal performance improvements *despite* significantly reduced cognitive anxiety and increased self-confidence. Maynard and colleagues (Maynard, Smith, & Warwick-Evans, 1995) used a cognitive (self-talk) procedure to reduce cognitive and somatic anxiety as well as enhance competitive performance (decision making and skill execution) in semiprofessional soccer players and found similar results. Anxiety was reduced as hypothesized, but actual competitive performance did not improve. Studies by Murphy and Woolfolk (1987) and Weinberg and colleagues (Weinberg, Seabourne, & Jackson, 1981) also suggested that PST interventions focusing on imagery, relaxation, and self-talk, while successfully reducing both state and trait anxiety, resulted in inconsistent and generally nonsignificant improvements in actual athletic performance.

These studies all suggest that reducing supposed mediating variables such as anxiety (with corresponding reductions in negative thinking) and increasing other assumed mediating variables such as confidence have little impact on competitive performance enhancement. This in turn suggests that while possibly valuable in their own right, anxiety reduction, confidence enhancement, and reduction in negative thinking are not correct (or necessary) mechanisms of change for interventions targeting athletic performance enhancement.

Conversely, keeping consistent with contemporary acceptance-based interventions, Crocker and colleagues utilized a stress management intervention including meditation and in-practice integration of coping skills to develop the athlete's capacity to *focus* on performance, *attend* in the moment, and *cope* with experienced emotion (Crocker et al., 1988). In this study, while competitive anxiety was *not* reduced and changes in negative cognitions were minimal, performance *was* significantly improved and remained improved at a 6 mo follow-up. This study further questions the relationship between internal states and athletic performance and certainly raises conceptual concerns for both researchers and practitioners.

In a recent study utilizing qualitative analytic methods, D'Urso and colleagues assessed the contribution of psychological and skill-based differences between best and worst performances and found that only the skill-based constructs were reliably related to performance differentiation (D'Urso, Petrosso, & Robazza, 2002). The authors also studied the competitive athletes' intra- and interindividual differences regarding the facilitating or debilitating role of a variety of cognitive and affective states. According to the authors and consistent with contemporary acceptance theory, personal differences in how internal states affect overt athletic performance must be carefully accounted for, as "both positive and negative emotions may exert beneficial or detrimental effects depending on their idiosyncratic meaning and intensity" (p. 174).

A metacognitive and acceptance-based theoretical position can explain D'Urso and colleagues' empirical findings by challenging the suppositions underlying traditional PST strategies. PST procedures fundamentally assume that reducing negative affective states and negative cognitive activity while increasing personal confidence directly influences and enhances athletic performance. However, the empirical evidence does not support the contention that these intervention goals (reduced anxiety and negative cognitions, increased confidence) are necessary, essential, or even related to enhanced performance. Actually, traditional PST approaches are likely to result in overly cognitive (controlled, verbal-semantic, self-focused) activity, possibly leading to counterproductive efforts to control such activity and potentially decrementing performance. The overly cognitive, self-focused process is likely to reduce the athlete's capacity to automatically engage (trust) developed athletic skills, respond to contextual cues, and attend to the necessary aspects of competition.

Recent evidence also raises questions of whether traditional PST approaches may indirectly promote self-blame as an inherent feature of control methods. Might competitive athletes, particularly those with adequacy (i.e., perfectionist) schemas, view unsatisfactory performance as a result of not sufficiently controlling their cognitive processes? Could this then result in further (dysfunctional) self-focus, efforts to control internal processes, and scanning for threat? While these are clearly open empirical questions, they are appropriate for theoretical study.

New Theoretical Constructs

The empirical and theoretical limitations of traditional change-based PST approaches to athletic performance enhancement justify an introduction to, and utilization of, innovative approaches based on contemporary theory and research in metacognitive processes, acceptance, and self-regulation. Specifically, rapidly growing mindfulness and acceptance approaches to understanding behavior change theoretically relate to performance enhancement efforts. These innovative approaches have growing empirical support suggesting their utility in clinical applications, and have demonstrated preliminary success in reducing work-related difficulties (Bond & Bunce, 2000) and in enhancing athletic performance with collegiate softball players (Little & Simpson, 2000). This later study utilized an intervention somewhat similar to acceptance and commitment therapy (Hayes et al., 1996), in which athletes were helped to view negative thoughts about themselves or their performance as a result, and not a cause, of performance difficulties. They were also helped to view internal events (thoughts and emotions) as normal and passing, not inherently or inextricably connected to actions, choices, and outcomes. The intervention emphasized a direct focus on contextual cues and contingencies in athletic competition. The study demonstrated promising results in enhancing direct measures of competitive athletic performance. Yet, this study did not utilize adjunctive mindfulness procedures in the delivered intervention.

Rather than controlling or reducing internal experiences, mindfulness and acceptance based interventions emphasize the development of a mindful, nonjudging awareness and acceptance of in-the-moment cognitive, affective, and sensory experiences. Internal experiences (thoughts, feelings, sensations) occur naturally, coming and going as normal facets of existence. Athletic performance requires these same internal phenomena. From the overarching theoretical perspective, human difficulties evolve when individuals fuse with their internal experiences (thoughts, feelings, and self–other evaluations), and thus view internal processes as absolute truths that provide reasons for events and guide or cause behavioral choices. As a result, rather than behaving in ways that reflect a commitment to personal athletic values (such as practicing and training hard, competing aggressively, maintaining strategic plans and choices, taking care of self), athletes often choose to avoid or control internal experiences they judge as unacceptable or uncomfortable (Hayes et al., 1996).

A series of recent studies by Tice and colleagues (Tice, Bratslavsky, & Baumeister, 2001) both describes and offers substantial empirical support for the theoretical underpinning of mindfulness and acceptance approaches. In these studies, individuals who believed that their affect (mood) was frozen and unchangeable, significantly reduced or even eliminated the behaviors that aimed to immediately relieve the negative mood. In the experiments, individuals reduced their tendencies to eat fattening snacks, increased their willingness to delay gratification, and reduced their tendencies to procrastinate when they began to believe that their mood did not need to be changed. The authors concluded that when people experience negative affect, they naturally give in to their immediate need to feel better and therefore often engage in strategies to instantly regulate their affect. Most individuals engage in these short-term strategies to quickly eliminate negative mood, instead of focusing on long-term self-regulation in the pursuit of distal goals (such as athletic achievement). In essence, when negative affect increases, individuals quickly respond to reduce or control their uncomfortable feelings and thoughts (a process known as experiential avoidance), often at the expense of their desired (albeit long-term) personal values. However, when they view affect as either unchangeable or *not requiring change,* experiential avoidance (for short-term affect regulation) is markedly reduced and goal-directed self-regulatory behaviors are enhanced. These results are wholly consistent with the theoretical foundations of contemporary acceptance-based approaches, and they strongly support their potential utility in applied sport psychology.

Commitment is particularly important in acceptance-based models. In this context, the term *commitment* refers to engaging in behaviors that lead to the attainment of personal values and do not promote experiential avoidance or the maintenance of internal rule systems ("I can't

play for someone like that") (Hayes et al., 1999). Generally, acceptance-commitment interventions promote nonjudging acceptance of thoughts and feelings and assert that these internal experiences are not literal truths and realities, do not need to be avoided, and do not require instant reduction or control. In fact, when individuals view internal experiences (thoughts and feelings) as unwavering truths and incorporate experiential avoidance, they typically make ineffective behavioral choices. To reiterate, acceptance-commitment approaches promote internal experiences as naturally occurring, time-limited events that regularly come and go throughout life; promote a willingness to fully experience these events; and enhance a commitment to act consistently with the pursuit of chosen values.

Mindfulness is closely associated with acceptance and commitment. Mindfulness, as an awareness of the present moment, stems from eastern philosophical traditions and has been defined as "paying attention in a particular way: on purpose, in the present moment, and non-judgmentally" (Kabat-Zinn, 1994, p. 4). Mindfulness has been a key component in therapeutic interventions targeting diverse problems such as chronic depression (Segal et al., 2002), borderline personality disorder (Linehan et al., 2001), stress (Kabat-Zinn, 1994), panic disorder (Miller, Fletcher, & Kabat-Zinn, 1995), and generalized anxiety disorder (Roemer & Orsillo, 2002).

Mindfulness techniques emphasize nonjudging attention to present realities, including both external stimuli and internal processes. Stimuli that enter awareness are observed, but not evaluated as good or bad, right or wrong. This skill of self-regulated, present-moment attention is developed through regularly practicing mindfulness exercises (Kabat-Zinn et al., 1992). Accumulated evidence from self-regulatory models of human performance suggests that optimal performance requires on-task, nonjudging attentional focus (Barlow, 2002; Gardner & Moore, 2004a; Gardner et al., 2005; Moore & Gardner, 2001, October; Wolanin, 2005). As such, mindfulness offers great promise as a logical component of effective athletic performance enhancement.

In addition to enhancing present-moment attention, mindfulness techniques have also effectively reduced the verbal-linguistic component of anxiety and worry (Roemer & Orsillo, 2002). As studies by Crews and Landers (1993) have demonstrated decreased verbal-linguistic activity in high-performing athletes, integrating mindfulness techniques into performance enhancement interventions appears particularly appropriate. It has also been suggested that mindfulness techniques help individuals develop greater self-awareness (Roemer & Orsillo, 2002) and identify habitual responses to external cues. Greater self-awareness and an understanding of personal response tendencies invariably promote alternative perspectives and enhance behavioral flexibility when responding to situational demands. Whereas the cognitive awareness suggested in traditional PST may promote excessive self-focus and cognitive activity relating to past, present, and future judgments and predictions, mindfulness emphasizes an in-the-moment awareness of internal states and external cues. This awareness promotes attention to performance cues and enhances behavioral flexibility as competitive demands and resultant internal experiences fluctuate.

A study by Klinger and colleagues (Klinger et al., 1981) elucidates the important role of task-relevant, in-the-moment focus and associated attention to contextual cues. In this study, reversals in game performance and an increased level of play by the competition shifted the attentional focus of collegiate basketball players from external, game-related cues to a self-judging, future-oriented anticipatory focus. Not surprisingly, the attentional shift impaired athletic performance. This attentional shift was also associated with momentum changes, minislumps, and more long-term performance dysfunction. These findings are consistent with predictions of performance dysfunction by contemporary self-regulatory models (Barlow, 2002; Gardner & Moore, 2005a; Moore & Gardner, 2001, October), in that when attention is diverted from a task-relevant external focus to task-irrelevant internal processes, performance difficulties typically ensue.

Mindfulness-Acceptance-Commitment (MAC) for Performance Enhancement

The mindfulness-acceptance-commitment (MAC) approach to performance enhancement integrates and adapts acceptance and commitment therapy (ACT) developed by Hayes et al. (1999) and mindfulness-based cognitive therapy developed by Segal and colleagues (2002). The MAC approach also draws on the extensive research on rule-governed behavior (Hayes et al., 1999). Hayes and colleagues suggest that when an individual

has a negative emotional response to an external stimulus (such as anxiety in response to a skilled opponent) and then directly thinks about the stimulus (such as "I can't keep up"), he will likely develop a negative emotional response directly to those thoughts. In the future, either the emotional response *or* the external stimulus triggers those same thoughts. As such, both cognitive and emotional responses become cues in and of themselves and often lead to forms of avoidance (overt task disengagement) or worry and concentration loss (covert task disengagement).

What we don't want are athletes to respond to their thoughts and emotions as if they are actual realities and subsequently guide their actions based on these seeming truths. Such actions are frequently engaged in to avoid or escape from negative or uncomfortable internal experiences. For example, an individual may lose aggressiveness or ask to be taken out of the game in response to the anxiety of facing a superior athlete. This process has been termed "experiential avoidance" (Hayes et al., 1996). Experiential avoidance can take many forms and can be triggered in an instant if the individual wishes to avoid an uncomfortable or negative internal process. For example, if an athlete experiences anxiety, anger, or frustration (related or unrelated to athletic participation) before practice, and this experience leads to thoughts such as "I'm too stressed to practice," she may decide to skip practice. The experiential avoidance in this example is based on rule-governed behavior, as the cognitive response to the emotion (a personal rule established by the individual) directly governs the avoidant behavior. The avoidant behavior is not consistent with the valued goals of improving performance, successfully competing, and enjoying athletic participation.

Certainly, athletes of all skill levels must consistently self-regulate their behavior so that it serves distal goals even at the expense of immediate emotional gratification. The distinction between rule-governed and values-directed behavior is particularly important. One of the hallmarks of the MAC approach is that it promotes both the competitive (present-moment) self-regulation necessary for optimal competitive performance and the commitment to personal athletic values necessary for quality practice, intense training, and long-term skill development.

For example, comments such as "I just can't play for him. He's a jerk" or "I didn't take that shot because I wasn't confident" are often made by those athletes using their internal processes

Internal rules can be difficult to ignore and disrupt an athlete's ability to concentrate on the competitive task.

(cognitive-emotional responses) to explain and guide behavior rather than the environmental contingencies they most value. These may include contingencies that contextually require sport-specific behavior (taking the shot when available), working to improve performance (quality practice), and enjoying competing in their chosen sport.

Note that in these circumstances, the athlete responds to his thoughts as though they reflect reality ("I just can't play for him. He's a jerk" or "I didn't take that shot because I wasn't confident"). In turn, the athlete behaves to reduce internal experiences such as frustration and anxiety (experiential avoidance) and not to achieve personal values (optimal athletic participation). In contrast, MAC promotes accepting internal experiences while at the same time focusing on the appropriate external contingencies and behavioral responses required to effectively navigate situations and achieve both immediate and long-term valued outcomes. In this way, the MAC approach is consistent with the suggestion by Murphy and Tammen (1998) that in addition to focusing on performance enhancement and regulation of internal experiences, sport psychologists should also promote pragmatic issues such as effective problem solving, decision making, and sound practice behaviors of competitive athletes. While the MAC approach includes self-regulation

during practice and competitive performance, it also directly promotes clarifying values and the commitment to engage in behaviors that can realistically achieve those values. Thus, MAC targets not only athletic performance enhancement, but also the athlete's decision making, problem solving, and behavioral processes regarding day-to-day athletic development and enjoyment issues. Such issues include training, practice, self-care, and many others requiring daily consideration.

This discussion highlights the connections between the self-regulatory processes associated with optimal athletic performance and the theoretical rationale for mindfulness, acceptance, and commitment concepts. As such, these connections have led to the integration of mindfulness (Segal et al., 2002) and acceptance-commitment (Hayes et al., 1999) strategies into the MAC protocol for performance enhancement. The MAC is an integrated approach targeting mindful, nonjudging, present-moment attention (mindfulness), acceptance of internal experiences as natural occurrences, willingness to remain in contact with internal experiences, and values-directed action (commitment). These skills are intended to replace the often unhelpful efforts at internal self-control and the behavioral restrictions that typically accompany both dysfunctional and underdeveloped performance (Gardner & Moore, 2005a; Moore & Gardner, 2001, October). Similar to the clinical uses of mindfulness and acceptance-commitment procedures, athletes receiving the MAC intervention demonstrate enhanced attentional awareness, nonjudging task-relevant attentional focus, and behavioral flexibility. In turn, these processes improve practice and training quality, competitive performance, and enjoyment of the athletic experience.

Empirical Status of MAC

MAC intervention methodology has been developed and empirically evaluated sequentially in three phases. Phase I, a series of individual case study evaluations and uncontrolled trials of MAC, was recently completed with Division I collegiate athletes and older elite athletes across a number of sports. Phase II involved open, controlled trials of the MAC protocol with Division I collegiate athletes. Phase III, which is now well under way, involves randomized controlled trials of the MAC approach compared to traditional psychological skills training interventions.

Intervention Protocol

The basic components of the MAC protocol are highlighted in the following sections. The format has been conducted in eight 1 h sessions.

Educational Phase

The educational phase addresses the athlete's need to understand and collaboratively participate in the intervention. This component includes intervention rationale, a discussion of athletic performance from a self-regulatory perspective, the athlete's personal performance experiences, and the contradiction of trying to control internal experiences such as thoughts, emotions, and bodily sensations by traditional forms of self-regulation. In this phase of the MAC protocol, athletes begin to recognize external events (early cue detection) related to performance difficulties or blocks and their relationship to internal experiences (thoughts and emotions) and the behavioral choices that follow.

Mindfulness Phase

Mindfulness is introduced as an important variable in attaining optimal athletic performance, and mindfulness techniques are introduced to heighten awareness of internal experiences (mindful awareness) and to develop nonjudging, present-moment attention. Special care

is taken to not use these techniques to avoid uncomfortable or troubling experiences, as doing this would simply be another form of the experiential avoidance so common to the human experience. Rather, the appropriate use of mindfulness helps the athlete notice and then let go of negative or distressing internal events and simply experience them without judgment or avoidance. In session, athletes learn specific mindfulness, attentional training, and situational attentional refocusing exercises (Wells, 2000) that they practice in session, at home, and during practice and competition. In addition, athletes learn to contrast these skills with typical habits of avoiding internal experiences and ruminating or worrying about their internal discomfort or behavioral choices.

Values Identification and Commitment Phase

This component explores the distinction between goals (outcome destination) and values (process journey). The overarching purpose is to increase effective actions that serve individual values. The discussion focuses on choosing valued directions in sport and other important life domains. Following this exploration, athletes are introduced to cognitive defusion, which is the process of disconnecting actions and behavioral choices from internal rules and experiences (known as rule-governed behavior). The athlete learns to act in a manner consistent with valued goals, regardless of negative or distressing internal states.

Acceptance Phase

In the fourth component of the MAC protocol, athletes further develop their abilities to recognize the connections between their thoughts, feelings, and behaviors. Rule-governed behavior is continuously discussed so that they become aware of their personal response tendencies and learn to disconnect previous automatic links among thoughts, feelings, and behavioral choices. Discussion includes the relationship between internal language and behavior, especially as it relates to athletic performance. Cognitive fusion receives elaboration, and direct efforts to defuse thoughts and emotions from choices and actions continue. The focus is again on accepting events and associated thoughts and emotions as opposed to controlling negative experiences. All of these concepts are intertwined with previous discussions of both self-regulation in athletic performance and mindfulness.

Integration and Practice Phase

In the final component of the MAC protocol, the athlete integrates, consolidates, and practices mindfulness, acceptance, and commitment skills, integrating them daily into both sports and everyday life. In vivo experiences (during practice and competition) allow athletes to further utilize and practice the techniques. Additionally, problems in using the techniques are thoroughly processed, and the MAC approach to dealing with external demands and internal experiences is continuously practiced, reinforced, and shaped. Finally, special attention is given to continually using these new skills in practice and competition, as well as in relevant nonathletic situations.

Case Example of the MAC Approach

The following case example highlights the basic components of the MAC protocol. In this case, an individual sought sport psychology services to enhance her performance and enjoyment of competitive activities.

Case Study: Masters-Level Female Powerlifter

LD is a 37-year-old masters-level female powerlifter who, while in her twenties, won several world championships at her weight level. Over the last three years, she has begun competing again in masters events with little success. Her weight training plateaued, and she reported no progress over the past two competitive seasons. A comprehensive assessment determined that LD could benefit from performance development, and an MCS-SP classification of PD-II was given to her case.

LD described her workouts as inconsistent and unfocused and her occupational and social functioning as positive and highly effective. Before beginning the MAC protocol, LD completed several assessment measures, taking a total of 20 min. LD scored a 27 on the distraction subscale of the Sport Anxiety Scale (SAS) (Smith, Smoll, & Schutz, 1990), suggesting significant competitive attentional difficulties. She also scored a 77 on the Acceptance and Action Questionnaire (AAQ), a measure of avoidance or acceptance of internal states and of willingness to act in pursuit of valued goals (Hayes et al., 1999). All other self-report data were within normal limits. The intervention goal was to enhance training behavior, including focus and intensity, as well as competitive performance. The MAC intervention focused on enhancing present-moment attention and commitment to training behaviors consistent with personal goals of competitive success.

These athletes are learning to integrate mindfulness skills into both practice and competitive situations.

The MAC intervention began with education about MAC and related issues. Following this phase, the protocol focused on practicing and developing mindfulness skills. This helped LD recognize the degree to which her thoughts were task irrelevant during practice. She diligently pursued mindfulness practice and then worked on accepting her thoughts and emotions during training instead of trying to limit or control them. LD found the discussion regarding personal athletic values particularly important. She evaluated her commitment to weight training and determined that her approach did not accurately reflect her desire to fully engage in training. She began training harder and more efficiently and reported significant increases in enjoyment. By the end of the intervention, her AAQ score decreased to 43, suggesting significantly reduced experiential avoidance and increased willingness to tolerate discomfort in the pursuit of her personal values. In addition, her score on the SAS distractibility component fell to 12 (well within normal limits), suggesting increased task-focus.

Behaviorally, her self-reported (and recorded) training intensity increased dramatically, as did her weightlifting performance (maximum and total volume of weight lifted) during practice. Following week six of the eight-week protocol, LD finished third in her first competition, her best performance since competing at this level, and lifted 15% beyond her best masters-level competitive performance.

While individual case studies do not provide conclusive intervention efficacy data, they can, during early research phases, guide the elaboration of intervention protocols, the development of intervention manuals, and the development of hypotheses to be tested later in controlled research. In the next section, we summarize a recently reported preliminary investigation utilizing the MAC approach (Gardner et al., 2003, October; Gardner et al., 2005; Wolanin, 2005).

Preliminary Investigation of the MAC Protocol

Recently, a study investigated the potential efficacy of the mindfulness-acceptance-commitment (MAC) approach with Division I collegiate athletes (Gardner et al., 2005; Wolanin, 2005). Eleven female field hockey and volleyball athletes participated in an eight-week MAC protocol and were compared to a control group of seven same-sport athletes. The MAC group was 64% sophomores, 18% juniors,

and 18% freshman. The control group was 57% sophomores, 29% seniors, and 14% freshman. Before receiving the intervention, each member of the experimental group was classified according to the MSC-SP by using the MCS-SP semistructured interview (see chapters 3 and 4). Within the treatment group, six participants (55%) were classified as PD-II, and five (45%) were classified as Pdy-II. No PI classifications were given. Performance was measured by coach ratings through the use of a questionnaire designed specifically for the study. The instrument was designed to assess athletic performance and related performance variables, since athletic statistical measures (such as points scored) do not necessarily accurately reflect athletic performance. In addition to an overall performance rating (a rating of the head coach's evaluation of the *current* competitive performance of each athlete), the rating scale also evaluated constructs such as concentration and aggressiveness. These constructs were theorized to reflect targeted processes of the MAC intervention, as concentration and aggressiveness are believed to be overt manifestations of increased attention and behavioral commitment. The Sport Anxiety Scale (SAS) (Smith et al., 1990) was also given, which is a 21-item self-report measure of somatic and cognitive trait anxiety.

Nonparametric data analysis offered preliminary support for MAC for enhancing the athletic performance of collegiate athletes *without* subclinical issues. The data further suggest MAC's potential as a promising new intervention model for psychologically healthy athletes seeking performance enhancement.

The initial comparison of performance ratings for MAC treatment and the control group suggested that a small treatment effect may have occurred, with 37% of MAC participants increasing performance ratings as compared to 14% of the control participants (see figure 6.1). However, when combining all the athletes regardless of intervention needs (and of MCS-SP subtype), the MAC protocol produced results similar to the majority of traditional psychological skills training outcome studies (Moore, 2003b; Moore & Gardner, 2005), in which performance enhancement interventions demonstrate minimal gain. For example, the participants who received the MAC intervention demonstrated only a 3.2% increase in their performance ratings (compared to an average *reduction* in performance ratings of approximately 7% for controls), which suggests MAC has minimal real-world applicability (see figure 6.2). This finding

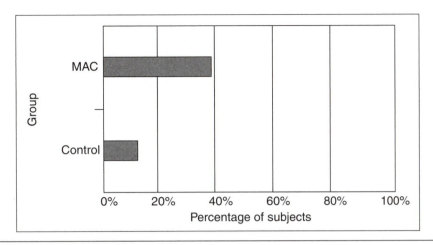

Figure 6.1 MAC (*n* = 11) and control (*n* = 7) group comparison based on the percentage of participants who increased performance ratings.

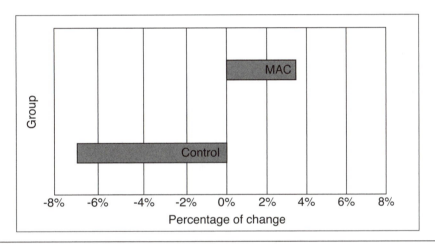

Figure 6.2 Mean performance ratings change of MAC (*n* = 11) and control (*n* = 7) groups.

highlights the limitations of studying athletes as a homogeneous population, in that when all athletes seeking performance enhancement are viewed as a single, homogeneous group and receive non-specialized interventions, minimal performance enhancement is noted.

At first glance, these results may seem disappointing. However, when MAC efficacy is viewed in the context of preintervention MCS-SP classification, more substantial treatment effects appear. Specifically, the data suggest that MAC holds considerable promise for enhancing the performance of athletes who have *minimal* psychological barriers (PD-I or PD-II classifications). The fact that 67% of the participants classified as PD and 0% of the participants classified as Pdy

improved their coach's ratings suggests that MAC may be an efficacious protocol for performance enhancement with athletes *without* subclinical concerns (see figure 6.3). Thus, viewing competitive athletes as a *heterogeneous* population can help demonstrate true intervention effects that may otherwise be hidden.

PD athletes receiving the MAC intervention *increased* performance ratings by approximately 14%, while both Pdy athletes and the control group *decreased* performance ratings by about 7%. The Pdy decrease in performance ratings was similar to that of the control group, who demonstrated a decrease in performance ratings of about 6% (see figure 6.4). A truly significant finding is the little impact MAC had on athletes

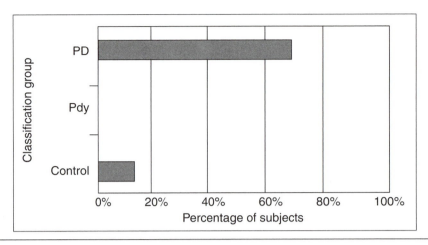

Figure 6.3 Percentage of participants with increased performance ratings.

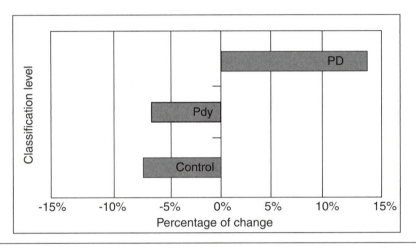

Figure 6.4 Mean amount of performance ratings change for MAC PD, MAC Pdy, and control groups.

experiencing subclinical levels of psychological distress (Pdy). Figure 6.5 pictorially compares the differential impact of MAC on athletes classified as either PD or Pdy. From these results, we can initially hypothesize that a more clinically oriented intervention with a greater focus on psychological barriers affecting performance may be more likely to enhance the performance of subclinical athletes by initially targeting dispositional or problematic characteristics such as worry or perfectionism (Gardner & Moore, 2003, August; Gardner & Moore, 2005a) and only secondarily focusing on enhanced behavioral self-regulation. It is also possible that participants classified as Pdy may benefit from traditional cognitive-behavioral therapeutic interventions. While this possibility is certainly an open empirical question requiring additional investigation, a finding from Wolanin (2005) and

Gardner and colleagues (2005) supports this suggestion. Specifically, Pdy athletes tended as a group to score in the higher (subclinical) range of experiential avoidance and worry when compared to the PD group. This is a finding consistent with the theoretical foundation of the IMAP model presented in chapter 2. These results initially support the suggestion that more clinically based intervention protocols may enhance the performance of Pdy participants with a subclinical expression of generalized anxiety symptoms such as worry and rumination.

This study is particularly important as it is the first empirical research study to support the idea that athletes desiring performance enhancement must *not* be viewed as a homogeneous population. Although not formally tested, other sport psychology professionals have supported this

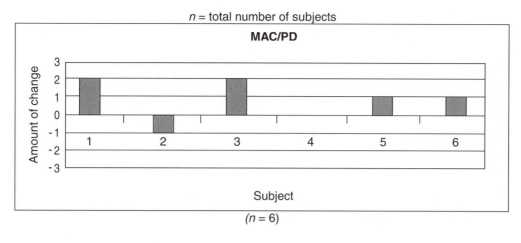

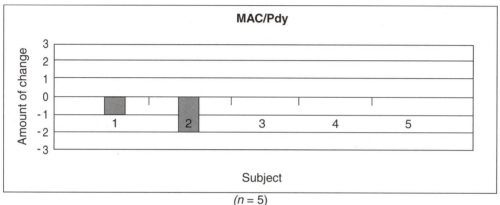

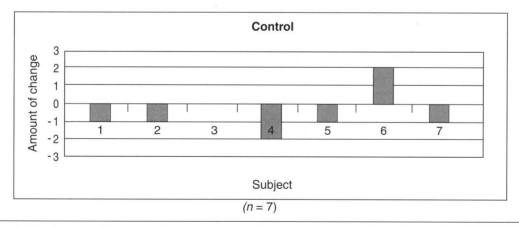

Figure 6.5 Comparison of changes in individual performance ratings among MAC PD (*n* = 6), MAC Pdy (*n* = 5), and control (*n* = 7) groups.

basic assertion for some time (Meyers et al., 1996; Vealey, 1994a). The necessity of viewing athletes as heterogenous also supports the rational employment of classification systems such as the MCS-SP in both research and practice settings. As suggested in chapters 5 and 14, one of the possibilities for poor outcome studies in the sport psy-

chology literature is the continued assumption of homogeneity in athlete populations. The Wolanin (2005) and Gardner et al. (2005) results suggest that when subjects are classified by the MCS-SP, differential treatment outcomes emerge. One can only speculate how the results of previous studies on traditional psychological skills training might have appeared if researchers had utilized classification systems before intervention to determine what athletes actually need.

Another important finding in the Wolanin (2005) and Gardner et al. (2005) studies was that MAC did *not* reduce anxiety (as measures by the SAS) even in athletes who increased performance ratings. This indicates that as anticipated, the MAC intervention successfully helped athletes interpret their sensations of anxiety as functional, minimally attend to anxious cues, and accept anxious states. This finding is theoretically consistent with the acceptance-based literature in which a person becomes aware of his bodily sensations in the moment, but focuses attention on the task at hand rather than on controlling his internal state. This finding is also consistent with recent results (Cohen, Pargman, & Tenenbaum, 2003; Craft, Magyar, Becker, & Feltz, 2003; Maynard et al., 1995) suggesting that anxiety reduction may not truly be a mechanism of change for increased performance in competitive athletes.

A careful analysis of possible change mechanisms in the Wolanin (2005) and Gardner et al. (2005) studies suggested that increases in ratings of performance strongly related to ratings of concentration ($r = .573$, $p < .05$, two-tailed) and aggressiveness ($r = .634$, $p < .01$, two-tailed). These data initially support the theoretical expectation that the MAC protocol helps athletes concentrate on cues related to the athletic task rather than on internal states. Furthermore, increased ratings of aggressiveness suggest that enhancing focus on behaviors connected to valued goals and relevant environmental cues and contingencies (inherent in the MAC protocol) may increase aggressive sport-specific behaviors believed necessary for optimal performance. Consistent with acceptance-based theory, these data suggest that optimally performing athletes may be more focused on behaviors (causes, contingencies, choices) consistent with how they want to act (values) rather than on thoughts or emotions contrary to their desired outcome.

Results also indicate that participants who increased their performance ratings were those who learned to hold fewer beliefs about the uncontrollability of their thoughts, emotions, and the potential consequences of their internal processes. This finding is also consistent with the MAC theoretical model, which hypothesizes that the ability to be aware of thoughts and emotions, view them as passing events, and defuse them from behavioral decision making can increase per-

formance (Gardner & Moore, 2004a). While the evidence for these mediating mechanisms of change is preliminary and needs further investigation, the mechanisms are exciting in their implications. An additional randomized controlled trial of MAC is currently being carried out with larger numbers of athletes classified as PD and Pdy across a wide range of sports. Preliminary results demonstrate similar findings at this time.

Final Thoughts

For any psychosocial intervention to be part of an evidence-based practice within applied psychology, whether within the clinical, counseling, or sport disciplines, it must be utilized consistently, meet accepted standards of empirical support, and demonstrate that it works through processes directly related to the outcomes in question. Promoting and disseminating interventions failing to meet these fundamental criteria reduce a professional discipline to a pseudoscience (Lilienfeld et al., 2003), which can lead to shallow consumer acceptance and place clients at risk. Specifically within sport psychology, recent critical reviews of traditional psychological skills training approaches for athletic performance enhancement suggest a troubling lack of empirical support (Moore, 2003b; Moore & Gardner, 2005). Similarly, on both theoretical and empirical grounds, there are sound reasons to question the assumptions traditional psychological skills training holds regarding the relationship between internal psychological processes and athletic performance.

After many years of study and use, traditional self-regulatory (cognitive-behavioral) PST approaches to enhancing athletic performance have gathered limited empirical support, appear to be based on questionable theoretical grounds, and require reconsideration. Recently, metacognitive mindfulness and acceptance approaches to understanding and enhancing behavioral functioning have emerged in the clinical science literature, all with promising empirical support across a variety of human behavioral issues and conditions. The goal of this chapter was to provide the theoretical rationale for an intervention based on and adapted from an integration of these sound conceptualizations and to overview the new approach to enhancing athletic performance and engagement, mindfulness-acceptance-commitment (MAC). We envision that this relatively new theoretical position and its intervention strategies will gain the empirical support that is so critical. While it is a new intervention just beginning to establish empirical support, we encourage practitioners to join us in its investigation and follow its development. Finally, we hope that the discussion of new theoretical frameworks will spur sport psychologists to move beyond the traditional approaches in applied sport psychology and begin to develop efficacious evidence-based methodologies for enhancing athletic performance.

CHAPTER 7

Performance Dysfunction (Pdy)

Athletes are no more or less likely to struggle with personal issues and situational stressors than the rest of us. Dispositional characteristics and life demands affect the athlete at least as much as they affect the general population, especially given the intense demands the competitive sports world places on an athlete to be consistent, focused, and optimally productive. Athlete-specific pressures such as training demands, physical injury, and constant external and internal performance evaluation interact with life pressures found in home, school, work, and friendships to extraordinarily challenge the athlete.

Performance dysfunction, introduced in chapter 3, refers to a significant performance disruption caused by either personal characteristics or an interaction between personal characteristics and external factors. These external factors could be part of the athletic environment (such as a coach conflict) or personal experience (such as the loss of a significant relationship). The defining feature of performance dysfunction is that the athlete's personal characteristics and responses to external factors are subclinical (subsyndromal), which means that while disruptive, they do not reach clinical levels. Although not fully clinical, these characteristics and responses require a clinical intervention as the first-line treatment. Such interventions ameliorate the subclinical difficulties and typically result in subsequent performance improvements (secondary to the primary concern).

The athlete who consults a clinical sport psychologist is likely to present an array of initial complaints. While one athlete may directly describe a problem with a coach, another may vaguely complain of dissatisfaction, lack of motivation, and problems concentrating. Careful assessment (discussed in chapters 3 and 4) will establish whether issues of performance development, performance dysfunction, performance impairment (clinical disorders), or performance termination underlie the presenting complaints. We have already discussed performance development (PD) and its relevant interventions. We now turn to the second MCS-SP classification, performance dysfunction (Pdy). To review, the Pdy athlete typically desires to enhance performance, has experienced more consistent and higher levels of performance in the past, or is not experiencing performance gains as expected. Unlike PD athletes, Pdy athletes have identifiable psychological barriers that are negatively affecting either athletic performance or general life functioning. These psychological barriers can include interpersonal, intrapersonal, developmental, and transitional difficulties, which require psychological intervention as the first-line treatment. Although self-regulatory approaches may be helpful, the psychological intervention takes initial precedence over performance enhancement procedures until the barriers have been reduced or eliminated.

As the reader will recall, there are two distinct subtypes within performance dysfunction. The first subtype, Pdy-I, occurs when developmental, transitional, interpersonal, or exogenous life events trigger psychological reactions, with dysfunctional athletic performance as a consequence. The Pdy-I category is based primarily upon external factors and secondarily upon their interaction with personal characteristics. The second subtype, Pdy-II, involves internal or personal characteristics primarily and the external factors surrounding them secondarily. These endogenous psychological factors can include core cognitive schemas (enduring behavioral characteristics) such as unrelenting standards (extreme perfectionism), excessive fear of failure, irrational need for approval, and low frustration tolerance. Performance cues and the competitive environment typically trigger these endogenous factors, leading to dysfunctional athletic performance.

Once assessment determines a Pdy classification, the clinical sport psychologist's primary task is to determine the relationship between the performance problem and personality variables, and to develop an empirically informed intervention plan. Note that the performance problems described here *are* psychological issues and are often as complex as more serious psychological disorders.

When an athlete comes for assistance with psychologically based performance concerns, it is likely that competitive performance difficulties motivated the request for assistance, even if the clinical sport psychologist ultimately determines that the performance concern is secondary (Bond, 2001). The clinical sport psychologist's goal in these circumstances is to describe to the athlete the relationship among internal and external factors and the dysfunctional performance that is of significant concern to the athlete. Athletes desiring assistance typically understand (and agree) with these intervention rationales and are comfortable knowing that the practitioner has taken the time to understand their athletic and life concerns.

This perspective differs from the binary view of presenting complaints common in applied sport psychology (described in chapters 1, 3, and 4) in which difficulties are often assumed to discreetly fall into the categories of clinical or performance concerns. As previously discussed, dichotomously separating issues in this way is both overly simplistic and remarkably unhelpful in the real world of professional practice. Unfortunately, practitioners often believe that only athletes experiencing a diagnosable psychological disorder have definable psychological barriers to overcome. What follows from this tendency is the supposition that all other performance phenomena directly relate to psychological skills, and thus all other athletes are likely to benefit from mental skill development.

Our conceptual understanding of athlete needs and the interventions based therein resist this tendency. We view all athletes as individuals who exist and develop in the athletic world, occasionally struggle with athletic demands, and also thrive and struggle with endogenous states and exogenous life realities. As such, athletes desiring professional support need to be understood as individuals engaged in a complex, high-pressure environment who can benefit from holistic assessment and interventions to increase their functionality in both the sport world and broader life environments.

Interventions for athletes presenting with subclinical concerns, or performance dysfunction (Pdy), somewhat differ from that for athletes simply requiring enhanced performance. Yet, much to the athlete's pleasure, performance improvements are a likely secondary benefit to Pdy interventions. Typically, minimizing the Pdy athlete's endogenous and exogenous subclinical difficulties reduces related performance decrements.

What does subclinical (or subsyndromal) mean when discussing the athlete? The sport psychology literature often refers to subclinical concerns as psychological barriers (Giges, 2000). They are issues that do not fall into clear categories of clinical disorders, but nevertheless exist due to intrapersonal factors or personal reactions to external events. These difficulties often require psychological interventions inconsistent with traditional psychological skills training procedures. Interventions for Pdy cases are traditionally thought of as psychological counseling or psychotherapy. Such interventions both ameliorate the subclinical difficulties and ultimately result in performance improvement. Pdy athletes are in a particularly interesting position in that they demonstrate no clear clinical issues *requiring* psychotherapy (as defined as an intervention to correct problematic behavior). Yet, Pdy athletes can still *benefit* from psychological counseling to develop behavioral strategies for more effectively responding to their personal barriers. From this perspective, psychological counseling is a performance enhancement strategy.

Some sport psychologists commonly assume that if subclinical issues are not blatantly stated during the athlete's initial presentation or are not intense enough to warrant a clinical diagnosis and treatment, the appropriate strategy is traditional psychological skills training. However, research on the efficacy of traditional self-regulatory approaches to performance enhancement provides poor to inconclusive empirical results (as discussed in chapter 5), and these traditional efforts are often used without consideration of the real and complex client needs that do not easily fit into strict performance or clinical categories. Sport psychologists have previously noted this, reporting that though many athletes initially seek sport psychology services for performance concerns, it soon becomes clear that personal issues and lifestyle management are primary foci for intervention (Bond, 2001; Meyers et al., 1996; Bauman, 2000, October). Even athletes who frequently use psychological skills can struggle with subclinical issues and dispositional factors that interfere with optimal sport and life functioning. As such, the sport psychologist practicing within the framework presented in this text should make few assumptions about initial athlete presentations and should resist the immediate utilization of psychological skills training until a full client picture is clarified.

Dispositional Variables

To truly understand performance dysfunction, it is necessary to return to the cognitive schemas presented in chapter 2. Like all human beings, athletes possess dispositional characteristics that are based on their unique histories and that serve as a template for assimilating and accommodating environmental stimuli. Through repeated interactions with their world, all individuals develop an interactive pattern of self and other mental schemas (internal rule systems) as cognitive representations of the self and its relation to the world (Safran & Segal, 1990). These cognitive schemas and their characteristic behavioral patterns serve as a basis for understanding the world and controlling affective responses. Response patterns such as experiential avoidance often result, but such behavioral responses can be self-defeating. Although these response patterns are intended for psychological self-protection (such as avoiding a feared situation), they often occur at the expense of more functional behavior (such as goal-directed athletic behavior). These behavioral patterns commonly develop in childhood, yet they typically do not serve the same self-protective function into adulthood. Although these behaviors may be initially adaptive responses to the environment, they are reinforced over time by naturally occurring contingencies and then become incorrectly generalized to situations for which they were not intended. These behavior patterns, often referred to as contingency-shaped behaviors (as they are learned from repeated exposure to life contingencies), form cognitive schemas (unspoken verbal rules). These learned behavior patterns become the fundamental operating systems by which individuals organize and respond to the world.

In the athletic domain, the personal meanings and importance the athlete places on performance help form an organizing system by which the athlete evaluates, interprets, and responds

This athlete's response to performance setbacks will be largely determined by her learning history, which sets the stage for self-evaluation and performance expectations.

to her competitive world. The athlete interprets performance events such as successes, failures, coach conflicts and so on using these preexisting templates (cognitive schemas) and responds according to previously adaptive behavior patterns (contingency-shaped behaviors). Although the behavior patterns may have been adaptive in childhood, these responses may be less adaptive and at times dysfunctional in adulthood. An example is the male athlete who as a child learned that even during high achievement in school, on the playing field, or in basic tasks at home, he would either be ignored or yelled at by his parents. Thus, as a child he developed a tendency to avoid difficult tasks not readily learned. He also carefully evaluated the responses of those around him (parents) so that he would be able to correct or escape from situations that may lead to a negative response from others. This behavior pattern allowed him to please the primary adults in his life and thus control his own negative affect. It also allowed him to maintain necessary levels of relatedness to significant others in his life. This pattern was initially adaptive by allowing him to experience a more pleasant life given the reality of his early environment. As an adult, however, this schema (based on failure and unrelenting standards) results in a behavior pattern in which he avoids challenge, gives up when faced with difficulty, seeks excessive reassurance, and overly responds to helpful (negative) feedback.

As noted in chapter 2, internal rule systems (cognitive schemas) tend to be self-perpetuating and highly resistant to change efforts. They generally develop in childhood, are based on a pattern of early events, and form the core of an individual's self-concept, interpersonal functioning, and overall worldview and expectations. This worldview spans many domains and sets the stage for the development of performance needs, expectations, and standards. Both schemas and their resultant coping styles can be viewed as trait-like functions that organize the individual's world and how she interprets, views, and responds in competitive performance situations and to life events. Thus, for some athletes, the surrounding environmental stimuli are often distorted to maintain the validity of these schemas (Young et al., 2003), and the athlete may engage in "selective inattention" by only seeing those aspects of a situation that confirm their rules and expectations about the world. As such, these athletes are likely to respond similarly to many different situations that even slightly resemble the early events that developed the schema.

The process by which an individual generalizes one situational response to a different, yet slightly similar situation is stimulus generalization. Stimulus generalization is important in that the individual is likely to respond to even the most minute aspect of a situation that he perceives is similar to previous situations. This process triggers his cognitive schema and results in associated overlearned behavior patterns (see figure 7.1). Conversely, he will *not* focus on and respond to the elements that differentiate a previous situation from the current one (stimulus discrimination). In many respects, the intervention for such dispositional issues is stimulus discrimination training, where the individual expands his range of response options as he learns to recognize the nuances of external events (triggering stimuli). Through stimulus discrimination training, the individual develops the capacity to discriminate the old situation that led to the dysfunctional behavior from the slightly similar current situation. In the example of the athlete with the overbearing parents, the psychological intervention would hopefully result in the client differentiating his father from his coach while understanding why he responds so poorly to coaching feedback. In addition, the athlete would learn that his desire to avoid the negative feelings associated with perceived failure (also learned as a child) currently interferes with his commitment to athletic success. The intervention would help him recognize that his thoughts are not necessarily realistic (just manifestations of his early learning history) and that he can focus his behavior on achieving valued pursuits rather than on regulating his affective states.

After reading the list of schemas in chapter 2 that particularly relate to the athletic domain, readers can probably think of several athletes who fit the descriptions. This is because schemas do not exist just in individuals with significant psychological difficulties, but exist in all people.

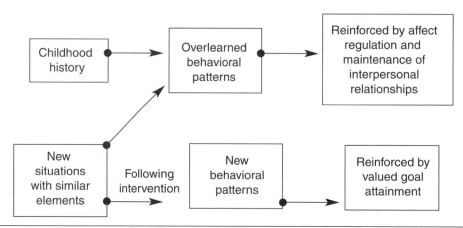

Figure 7.1 Training in stimulus discrimination leads to new behavioral patterns.

Again, the schema is not the concern. The concern arises when an individual's schema, triggered by a single event or series of events, interferes with adaptive functioning. Thus, the remainder of this chapter elaborates on the common types of performance dysfunction encountered by clinical sport psychologists.

Performance Dysfunction-I (Pdy-I)

Common to Pdy-I are life-role conflicts, reactions to role change (transition), lack of organizational fit, problematic interpersonal relationships, and other developmental and transitional events such as death and loss and acute stress responses. We discuss each separately.

Life-Role Conflicts

There are times that stressors occurring away from athletics cause stress and reduced effectiveness in the athletic venue. The converse is true as well, as stress and pressures in competitive athletics can negatively affect other life domains. The impact of sport on life-role adjustment and the impact of life-role conflicts on athletic performance are fundamental to practice in clinical sport psychology (Murphy, 1995). Life-role conflicts can reduce the athlete's task-focus, increase her cognitive and emotional interference, and reduce her motivation.

We as humans bring our cognitive schemas to every life situation. Thus, as with all people, athletes are more or less vulnerable to life-role stressors depending upon their unique social learning histories. Athletes with dependence or vulnerability schemas are more likely to react to living alone or moving away from home for the first time, while athletes holding mistrust or abandonment schemas are more likely to respond intensely to relationship turmoil or disruption. As no two people respond the same way to life-role stress, the clinical sport psychologist needs to accurately assess the schematic interpretations of an athlete's life events.

Typical life-role conflicts include family, relationship and marital, school-related, and work-related stress. Often, not these stressors by themselves, but rather their interconnectedness to athletic pressures and competitive performance, cause the life-role difficulties. An athlete is particularly vulnerable to life-role conflicts when competitive pressures and pressures inherent in

work, school, family, or relationships combine to tax the coping resources of even the most well-adjusted individual. How problematic life-role conflicts become is most often determined by situational circumstances, dispositional factors, preparedness, history with similar situations, and available support systems.

While interventions vary depending on the history, severity, functional impairment (in either general life or athletics), and intensity of the cognitive schemas, generally the clinical sport psychologist may best start with a solution-focused approach that addresses the immediate conflict and then follow with interventions directed at any remaining psychological symptoms. Finally, if necessary and desired by the athlete, interventions can address more long-term dispositional behavioral patterns. Family, relationship, or marital counseling may be helpful, or an individually based, empirically supported intervention such as interpersonal psychotherapy (IPT) (Klerman & Weissman, 1993) or brief cognitive therapy (CT) (Beck, 1976) may be required to ameliorate role conflicts.

Role disputes can occur with life partners, roommates, good friends, and so on and can include overidealized expectations of others or unresolved (spoken and unspoken) interpersonal conflicts (Gillies, 2001). These conflicts often occur due to interpersonal deficits such as lack of assertiveness skills necessary for problem-solution, lack of social initiative and its resulting alienation and isolation, and lack of interpersonal problem-solving skills (with associated deficits in alternative and consequential thinking).

The brief interventions for life-role conflicts center on helping the athlete clearly understand his current life-role challenge, his unique contribution to his life-role conflict (either behavioral or cognitive), and the choices and behaviors required to ameliorate the current conflict. The intervention should follow a sequential pattern for optimal effectiveness. After establishing a strong working alliance, the intervention should focus on understanding the external and internal triggers for the current situation and developing active behavioral responses and problem-solving approaches to stressors in order to enhance positive outcomes and expose the athlete to natural reinforcement.

Individuals experiencing life-role events commonly experience varying degrees of associated anger, anxiety, and depression. Life-role difficulties, while possibly meeting *DSM-IV-TR* criteria for an adjustment disorder, are typically treated with brief yet targeted counseling. Although these difficulties often remit with basic supportive counseling (and in some cases with no intervention at all), they can just as readily worsen, resulting in clinical disorders such as major depressive disorder (discussed in the next chapter). Life-role difficulties are frequently found in individuals with chronic mild depression (often referred to as dysthymic disorder), as characteristically these clients lack social skills, view themselves as helpless in a challenging world, and incorrectly interpret the actions and intentions of others (McCullough, 2000). Life-role conflicts often trigger more intense reactions in such individuals, and potential dysthymic disorders must be assessed before beginning formal intervention efforts. Individuals suffering from dysthymic disorder often do not describe themselves as depressed (unless the depression is exacerbated), as they typically are used to their chronic dysphoric mood. They often report experiencing little joy and happiness even when engaged in activities (such as athletics) that should result in pleasure and enjoyment. Dysthymic disorder is discussed in the next chapter.

Reactions to Role Change

Role changes occur as life and sport stressors rapidly or gradually alter a person's functioning, correspondingly altering daily social exchange and reinforcement (Wheeler, Christensen, & Jacobson, 2001). These role transitions can be as complex as a new marriage, the end of a relationship, or a move away from home that entails living without family support for the first time. The most problematic life-role changes for athletes are usually changes in their personal athletic roles, such as being demoted from starter to reserve in a team sport, dropping from top challenger to the middle of the pack in an individual sport, or encountering new organizational demands. These changes can result from numerous factors such as increasing age, injury, a trade, transfer to a new school, or a new coach. Once again, these transitional events interact with dispositional factors (schemas) to make individuals respond well or poorly.

The clinical sport psychologist can respond to an athlete's intense psychological reaction to role changes in several ways. First, for inevitable transitions (such as retirement or leaving for college), the clinical sport psychologist can provide proactive education targeting life skills and realistic expectations and planning (Danish et al., 1995; Murphy, 1995). Second, the clinical

sport psychologist can support and normalize the responses that seem overwhelming to the athlete but are in fact normal responses to life transitions. Third, when affective and behavioral responses are abnormal, reducing adaptive functioning in one or more major life domain (including competitive athletics), the practitioner may intervene with clinical or counseling interventions. These solution-focused interventions are similar to those utilized in role conflicts, and they focus on providing the client with guidance and modification of situational difficulties, proper interpretation of the role change, maintenance of necessary functional behaviors that pursue personal values, and, later, possible schema modification (Young et al., 2003). For clarification, *personal values* are the journey of life as opposed to the end-point destination of achievement goals.

Athletes dealing with role change often respond well to basic counseling skills, including empathy, support, and normalization. However, the athlete's idiosyncratic interpretations of the role change (including the personal meaning in the particular transitional situation) may exacerbate affective responses (Beck, 1976) so that the athlete loses the perspective necessary to effectively cope with the change. The clinical sport psychologist can contribute to the athlete's transition adjustment by helping him objectively and realistically view the events and requirements of the changed life circumstance. For athletes predisposed to such difficulties, the intensified affect caused by the transition may result in behaviors focused on immediate emotion regulation rather than solution-focused behavior. These emotion-focused behaviors can exacerbate the situation and counter the athlete's ultimate goals. In these circumstances, interventions should ensure that the athlete maintain focus on and commitment to his personal values and accept that increased levels of affect and distress are time-limited, expected, and tolerable (Hayes et al., 1999).

Lack of Organizational Fit

Athlete difficulties are not always internal. Problems in an athlete's organization, such as a professional team, Olympic team, university, or club, may also result in performance dysfunction. The changing or challenging characteristics of the competitive environment and organization may partially or completely cause the conditions culminating in performance dysfunction. The model of functional and dysfunctional athletic performance (IMAP) presented in chapter 2 suggests that in the preparatory stage, athletes must integrate their skills and abilities with personal dispositional variables and with external factors (including explicit performance demands and organizational realities) in order to perform optimally. Unrealistic competitive demands, defective coaching, and dysfunctional interpersonal relationships often cause performance dysfunction by disrupting this first (preparatory) stage of the self-regulatory process.

The clinical sport psychologist's first challenge in such situations is to accurately assess the extent to which performance difficulties are caused by working conditions, the athlete's psychological dynamics (such as dispositional cognitive schemas and behavior patterns), or both. The practitioner may not be educated, trained, available, or able to promote change in the athlete's competitive environment, but she should make all reasonable efforts to assess its contribution to the performance dysfunction. The practitioner can then work with the athlete to either accept circumstances and problem solve more effectively (emotional acceptance with corresponding goal-promoting behavioral choices) or consider ways of removing himself from the problematic situation (transfer, new personal coach, trade request) if deemed necessary. When confronted with claims that performance difficulties are due to external factors, the clinical sport psychologist should not immediately conclude that external factors are the primary source of difficulty and must maintain a third-party perspective. This perspective, objective and open to all possible explanations, can help determine if the specific competitive and organizational environment or the athlete's response, lack of adjustment, or adaptation to reasonable organizational demands is problematic.

In such situations (and in all consulting roles), it is helpful if the clinical sport psychologist can develop a consulting relationship with an organization that allows for a full understanding of its history, mission, and culture. This relationship has been described as an *internal consultant professional role* (Gardner, 1995). This role allows the practitioner to influence the organizational system to benefit both it and the individual athlete (Gardner, 1995, 2001). However, this professional role is rare. If this role develops, it will develop gradually, and must never be forced. If it develops, the clinical sport psychologist should remain within her professional areas of competence as well as within the job description for which she was contracted. Additionally, the internal consultant role should only occur when organizational

change is possible, appropriate, and when administration is open to such changes. As discussed in chapter 12, the clinical sport psychologist must carefully consider ethical issues in effecting organizational change to aid an athlete or the organization. Competence, contract status, confidentiality, and the best interests of both the organization and the athlete must be considered in all organizational interventions. Further, the practitioner must carefully consider who his client actually is, whether the athlete or the larger organizational system. This question is typically answered by prearranged agreements, consents, and the sport psychologist's contract.

Problematic Interpersonal Relationships

Problematic interpersonal relationships create some of the most volatile and destructive problems in the athletic domain and can devastate both individual and team performance. Problematic interpersonal relationships can cause individual performance dysfunction by reducing task focus, disrupting motivation, increasing cognitive and affective activity, and reducing behavioral commitment to training. These negative consequences can affect individual athletes, subgroups, or even entire teams. Problematic relationships can be intense for a limited time, as when romantic partners break up, or can be chronic and cyclical, as during long dysfunctional relationships with a history of violent disputes.

Often, the emotional reactions these problematic interpersonal relationships engender become disproportionately disruptive (more than the precipitating conflict or event would suggest), and individuals become locked into dysfunctional interactional patterns with others. In some circumstances, these conflicts become public and affect a number of initially uninvolved people, such as friends, family, staff, and teammates. Problematic relationships are often triggered by characteristic dysfunctional response patterns to authority figures (discussed later in this chapter), a lack of interpersonal skills (including communication and conflict-resolution skills), or a particular interpersonal dynamic with a coach, teammate, or personal friend (including a romantic partner). These problematic relationships can be intense and acute or more subtle and chronic. However, all problematic personal relationships tend to distract and mentally exhaust the athlete and can residually affect the entire team.

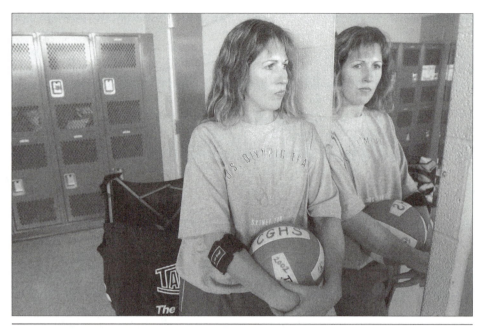

Difficulties with establishing and maintaining effective interpersonal relationships can lead to truancy, motivation loss, alienation, and disputes with teammates and coaches.

The clinical sport psychologist should carefully evaluate dispositional variables and situational demands before intervening with an individual or a group (team). Often, the required intervention is simple communication training or conflict management. In other circumstances, the intervention of choice may integrate problem-solving skills with a more cognitive approach. Cognitive interventions (which include problem-solving skill development) foster accurate interpersonal interpretations and also focus on developing and reinforcing actions that lead to more positive relationship outcomes while maintaining focus on necessary sport-related choices and behaviors. These interventions often involve multiple team members or even entire teams. The clinical sport psychologist should understand the impact of the interpersonal conflict on the larger team system and understand that since these groups tend to be closely bonded and closed systems, efforts to change the problematic interpersonal behavior of one member can readily affect the others.

Other Developmental and Transitional Events

In addition to the difficulties already listed, other developmental and transitional occurrences may provide obstacles for the athlete. Some additional obstacles include death and loss and acute stress responses.

Death and Loss

All people must face the deaths of acquaintances and loved ones as a natural part of life. Athletes are certainly not immune to this reality, and they must deal with expected and unexpected loss. Such losses can be real, as in the case of a parent's death, or symbolic, as in the case of an injury terminating a career (discussed in chapter 10). A sense of loss also occurs when a long-term relationship breaks up or living status and style significantly change.

As with all responses to life events, the athlete's dispositional characteristics, available support systems, and characteristic coping behaviors contribute to the emotional intensity, general life and specific performance impact, and overall adaptation to loss. Kubler-Ross (1969) suggested that an individual's response to death follows, either linearly or nonlinearly, a series of identifiable stages. These stages include denial, anger, bargaining, depression, and, ultimately, acceptance.

Most responses to death and loss follow a relatively brief course of normal grieving that likely includes some alteration of mood, energy, and concentration. In a relatively short time, usually after several weeks, the individual's affective and behavioral states return to pre-event levels. In these circumstances the clinical sport psychologist can offer support and empathic counseling to help the grieving process resolve normally.

However, in some situations, due to personal dispositional factors (typically related to unresolved relational issues or early learning histories), grieving does not proceed normally and extends for an undetermined time. These situations usually involve a blocking of the normal grief response, wherein the individual does not allow himself to progress through the grieving process or wherein psychological factors interfere with the completion of grieving. The extended grief response often requires therapeutic intervention to fully and successfully complete the grieving process. An empirically supported intervention for these situations is interpersonal psychotherapy (IPT) (Klerman & Weissman, 1993), which places focus on the completion of unresolved grief.

Acute Stress Response

While there are no prevalence data for acute stress response, termed acute stress disorder (ASD) in the *DSM-IV-TR* (APA, 2000), a large number of people experience short-term, intense responses to a variety of traumatic events. We place ASD in the performance dysfunction classification because it is a short-term response with time-limited performance and general life ramifications. It does not reach the severity or duration levels characteristic of serious clinical disorders and does not result in profound performance impairments. ASD also tends to affect teammates as well as the traumatized individual.

The essential features of ASD are anxiety, numbing, or other psychological symptoms that develop within 1 mo of a traumatic event. Motor vehicle accidents and sexual assault (or the sexual assault of a teammate) are some of the many situations that may trigger an acute stress response. The affected individual may reexperience the traumatic event (in dreams and flashbacks), avoid associated situations or stimuli, demonstrate markedly reduced general functioning, and experience decrements in specific domains of functioning such as sport participation. The acute stress response can be as brief as 2 d or as long as 4 wk. The more time-limited response can have intense, albeit short-term, effects on both the individual and his teammates. For many who experience traumatic events, either directly or vicariously through those close to them, this acute response can become chronic (lasting beyond 4 wk), and the serious psychological difficulties of posttraumatic stress disorder (PTSD) can ensue (discussed in chapter 8).

In addition to numbing and anxiety, individuals who experience an acute stress disorder may respond with despair and hopelessness. Individuals who experience traumatic events with another person who faces greater consequences (such as surviving a motor vehicle accident in which a friend dies) may experience overwhelming guilt about not providing enough help or having remained relatively unhurt. Individuals experiencing acute stress often believe they are more responsible for negative consequences than is rationally warranted. Impulsivity, risk taking, and neglecting basic health and safety are not uncommon during an acute stress response, especially in adolescents and young adults. Athletes, mostly young and in good health, often feel strong and omnipotent and can be intensely affected by traumatic events, either their own or traumatic events of their teammates (even events for which they're not directly present). The natural bond inherent to and critical for success in competitive team sports can result in acute stress responses that affect one or more teammates. Individuals with early histories of trauma and preexisting psychological difficulties are understandably at greater risk for ASD, and the duration, severity, and proximity of a traumatic event to an individual are most predictive of ASD.

Unfortunately, there is currently no empirically supported treatment for ASD. Although its proponents suggest that critical incident stress debriefing (CISD) is appropriate for both ASD and PTSD (Kirk & Madden, 2003; Rank & Gentry, 2003), controlled studies of CISD suggest the contrary and even suggest that CISD can result in negative reactions and increased PTSD symptomatology (Lilienfeld et al., 2003; Litz, Gray, Bryant, & Adler, 2002). The purpose of CISD (also known as crisis debriefing) is to minimize the potential development of PTSD by conducting a one-session debriefing session immediately following a traumatic event (within the first 3 days). Data not only demonstrate ineffective and possibly harmful effects of CISD, but also show that victims treated with CISD show significantly greater levels of PTSD symptomatology, depression, anxiety, and general psychopathology and remain symptomatic significantly longer than those who do not receive CISD (Bisson, Jenkins, Alexander, & Bannister, 1997; Mayou, Ehlers, & Hobbs, 2000).

Since no clear empirically supported treatments are available for acute stress disorder and CISD is clearly contraindicated, we make several suggestions based on available data. Since ASD is

Summary of Typical Pdy-I Issues

Common Pdy-I Difficulties
Primarily external concerns, such as

- Life-role conflicts
- Reactions to role changes and transitions
- Lack of organizational fit
- Challenged interpersonal relationships
- Other transitional events
  - Death and loss
  - Acute stress response

a relatively normal and expected response, individuals experiencing ASD can be provided with therapeutic support, should be encouraged to seek social supports, and should continue with their daily routines as much as possible. If the practitioner deems that formal interventions are necessary, a five-session intervention (conducted within 2 wk of the trauma) using exposure or exposure with anxiety management may reduce the likelihood of PTSD development (Bryant, Sackville, Dang, Moulds, & Guthrie, 1999). Regardless of the chosen intervention strategies, the clinical sport psychologist should monitor the athlete's reactions closely and intervene with cognitive processing therapy (CPT) (Resick & Calhoun, 2001) if the athlete's symptoms intensify, become more chronic, and evolve into PTSD. CPT is the most empirically supported treatment for PTSD at this time, and is covered in further detail in chapter 8.

Performance Dysfunction-II (Pdy-II)

Now we turn our attention to the common Pdy-II difficulties. These typically include patterns of avoidance and underinvolvement and patterns of overinvolvement. We highlight each separately.

Avoidance and Underinvolvement

Experiential avoidance has been defined as avoiding negatively evaluated thoughts or emotions (Hayes et al., 1996). As discussed in chapter 2, an avoidance-based coping style is frequently associated with performance dysfunction. This style may be dispositional or develop gradually in response to the repeated failure of more adaptive efforts at success. Additionally, negative outcome expectancies develop and strengthen over repeated dysfunctional experiences, and avoidance behaviors are therefore negatively reinforced, becoming the characteristic style of the individual. Athletes (like all individuals) engage in tasks as long as their behavior results in positive consequences and they reasonably believe that positive outcomes are likely. Conversely, they tend to disengage when negative outcomes occur frequently and become anticipated. Thus, the athlete experiencing persistent performance dysfunction is likely to respond by covert or overt avoidance or task disengagement.

Inherent in our conceptualization of performance dysfunction, and supported by recent research on behavioral disorders (Hayes et al., 1996), experiential avoidance provides individuals experiencing high levels of negative affect with a short-term means of emotion regulation. While this regulation does not fulfill long-term valued goals (such as performance), it does immediately reduce affect and as such is strongly (negatively) reinforced. For example, if an athlete has been in conflict with a coach and therefore experiences negative affect during practice, the athlete may skip practice to avoid the interpersonal conflict. By doing this, the athlete's negative affect decreases, and is therefore negatively reinforced. However, while the experiential avoidance led the athlete to feel better for the moment, it has gotten in the way of valued goals (such as sport success). This reinforced pattern is often well-learned and used in a variety of contexts. Experiential avoidance can develop in other life domains and become generalized to the athletic environment, or can develop specifically in the athletic milieu based on situational factors.

Experiential avoidance can take many forms, and the clinical sport psychologist should carefully evaluate for its presence by conducting a functional analysis of behavior during performance situations (the Action and Acceptance Questionnaire [AAQ] is also very helpful, as described in chapter 6). For example, the athlete frequently demonstrating behaviors such as poor training and lack of responsiveness to staff efforts may be engaging in avoidant behavior. In fact, though a lack of motivation may seem like the obvious explanation, the problematic behavior may just as easily reflect a lack of commitment to behaviors serving distal (long-term) athletic goals. While clearly not serving athletic goals, avoidant behavior may less obviously benefit the athlete by briefly reducing negative thoughts and emotions. Research suggests that the short-term benefit of avoidant behavior is strongly reinforced and is therefore highly motivating (Tice et al., 2001). This avoidant behavior may predominate as a primary coping style and manifest itself in both obvious and subtle ways.

Avoidance-based coping strategies are the behavioral manifestation of many performance schemas. Avoidance strategies can result in an athlete's underinvolvement in athletic pursuits, therefore making her less effective than her ability or athletic history suggests she should be. The central theme in forms of underinvolvement is the athlete's failure to commit to the requirements of the athletic role so that she does not reach her potential or so that there is a significant discrepancy between typical performance and competitive requirements. Underinvolvement is often cyclical, occurring at sporadic intervals, but in some cases it persists and becomes highly characteristic of the athlete. Underinvolvement commonly includes

1. resistance to authority and necessary training,
2. procrastination,
3. temporary performance dysfunction (slumps), and
4. fear of failure or success.

These four forms of underinvolvement most often result when the various cognitive schemas noted earlier are triggered. While schemas (rule systems related to contingency-shaped behavior) associated with avoidance-based difficulties have not been formally studied in the sport domain, there is no reason to believe that avoidance-based difficulties in other human activities would differ in competitive sports. With this in mind, let's discuss each of these four forms of underinvolvement.

Resistance to Authority and Necessary Training

This behavior pattern most often results from entitlement or low frustration tolerance schemas. Individuals experiencing these schemas often become easily angered and demonstrate little tolerance

for frustration. In response to their frustration, behavioral avoidance is initiated to remove the discomfort (frustration) and to create a more pleasant affective state. Often, the anger these athletes experience is directed at authority (staff) and is triggered when self-discipline or compliance with organizational standards is expected. Often, these athletes constantly frustrate staff and teammates, who find it difficult to get them to conform to a team environment and accept the same rules the others accept. Conflict with teammates and staff is likely cyclical and repetitive. Similar difficulties in nonathletic arenas (such as home and school) are not uncommon. At extreme levels, these behavioral characteristics are the core components of personality disorders, substance use disorders, or anger disorders and domestic violence (discussed in chapter 9). In our experience, these behavioral characteristics are particularly triggered by coaches who utilize either an overcontrolling or a permissive style, both of which interact with the athlete's interpersonal characteristics to trigger the less adaptive aspects of his personality.

The dispositionally based and situationally triggered difficulties can readily result in performance dysfunction by leading to problematic responses in the preparatory phase of athletic performance (described in chapter 2). In this phase, schemas can be triggered by explicit performance demands inherent in the competitive environment or by the behavioral (possibly authoritative) style of a particular staff member. The triggered schema increases affective responses and associated behaviors as previously noted. The maladaptive coping behaviors are intended to regulate the affect that occurs when the schema is triggered, but this rarely leads to valued goal attainment. This is why nonprofessionals frequently view these behaviors as obviously self-destructive and not understandable.

Intervening with this particular performance dysfunction is complex. First, using standard goal setting as often suggested in the traditional sport psychology literature (Burton et al., 2001) is unlikely to succeed if the goal setting is used as a motivational and self-regulatory technique. In addition, self-talk (Williams & Leffingwell, 2002) and precompetitive routines (Hardy et al., 1996) are unlikely to succeed, based on both limited empirical findings (Moore, 2003b; Moore & Gardner, 2005) and a poor theoretical match. The issue for these athletes is not motivation, negative self-talk, or a simple case of behavioral self-regulation, but instead is the overlearned avoidance of negative internal experiences (cognition and affect). Any intervention effort should target the use of experiential avoidance as a maladaptive form of emotion regulation. Intervention success is unlikely unless the athlete learns to accept and tolerate distress, recognize the degree to which she automatically responds with rule-governed behavior (based on cognitive schemas and their automatic behavioral responses), act toward her personal goals (commitment), and become reinforced by the natural contingencies in her environment. From this conceptual position, traditional psychological skills training, most likely goal setting or self-talk, is inconsistent with the dysfunctional cognitive and behavioral processes at work. Without focusing on distress tolerance and values-directed behavior, these self-regulatory interventions are unlikely to have a positive effect and may additionally frustrate the athlete and staff.

Procrastination

Procrastination is a persistent and often cyclical behavior pattern in which the athlete avoids the timely initiation and completion of goals (including sport tasks) or activities (including training and preparation for competition) required for optimal performance. Procrastination is most common in athletes holding either failure or extreme standards schemas. In both of these schemas, athletes give up easily or avoid situations where failure or performance judgment is a real or perceived possibility. Procrastination typically involves three distinct components (not all of which may occur in every athlete):

1) Failure to initiate goal-directed activity in a timely manner, as seen in the distance runner who delays the onset of training

2) Perseverance in activities that prevent the completion of goal-directed tasks, as seen in the athlete who repeatedly stays out late with friends and thus impairs his strength training

3) Failure to sustain (and possibly complete) goal-directed tasks previously initiated, as seen in the athlete who starts to spend extra time working with a coach and then increasingly misses these prearranged meetings

Typically, procrastination is not based on a lack of motivation (defined as the desire to develop and succeed) or a lack of concentration. Instead, procrastination reflects an avoidant coping style

intended to reduce (regulate) negative cognition and affect. Once again, this behavior pattern occurs at the expense of goals the athlete deems important. Although it may seem clear to the observer, procrastinators typically do not consider these consequences.

In cases of procrastination, athletes may not respond to performance demands with necessary effort, but may respond with task avoidance to control the negative thoughts and emotions triggered by external demands or self-perceptions of negative performance. The athlete's expressed desire to succeed and her occasional disregard for activities necessary to success are incongruent. Since the athlete's primary goal becomes immediate emotion regulation rather than goal attainment, the athlete fails to engage in the behaviors required by external demands and contingencies. The athlete also commonly displays this pattern in nonsport activities such as school or family responsibilities when failure or being judged is a possibility.

Performance dysfunction due to procrastination is most likely found in the preparatory phase of athletic performance (see chapter 2) and also is not likely to be amenable to standard psychological skills training interventions. While these athletes may seem to have deficits in motivation or concentration, their minimal self-confidence and overinterpretation of real or possible failure form the core psychological barrier to their success. As the issue is not lack of goal setting, poor concentration, negative self-talk, or absent images of success, traditional self-regulatory skills training is not likely to succeed alone. Instead, specialized interventions should be based on the core issues inherent in the maladaptive process, focusing on

a) behavioral assignments exposing the athlete to his negative affect to develop greater distress tolerance (task completion exercises);

b) monitoring and understanding relevant core beliefs (schemas) relating to failure (self-monitoring of automatic thoughts);

c) directly defusing these automatic thoughts; that is, developing mindful awareness without judging automatic thoughts as true or false, right or wrong (mindfulness and cognitive defusion exercises); and

d) determining valued objectives and the choices and behaviors necessary to achieve them (values clarification and behavioral activation).

In the *later* stages of interventions for procrastination, adjunctive stimulus control techniques such as precompetitive or prepractice plans may help the athlete develop necessary stimulus discrimination and increase appropriate behavior.

In addition to being found in the preparatory phase of athletic performance, both resistance to authority and procrastination can also occur in the postperformance response phase of athletic performance (see chapter 2), during which the athlete subtly or overtly avoids full or partial reengagement in practice or competition. The dysfunctional process and the needed interventions are the same in the two phases.

Temporary Performance Dysfunction (Slump)

Some athletes respond to negative performance events with debilitating and possibly chronic performance dysfunction. In chapter 2, we described the sequence of both functional and dysfunctional performance. For some athletes, difficulties in the performance phase, particularly those related to appropriate discrepancy adjustment, can negatively affect performance. Of course, many athletes recover quickly from these inevitable experiences due to adaptive dispositional characteristics or positive outcome expectancies that isolate the temporary dysfunction as situational and non-threatening. Other athletes, however, go through a period of persistent performance dysfunction that may be time limited or may become chronic and pervasive. For these athletes, performance dysfunction typically ensues due to new or changing external circumstances (such as a new and possibly more intense level of competition), the triggering of preexisting performance schemas, or athletic skill disruption (such as injury).

Temporary performance difficulties typically result from a significant disruption in the performance phase of athletic performance. Most often, disruption begins with failed discrepancy adjustment, which is essentially when an automated task-oriented process becomes a more controlled and self-focused process. Failed discrepancy adjustments enhance threat interpretations, increase negative cognitive and affective responses, increase arousal, and reduce task-relevant attentional focus. While failed discrepancy adjustment is the most common starting point for this dysfunctional process, disruption can also occur later in the self-regulatory process during periods of excessive self-focused (and possibly negative) cognitive content or unexpected (and possibly

misinterpreted) increases in emotional arousal. Dysfunctional athletic performance inevitably results when some aspect of negative performance triggers an excessive internal focus, which then predominates and replaces performance-relevant behavior. As noted earlier, disrupted performance is not uncommon and is most often self-corrected. It also typically remains brief, minimally affecting long-term competitive performance. Yet, when negative performance events trigger performance schemas such as failure, approval seeking, negativity, extreme standards, or self-punishing schemas, the dysfunctional spiral begins more readily and is more likely to become chronic and difficult to overcome. As a result, athletes with these schemas, which are based upon their personal social-learning (and possibly competitive) history, are more vulnerable to excessive self-focus and to avoidant responses (to negative internal states) when confronting natural performance decrements. Furthermore, they are likely to have a more difficult time recovering from these events, as they focus on internal processes (thoughts and emotions) instead of external performance cues and contingencies. In such situations, self-focus replaces task-focus, disrupting automated athletic performance and increasing cognitive activity (such as potentially debilitative worry and rumination).

The conceptual weakness of traditional psychological skills training is most clear with temporary performance dysfunction. As noted in chapter 1, theories behind PST interventions typically assume that deficits in appropriate behaviors (often described as psychological skills) are the primary causes of dysfunctional performance, and thus interventions focus on developing behavioral (goal setting) and cognitive (self-talk, imagery, attention control) skills to aid self-regulation. More specifically, these procedures essentially teach athletes that

a) thoughts and feelings (internal experiences) are causative and thus directly linked to success or failure in competitive performance;

b) optimal success requires athletes to master (control or reduce) internal states;

c) the sport psychologist should provide techniques to achieve mastery (and control) over internal experiences; and

d) athletes who practice hard and consistently use these techniques will achieve greater athletic success.

Unfortunately, the empirical data do not support the assumptions inherent in traditional psychological skills training nor its efficacy to enhance performance. This is particularly poignant in Pdy cases, in which performance dysfunction is due to overemphasizing internal processes at the expense of performance cues and contingencies.

One option for the clinical sport psychologist is to utilize interventions that integrate acceptance and mindfulness procedures (Hayes, Jacobson, Follette, & Dougher, 1994) with traditional exposure-based principles. We stated in chapter 6 that preliminary data indicate that the original MAC protocol appears most effective with athletes classified as PD-I or PD-II (Gardner et al., 2005; Wolanin, 2005). The MAC intervention requires slight modification to meet the differing needs of Pdy athletes. This modification combines the MAC protocol, which focuses on clarifying personal values and defining the behaviors necessary to achieve them and a willingness to experience negative internal states, with a variation of the worry exposure procedures often utilized to treat generalized anxiety disorder (Barlow, 2001). The clinically enhanced MAC protocol, termed MAC-worry-exposure (MAC-WE), teaches the athlete to become aware of his worry states and view them as passing events. The athlete experiences his thoughts and emotions, becomes present with them, and allows them to gently pass as his focus becomes more task oriented. Directly related to our decision to integrate these procedures is the finding in our research lab that athletes demonstrating temporary performance dysfunction tend to score at borderline clinical levels on the Penn State Worry Questionnaire (PSWQ) (Meyer, Miller, Metzger, & Borkovec, 1990), which measures pathological worry. This finding suggests that temporary performance dysfunction is similar, albeit at subclinical levels, to generalized anxiety disorder, a clinical disorder distinguished by anxiety, worry, and avoidance (Barlow, 2001). Based on the avoidant nature of worry, it is rational to include worry-based temporary performance dysfunction as a special subset of avoidant behavior patterns. We have also found that procedures such as MAC-WE can be effectively utilized with athletes who are not worrying, but are focusing on negative self-image, poor responses of those close to them, and so on.

For such athletes, MAC-worry exposure (MAC-WE) targets the worry underlying dysfunctional performance by focusing on the athlete's overemphasis on internal scanning and efforts at internal control, which comes at the expense of the more functional external focus of attention and the athlete's trust in his performance abilities (known as automatic performance-cued behavior). This protocol helps the athlete develop mindful attention, clarify values, accept negative affective states, and commit to the behaviors necessary for successful athletic performance (skills basic to the MAC intervention). The worry exposure component utilizes mindfulness meditation to help athletes increase contact with and awareness of internal states, and habituation to their worries so that they view internal states as normal, passing, and less "real." In addition to using MAC-WE with such athletes, practitioners can also utilize other traditional cognitive behavioral interventions (Beck, 1995) or more contemporary third-wave behavioral interventions such as acceptance and commitment therapy (Hayes et al., 1999).

Many athletes seeking consultation from a sport psychologist certainly want to perform better, but many also do not like how they think or feel. Often, reducing personal discomfort takes precedence over the disruptive consequences caused by the athlete's internal states. In many cases, the negative internal states (thoughts and feelings) are disruptive *because* they receive such attention and the athlete develops increasingly rigid behavioral responses (even during competitive situations) to his internal states in order to control or reduce the negative experience. Unfortunately, using rule-governed behavior, some athletes will actually describe their thoughts and feelings as a *good* reason to respond less effectively, such as the athlete who says, "I'm stressed out so I'm not going to train until I feel better." In such cases, interventions should focus on accepting (not controlling) internal states and disconnecting task-relevant behavior from them. The major intervention goal is to replace *but* with *and*. So, instead of saying, "I know I need to train *but* I feel too stressed right now," and choosing to act against athletic values, the athlete can engage in necessary training while feeling poorly (and will resist avoidance behaviors used to reduce internal states). The athlete will therefore now say, "I know I need to train *and* I feel stressed right now." The intervention promotes having a negative internal experience and still fulfilling athletic responsibilities.

Values identification may be a rational adjunctive intervention, as this promotes behavioral activation while the athlete learns to remain in the moment and tolerate the discomfort he has previously avoided. Conversely, positive imagery

Focusing on internal processes such as thoughts, emotions, and physical sensations during a match instead of athletic cues and contingencies can lead to debilitating performance effects.

and particularly self-talk interventions are contraindicated because they are self-regulatory interventions for enhancing internal control and they increase internal scanning and cognitive activity.

Other forms of subclinical anxiety are also related to performance dysfunction. For example, subclinical forms of social-performance anxiety and obsessive-compulsive disorder can disrupt the self-regulatory process, requiring an intervention adapted from the clinical literature and tailored to an athlete's specific needs. These treatment protocols are described in chapter 8.

When performance dysfunction becomes chronic, avoidant patterns of behavior may result in complete task disengagement. Left untreated, this withdrawal may become overt and complete. Repeated failure to perform at expected standards is likely to extinguish necessary effort (approach behaviors) and to negatively reinforce avoidant behaviors such as withdrawal from sport participation. As Smith (1986) has suggested, the balance between reinforcement and aversive consequences of continued athletic involvement becomes such that dissatisfaction and negative affect predominate. In these circumstances, the athlete may determine that the benefit to continued athletic participation is minimal, may experience greatly reduced motivation, and may ultimately disengage completely from sport participation. Smith (1986) and others (Hardy et al., 1996) have termed this phenomenon *burnout*. In such cases, interventions need to address the decisional imbalance (whether the reasons for withdrawing are greater than the reasons for remaining engaged). This can be done by using self-monitoring of automatic thoughts, pleasure and mastery logs, or cognitive restructuring if perceptual errors (cognitive distortions) are resulting in unrealistic negative interpretations of performance (Beck, 1976). In situations where a negative decisional balance has developed due to actual, repeated competitive failure, it is critical that the athlete first identify and clarify his values to determine if he is truly willing to do what is necessary to perform well. This should be followed by direct skill enhancement (most likely in consultation with coaches and staff). Even if these enhanced training regimens are appropriately implemented and accurately defined, the athlete may be at a point where repeated failure leads the athlete to give up, thereby keeping the athlete from actively engaging in consultation. In these circumstances, behavioral activation through techniques such as weekly goal setting, stimulus control, and direct behavioral assignments to increase the athlete's effort are likely to help.

Fear of Failure or Success

Both fear of success (FOS) and fear of failure (FOF) are organizing constructs that help explain the underinvolvement occasionally found in the athletic setting (Mulig, Haggerty, Carballosa, Cinnick, & Madden, 1985). Conroy and Meltzer (2004) recently found a strong and distinct pattern of self-talk associated with FOF and a somewhat weaker pattern associated with FOS. In another study, psychometric evaluation found FOF to be strongly associated with high levels of worry, somatic anxiety, cognitive disruption, and general sport anxiety and with low levels of optimism (Conroy, Willow, & Meltzer, 2002). Interestingly, this study also found that FOF was unrelated to, and thus independent of, perceived competence. Finally, extensive interview data from both athletes and performing artists suggest that athletes are concerned about failure and success and the resultant consequences, thus allowing the authors to develop multidimensional models of FOF and FOS (Conroy, Poczwardowski, & Henschen, 2001). Performance schemas theoretically consistent with FOF and FOS include approval and recognition seeking, negativity, extreme standards, and self-punishing schemas (see chapter 2).

Fear of failure is essentially a failure-threatened dispositional style. The most characteristic coping behavior is taking on very low levels of task difficulty (and avoiding challenging competitive situations) in order to create excusable failure: "I could have done better but I didn't really try . . . so I didn't *really* fail!"

Fundamental to FOF is a core belief of failure and associated beliefs that attaining desired goals is not likely. In addition, failure is commonly associated with predictions of social and familial rejection, an expectation of external punishment, and a sense of reduced social value (Burney, Burdick, & Teevan, 1969). The athlete who fears failure is likely to avoid training and preparation, thereby actually ensuring her failure and reinforcing her failure-based belief system. Those with high FOF often cease active effort, although they rarely verbalize that fact to others. They often appear motivated but inconsistently committed, especially when goals appear particularly close to fruition. They tend to be excessively ingratiating to others and seek to favorably impress those close to them, to the exclusion of more goal-relevant behaviors. Effective problem solving is often missing in these individuals. Rather, they may spend too much time on unnecessary tasks, take high risks (make seemingly impulsive decisions) regarding training and preparation, and set goals in an overly restricted range. The primary motivation of athletes with FOF is failure avoidance, *not* success attainment.

Fear of success (FOS) is another construct that explains underinvolved behavior. FOS is a persistent tendency to avoid activities that would result in achievement, particularly when success appears imminent (and the athlete thus appears self-destructive). In addition, individuals with FOS minimize accomplishments and attribute success and the achievement of goals to factors not under their direct control (Kirkpatrick, 1982). Consistent with the relevant performance schemas are FOS characteristics such as low self-esteem and preoccupation with external evaluation (and fear of appearing incompetent) (Pappo, 1983). Evaluative performance anxiety is also common. FOS is in many ways the fear of failure, as the true fear is that success will be fleeting and not maintained. In essence, the athlete feels less competent than she actually is and views success as a mistake that will be ultimately found out by others. Despite what appears to others as clear success, the athlete

experiencing FOS views success as one step closer to being discovered, embarrassed, and possibly humiliated when the eventual (and seemingly unquestionable) failure occurs. Therefore, FOS can be viewed as a form of FOF in which success and achievement are stimuli that trigger the relevant performance schemas and associated concerns about failure.

Some evidence suggests that individuals with high FOS and low achievement motivation are particularly prone to performance dysfunction (Tresemer, 1976). Individuals who experience FOS may be more vulnerable to the effects of staff and coach evaluations, family involvement in their athletic careers, and higher levels of competition that come with inherent public scrutiny.

Psychological interventions for FOF and FOS should directly address the athlete's subjective estimations of success and his predictions of the consequences of failure. As the FOF or FOS athlete's thought process is often highly overlearned and automatic, it is possible that the athlete will not directly articulate success and failure predictions, avoidance of anticipated outcomes, and the consequences of avoidance. The first step in effective treatment is developing self-awareness of the personal rules the athlete holds regarding success and failure, such as, "If I'm successful, my old friends won't like me, and they'll just laugh when I ultimately fail," and, "If I fail it will be a tragedy, my family will be disappointed in me, and I will be humiliated for the rest of my life." Cognitive restructuring of false or unproven assumptions and conclusions can assist the athlete in developing a more realistic approach to his career and athletic pursuits.

Athletic performance cannot always be altered to the degree that we and our athletes would like. Thus, relative ability needs to be carefully considered before intervening with FOF and FOS. For many athletes, especially nonprofessional athletes, accomplishing lesser goals may be much more satisfying than accomplishing the more ambitious (but possibly less realistic) goals that have resulted in anxiety and avoidance. In this regard, values clarification and competitive and precompetitive plans that incorporate reasonable achievement goals are often necessary intervention strategies. By developing realistic goals, increasing effort, and seeking supportive assistance from staff, the athlete may develop more approach-based (rather than avoidance-based) behaviors, achieve goals more readily, and enhance self-efficacy.

Overinvolvement

As with underinvolvement, when discussing overinvolvement, the reader should recognize that there is a fine and sometimes imperceptible difference between normal behaviors and problematic behaviors. For example, when assessing a potentially underinvolved athlete, the clinical sport psychologist should determine if the athlete's behaviors are simply ineffective or result from avoidance behaviors. Likewise, when assessing a potentially overinvolved athlete, the practitioner needs to consider if the athlete presents with compulsive overcommitment or productive achievement-oriented behaviors (Hayes & Feldman, 2004). Although this distinction is important in both, underinvolvement and overinvolvement involve very different processes. Overinvolvement has been referred to as "workaholism" (Naughton, 1987) and is less likely to be viewed as problematic in the "win at all costs" culture of competitive sports. In fact, the drive and obsessive concern for success is most often seen as a positive personality trait and is typically highly valued in the sport milieu. Overinvolvement can be the acceptable price of success in the goal-directed, success-oriented athlete, or it can be based upon unhealthy motives and result in an unhappy and distressed individual who experiences burnout.

The rewards within the sport culture for compulsive and ultimately successful competitive pursuits and behaviors cannot be underestimated when working with highly success-oriented athletes, and these rewards should always be carefully assessed and considered when determining interventions for the overinvolved athlete. The defining features of overinvolvement are

a) a lack of overt enjoyment of sport participation;

b) a lack of engagement and enjoyment in nonathletic activities;

c) a tendency to minimally engage in social activities;

d) a willingness to risk health for additional success (use drugs to enhance performance, overtrain to the point of injury, and so on); and

e) a possible reliance on potentially self-destructive coping behaviors such as using alcohol and drugs.

For many overinvolved athletes, life is single-mindedly (obsessively) directed toward accomplishing defined athletic and competitive goals, while pleasure is an adjunctive (and possibly unnecessary) consequence of success.

It is difficult to imagine any sport organization, particularly those at high levels in which winning and economic rewards are of prime importance, not valuing the obvious elements of overinvolved, possibly compulsive behavior. In fact, many readers may have difficulty imagining these behaviors as problematic in the sport milieu. At the individual level, however, compulsive preoccupation with success can come at a heavy price. Such individuals commonly experience significant relationship difficulties and possibly experience medical complications such as injuries from overtraining. Of course, the numerous positive outcomes associated with overinvolvement and its daily positive reinforcement make acknowledging it as a problem difficult even in the best circumstances.

It is most often when compulsive efforts stop being effective, possibly to the point of causing negative consequences, that overinvolvement comes to the attention of the clinical sport psychologist. The negative consequences of overinvolvement may include overconfidence and unrealistic career goals, reduced performance due to poor maintenance of physical or mental energy, reduced physical capacity to perform due to overtraining, poor recovery from injury or setbacks in physical therapy following injury, depression, and considering a premature separation or termination from sport. Yet while some athletes seek help for the negative consequences of their overinvolvement, other circumstances may lead to consultation with the sport psychologist. Athletes with a compulsive approach to sports may seek services when they have lost or are threatened with the loss of a significant other (due to their lack of availability in the relationship), when substance abuse or similarly destructive compulsive behaviors develop as a means of coping with the excessive stress associated with overinvolvement, and *following* the termination of their careers, having lost their major, and possibly only, source of self-esteem (discussed in chapter 10).

Overcompensation for failure and negativity, extreme standards, and self-punishing schemas may all be associated with overinvolvement and need to be carefully assessed by the clinical sport psychologist. Exploring these cognitive schemas often reveals a contingent environment in which the individual had to perform well in order to receive praise and acceptance and maintain interpersonal connection to significant caretakers. In some circumstances, compulsive perfectionistic efforts were the primary escape from stressful or chaotic home environments.

The primary coping behaviors associated with each of these schemas are compulsive, perfectionistic behaviors. Perfectionism is a poorly understood phenomenon that has recently garnered attention in the sport and clinical science literature (Anshel, 2003; Ellis & Knaus, 1977). It has been conceptualized as a coping strategy to reduce or avoid negative affective states such as anxiety. A recent study by Wagner and Gardner (2005) investigated the relationship between perfectionism, experiential avoidance, and psychological distress among 120 university student athletes and nonathletes. Experiential avoidance was found to mediate a strong relationship between perfectionism and psychological distress. Interestingly, this study also indicated that there were no differences in level of perfectionism or in the psychological distress related to perfectionism, when comparing athletes and nonathletes.

There is an obvious relationship between perfectionism and overinvolved, compulsive approaches to athletic performance. Some have argued that there is a healthy form of perfectionism in which attention to detail and systematic goal-directed behavior predominates. It is the compulsive unremitting perfectionism at the expense of life satisfaction, and not the healthy striving for success, that is problematic. Extreme perfectionism often results in misplaced training efforts, as the larger picture is masked by each and every minor detail of training.

Because of the positive rewards associated with compulsive overinvolvement in sport, intervening to promote change is not easy. The majority of athletes seeking consultation for overinvolvement come in the door looking for help dealing with the *consequences* of this pattern, such as marital conflict, overtraining, or substance use, and not for help altering the compulsive and perfectionistic involvement in sport that leads to these consequences. Since this athlete typically views only the consequences of overinvolvement as the problem (and not the overinvolvement itself), readiness for change may be a viable concern. Prochaska, DiClemente, and Norcross (1992) have described stages of change that are particularly relevant in these circumstances. In their model, behavior change follows discrete phases that essentially correspond to

a) the period in which an individual is not fully cognizant of the need to change and seeks consultation on the advice or requirement of others (precontemplation stage);

b) the period in which an individual considers the costs and benefits of change and is facing her behavioral patterns and their consequences for the first time (contemplation stage);

c) the period in which an individual determines that change is necessary and becomes committed to the idea that active effort at change is in his best interests (action stage); and

d) the period in which an individual actively engages in maintaining and reinforcing change (maintenance stage).

This model was developed primarily in working with individuals requiring behavioral change who were typically forced into treatment by society or those close to them.

Interventions for the overinvolved athlete can include motivational interviewing and schema-focused cognitive behavioral interventions, both targeting different processes. Motivational interviewing can be used as a pretreatment strategy or as a complete intervention to help individuals move from the precontemplation stage to the action stage, where the athlete is ready to make an effort to change (Burke, Arkowitz, & Menchola, 2003). Motivational interviewing has gathered some empirical support and may be a sound first step in counseling these individuals. Once motivational interviewing has helped the athlete commit to change, a schema-focused cognitive-behavioral intervention (Young et al., 2003) will help them recognize their overlearned and dysfunctional patterns, modify both cognitive and behavioral processes associated with early maladaptive cognitive schemas, and develop greater tolerance for uncertainty and lack of control (features essential to modifying worry and perfectionism). An accepting and nonthreatening therapeutic relationship is important in such interventions, as these athletes tend to overinterpret and respond intensely to perceived judgments, frustration, and rejection. The clinical sport psychologist needs to fully understand and respect the athlete's fear of loss of identity and loss of control as change efforts are initiated.

An additional strategy is developing personal valued goals apart from athletic valued goals based on athlete status. Again, valued goals (as opposed to achievement goals) refer to the journey and process of life, not the end-point destina-

Summary of Typical Pdy-II Issues

Common Pdy-II Difficulties

Primarily internal concerns, such as

- Patterns of avoidance and underinvolvement
- Resistance to authority
- Procrastination
- Temporary performance dysfunction and slumps
- Fear of failure or success

Patterns of overinvolvement

- Workaholism
- Extreme perfectionism

tion (Hayes et al., 1999). Discussing which type of person the athlete wants to be known as and which nonathletic relationships or activities have personal meaning can adjunctively help a comprehensive intervention. Many athletes believe that athletic success and overinvolved behaviors are inextricably connected. As such, they must learn slowly and patiently that they can intertwine hard work and goal-directed behavior with other life pursuits, and that reducing intensity can actually effectuate achievement of athletic and other valued goals.

Final Thoughts

Over the course of this chapter we have reviewed numerous examples of performance dysfunction. Typically, the primary causes of performance dysfunction are dispositional psychological characteristics and external events. These exogenous and endogenous factors can be barriers to the ultimate goal of optimal athletic performance. At the same time, these subclinical psychological characteristics and responses to external factors can cause personal distress and reduce quality of life apart from competitive sports. These characteristics and events do not typically reflect diagnosable clinical disorders, although at times they may be subclinical forms of similar clinical concerns. These difficulties and barriers require psychological treatment and are typically inappropriate (at least initially) for traditional psychological skills training for performance enhancement.

This discussion highlights the need to view athletes and their performance concerns holistically, understanding that competitive sports involve a complex combination of personal, sport, and nonsport issues. There are numerous reasons for athletic performance dysfunction, as is the case with general life dysfunction. We hope we demonstrated the need to consider the balance of psychological, physical, technical, and situational factors and to guard against readily assuming that simplistic or nonspecific interventions can have an effect on this complex balance. In the next chapter, we discuss the more clinical athlete concerns such as anxiety disorders, depressive disorders, eating disorders, and attention deficit disorders associated with the MCS-SP classification of performance impairment-I (PI-I).

CHAPTER 8

Performance Impairment-I (PI-I)

This chapter and the next discuss the wide range of clinical disorders that impair both athletics and other major life domains. We also describe the most well-established, evidence-based interventions for the clinical disorders commonly encountered by clinical sport psychologists.

As discussed in chapter 3, clinical disorders are most appropriately classified as performance impairment (PI) by the MCS-SP. PI classifications are characterized by decrements in competitive performance that, while quite possibly the initial reason for referral, are secondary to significant psychological distress and disruption in overall life functioning. PI referrals are most commonly associated with specific *DSM-IV-TR* (APA, 2000) diagnoses and require clinical treatment as the first-line intervention despite concomitant impairments in athletic performance.

Differentiating psychological disorders from other factors (performance changes, health concerns, and so on) is conceptually and clinically complex and requires careful assessment (see chapter 4). Many individuals who seek consultation from a clinical sport psychologist are experiencing anxiety, depression, or other symptoms that require clinical attention and treatment. Of course, since athletes with such difficulties do not always directly present these issues during initial sessions, the practitioner must remember to thoroughly assess for clinical symptomatology.

To review, in the MCS-SP, performance impairment (PI) classification refers to athlete's presenting with clear clinical issues that involve significant emotional distress or behavioral dysregulation that affects both their athletic pursuits and overall functioning in other important life domains. These clinical issues can be either intrapersonal or interpersonal in nature, and require direct clinical treatment instead of performance enhancement.

As you will recall, there are two PI subtypes within the MCS-SP. PI-I designates clinical disorders or comorbid clinical conditions that severely impair general functioning (including athletic performance). The specific disorders included in this category are anxiety disorders, affective (mood) disorders, eating disorders, and attention deficit disorders. PI-I is the focus of this chapter. The second PI subtype, PI-II, is covered in detail in the next chapter, though this chapter covers the basic elements of both subtypes together. PI-II also indicates severe impairment among major life domains and athletic participation. However, the PI-II subtype includes athletes who are experiencing significant behavioral dysregulation such as anger and impulse control disorders, alcohol use disorders, drug use disorders, and personality disorders. Such behavioral dysregulation eventually results in interpersonal, familial, and occupational impairment, and the behavioral disruption frequently places the athlete at risk for termination from athletic participation.

While athletes experiencing PI will likely report (at least intermittently) significant difficulties in competitive performance, the clinical sport psychologist *must* maintain perspective and view these performance decrements as secondary to the general psychological distress and reduced functioning characteristic of PI disorders. In fact, these athletic performance decrements are likely a direct result of the athlete's psychological distress or behavioral dysregulation. This is analogous to a nonathlete with similar psychological distress who presents with reduced efficiency in the work place.

As noted in chapter 4, sport psychologists should carefully assess the overall psychosocial functioning of athletes to either rule out or confirm PI. When PI is noted by a practitioner not certified or licensed to engage in psychological treatment, it must be referred to a professional trained to treat such complex cases. PI cases cover the entire range of psychological difficulties experienced by human beings. The most frequent examples of PI encountered by the clinical sport psychologist are anxiety disorders, mood disorders, eating disorders, attention deficit disorders, anger and impulse control disorders, alcohol use disorders, substance use disorders, and personality disorders.

One important question to answer is: If these problems are within the traditional purview of clinical psychology, psychiatry, and similar mental health professions, what does the clinical sport psychologist offer that the mental health practitioner not trained in sport psychology does not? The answer requires us to view the sport experience and the experience of competitive athletics in terms of culture. While the influence of culture on psychosocial treatment variables is commonly accepted, cultural influences in professional psychology typically focus on race, gender, socioeconomic status, sexual orientation, and ethnicity. These factors are certainly all important. However, when considering the full context within which motor skills merge with individual psychological strengths and weaknesses to result in athletic performance, both the general and specific sport culture are important components of that context.

Sport culture refers to the attitudes and expectations inherent in competitive sports. The ever-present focus on personal and team success, the ongoing pressure to win, the physically demanding lifestyle, and the ongoing physical comparisons and physical competition among athletes all contribute to the context within which specific performance concerns and personal psychological functioning must be understood. The specific aspects of the sport culture refer to specific sport, team, and organizational realities, such as the inherent machismo realities of American football, the weight requirements in wrestling or gymnastics, the team atmosphere created by specific coaches, and the specific expectations and climate that exist within certain organizations.

To comprehensively understand the athlete's issues and needs and to subsequently decide on treatment approaches, sport-specific cultural factors should be considered and appropriately integrated. This is true for both the performance and clinical issues presented to the clinical sport psychologist. Sport cultural influences need to be considered to the same degree that racial, ethnic, and other traditional cultural factors are considered.

Issues such as gender, ethnicity, socioeconomic status, race, and sport-specific culture are important to consider when working with an athlete or team.

The remainder of this chapter discusses in detail the specific disorders that lead to an MCS-SP classification of PI-I, which are also the disorders frequently confronted by the clinical sport psychologist. The following chapter discusses the disorders leading to an MCS-SP classification of PI-II. Readers interested in a more comprehensive discussion of particular disorders should refer to *A Guide to Treatments That Work, Second Edition* (Nathan & Gorman, 2002), which details the empirically supported interventions for *DSM-IV* disorders. Our discussion of each problem domain includes

- an overview of diagnostic considerations and presenting complaints;
- relevant issues, how sport cultural factors may affect treatment, and how athletic performance may be affected by (and possibly mask) the disorder;
- a brief guide to assessing the clinical disorder; and
- descriptions of the empirically supported treatments available at this time (when available).

Anxiety Disorders

The salient feature of all anxiety disorders is intense personal discomfort, typically in the form of specific or generalized fears, which results in ongoing efforts to reduce or completely avoid the discomfort (Barlow, 2002). The discomfort is often described as apprehension, fearfulness, concern about going crazy, or even terror, and associated physical symptoms include palpitations, choking sensations, and muscle tremors. Various forms of mental and physical avoidance such as worry; physical avoidance of people, places, or things; repetitive rituals; and similar internal or external behaviors temporarily reduce the client's negative affect (personal distress) and negatively reinforce even greater avoidance. As such, the avoidant behavior that typifies anxiety disorders tends to increase over time, disrupting the client's overall functioning and further exacerbating the anxiety itself. The behavioral avoidance seen across all anxiety disorders is considered to be the major source of life disruption (Hayes et al., 1996).

The next sections discuss the specific forms of anxiety disorders clinical sport psychologists most often see. For the complete diagnostic criteria for these disorders, readers should refer to the *DSM-IV-TR* (APA, 2000).

Panic Disorder

Epidemiological data suggest that 2 to 6% of the population (including athletes) experience symptoms of panic disorder at some point. For most of these individuals, symptoms begin between adolescence and the mid-30s, and 72% report a significant life stressor such as injury, illness, relationship breakup, job loss, or death of a significant family member as a direct causative event (APA, 2000; Craske & Barlow, 2001).

Characteristics

Panic disorder is characterized by periods of intense fear or discomfort accompanied by symptoms such as palpitations, sensations of choking, nausea, dizziness, lightheadedness, fear of going crazy, and tingling or numbness (Craske & Barlow, 2001). Individuals with this disorder report recurrent and seemingly unexpected attacks of anxiety or panic and its associated physical symptoms. In addition, these individuals continually worry over the threat of additional attacks and the anticipated consequences. This disorder often resembles cardiac distress and results in emergency room visits for (misinterpreted) possible cardiac emergencies. Clients focus on these panic attacks to the point that fear of a panic attack (anxiety *about* anxiety) becomes the central feature of the condition. Scanning bodily sensations, including physical signs that are normally ignored, dominates conscious awareness. Individuals engage in behavioral avoidance in an attempt to prevent further attacks. However, this avoidance tends to occur in response to a widening variety of external or internal stimuli, substantially reducing behavioral flexibility and impairing life functioning up to and including self-restriction to the home environment (agoraphobia).

Particularly troubling to the athlete experiencing panic disorder is that physical activity, with its natural bodily changes (increased heart rate, increased respiration, and so on) often triggers attacks, as the athlete interprets the natural physiological changes as signaling impending danger (i.e., a new attack). This false-alarm response to normal physiological processes has been noted as a primary clinical component of panic disorder (Barlow, 2002). Athletes experiencing panic disorder often lose energy, concentration, and motivation, and may appear poorly conditioned to staff and teammates (based on shortness of breath, rapid heart rate, dizziness, and so on). Even worse, others may misinterpret their inattentiveness to team activities and mistakenly view these athletes as lacking effort. Competitive athletes experiencing panic disorder may find it hard to accept the lack of clear medical explanation or cause of their symptoms and may be reluctant to discuss these symptoms for fear of being seen as crazy (a concern that they themselves may actually hold). The symptom cluster of panic disorder and the cognitive focus on internal processes at the expense of external sport focus make this condition particularly likely to affect athletic performance as well as other major life domains.

Assessment

Assessment for panic disorder should include a careful functional analysis of behavior (described in chapter 4) in order to fully understand the situational triggers, affective and physiological responses, and negative reinforcement properties of the specific avoidance behaviors adopted by the athlete. In addition, a medical evaluation is suggested to rule out potential cardiac explanations as well as other medical explanations such as thyroid conditions, caffeine or amphetamine abuse, drug withdrawal, or adrenal cancer (Craske & Barlow, 2001). Some medical conditions such as mitral valve prolapse, asthma, allergies, and hypoglycemia can exacerbate, although typically not cause, symptoms of panic disorder by initiating physical symptoms that the client misinterprets as evidence of impending attacks.

It is also critical to evaluate the specific contexts in which panic attacks occur. Although the occurrence of panic attacks is only a specific criterion for a diagnosis of panic disorder according to the *DSM-IV-TR*, panic attacks can occur in the context of other anxiety disorders, such as social anxiety disorder and generalized anxiety disorder, and can even occur in individuals who have no diagnosable psychological disorders (Beidel & Nay, 2003). A diagnosis of panic disorder should never be given when the panic attacks only occur during social and evaluative situations, as this context suggests a more accurate diagnosis of social anxiety disorder. Clinical sport psychologists should never assume that the presence of panic attacks automatically warrants a panic disorder diagnosis, and should conduct a thorough assessment of situational triggers and contexts in which panic attacks occur prior to diagnosing this disorder.

Several self-report measures are available to help assess panic conditions. The Albany Panic and Phobia Questionnaire (APPQ) (Rapee, Craske, & Barlow, 1995) comprehensively assesses fear and avoidance of activities that heighten physical sensations via a 32-item standardized questionnaire. Other standardized self-report tools for panic disorder include the Agoraphobic Cognitions Questionnaire (ACQ), which measures fearful cognitions (Chambless, Caputo, Bright, & Gallagher, 1984); the Body Sensations Questionnaire (BSQ), which measures fear intensity, arousal, and associated physical symptoms (Chambless et al., 1984); and the Anxiety Control Questionnaire (Rapee, Craske, Brown, & Barlow, 1996).

Treatment

The well-established empirically supported treatment for panic disorder, as most clearly articulated by the panic control treatment protocol of Craske and Barlow (2001), is a structured, 15-session cognitive-behavioral intervention that focuses on

- client education about anxiety and panic;
- cognitive restructuring to correct misconceptions about anxiety and automatic thoughts that overestimate threat and danger;
- interoceptive exposure to help clients systematically experience increasingly intense physiological sensations without the usual pattern of avoidance;
- situational exposure to allow clients to systematically approach and experience previously avoided life situations; and
- acquisition of coping skills such as controlled breathing.

A recent review of treatment data suggests that cognitive behavioral therapies for panic disorder significantly improve panic disorder in up to 80% of participants, with maintenance up to 2 y (Craske & Barlow, 2001). A review of randomized controlled trials of CBT for panic disorder, psychopharmacology, and the two combined suggests that CBT for panic disorder results in an effect size of 0.88, with dropout rates of approximately 5.6%. Psychopharmacology alone and the combined use of psychopharmacology and CBT result in effect sizes and dropout rates of 0.47 and 9.8% and 0.56 and 22%, respectively (Gould, Otto, & Pollack, 1995). Given that there are currently no data on how psychotropic medications for panic disorder may affect athletic performance, the clinical sport psychologist should carefully collaborate with the athlete and a sports medicine practitioner in order to provide treatment options and discuss the potential costs and benefits of combining CBT with psychopharmacology.

Generalized Anxiety Disorder

Lifetime prevalence rates for generalized anxiety disorder (GAD) indicate that 2 to 5% of the population (including athletes) suffer from this disorder (APA, 2000). Symptoms usually begin during childhood or adolescence, and most individuals with GAD report that they have always felt some anxiety. Without treatment, individuals with GAD typically experience an unremitting, chronic course of anxiety that worsens during periods of stress.

Characteristics

Generalized anxiety disorder is characterized by excessive worry (often referred to as apprehensive expectation) that is difficult to control and results in symptoms such as concentration difficulties, fatigue and sleep disturbance, restlessness, muscular tension, and irritability (APA, 2000). This anxiety and its associated avoidant behaviors can lead to distress and impairment in social, occupational, and family functioning (Beidel & Nay, 2003). The nature and function of worry (see chapter 2) should be considered the single most distinguishing feature of GAD. Although GAD is often comorbid with other anxiety disorders (and depression) (Brown, O'Leary, & Barlow, 2001), it is markedly different than other anxiety disorders. GAD appears to be more characterological than other anxiety disorders, in that individuals suffering from it typically experience chronic worry their entire lives (Barlow, Raffa, & Cohen, 2002).

The symptom cluster for GAD often precludes successful competitive performance. As with panic disorder, the symptoms of GAD can easily be misunderstood by both the athlete and team staff, and can be misinterpreted as a medical condition, case of substance abuse, or lack of personal motivation. Once again, athletes with GAD may hesitate to seek help. Further, although the pathological worry central to GAD is quantitatively different than normal, adaptive forms of worry, athletes may see their pathological worry as necessary, or even responsible, for athletic success. An example of this would be an athlete who worries excessively about his health, grades, family, relationships, and sport experience, and scans the world for possible misfortune. By engaging in excessive worry and continuously scanning his environment, he believes he is less prone to misfortune, and believes this worry is a primary cause for his success.

As previously noted, subclinical worry, while not meeting GAD criteria, may also interfere with athletic performance and would thus be classified as Pdy-II by the MCS-SP. The clinical sport psychologist should carefully assess clients presenting symptoms consistent with GAD to discriminate subclinical and clinical levels of worry, particularly when athletic performance is a central worry domain. While it can disrupt athletic performance, subclinical worry is less pervasive and less severe than GAD, and culminates in less functional impairment for the athlete. Thus, subclinical and clinical manifestations should be differentiated in order to determine intervention needs.

Assessment

Assessment of generalized anxiety disorder begins with a careful interview. This can be done through an interview format such as the Anxiety Disorders Interview Schedule for *DSM-IV* (ADIS-IV-L) (Brown, DiNardo, & Barlow, 1994; DiNardo, Brown, & Barlow, 1994). The ADIS-IV is a semistructured interview based on *DSM-IV* anxiety disorder criteria that provides differential diagnoses for the entire spectrum of anxiety disorders. When diagnosing GAD, it is particularly important to evaluate the excessiveness, pervasiveness, and perceived uncontrollability of worry. The Penn State Worry Questionnaire (PSWQ) (Meyer et al., 1990) is also often utilized to diagnose GAD. This questionnaire is a self-report form measuring worry from normal to pathological levels. The questionnaire is incredibly quick to administer (3 min) and assesses both the intensity and the excessiveness of the client's worry. Translated and child and adolescent versions are available.

Treatment

To date, the most empirically supported treatment for GAD has been a form of cognitive behavioral therapy (CBT) specific for GAD (Brown et al., 2001). This treatment typically consists of 15 sessions and includes

- psychoeducation on the nature and function of worry, the development of GAD, the treatment protocol, and expectations for treatment;
- self-monitoring to understand the client's responses to the intervention, to gain a full functional analysis, and to track treatment compliance;
- cognitive restructuring with an emphasis on identifying automatic thoughts, a specific focus on the client's tendency to catastrophize (thinking one is unable to handle a

negative event) and engage in "probability overestimation" (overestimating the likelihood of a negative event happening), and an effort to counter cognitive distortions;

- progressive muscle relaxation exercises to combat the physiological aspects of GAD by appropriately interpreting physiological sensations;

- exposure to major hierarchical spheres of worry (worry exposure), imagery training, and worry-behavior prevention, all of which address the behavioral component of GAD; and

- training in problem solving (particularly within the interpersonal domain) and time management, also addressing the behavioral component of GAD.

Generalized anxiety disorder is a more chronic, characterological disorder than the other anxiety disorders, and as such, it is more difficult to effectively treat. Randomized controlled trials have demonstrated the superiority of cognitive behavioral treatments to applied relaxation or nondirective counseling (Borkovec & Costello, 1993), behavior therapy (Butler, Fennell, Robson, & Gelder, 1991), and psychodynamically oriented psychotherapy (Durham et al., 1994). Despite numerous clinical trials demonstrating its efficacy, CBT helps only 55 to 60% of clients reach high-end functioning (so they no longer meet criteria for diagnosis), though a far greater percentage demonstrate significant improvement (although still meeting criteria for diagnosis). Newer interventions not yet attaining the well-established level of empirical support have demonstrated promising initial results. These newer treatments integrate the effective components of CBT, such as psychoeducation and self-monitoring, with acceptance-based approaches similar to those described in chapter 6. These approaches develop mindful action in the pursuit of valued goals as an alternative to the habitual inaction and avoidance that accompanies pathological worry (Orsillo, Roemer, & Barlow, 2003).

Social Anxiety Disorder

Prevalence data suggest that up to 13% of all adults (including athletes) experience social anxiety disorder (SAD) during their lifetime (Kessler et al., 1994) and that the prevalence of SAD is actually increasing (Magee, Eaton, Wittchen, McGonagle, & Kessler, 1996). Symptoms can develop gradu-

ally or quickly following a highly stressful event. Onset typically occurs during childhood or adolescence, and symptoms may fluctuate over time due to changing life circumstances and demands (APA, 2000).

Characteristics

Social anxiety disorder, frequently referred to as social phobia, is an often disabling disorder marked by fear of scrutiny in social situations. This form of anxiety revolves around concerns about humiliation, inadequate performance, or the display of outwardly visible signs of anxiety. Many athletes with this disorder report that the fear of scrutiny or negative evaluation includes situations involving competitive performance. As such, this category subsumes problems of competitive anxiety discussed in the sport psychology literature. Individuals suffering from SAD may fear the negative evaluations inherent in social interactions, public speaking, or performances of complex motor tasks (such as athletic or musical performances) that could be disrupted by muscle tremors or lack of concentration. As this fear typically leads to avoidance of particular or generalized social performances, SAD can significantly impair day-to-day routines and social or occupational functioning (Beidel & Nay, 2003; Turk et al., 2001). In addition, the avoidance, functional impairment, and reduced quality of life inherent in SAD commonly result in comorbid clinical depression (Turk et al., 2001), as social reinforcement decreases and negative beliefs regarding the self, others, and the future subsequently increase.

Understanding social anxiety disorder is particularly important for the clinical sport psychologist, as this disorder involves both social-evaluative and performance-evaluative anxieties. Obviously, athletes commonly experience anxiety (before and during competition) to some degree, but it is only situations of excessive or functionally disruptive anxiety that warrant a diagnosis of SAD. Athletes with nonpathological competitive anxiety typically demonstrate periods of self-focused attention during which they may be distracted and inattentive to performance-related demands. Yet, such individuals are able to regain focus and continue to meet the demands of competition. On the other hand, athletes with SAD will experience more severe anxiety based on ongoing social and performance evaluation, will be less able to regain task-focused attention, will respond poorly to (real or perceived) performance failures, and may begin to avoid performance situations altogether to minimize their psychological distress. Of course, many athletes without clinical levels of anxiety report that feeling anxious before and during competition allows them to get pumped up, gain focus, and prepare for the performance situation. Based on such self-reports, the clinical sport psychologist may begin to view such concerns as contextually appropriate, and may therefore minimize the presence of a clinical disorder. Performance-related worry, anxiety, and fears should therefore be carefully evaluated to determine if the athlete excessively incorporates an audience effect. The audience effect is the degree to which anxiety is based on fears of humiliation and external evaluation of moment-to-moment performance. It is not difficult to imagine how a competitive athlete could justify performance anxiety as a normal and even necessary part of athletic life, but the clinical sport psychologist must be able to differentiate nonclinical, subclinical, and clinical levels. It is therefore essential that the clinical sport psychologist carefully assess for SAD, especially with athletes reporting at least moderate levels of competitive anxiety. Automatically assuming SAD is absent and engaging in interventions directed at self-regulating athletic performance may harm the athlete who does battle this disorder, as untreated SAD can quickly lead to situational or competitive avoidance and eventually to athletic disengagement. In addition to the audience effect, several other factors help diagnose SAD. Generally speaking, the athlete with SAD (Turk et al., 2001)

- allocates significant attention to indicators of negative performance evaluation by others;
- perceives internal cues (i.e., physiological signs of anxiety) as clearly observable by an audience; and
- demonstrates a predominant mental representation of the self as seen by others and compares that representation to an assumed audience standard.

While these characteristics are typically not as intense in nonpathological levels of competitive anxiety, the differences between nonpathological and pathological anxiety are usually more quantitative than qualitative. As such, nonpathological (subclinical) levels of SAD are found in many presentations of performance difficulties.

Assessment

Assessment of SAD requires a careful interview, possibly using the ADIS-IV (Brown et al., 1994; DiNardo et al., 1994) for differential diagnoses. Additional useful measures include self-report instruments such as the Social Phobia Scale (SPS), which measures fears of negative evaluation based on routine activities (Mattick & Clarke, 1998), and the Social Interaction Anxiety Scale (SIAS), which assesses fears related to general situations and social events (Mattick & Clarke, 1998). The Social Phobia and Anxiety Inventory (SPAI) assesses the symptom severity of social anxiety (Turner, Beidel, Dancu, & Stanley, 1989) and the Fear of Negative Evaluation Scale (FNE) (Watson & Friend, 1969) targets the core constructs related to negative evaluation and performance evaluation concerns. Sport-specific instruments such as the Sport Anxiety Scale (SAS) (Smith et al., 1990) and Sport Competition Anxiety Test (SCAT) (Martens, 1977) may also be useful, but they should be used cautiously as they have not been standardized with the goal of identifying social anxiety disorder.

Treatment

At this time, cognitive behavioral treatments incorporating client education about SAD and CBT, cognitive restructuring, and graded prolonged exposure to increasingly challenging social-performance situations meet the well-established criteria for empirical support and are clearly the psychosocial treatments of choice (Barlow et al., 2002). A particularly well-researched SAD treatment protocol is cognitive-behavioral group therapy (CBGT) (Turk et al., 2001). Although CBGT delivers the prescribed treatment to a group of clients, an individual version of the protocol is available. Since individuals who engage in behavioral restriction to minimize social-evaluative fears often limit the number of social interactions they have, CBGT provides a logical treatment format. For the athlete with less severe symptomatology, the individual format can be used. Effective treatments of SAD usually include 12 to 24 sessions, depending on the severity of the disorder. Current research indicates that 70 to 75% of SAD clients treated with CBT reach high-end functioning (no longer meeting the criteria for SAD). Very few of these clients relapse within 6 mo of treatment (Barlow et al., 2002).

Results from treatment studies comparing psychopharmacology (Phenelzine) and CBT for social anxiety disorder are mixed (Heimberg et al., 1998). At present, evidence suggests that both treatment approaches are effective interventions for SAD, although competitive athletes should consult with a sports medicine practitioner to ascertain the likely performance effects of the SAD medication (Heimberg et al., 1998).

Obsessive-Compulsive Disorder

Obsessive-compulsive disorder (OCD) occurs in approximately 2.5% of the population (APA, 2000) and tends to vary in intensity throughout one's life if left untreated. Symptoms occasionally begin during childhood, but OCD typically comes on gradually during adolescence or early adulthood (Foa & Franklin, 2001). Similar to social anxiety disorder, OCD symptomatology may remit at times and is usually heightened during significant distress.

Characteristics

Obsessive-compulsive disorder is characterized by recurrent obsessions or compulsions that substantially interfere with daily functioning and cause significant personal distress. At some time during the disorder, the individual must recognize that his symptomatology is illogical or irrational (APA, 2000). The characteristic obsessions can best be described as "persistent ideas, thoughts, impulses, or images that are experienced as intrusive and inappropriate and that cause marked anxiety or distress" (APA, 2000, p. 457). The client responds by engaging in compulsive behaviors, which are repetitive overt or covert behaviors that serve to reduce the anxiety and related psychological distress (Beidel & Nay, 2003). By reducing the anxiety or distress, these compulsive behaviors are repeatedly negatively reinforced and thus overlearned. As with all anxiety disorders, the goal of anxiety avoidance inherent in OCD leads to growing behavioral restriction that increasingly impairs social and occupational domains (Foa & Franklin, 2001).

While the competitive athlete is generally no more or less prone to OCD than the rest of the population, there are two particular situations in which OCD may prevail. The first involves precompetitive routines. While most athletes develop personal precompetitive routines, which the professional literature suggests strongly relate to positive athletic performance (Hardy et al., 1996), these routines may at times become superstitious rituals. Superstitious rituals are not problematic in and of themselves and are not inherently related to OCD. However, athletes predisposed to anxiety disorders (individuals with extreme moral standards and guilt) (Foa & Franklin, 2001) may view these superstitious rituals as the primary reason

for positive athletic outcomes, and may also use them to reduce competitive anxiety. When used excessively, used as a form of avoidance (of distress), and when performance success is attributed only to their use, these superstitious rituals can negatively affect both athletic and social functioning and fulfill criteria for OCD. While we must state that the development of OCD through competitive rituals is certainly not common, the clinical sport psychologist may be called upon to evaluate and possibly intervene in cases where the athlete predisposed to anxiety refuses to perform when his preset conditions are not right.

The second situation is body dysmorphic disorder (APA, 2000), in which preoccupation with perceived flaws in appearance markedly distress the athlete and impair life functioning. In this very specific disorder, often viewed as a type of OCD, an athlete may become preoccupied with an imagined physical defect or become excessively concerned with one or more physical features. Athletes who engage in sports that evaluate physical attributes, such as body builders or figure skaters, may be contextually vulnerable.

Assessment

In addition to a careful and comprehensive interview, several scales can help assess OCD. In addition to the ADIS-IV, the most common scale for diagnosing OCD is the Yale-Brown Obsessive-Compulsive Scale (Y-BOCS) (Goodman, Price, Rasmussen, Mazure, Fleischmann, et al., 1989; Goodman, Price, Rasmussen, Mazure, Delgado, et al., 1989), which is a standardized, semistructured 10-item questionnaire measuring symptom presence and severity. This questionnaire is useful, as there are versions adapted for children (Scahill et al., 1997) and for those with body dysmorphic disorder (Phillips et al., 1997). Also, the Compulsive Activity Checklist (CAC) (Freund, Steketee, & Foa, 1987; Philpott, 1975) is a self-report tool that measures the degree to which compulsive behaviors interfere with daily life activities. The CAC can be administered in 5 min.

Treatment

The treatment for OCD that has attained the well-established level of empirical support is a 15 session behavioral intervention conducted in either an individual or group format. The intervention begins by educating the client about the disorder, followed by a structured intervention referred to as exposure and ritual prevention (EX/RP) (Foa & Franklin, 2001; Meyer, 1966). Due to the nature of

OCD and the obvious need for intense treatment to break the strongly overlearned obsessive thoughts and compulsive rituals, the 15 sessions are often massed into a 3 wk, 5 d/wk, 2 h/session format (Foa & Franklin, 2001). The EX/RP component involves both "prolonged exposure to obsessional cues and procedures aimed at blocking rituals" (Foa & Franklin, 2001, p. 217). The exposure evolves from imaginal exposure exercises (thoughts and images related to the feared stimuli) to in vivo exercises (real-life exposure to the feared stimuli), focusing on a wide variety of both external and internal anxiety-producing stimuli. This strategy is based on the supported theory that "repeated, prolonged exposure to feared thoughts and situations provides information that disconfirm mistaken associations and evaluations held by the patients and thereby promotes habituation" (Foa & Franklin, 2001, p. 217).

Another critical component of this behavioral treatment is ritual prevention (i.e., refraining from self-inspection), which often utilizes family members for support. Following the 15 sessions of intensive intervention, there are often up to 12 additional maintenance sessions, which appear to substantially reduce relapse (Foa & Franklin, 2001). While many practitioners add cognitive restructuring (cognitive modification) to this treatment package, the available outcome data suggest conflicting evidence as to its value (Hiss, Foa, & Kozak, 1994). Body dysmorphic disorder is the exception to this finding, as clinical trials indicate that a combination of exposure to anxiety-producing situations, ritual prevention, cognitive restructuring focusing on identifying and challenging distorted body perceptions, and interruption of self-critical thought processes demonstrates improvement in 50 to 75% of clients (Franklin & Foa, 2002).

In clinical trials of EX/RP for obsessive-compulsive disorder, up to 75% of treated individuals demonstrate high-end functioning at the end of treatment (particularly with the additional maintenance sessions), and most remain symptom free at 6 mo follow-up (Hiss et al., 1994). There is, however, a subset of the population for whom this treatment remains ineffective, and for those individuals, psychopharmacology is indicated (Kozak, Liebowitz, & Foa, 2000).

Posttraumatic Stress Disorder

Epidemiological studies suggest that at least 20.4% of women and 8.2% of men are likely to develop posttraumatic stress disorder (PTSD) following exposure to trauma (Resick & Calhoun, 2001), and approximately 40% of these individuals develop it within 3 mo following the traumatic event (Rothbaum & Foa, 1993). The disorder can develop at any age (including childhood). However, following a traumatic event, the amount of time prior to the onset of symptoms can vary greatly among individuals. Symptoms can develop quickly following exposure or may be delayed for months or even years before fully developing into a clinical disorder (APA, 2000). Possible traumatic events include combat, terrorism, motor vehicle accidents, sexual assault, natural disaster, crime victimization, and physical injury (Kessler, Sonnega, Bromet, Hughes, & Nelson, 1995; Resick & Calhoun, 2001).

Characteristics

The *DSM-IV-TR* describes posttraumatic stress disorder as a response to witnessing, experiencing, or otherwise confronting an event that involves (actual or possible) death or injury (APA, 2000). In addition, a PTSD diagnosis requires an intense emotional response to the event. Symptoms of PTSD fall into three general categories (APA, 2000):

- Reexperiencing symptoms (flashbacks, intense psychological reactions to cues associated with the traumatic event)
- Avoidance and numbing symptoms (not thinking about or avoiding any and all cues associated with the trauma, emotional detachment)
- Physiological hyperarousal (hypervigilance, extreme startle response, irritability, decreased attention and concentration)

These symptoms often result in heightened behavioral restriction and impaired interpersonal relationships. Trauma leads to PTSD through the incomplete processing of intense emotion (such as fear) at the time of the trauma, along with altering cognitive schemas related to trust, intimacy, safety, personal competence, and responsibility (Resick & Calhoun, 2001).

With the high epidemiological rate of PTSD among both females and males (including athletes), the clinical sport psychologist will inevitably encounter this clinical presentation among athletes. PTSD is particularly concerning to the clinical sport psychologist in that its onset is unpredictable and its consequences can be extreme. In addition to the trauma victim's personal experience, the traumatic event may also residually affect those close to the athlete, including teammates. Furthermore, indirect trauma that occurs through watching or in some way intimately reliving an event can lead to PTSD symptoms in those who have previously experienced personal tragedy themselves. For example, an athlete who has a history of sexual trauma may experience PTSD symptoms following the sexual assault of a teammate. As such, the clinical sport psychologist working with teams should be both prepared for and open to subtle signs of these residual effects.

Athletic contexts deserving thoughtful consideration include the response of a close-knit team to one member's trauma and the culture of "show no emotion" often demonstrated in highly physical, male-dominated sports like American football. Realities such as these (and many more) could complicate intervention efforts. In the case of the close-knit team, a group intervention for the nonaffected athletes is also recommended. In a "show no emotion" situation, experiential avoidance will likely be extremely high, resulting in incomplete emotional processing (including verbal expression), which is thought to be a central mediator in PTSD development (Hayes et al., 1996).

There is a special subclass of traumatic events that is somewhat specific to competitive athletes. PTSD symptomatology and other forms of marked distress can follow severe and career-threatening injury. In fact, the prevalence rate for developing PTSD following injury has been reported as at least 9% of the general population (Resnick, Kilpatrick, Dansky, Saunders, & Best, 1993). This specialized topic is covered in chapter 10.

Assessment

The Structured Clinical Interview for *DSM-IV* Axis I Disorders (SCID-I) (First et al., 1997) is the most widely used tool for diagnosing PTSD. Also available are the Diagnostic Interview Schedule (DIS) (Robins, Cottler, Bucholz, & Compton, 1995), the ADIS-IV (Brown et al., 1994; DiNardo et al., 1994), and the PTSD Symptom Scale (Foa, Riggs, Dancu, & Rothbaum, 1993), which is a brief, semistructured measure including an interview and a 17-question self-report that provides diagnostic clarity and assesses symptom severity. The Purdue PTSD Scale-Revised (PPTS-R) (Lauterbach & Vrana, 1996) and the PTSD Checklist (PCL) (Blanchard, Jones-Alexander, Buckley, & Forneris, 1996; Weathers, Litz, Herman, Huska, & Keane, 1993, October) are additional 10 to 15 min self-reports with sound

psychometric properties that clarify diagnosis and symptom severity. Along with the clinical interview, each of these adjunctive measures can assist in correctly diagnosing posttraumatic stress disorder.

Treatment

Currently, cognitive processing therapy (CPT) is the most empirically supported intervention for PTSD. CPT integrates the cognitive components of traditional cognitive therapy with exposure-based interventions. The treatment consists of processing the traumatic memory, systematic imaginal exposure to traumatic cues, and restructuring the cognitions (belief systems) most typically related to trust, competence, and safety that the traumatic event altered (Resick & Calhoun, 2001). According to Foa and colleagues (Foa, Steketee, & Rothbaum, 1989), "systematic exposure to the traumatic memory in a safe environment serves to alter the feared memory, such that threat cues are reevaluated and habituated" (p. 172). CPT exposure involves having the client write accounts of different elements of the traumatic event, read the accounts to the therapist during the session and to themselves each day, and identify the discrepancies between the old belief system and the new information causing conflict. Thus, the exposure and cognitive restructuring components are integrated during treatment.

The goal of the exposure exercises is to eradicate threat cues. Yet, even once these threat cues are eliminated during treatment, the individual still has an altered set of beliefs about the self and the world based on the traumatic experience. Although the client will no longer excessively respond to threat cues in the environment, the altered cognitions will continue to cause marked distress. Thus, CPT includes cognitive restructuring as a core focus of treatment. Cognitive restructuring ameliorates this component of PTSD by eliciting the connection between previously held belief systems, the traumatic event, and the newly altered belief systems that now imply vulnerability, lack of safety, fear of intimacy, threats to personal competence, and lack of trust in the self, others, and the environment. The discrepancy among the old belief system and the new information causes an array of symptomatology, including heightened physiological arousal, cognitive distortions, and behavioral avoidance. As such, the cognitive restructuring component of CPT seeks to challenge the discrepancy between the previous belief system and the new belief system formed by the trauma. For example, prior to a sexual trauma, Lysette felt competent as an athlete, student, and friend; trusted others close to her; and held a fundamental belief that the world was generally a safe place. During her sophomore year in college, a friend sexually assaulted Lysette during a social engagement. Following the event and the subsequent onset of PTSD symptomatology, Lysette developed a belief system that challenged her previous view of herself, others, and the world. She began to experience low self-esteem, lost motivation in athletics, and disengaged from her previously valued friendships. In addition, Lysette became increasingly afraid of developing male relationships, trusted few people, and saw the world as inherently dangerous. Overcoming the alteration in Lysette's belief system is precisely the goal of CPT's cognitive restructuring component.

CPT is typically administered in an individual format across 9 to 12 sessions (Resick & Schnicke, 1993; Rothbaum & Foa, 1992), and it combines exposure exercises with direct efforts to alter the dysfunctional core beliefs of those experiencing PTSD symptoms. Between-session homework, often including narrative descriptions of various aspects of the traumatic event, is a major component of this treatment. Empirical data suggest that up to 90% of patients meeting pretreatment criteria for PTSD no longer meet criteria at posttest and follow-up when treated with CPT (Resick & Calhoun, 2001). Although the data suggest significant treatment gains are possible, readers interested in this treatment approach are encouraged to become very familiar with the specific components of this protocol prior to using it. Improper use of these procedures with PTSD victims can be retraumatizing and very detrimental to the client's overall well-being.

Mood Disorders

Mood disorders constitute a large number of psychotherapy referrals and represent a substantial number of athlete concerns. In fact, one reason why mood disorders prevail in clinical sport psychology is because they cause marked emotional distress and affect daily functioning to the point that individuals recognize they need assistance in order to feel and function better. Understandably, symptoms such as diminished interest in once enjoyable activities, dysphoric mood, fatigue, difficulty sleeping, and altered concentration

concern the athlete, as such symptoms inevitably affect both performance and daily functioning. Even if the athlete personally delays assistance, it is not uncommon for those close to the athlete (family, coaches, friends) to recommend treatment for what is obviously negatively affecting the athlete. Among the mood disorders classified in the *DSM-IV-TR* (APA, 2000), the most common mood disorders seen by sport psychologists are major depressive disorder, bipolar disorders, and dysthymic disorder, which all include a substantial deviation from normative mood states and have additional cognitive, behavioral, and physical symptomatology (Truax & Selthon, 2003). We discuss each separately.

Major Depressive Disorder

Major depressive disorder (MDD) is the most common psychological disorder among adolescents and adults, with a lifetime prevalence rate of 20 to 25% for women and 10 to 12% for men (Kessler et al., 1994). Although MDD can begin at any age, the peak years for onset are between ages 15 and 29 (Burke, Burke, Regier, & Rae, 1990). Clinical sport psychologists working in high school through postcollege athletic environments are certainly likely to encounter MDD. Depression is also the leading cause of disability in the United States, and it increases the risk of heart attack, stroke, diabetes, and cancer (National Institute of Mental Health [NIMH], 1999). Certainly, it is not easy to predict who will experience depression, but more than two-thirds of all individuals who experience one episode of depression experience additional episodes unless effectively treated (Teasdale et al., 2000). Early detection of this disorder is critical, as untreated MDD can have devastating effects in all major life domains (Truax & Selthon, 2003).

Characteristics

The salient feature of major depressive disorder is an almost daily dysphoric mood (lasting for at least 2 wk before examination) associated with low levels of pleasure or a loss of interest in most activities, particularly those which were previously satisfying (APA, 2000). Additional symptoms include psychomotor agitation or retardation, significant nonvolitional weight change, fatigue or loss of energy, sleep disturbance, decreased concentration, feelings of guilt or worthlessness, and recurrent suicidal ideation or thoughts of death. As many as 15% of individuals with severe MDD die by suicide (APA, 2000).

While depression can significantly disrupt functioning in nonsport domains, it also weakens the athlete's ability to handle minor performance errors, adjust to role changes, and recover from interpersonal disputes.

MDD usually reduces daily functioning across several life domains, and the athlete may display irritability with teammates or staff, loss of interest, lethargic behavior, and reduced concentration during practice or competition. The clinical sport psychologist should be especially aware of these symptom patterns, as they can readily be misinterpreted in the sport environment as loss of motivation, drug or alcohol use, lack of attention to self-care and training, and so on (Cogan, 2000). Such misinterpretations by teammates and staff can exacerbate depressive symptomatology, as those who are unaware of the depression may treat the athlete as if he is doing something *wrong*.

The most empirically supported pathological process associated with MDD is a stress-diathesis model in which biological and psychological vulnerabilities (early maladaptive schemas) are triggered by a significant event or series of events. When triggered, these schemas, or learned cognitive structures for appraising and interpreting the world, lead the individual to negatively interpret the self, others, and the future and to systematically withdraw from interpersonal and other activities that were previously rewarding (Young, Weinberger, & Beck, 2001). As a result, this withdrawal reduces positive (particularly social) reinforcement in the athlete's life and further exacerbates the depressive symptomatology.

Assessment

As with other disorders, correctly diagnosing the various mood disorders requires a careful and comprehensive interview and client history. The Structured Clinical Interview for *DSM-IV* Axis I Dis-

orders (SCID-I) (First et al., 1997) and the Diagnostic Interview Schedule (DIS) (Robins et al., 1995) are two interview formats that carefully examine signs and symptoms of the various *DSM* mood disorders. The Diagnostic Interview for Children and Adolescents (DICA) (Herjanic & Campbell, 1977) is especially helpful with clients aged 6 to 17, assessing interpersonal functioning between the child and her peers, behaviors demonstrated at school, and behaviors demonstrated at home.

In addition to the interview formats, the two self-report measures that are most frequently used in diagnosing mood disorders (particularly MDD) are the Beck Depression Inventory II (BDI-II) (Beck et al., 1996) and the Center for Epidemiological Studies Depression Scale (CES-D) (Radloff, 1977). The BDI-II assesses the full spectrum of symptoms found in depressive disorders and symptom severity in people 13 years and older (Beck et al., 1996). Additionally, it provides severity cutoffs corresponding to minimal, mild, moderate, and severe levels of depression. The CES-D focuses on the affective components of depression and also has cutoff scores indicating the presence or absence of clinical depression.

Treatment

There are currently three therapy approaches that are well-established as empirically supported treatments for MDD: behavior therapy (BT) (Jacobson et al., 1996), cognitive behavioral therapy (CBT) (Beck et al., 1979), and interpersonal psychotherapy (IPT) (Gillies, 2001; Klerman & Weissman, 1993). For clarity, we discuss each treatment separately.

Behavior Therapy for Depression

There are two distinct treatment types when using behavior therapy (BT) for depression. The first type utilizes active-directive behavioral methods, such as activity logs, graded behavioral assignments to increase behavioral activation (to increase the frequency of previously enjoyed activities), and skills training interventions to develop more effective problem-solving and social skills (Jacobson et al., 1996).

The second BT treatment approach utilizes behaviorally based marital therapy with individuals who are suffering concurrently from MDD and marital distress (Beach, Sandeen, & O'Leary, 1990; Jacobson, Dobson, Fruzetti, Schmaling, & Salusky, 1991). In this treatment, clients enhance their communication skills, more consistently reinforce appropriate relationship behavior, provide the specific behaviors that are most desired by each member of the couple, and accept aspects of each other that are unlikely to change.

Cognitive Behavioral Therapy for Depression

Cognitive behavioral therapy (CBT) is a directive form of psychotherapy that modifies dysfunctional attitudes and beliefs such as the individual's negative view of the self, others, and the future (Beck et al., 1979). The first half of this treatment actively and objectively analyzes thinking patterns, directly enhances daily behavioral activity, and logically challenges the accuracy of moment-to-moment thoughts (automatic thoughts) associated with depression. These automatic thoughts often contain cognitive distortions that exacerbate negativity and depressive symptoms. The most common cognitive distortions (Beck, 1995) are the following:

- **Catastrophizing.** Making negative predictions about the future without weighing the evidence of the negative event actually occurring or considering other likely outcomes.

- **Emotional Reasoning.** Believing that feelings are based on reality and therefore must be true, regardless of contradictory information.

- **Negativistic Thinking.** Believing that positive events have little meaning while magnifying negative events.

- **Mind Reading.** Believing that you can predict what another person is thinking (typically negative), regardless of evidence to the contrary.

- **Personalization.** Believing that other people's negative actions or feelings are because of you, without considering other possible causes.

- **Tunnel Vision.** Focusing exclusively on the negative components of a situation, instead of also seeing the positive or more realistic aspects.

- **All-or-Nothing Thinking.** Viewing a situation in dichotomous, opposite ways; also known as black-and-white thinking.

- **Labeling.** Holding a rigid (typically negative) view of the self, others, or an event without considering alternative, possibly more realistic hypotheses.

- **Mental Filter.** Focusing excessively on one negative aspect without seeing the broader situation.

- **Overgeneralization.** Making broad conclusions (typically negative) based on one aspect of a situation.

- **Shoulds and Musts.** Rigidly thinking that there is one way that the self and others should be and magnifying how uncomfortable deviations from these self–other expectations would feel.

The second half of CBT treatment involves recognizing and modifying the core beliefs (early maladaptive schemas) assumed to make the patient vulnerable to MDD. To review the prevalent schemas affecting athletes, refer to chapter 2.

Interpersonal Psychotherapy for Depression

Interpersonal psychotherapy (IPT) is the third empirically supported intervention for MDD. IPT makes no assumptions about the causes of depression (Klerman & Weissman, 1993). IPT is a manual-based intervention that identifies and modifies the patient's interpersonal functioning associated with the MDD. The intervention focuses on problems such as unresolved grief, interpersonal disputes, interpersonal (skill) deficits, relationship issues, and role transitions. It is recommended for "symptom removal, prevention of relapse and recurrence, correction of causal psychological problems for secondary symptom resolution, and correction of secondary consequences of depression" (Gillies, 2001, p. 311). The goal of IPT is to help the client resolve current interpersonal situations, and in so doing, increase productivity and reduce negative affect.

Since clinical sport psychologists frequently work with athletes aged 13 to 22, it is important to note that IPT is considered particularly helpful with adolescents with depressive symptomatology. The very nature of IPT, with its focus on interpersonal functioning, role transitions and disputes, and depression seems to logically fit with the changing needs of the adolescent. Teenage-friendly characteristics of IPT include a focus on the present, flexible session frequency, telephone consultation, active and supportive practitioner involvement, and practitioner advocacy for the adolescent regarding school and parent issues. IPT can be tailored to meet the demands of adolescent athletes, especially those training under strict regimens or away from home.

All three of these psychotherapeutic interventions (BT, CBT, and IPT) have demonstrated clinically significant reductions in both depression

Treatments for Major Depressive Disorder

Behavior Therapy

Active-Directive Methods

- Behavioral activation and problem-solving skills training

Behavioral Marital Therapy

- Enhanced communication skills, consistent reinforcement, and acceptance

Cognitive Behavioral Therapy

- Modification of dysfunctional thinking patterns
- Behavioral activation
- Modification of core beliefs

Interpersonal Psychotherapy

- Modification of interpersonal patterns of functioning by focusing on role disputes, dysphoria, role transitions, and unresolved grief and by modifying skill deficits

---

ratings and the number of clients meeting MDD criteria at posttreatment follow-up. Yet how does the clinical sport psychologist determine which one to utilize when working with a depressed athlete? While there is probably no definitive answer to this question, recent evidence suggests several general conclusions (Craighead, Hart, Craighead, & Ilardi, 2002):

- Clients with comorbid personality disorders appear to respond better to cognitive behavioral therapy (CBT).

- Clients reporting more existential explanations for their depression appear to do better with cognitive behavioral therapy (CBT) than with behavior therapy (BT).

- Clients holding significant dysfunctional beliefs (cognitive distortions) respond better to interpersonal psychotherapy (IPT) than to cognitive behavioral therapy (CBT).

- Clients with severe interpersonal dysfunction respond better to cognitive behavioral therapy (CBT) than to interpersonal psychotherapy (IPT) (Sotsky et al., 1991).

- Cognitive behavioral therapy (CBT) is the treatment of choice for clients with low levels of pretreatment depression, high levels of resourcefulness, decent interpersonal relationships, and stable intimate relationships.

These latter three findings suggest that evidence-based therapy for depression may work best when focusing on building upon preexisting strengths or ameliorating less significant weaknesses, rather than on attempting to compensate for, or eliminate, the most significant weaknesses.

Psychopharmacological treatments of moderately to severely depressed individuals result in outcomes comparable to the psychosocial treatments (Craighead et al., 2002). To date, adequate data do not exist to determine if the combination of an empirically supported therapy and psychopharmacology is superior to the individual psychotherapeutic interventions.

Bipolar Disorders

Lifetime prevalence rates indicate that bipolar disorders may affect 2.5% of the U.S. population (Kessler et al., 1994). Bipolar disorders run a long, recurrent course and are highly heritable, with concordance rates of approximately 70% in identical twins. Although individuals typically function very well between depressive, manic, and hypomanic episodes (APA, 2000), the symptoms experienced during episodes can be extremely distressful and can lead to dangerous results. Bipolar disorders are the sixth-leading cause of disability worldwide (Murray & Lopez, 1996), and 25% of clients with bipolar disorders attempt suicide (Hopkins & Gelenberg, 1994).

Characteristics

Bipolar disorders are severe, cyclical, and recurring disorders characterized by disturbances of mood, cognition, and behavior (APA, 2000; Miklowitz, 2001). The core element of bipolar disorders is extreme affective dysregulation often consisting of alternating low (depressive) and high (hypomanic or manic) mood states. These alterations can occur within the same day or over several months.

The diagnosis of a bipolar disorder, as with all psychological diagnoses, requires that symptoms impair one or more major life domains (work, school, social, marital, and so on) (APA, 2000). Bipolar disorders are diagnosed as bipolar I (which includes mania) or bipolar II (which includes hypomania) (APA, 2000; Truax & Selthon, 2003). Bipolar I disorder is the more severe of the two subtypes, as clients with manic symptoms can be extremely elevated, distressed, expansive, and potentially delusional. Clients experiencing a manic episode demonstrate an euphoric mood that can be elevated or irritable, a decreased need for sleep, increased goal-directed behavior often involving high-risk or self-destructive activities (binge drug use, sexual activity, spending), increased or pressured speech, and disrupted cognitive content (grandiose delusions, flight of ideas, distractibility) (Miklowitz, 2001). These symptoms must persist for more than 1 wk for a diagnosis of a manic episode. Clients experiencing a bipolar II (hypomanic) episode demonstrate many of these same symptoms, but most often for a shorter duration, at a lesser intensity, and with lower levels of functional impairment.

As many as 40% of patients with Bipolar I disorder experience mixed episodes in which they meet criteria for a major depressive episode *and* a manic episode every day for at least 1 wk (Calabrese, Fatemi, Kujawa, & Woyshville, 1996). In the rapid cycling type of bipolar disorder (more common for bipolar II clients), the individual experiences at least four discrete depressive, manic, hypomanic, or mixed episodes within 1 yr. Bipolar disorders are commonly comorbid with anxiety disorders, personality disorders, and substance use disorders (Miklowitz, 2001). These disorders all involve affect dysregulation, and some people have argued that many patients diagnosed with substance use or personality disorders are in fact also suffering from an undiagnosed and untreated bipolar disorder (Akiskal, 1996).

A bipolar disorder may present in many different ways in athletes. It may present as sudden, extreme, or atypical behavior in previously well-functioning athletes or may present as extreme self-destructive, violent, or substance-related behaviors. Additionally, bipolar symptoms may be misperceived as hyperactivity in athletes who at other times appear sluggish and unfocused. While the manic episode is often quite recognizable (as it is more severe), the hypomanic episode is often wrongfully diagnosed and misinterpreted as the result of drugs, alcohol, or attention deficit disorders. Overall, the extreme behaviors associated with bipolar disorders frequently culminate in erratic behavioral disruptions (including missing practices), both short- and long-term suspensions from play, and even early career termination.

Assessment

As is the case with MDD, assessing a bipolar disorder requires a careful interview and possible use of adjunctive psychometric instruments. Since individuals with bipolar symptomatology are often misdiagnosed with personality disorders, substance use disorders, and attentional disorders, the SCID-I section on mood disorders (First et al., 1997) can provide excellent diagnostic clarity. Additionally, the Altman Self-Rating Mania Scale (ASRM) (Altman, Hedeker, Peterson, & Davis, 1997) was developed specifically for screening suspected manic episodes. However, it does not by itself constitute a diagnosis of a bipolar disorder, and it may potentially overidentify the presence of these disorders (Altman, Hedeker, Peterson, & Davis, 2001).

Treatment

Unfortunately, there is currently no clear empirically supported psychosocial treatment for bipolar disorders. However, since it is believed that life events and family stressors exacerbate mood disorder symptoms (Miklowitz, 2001), psychological interventions focusing on these stressors may help reduce associated symptoms. In addition, the empirical evidence currently suggests that combining psychopharmacological interventions with family focused therapy results in better outcomes than psychopharmacology alone (Craighead, Miklowitz, Frank, & Vajk, 2002).

Of the available treatment options, family focused treatment (FFT) (Miklowitz & Goldstein, 1997) has garnered the most empirical support for treating bipolar disorders. It typically lasts 20 sessions and consists of

- family psychoeducation about the nature and course of the specific bipolar disorder;
- family communication enhancement training focusing on reducing high levels of emotional expression among family members;
- family problem-solving skills training; and
- full family cooperation in medication compliance.

Within these particular components, FFT works with both the client and his family to define six treatment objectives (Miklowitz, 2001). These include integrating the individual and family experiences of bipolar disorder, recognizing that future bipolar episodes may occur, understanding the importance of psychotropic medication in reducing symptoms and increasing effective functioning, distinguishing between the client's mood disorder and his personality, learning coping strategies that can be utilized during stressful events, and repairing and maintaining interpersonal relationships that may be tested during bipolar episodes.

At this time, as a newer intervention, FFT has not attained full empirical support and has been primarily administered to adults with close access to family members. Utilizing the FFT protocol with adolescents is under way, and although components such as communication enhancement and problem-solving skills training may help younger clients, the efficacy of FFT with children and adolescents is presently unknown (Miklowitz, 2001).

Dysthymic Disorder

The lifetime prevalence rate of dysthymic disorder (DD) is approximately 6% of the United States population (APA, 2000; Kessler at al., 1994). Although it occurs equally among males and females during childhood, women are significantly more likely to develop the disorder during adulthood (APA, 2000). Dysthymic disorder tends to have an early onset (childhood, adolescence, or early adulthood) and runs a more chronic course than the other mood disorders.

Characteristics

The essential characteristic of dysthymic disorder is a mildly to moderately depressed mood lasting at least 2 y (APA, 2000). Children with this disorder may not seem particularly depressed, yet they may appear irritable and may demonstrate poor social skills. Individuals experiencing DD often do not describe themselves as depressed, as they have habituated to the chronic affective

state and therefore experience the mild to moderate depression as their normal mood state. For this reason, dysthymic clients typically do not describe depressive symptoms to the psychologist. Instead, despite clear depressive qualities, these individuals will often state, "This is just how I am." When such clients do describe depressive symptoms, it is usually during discrete periods in which the mood worsens from the typical dysthymic state. During these times, they may note lower energy, sleep disturbance, appetite changes, and lack of interest in activities. Increased feelings of hopelessness and low self-esteem are also likely during these times.

Individuals with dysthymic disorder characteristically describe difficulty making decisions, reduced concentration, and greater self-criticism, and they see themselves as essentially less capable or interesting than others (APA, 2000). While dysthymic disorder and major depressive disorder may present similarly, they are both diagnostically and functionally distinct. The depressive symptoms are relatively chronic, are milder, and have been present for several years in individuals with DD, while the depressive episodes are more acute and severe in individuals with MDD. From a functional perspective, during a discrete MDD episode, the MDD client is likely to experience greater impairment in daily living, report a greater level of subjective intrapersonal distress, and experience greater social and occupational disruption. On the other hand, the DD client demonstrates a more chronic style of associated behavior, experiences greater long-term interpersonal distress, and describes symptomatology as less problematic than her functional impairments indicate.

Dysthymic disorder is often seen by the clinical sport psychologist working in youth (through college) sport environments, as it is during this time that the disorder begins a slow, insidious development. Remember that children and adolescents with DD often appear as irritable, chronically unhappy children unable to experience consistent joy. These children are also difficult to soothe when distressed. Based on the symptom picture, particularly the low energy, low self-esteem, feelings of helplessness, and reduced concentration, ascension to elite competitive athletics may be less probable than the more emotionally regulated young athlete.

As we previously stated, adult athletes experiencing dysthymic disorder are not likely to initially present themselves as depressed, because their baseline affective state is a mild depression that they often describe as chronic boredom, irritability, minimal life enjoyment, chronic pessimism, and so on. Since they often view their affective state as normal, they may therefore not initially believe they are in fact depressed. As such, these athletes are more likely to seek treatment only when an acute, external event heightens their chronic level of depression (thereby leading to double depression). In the athletic domain, athletes with DD may appear brooding, difficult to please, may seem to lack enjoyment in athletic pursuits, and may require much time and attention to be placated (all often noted by the coaching staff). Frequent unhappiness, complaining, and pessimism may all suggest dysthymic disorder.

It is important to note that MDD can also be superimposed upon dysthymic disorder in what is referred to as "double depression" (McCullough, 2000; Truax & Selthon, 2003). As previously stated, many dysthymic athletes will not recognize their low-level depression as depression at all, but may instead describe themselves as pessimistic, cynical, and without positive mood states. Since DD typically has a gradual onset and runs a chronic course, the athlete may at times experience a major depressive episode based on situational variables that exacerbate DD symptomatology. Dysthymic disorder and major depressive disorder are conceptualized quite differently, thereby leading to important assessment and treatment considerations. McCullough (2000) has suggested that due to its early onset and chronic course, DD clients do not develop the necessary skills to reduce their chronic negative mood state. On the other hand, because MDD is a more situational and episodic disorder, these clients have previously had the opportunity to develop such skills and only have difficulty using them during discrete depressive episodes. As such, a double depression episode will leave the athlete more vulnerable to the devastating effects of these disorders. The clinical sport psychologist should therefore accurately assess for this combination, as it can be devastating to the athlete's well-being unless treated appropriately.

Assessment

Generally speaking, assessing dysthymic disorder requires the same interview (SCID-I) and psychometric evaluation (BDI-II, CES-D) as major depressive disorder. However, its chronic nature requires the clinician to carefully review the time line of the athlete's depression, and especially to ascertain times in which the athlete was truly happy or content. Typically, along with SCID results consistent with dysthymic disorder and BDI-II or CES-D scores consistent with mild to moderate depression, time line findings will indicate an individual who remembers rarely (if ever) feeling happy and content with life.

Treatment

While there is currently no clearly well-established, empirically supported treatment for dysthymic disorder, a structured intervention integrating cognitive, behavioral, and interpersonal strategies shows considerable promise. This newer intervention, referred to as the cognitive behavioral analysis system of psychotherapy (CBASP) (McCullough, 2000), has demonstrated impressive outcomes and is considered a probably efficacious intervention for dysthymic disorder at this time. This intervention awaits replication by an independent research team before it can be classified as a well-established intervention for dysthymic disorder.

The CBASP treatment focuses on improving social problem solving and empathic responsiveness to others and on developing specific behavioral skills required to produce desired interpersonal outcomes (such as assertiveness, parenting, and conflict-resolution skills). CBASP reduces chronic depression by enhancing perceived functionality and interpersonal relationships. Although a distinct approach, it integrates elements from both traditional cognitive behavioral therapies and interpersonal psychotherapy (previously mentioned in the MDD section).

According to the CBASP model, chronic depression develops from coping failures that affect the depressed individual's perception of relationships with others and the world and that disconnect the client from the environment (McCullough, 2000). The chronically depressed individual responds to the perceived relational challenges, ineffective coping responses, and environmental disconnection by further restricting her engagement with others and the world. As a result, she thus receives limited social feedback and reinforcement, leading to additional hopelessness and helplessness. This creates a circular pattern of dysphoria, disengagement, and withdrawal.

CBASP treatment creates a greater connection between the chronically depressed client and her environment by helping her recognize the specific consequences of her behaviors. Enhancing social problem solving, promoting empathic responsivity, and using negative reinforcement principles as a motivational tool are all integral components of the CBASP approach (McCullough, 2000).

Eating Disorders

The two most prevalent eating disorders are bulimia nervosa (BN) and anorexia nervosa (AN). In a review of the literature on eating disorders and athletes, Swoap and Murphy (1995) reported that eating disorders occur substantially more often in athletes than in the general population. According to these authors, a significant percentage of athletes (both men and women) utilize pathogenic eating or weight loss behaviors. These behaviors are sport specific, in that sports such as wrestling and gymnastics have higher prevalence rates than sports such as archery or soccer. Swoap and Murphy (1995) logically suggest that apart from the same sociological and psychological issues involved in disordered eating across the general population, issues such as sport-specific weight restrictions, evaluation criteria, peer and coach pressure, peer comparison, and athletic performance demands are additional factors related to the development of eating disorders and weight-related behaviors in athletes. Even more vexing for the clinical sport psychologist, characteristics of the sport culture can leave athletes more vulnerable to the development of these disorders, make athletes less likely to view their behaviors as problematic (Sherman & Thompson, 2001), and

reduce the likelihood that such athletes will seek (or accept) help (Petrie & Sherman, 2000). Since many eating disordered clients in the general population do not seek help on their own but instead enter treatment at the insistence of others close to them (Stein, Goodrick, Poston, & Foreyt, 2003), it can be hypothesized that eating disordered athletes will be even less likely to personally seek treatment due to sport requirements, pressures, and the constant comparison to other athletes.

Bulimia Nervosa

The prevalence of bulimia nervosa among young females is approximately 2 to 3%, and the disorder typically begins during later adolescence or early adulthood (APA, 2000; Fairburn et al., 1995; Hsu, 1990). It frequently coexists with other forms of psychopathology, including mood disorders, anxiety disorders, substance use disorders, and personality disorders. Unfortunately, BN typically follows a chronic and unremitting course (Fairburn et al., 1995). Although possible, BN is rarely found in males (Hsu, 1990) in the general population. Although possibly more prevalent among male athletes involved in sports that impose weight restrictions, prevalence rates for male athletes are unavailable at this time.

Sport culture and expectations can place added pressure on the athlete to remain thin, and harmful eating patterns may be overlooked or minimized.

Characteristics

Bulimia nervosa is characterized in the *DSM-IV-TR* by several clinical features (APA, 2000; Wilson & Pike, 2001), including the uncontrolled consumption of large amounts of food (binge eating); regular use of methods to influence weight and shape, such as purging through vomiting or laxative use, strict dietary control, and compulsive, rigorous exercise; and inordinate self-evaluation of weight and body shape. The individual typically engages in binge eating due to a negative mood, and the binge and purge activities serve to immediately alleviate the negative affective state. However, the short-term reduction in negative mood is truly time limited, as the individual quickly engages in significant self-criticism and experiences shame, lowered self-esteem, and guilt associated with her activities (APA, 2000).

Although the media has portrayed bulimia nervosa as involving both bingeing *and* purging, there are actually two distinct subtypes of BN characterized by either the presence *or* absence of purging (APA, 2000; Stein et al., 2003). For those that do not engage in purging activities (vomiting, laxative, and diuretic use), compensatory strategies typically include excessive exercise or periods of significant dieting. When binge eating does not involve purging, the disorder is often called binge eating disorder and can occur in various severities from mild to very severe. Regardless of subtype, the majority of clients suffering from BN are within their normal weight range (Wilson & Pike, 2001).

Assessment

There is a standard set of measures for assessing eating disorders (both BN and AN). When an eating disorder is suspected, such measures are typically given to identify the specific disorder and to rule out other disorders not specific to the client.

Assessment begins with a semistructured or structured clinical interview. The best known and most widely used interview format is the Eating Disorder Examination (EDE) (Fairburn & Cooper, 1993). Helpful self-report instruments include the Eating Disorders Inventory-2 (EDI-2) (Garner, 1991), the Binge Eating Scale (BES) (Gormally, Black, Daston, & Rardin, 1982), and the Eating Disorder Examination Questionnaire (EDE-Q) (Fairburn & Beglin, 1994), which is the self-report version of the EDE. These are all useful tools for understanding the behavioral patterns and psychological characteristics of the client, and for differentially diagnosing bulimia nervosa and anorexia nervosa.

In addition to the formal assessment of eating disorders, clinical sport psychologists should be aware of and assess for disordered patterns of eating that do not meet criteria for an eating disorder, but are nonetheless detrimental to the athlete's overall well-being (Sherman & Thompson, 2001). Careful assessment should also include the athlete's emotional, cognitive, and behavioral processes and the sociocultural and familial factors involved, in order to comprehensively understand the nature of any disordered eating patterns and the effects of such patterns on the athlete. Additionally, performance consequences of disordered eating should be assessed, such as changes in strength, power, and endurance (Sherman & Thompson, 2001). Such decrements in performance (resulting from disordered eating) may be the initial reason for consultation. As such, when the athlete reports these changes, the practitioner should assess whether disordered eating is the causative factor.

Treatment

The empirical evidence to date suggests that the first-line treatment for BN is a manualized cognitive behavioral (CBT) protocol that has multiple randomized controlled studies demonstrating its efficacy (Wilson & Fairburn, 2002). It reduces restrained eating behaviors through direct behavioral interventions (self-monitoring, scheduled eating) and by modifying the dysfunctional attitudes and beliefs that maintain these behaviors. CBT for BN has a fairly low dropout rate, appears to be the most effective means of reducing the dietary restraint and disordered eating behaviors associated with BN, and typically improves comorbid psychological problems such as low self-esteem and depression. The best predictor of success in CBT for BN is early response, as improvement is most often noted within the first four sessions (Wilson & Fairburn, 2002). In addition, both psychopharmacological interventions and interpersonal psychotherapy (IPT), with its focus on problematic relationship behaviors and circumstances, have demonstrated some efficacy in treating BN. However, the CBT protocol improves symptoms significantly faster than IPT. The CBT protocol also demonstrates a much lower relapse rate than psychopharmacology treatments and is the only intervention with a clear predictor of success (early response), making it the BN treatment of choice at this time. That being said, these other interventions are viable alternatives for those patients not responding to CBT.

Anorexia Nervosa

The prevalence rate for anorexia nervosa is 0.5 to 1% in females, and AN is rarely reported in males (Wilson & Pike, 2001) in the general population. These data are strongly suggestive of societal pressures on women relating to weight and shape. Although AN appears to seldom occur in males, it is possible that male athletes involved in weight-focused sports will be more likely to present with AN symptomatology. However, prevalence rates for male athletes are unavailable at this time. On average, AN develops during the teenage years, with the typical onset around age 17. Although AN can occur for one acute episode, it is considered to be a more chronic disorder with a fluctuating lifetime pattern (APA, 2000). As much as 10% of the clinical population with AN dies from complications of the disorder. It is therefore critical that clinical sport psychologists adequately assess for AN, and if personally unable to treat the disorder, should refer such athletes to another professional for immediate treatment.

Characteristics

Anorexia nervosa is characterized by several essential clinical features (APA, 2000). The client willfully maintains an abnormally low body weight, defined as at least 15% below expected levels. In females, there is an absence of three consecutive menstrual cycles (amenorrhea). AN is also characterized by a significant disturbance in body shape and weight perception and by an intense fear of gaining weight. Typically, the individual completely denies the seriousness of her low weight, irrationally describes and perceives her shape and weight, and places undue importance and centrality on weight and shape. Compulsive behaviors (not considered symptoms of OCD) are also common, such as frequently weighing oneself, looking in mirrors, and measuring the body (APA, 2000). By definition, clients diagnosed with anorexia nervosa are substantially underweight, tend to be highly resistant to treatment, and are at severe risk of death from the disorder.

Assessment

As previously discussed for bulimia nervosa, there is a standard set of measures for assessing disordered eating. A comprehensive assessment should also assess for decrements in performance that may result from disordered eating, and should consider the athlete's emotional, cognitive, and behavioral processes and the effects of sociocultural and familial factors. Please refer to the previous section for assessment methodology.

Treatment

The empirical evidence for treating anorexia nervosa is more complex and less clear than the evidence for treating bulimia nervosa. Inpatient treatment, including dietary counseling and behavioral reeducation, is often necessary to restore body weight in most cases of AN. Further, family-based interventions including parent-directed refeeding of the client, support for the parents, and support for the client in becoming increasingly autonomous have been the only interventions carefully studied among AN adolescents (Eisler & Dare, 2000). While results are promising, comparisons with alternative treatment approaches have not yet been undertaken. Given its success in treating bulimia nervosa, CBT may be viable for treating AN adults for whom family therapy is not indicated (Russell, Szmukler, Dare, & Eisler, 1987), but this empirical question needs further investigation. Yet, due to the physical exertion, weight pressures, and self-other evaluation found in the sport environment, interventions may need to be slightly modified for competitive athletes. For example, Sherman and Thompson (2001) have suggested that athletes with AN should be required to cease all involvement in sport activities until they no longer meet full diagnostic criteria for the disorder. This includes complete abstinence from exercise, training, practice, and competition, so that the athlete learns that her health is more important than athletic participation. For those meeting criteria for eating disorders other than AN, Sherman and Thompson suggest that sport participation is acceptable only if the athlete is engaged in treatment, participates in athletics due to personal choice, is not suffering from medical complications, does not exercise excessively, and if the athlete's disordered eating is not solely related to sport participation.

Regardless of type, eating disorders are highly dangerous and require careful attention and treatment. As the clinical sport psychologist frequently works with athletes whose body and physical appearance are critical (or perceived as critical) to their overall success, the practitioner must be thoroughly knowledgeable about these complex disorders, knowing physical warning signs, emotional signals, parental and coaching pressures, weight restrictions for competition, perceptions about body size and shape, perceived environmental control, self-worth, and a host of additional factors placing the athlete at risk for developing an eating disorder. The clinician who passes off low body weight or restricted eating patterns as contextually appropriate behaviors for a given sport is placing the eating disordered athlete in great physical and emotional danger.

Treating eating disorders is a fairly specialized process that should not be undertaken by sport psychologists lacking the appropriate knowledge, training, and experience. In this case, the practitioner is encouraged to compile a list of available outside treatment resources for assisting such athletes. Practitioners can then quickly refer athletes to the appropriately trained professional. For the clinical sport psychologist with training in this area, most eating disordered athletes can be treated during weekly sessions on an outpatient basis. However, athletes with severe anorexia nervosa will require inpatient hospitalization in order to save the athlete's life. Clinicians are encouraged to have referrals on hand to immediately begin hospitalization and are encouraged to frequently consult with and support the athlete's family during this period.

Attention-Deficit Hyperactivity Disorder

Prevalence rates for attention-deficit hyperactivity disorder (ADHD) are 3 to 7% of the school-age population. Diagnosis is usually made during childhood or early adolescence, and although the majority of those diagnosed with ADHD are male (Hinshaw, Klein, & Abikoff, 2002), females also struggle with this disorder. Most individuals with ADHD experience a decrease in symptoms as they progress through adulthood (APA, 2000), but during the peak of this disorder, they can experience a host of difficulties that can affect all major life domains, such as school functioning, sport participation, and interpersonal relationships.

Characteristics

Attention-deficit hyperactivity disorder is an impairing, cross-situational, chronic disorder of childhood and adolescence that can continue well into adulthood (Greenhill & Ford, 2002; Hinshaw et al., 2002). Its fundamental symptoms fall into two distinct clusters: inattention and disorganization, and hyperactivity and impulsivity. For a diagnosis of ADHD, 6 of 9 symptoms of both inattention and hyperactivity must be clearly noted and some impairment must occur before the age of 7. Impairment from these symptoms must occur in two or more settings such as school, work, and home environments (APA, 2000). It is not uncommon for this disorder to be comorbid with conduct disorder and oppositional defiant disorder (often seen as childhood precursors of adult personality disorders), mood disorders, anxiety disorders, and substance use disorders.

Assessment

ADHD assessment begins with a thorough interview, including a detailed medical, academic, social, and behavioral history. Psychological test batteries that measure cognitive ability, academic achievement, neuropsychological functioning, attention, and behavior often help in a differential diagnosis of ADHD (Barkley, 1998).

Causal factors of ADHD include genetic predisposition and early life (neonatal or early childhood) biological triggers, with negative family experiences and parenting patterns serving as escalating variables. A few indicators of childhood ADHD include stubbornness, difficulty concentrating, trouble sitting still, talking excessively, impulsive actions, fidgeting, and frequently interrupting others. Many of these indicators are normal childhood behaviors and, as such, practitioners must be extremely cautious not to over diagnose this disorder. Although ADHD has a low prevalence rate among school children (APA, 2000), this disorder is often overdiagnosed among children displaying ADHD behaviors in normal amounts, children with a low IQ in academic environments that are too challenging, and children with a high IQ in academic environments that are not challenging enough. All of these factors must be carefully considered.

Diagnosing adults with ADHD is even more challenging. Adults who manifest concentration difficulties, impulsive behaviors, anger dysregulation, job instability, and relationship difficulties often seek help for problems they believe stem from adult manifestations of ADHD. However, diagnosing adult ADHD is often difficult because adults typically do not accurately recall their childhood history of ADHD symptomatology. In addition, the high incidence of comorbid *DSM-IV-TR* Axis I disorders (typically depression and anxiety disorders) and Axis II disorders (typically antisocial personality disorder) makes it exceedingly difficult to differentiate ADHD from a potentially comorbid condition.

As competitive athletics require high levels of task-focused attention and personal discipline, any disorder causing inattention and impulsive behavior is problematic in the sport environment. The clinical sport psychologist should watch for signs and symptoms that may reflect ADHD. At the same time, the practitioner should use caution when considering an ADHD diagnosis, and should carefully consider all historical and psychosocial factors before making a final diagnostic decision. Inattention and impulsivity are not sufficient reasons to diagnose ADHD. A diagnosis of ADHD must be accurate, as it may result in special academic or work accommodations that might be desired by some whose constellation of symptoms, while serious, should be diagnosed as other Axis I or Axis II disorders.

Describing ADHD characteristics in a sport context may further clarify the picture. The athlete experiencing ADHD will likely be inattentive, and may in fact be referred to the clinical sport psychologist for distractibility and lack of focus. Others may interpret his inattention as poor attitude or lack of motivation, as he appears disinterested due to a short span of attention. The athlete can also be expected to make errors (even after repeated trials) due to both the inattention and a tendency to impulsively respond to situational (sport) demands. He may appear high strung and anxious and often relies on self-medication (drugs and alcohol) to feel right. When he is focused during a practice or game, he may have difficulty tolerating breaks in play, skill correction, and coach commentary. During these times, he may appear particularly irritated and frustrated. As can easily be seen in this example, athletes with ADHD may have substantial difficulties in several life domains, including sport performance, relationships with staff, and general life situations. This portrayal reflects just a few of the many possible ADHD characteristics that may present to the clinical sport psychologist.

Treatment

The treatment of ADHD has traditionally centered on psychostimulant medication. A substantial amount of controlled-outcome data supports the efficacy of medication, although anecdotal reports suggest that children and adolescents with ADHD relapse when the medication is withdrawn and respond anew when it is restarted (Hinshaw et al., 2002). Despite understandable parental fears, long-term side effects of psychostimulants appear minimal, especially when considering the rapid and often dramatic improvements of these medications. The combination of intensive behavioral intervention and medication is somewhat more effective than medication alone, especially in reducing treatment dropout (MTA Cooperative Group, 1999a; MTA Cooperative Group, 1999b).

Controlled studies of adults diagnosed with ADHD suggest that psychostimulant and antidepressant medications may significantly reduce ADHD symptomatology (Hinshaw et al., 2002). However, at this time there is not sufficient evidence to view medication as an empirically supported treatment among adult ADHD populations. Further, medication must be cautiously administered to adults presenting with a comorbid substance use disorder, a common disorder among adult ADHD clients. Systematic studies evaluating psychosocial treatments for adults with ADHD are not yet available, thus creating a difficult situation for the clinical sport psychologist attempting to treat the adult athlete with ADHD symptoms. We suggest the sport psychology practitioner target specific symptoms with interventions appropriate for the symptom cluster. These may include skills training for the social-interpersonal aspects of ADHD and may include cognitive behavioral therapies, particularly mindfulness interventions, for the impulsivity inherent in ADHD. Clinical sport psychologists working with younger athletes will undeniably encounter ADHD. When working with ADHD children, several research findings may guide intervention efforts:

- Contingency-management procedures conducted in the classroom reduce problematic behaviors and often enhance academic performance among children, and psychopharmacological treatments provide even more significant results.

- Behavior therapy approaches have been shown to be effective based on parent and teacher ratings of the child's behavior, but these approaches have not been as clearly observed by direct measure.

- Cognitive approaches have not been shown to be effective treatments for ADHD.

Summary of Typical PI-I Issues

Common PI-I Difficulties

- Clinical levels of emotional distress, typically meeting *DSM-IV-TR* Axis I criteria
- Impairment in general functioning (social, school, team, family, athletics)

- It has not been determined whether psychopharmacological and behavioral treatment gains are maintained once interventions are terminated.
- Psychopharmacology can be highly effective in children exhibiting aggression, and behavioral contingencies also show some success.

Final Thoughts

This chapter discussed the particular clinical disorders that make up the MCS-SP classification of PI-I. Clinical sport psychologists will likely see these disorders, including anxiety disorders, mood disorders, eating disorders, and attention deficit disorders, regardless of the specific athlete populations and settings in which they work. PI disorders (both I and II) require concerted interventions wholly separate from performance enhancement procedures, although such disorders inevitably affect the athlete's competitive performance. Luckily, there are empirically supported or empirically informed interventions available for the majority of these disorders, providing the clinical sport psychologist with clear treatment guidelines. The next chapter covers the second PI subtype, PI-II. PI-II disorders include anger and impulse control disorders, alcohol and drug use disorders, and personality disorders, all of which are likely to be presented by a percentage of all athlete populations.

CHAPTER 9

Performance Impairment-II (PI-II)

This chapter highlights the clinical presentations and disorders constituting a MCS-SP classification of performance impairment-II (PI-II). In these clinical concerns, the athlete experiences extreme emotional distress and also exhibits significant behavioral dysregulation that functionally impairs several life domains (likely including athletic participation). The PI-II athlete may exhibit disruptive anger, extreme impulsivity despite clear consequences, and explosive displays of negative affect. In addition, substance and alcohol abuse and personality disorders may be present, leading to interpersonal conflicts, poor social skills, and ineffective decision making. When these elements combine, the internal symptom picture reflects clear intrapersonal distress, and the external consequences of the behavior dysregulation negatively affect the athlete's ability to conduct loving relationships, resist the use of substances, regulate anger, engage in consequential thinking, and remain functionally integrated in the athletic domain.

It is not difficult to imagine how such athletes may end up in the office of the clinical sport psychologist. However, those challenged by such concerns often minimize endogenous symptomatology and negate their personal impact on those around them. In fact, individuals with long-standing characterological disorders, substance use histories, and anger difficulties traditionally fare poorly in psychological treatment (Young, 1999). There are several distinct reasons for this pattern. Generally speaking, PI-II individuals

- often hold enduring behavioral characteristics that exhibit behavioral inflexibility and cognitive and emotional rigidity;

- frequently minimize or have difficulty reporting feelings such as anger, sadness, frustration, guilt, anxiety, and depression;

- have difficulty accessing automatic thought content and therefore have trouble developing rational thinking patterns and positive coping skills;

- may not be motivated for treatment;

- typically believe their long-standing difficulties have been present for so long that they cannot be modified;

- may have difficulty engaging in a therapeutic relationship with the practitioner due to interpersonal concerns and skill deficits;

- frequently have an ego-syntonic view, believing that their difficulties are not difficulties at all; and

- often use avoidance strategies to minimize painful or distressing stimuli due to significant emotion regulation deficits.

These, of course, are generalizations and do not reflect every individual with a PI-II categorization. Nonetheless, treating the above concerns can be particularly challenging, and for this reason, evidence-based treatment approaches are sparse. Such athletes, however, do occasionally seek the assistance of the clinical sport psychologist and are even more frequently referred by coaches, trainers, and family members following a clear disruption of behavior. Yet without formal empirical guidance and well-tested intervention protocols, how should the clinical sport psychologist work with these athletes? For most of the PI-II difficulties, some helpful suggestions can be made. As in the previous chapter, we cover the characteristics, assessment, and treatment of each disorder in detail.

Anger and Impulse Control Disorders

Thorough epidemiological studies of anger have yet to appear in the professional literature, although anecdotal evidence suggests that anger and impulse control are common clinical concerns. In a survey, experienced psychologists and psychiatrists (n = 500) indicated that they work with anger-related problems as frequently as they work with anxiety (Lachmund & DiGiuseppe, 1997, August). Yet to date, *DSM* nosology does not specifically consider anger apart from its comorbid contribution to other mental disorders such as posttraumatic stress disorder, mood disorders, impulse control disorders, anxiety disorders, and borderline personality disorder. Anger has therefore received little formal attention in the professional literature.

This section focuses primarily on anger-related difficulties, on impulse control disorder not otherwise specified (NOS), and on intermittent explosive disorder (IED) (APA, 2000). Other impulse control disorders classified in the *DSM-IV-TR* such as kleptomania, pyromania, pathological gambling, and trichotillomania are beyond the scope of this text.

Characteristics

The *DSM-IV-TR* characterizes intermittent explosive disorder (IED) as "discreet episodes of failure to resist aggressive impulses resulting in serious assaults or destruction of property" (APA, 2000, p. 663). The displayed aggressiveness must be disproportionate to the actual nature of the event and is typically followed by arousal relief that may then be followed by remorse, guilt, or embarrassment over the display of aggression. In addition, the individual with IED may experience depression subsequent to aggressive actions. This disorder typically begins between childhood and the early 20s. Little is known about IED, as it has received little formal study within professional psychology. However, we do know that it can be either chronic or episodic and that it often results in relationship termination, job loss, disrupted interpersonal relationships, school dismissal or suspension, athletic dismissal or suspension, financial difficulties, legal action or jail time, vehicle accidents, and hospitalization for physical injury. A separate diagnostic category within the same *DSM* class is impulse control disorder NOS. This diagnosis is typically given when the individual does not meet all of the criteria for a specific impulse control disorder, but nonetheless exhibits significant difficulties with impulse control (APA, 2000).

Historically, anger dyscontrol has been viewed as a subset of impulse control disorders (particularly IED and impulse control disorder NOS), and is a common symptom in numerous mood, anxiety, and personality disorders. At present, anger disorders do not have their own *DSM* category, although some suggest that the next *DSM* version should include these disorders (Kassinove & Sukhodolsky, 1995; Lachmund & DiGiuseppe, 1997, August). Regardless of formal *DSM* inclusion, additional study is warranted, as anger dysregulation is commonly associated with aggressive behavior, family violence, substance abuse, and physical health problems (DiGiuseppe & Tafrate, 2003), all of which are frequently encountered by clinicians.

In the world of competitive sports, athletes at all levels occasionally experience difficulty controlling anger as well as behavioral impulsivity, dyscontrol, and dysregulation. These difficulties often manifest as domestic abuse, problems with authority (such as with coaches, staff, parents), substance abuse, and aggressive responses (such as to unruly fans and law enforcement officials). The sport culture naturally rewards athletes for *controlled* aggressivity and, at times, even uncontrolled aggressivity is rewarded if it leads to team success. For athletes who are psychologically predisposed to anger, impulsivity, or interpersonal violence, such reinforcements may exacerbate difficulties with anger dyscontrol and impulsivity. For such athletes, day-to-day conflicts or interpersonal disputes with family, friends, and even authorities can lead to overly aggressive responses resulting in suspensions, dismissals from athletic involvement, and civil or criminal sanctions.

Assessment

The assessment of anger and impulse control disorders is complicated by the limitations imposed by previous and current *DSM* nosologies, which do not designate anger disorders as a unique class of behavioral problems. As a result, diagnoses such as IED and impulse control disorder NOS are typically given for impulsive and explosive violent acts. However, these diagnoses are not always applicable, especially among those who experience more chronic anger and less frequent behavioral displays.

Athletes with aggressive or hostile dispositions frequently engage in impulsive behaviors, exhibit extremely low frustration tolerance, and experience significant and ongoing interpersonal conflict.

The assessment of anger and impulse control disorders (those discussed herein) can occur through a semistructured interview. The assessment should evaluate the topographical aspects of intermittent explosive disorder (IED) using the SCID-I (First et al., 1997) as well as functionally assess anger and impulsivity as affective responses. This functional assessment must carefully evaluate triggering stimuli, intensity of affective responses, range of behavioral responses, and behavioral consequences. In addition, Kassinove and Tafrate (2002) suggest obtaining client information by five primary methods (we modified their examples to reflect an athlete population):

- **Verbal reports** elucidate the degree to which the athlete endorses his anger. Are his reports embellished? Does the athlete rationalize his anger (perhaps stating that aggressivity is needed in sports)? Does the athlete easily discuss anger with or without affect?

- **Informant reports** can help confirm (or disconfirm) the athlete's report. Confirmation does not have to be the sole intent of informant reports, however, as reports by people close to the athlete (family members, coaches, teammates, friends) can fill in the diagnostic and behavioral picture. Close individuals can also assist the athlete in completing the necessary between-session homework prescribed by the clinical sport psychologist.

- **Observation** of the athlete is also a critical assessment tool. The attentive practitioner should note angry facial expressions, nonverbal behaviors, or physiological changes accompanying an anger episode that occurs during a session or accompanying discussion of an anger episode. Observation can also be conducted at the practice facility and during games, if in these environments the athlete is particularly vulnerable to anger episodes.

- **Self-monitoring** gives an accurate representation of the difficulties associated with the athlete's anger and can elucidate the particular contingencies related to anger episodes. Self-monitoring also indicates intervention progress and highlights difficulties that have yet to be appropriately addressed.

- **Formal psychometric evaluation** can provide reliable and valid information related to the athlete's difficulties with anger. One such measure, which we discuss in a moment, is the State-Trait Anger Expression Inventory-2 (STAXI-2) (Spielberger, 1999).

Once the semistructured interview or the listed methods clarify the full diagnostic picture, diagnosis can be made. Anger and impulse diagnoses are not warranted when expressions of anger or impulsivity occur only during alcohol or substance use; when difficulties are closely associated with antisocial or borderline personality disorders, oppositional defiant disorder, a manic episode, or conduct disorder; or when the individual is seeking secondary gain by malingering (APA, 2000).

When adjunctive psychometric assessment is necessary, three instruments may be useful. The State-Trait Anger Expression Inventory-2 (STAXI-2) (Spielberger, 1999) is clinically useful with both adolescents and adults. This is a self-report instrument that measures state anger (situation-specific anger), trait anger (anger across situations), angry temperament (anger without provocation), angry reaction (anger in response to criticism or perceived unfairness), anger-in (suppressing anger), anger-out (aggressively directing anger toward others), and anger control (monitoring and controlling anger expression). The STAXI-2 has been found to have sound psychometric properties and is particularly useful in its ability to provide adjunctive information when the practitioner only has the athlete's verbal report and observant reports of anger episodes (which we know to be subjective and unreliable). The second psychometric instrument that provides valuable data is the Anger Disorders Scale (ADS) (DiGiuseppe & Tafrate, 2004), which is a 74-item self-report measure that assesses and identifies aspects of anger that may lead to dysfunction and impairment in clinical populations. Additionally, the Gardner-Moore Hostility Scale (GMHS) (Gardner & Moore, 2005b) has been designed to assess hostile rumination, hostile anticipation, and key processes involved in clinical anger. This measure is currently undergoing psychometric evaluation, with initial results suggesting strong internal consistency and convergent validity with the STAXI-2.

Treatment

The empirical study of anger-related treatments lags behind that of other clinical problems, primarily due to the lack of clear diagnostic criteria for anger difficulties. Despite the want of hard data, anger management has become increasingly popular and can be frequently found in schools, community mental health centers, and correctional facilities (DiGiuseppe & Tafrate, 2003),

and sport organizations frequently suggest anger management for athletes exhibiting dysfunctional behavior.

A recent extensive review of the professional literature on treating anger-related disorders concluded the following (DiGiuseppe & Tafrate, 2003):

- To date, only cognitive-behavioral interventions (CBT) have appeared in the literature. As such, family interventions and psychodynamic and experiential theoretical models have not been evaluated. While this lack does not mean that these approaches are inefficacious, they must be used carefully, as currently there is no evidence supporting their use over more well-established treatments.

- Generally, cognitive-behavioral interventions produce moderate improvements that are sustained over follow-up.

- Anger treatment using the CBT model includes cognitive, physiological, and behavioral components, specifically, cognitive restructuring, applied relaxation training, assertiveness and social skills training, and exposure to anger cues.

- Cognitive-behavioral anger treatment appears to reduce aggressive behavior and increase prosocial behavior more than reduce the subjective experience of anger.

- Most of the interventions studied demonstrated some positive results within a brief (12 sessions) time.

Despite the meta-analytic findings, however, a recent qualitative review of the anger treatment literature (Santanello, Gardner, & Moore, 2005; Santanello, Gardner, Moore, & Turk, 2004, November) utilizing the stringent criteria established by the Division 12 Task Force on the Promotion and Dissemination of Psychological Procedures (Chambless et al., 1998) suggests that critical issues such as methodological concerns, inconsistent use of clinical populations, uneven use of manualized interventions, and a highly restricted range of research teams prevent the firm conclusion of efficacy for the variety of interventions that have been utilized to date. Although we currently have few substantial empirical directions, recent developments have increased treatment options and empirical data are growing for a new behavioral intervention protocol known as Anger Regulation Therapy (ART) (Gardner & Moore, 2005b).

ART is not anger management. It does not focus on the reduction of anger per se, rather aims at the development (addition) of more functional and adaptive behaviors and, in turn, greater acceptance and willingness to experience personal affect. As such, anger is not seen as problematic in and of itself. Instead, the problematic aspects of clinical anger lie in the behaviors that are engaged in to avoid, suppress, or minimize the experience of anger, which subsequently result in a rigid and narrow behavioral repertoire. General techniques of the ART treatment protocol (Gardner & Moore, 2005b) include

- education about the adaptive functions of both emotion in general and anger in particular;
- self-monitoring exercises (such as thought monitoring and mindfulness meditation), which are intended to disrupt perseverative hostile anticipation and in turn lessen the patterns of attention and memory retrieval biases that sustain problematic anger;
- experiential or exposure-based exercises intended to allow for an enhanced willingness to experience and process emotion, a more complete experiencing and processing of anger in particular, and a resultant modification of overlearned avoidance behaviors that take the form of hostile rumination (and) or overt aggression; and
- Interpersonal or social skill development to allow for a wider array of adaptive and opposite-action behaviors.

With these basic techniques in mind, the specific phases of the treatment protocol include: psychoeducation; self-awareness and emotion processing; and social problem solving and interpersonal skills training (including maintenance of treatment gains and preparation for termination).

Regardless of intervention choice, brief, cost-effective interventions can easily be integrated into the athletic milieu. However, in many cases, the sport psychologist should carefully present the need for intervention, as athletes frequently confuse necessary competitive aggression with inappropriate, anger-related behavior demonstrated away from the competitive environment. The practitioner must therefore patiently yet directly distinguish between competitive aggression and problematic anger and its behavioral manifestations.

Alcohol and Drug Use Disorders

Alcohol and drug use among athletes have clear consequences, not just as obstacles to performance success, but also as potential detriments to overall physical and psychosocial well-being. Although the patterns and consequences of alcohol use and drug use are similar, we discuss each separately.

Alcohol Use Disorders

Alcohol use disorders affect individuals across a wide spectrum of demographic, racial, ethnic, and occupational groups, although prevalence rates suggest that these disorders are more common in males and younger adults (McCrady, 2001). The onset of alcohol dependence typically occurs during the 20s and 30s, and alcohol dependence follows a long course with periods of consumption remission and relapse, and with periods of abuse (APA, 2000).

Characteristics

Alcohol use disorders constitute a variety of problems ranging from a heavily drinking college student missing classes and practices to a middle-aged adult whose long-term, severe drinking patterns result in significant medical and social consequences. As alcohol use and abuse are common, any practitioner working in the behavioral health field must be competent to identify and assess these issues.

The athletic environment is certainly not immune to drug and alcohol abuse, and authors have previously detailed the unique pressures and issues associated with drug and alcohol use in sports (Carr & Murphy, 1995). In describing alcohol use in athletes, Carr and Murphy (1995) summarized a number of studies, suggesting that 92.3% of high school, 88% of collegiate, and 90.4% of elite athletes consumed alcohol during the previous year. Family history, peer pressure, sensation seeking, adaptive emotion regulation deficits, and media pressures are possible contributors to drug and alcohol use. Male athletes have been reported to drink to intoxication significantly more often than female athletes (Carr, Kennedy, & Dimick, 1990). In addition, society promotes the cultural connection between sports and alcohol, most readily seen by the predominance of beer commercials on the television programming of major sporting events. Whatever the causes, professional work in the sport milieu requires that the clinical sport psychologist vigilantly watch for potential alcohol abuse. Complicating the issue further is the fact that athletes demonstrating problematic drinking behaviors often readily (and often accurately) point out that their entire friend and teammate group engages in alcohol consumption, quite possibly at equivalent levels.

The two primary alcohol use disorders noted in *DSM-IV-TR* (APA, 2000) are alcohol dependence and alcohol abuse. A diagnosis of *alcohol dependence* requires the individual to meet 3 of 7 criteria, including persistent efforts to cut down or stop, consuming larger amounts or drinking over longer periods of time, increased physical tolerance, physical withdrawal, neglecting other necessary activities, spending greater time using alcohol, and continuing use despite recurrent medical or psychological consequences. *Alcohol abuse* is diagnosed based on problem use, including failure to fulfill significant obligations (such as family, work, team, school), drinking patterns that repeatedly create the potential for harm (such as driving while intoxicated), incurring repeated legal or organizational consequences (such as arrests, team suspensions), or significant interpersonal consequences (such as failed relationships) (APA, 2000; Hodgins & Diskin, 2003). While the formal *DSM-IV-TR* diagnostic system (APA, 2000) is widely used, some clinicians suggest that it may be more useful to view alcohol problems on a continuum. Such a continuum could include abstinence and nonproblematic alcohol consumption on one end, acute and chronic patterns of problematic drinking behavior on the other end, and differing degrees of use throughout (McCrady, 2001).

Given the high comorbidity between alcohol use disorders and domestic and interpersonal violence, legal difficulties, suicidal ideation, and daily difficulties with personal responsibilities, these disorders are likely to come to the attention of the practicing clinical sport psychologist. The practitioner should carefully review mood fluctuations, unexplained changes in daily behavior, anger dysregulation including violent behavior, and reduced personal responsibility, especially in groups at higher risk for alcohol use disorders such as college students, for possible alcohol-related explanations. As alcohol and drug use commonly play a role in the seemingly frequent media presentations of athletes accused of domestic violence or other legal difficulties, in the future, professional and collegiate sports will likely rely

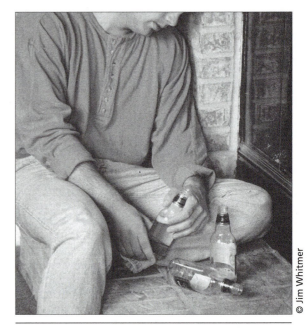

Although numerous athletes drink in moderation, the sport psychologist should be aware of signs of problematic drinking patterns and overuse.

on the clinical sport psychologist to understand, assess, and treat these serious issues.

Assessment

Treating alcohol use disorders begins with a thorough assessment that covers problem severity, coexisting life difficulties and psychological problems, client treatment expectations, client motivation for treatment, factors maintaining drinking behavior, familial history, consumption quantity, clinical comorbidity, and social supports (Hodgins & Diskin, 2003). In addition, the social, occupational, medical, legal, familial, financial, and spiritual consequences of drinking behaviors should be fully discussed.

Comprehensive assessment can include semistructured or structured interviews such as the SCID-I (First et al., 1997) and the Addiction Severity Index (ASI) (McLellan, Luborsky, O'Brien, & Woody, 1980), and self-report measures such as the Alcohol Dependence Scale (Skinner & Allen, 1982) and the Drinker Inventory of Consequences (DrInC) (Miller, Tonigan, & Longabaugh, 1995). Also useful is the Alcohol Use Disorders Identification Test (AUDIT) (Babor, de la Fuente, Saunders, & Grant, 1992), a questionnaire with 10 multiple-choice questions measuring general alcohol consumption, dependence, and associated problems. Additionally, as suicide is a particular concern with excessive alcohol users, practitioners are encouraged to frequently assess for suicidal ideation, plans, and intent. Importantly, during the initial interview, some athletes may significantly minimize drinking behaviors. This can be due to a host of influences, such as the belief that drinking is not problematic and the fear of team dismissal, suspension from athletic involvement, or losing an athletic scholarship. The clinical sport psychologist must understand this reluctance and patiently persist in a nondirective approach to the topic. Motivational interviewing (Miller & Rollnick, 1991), which utilizes nondirective counseling to discuss the decisional balance involved in drinking use, may help. See figure 9.1.

Treatment

The empirical evidence to date suggests that there is more than one effective treatment for alcohol use disorders (Project MATCH Research Group, 1998). This contrasts to treatments for many other of the discussed disorders, where one treatment typically demonstrates clear superiority. The treatments with the most substantial empirical findings for alcohol use disorders are behavioral marital therapy, which focuses on marital relationship issues (O'Farrell, Choquette, & Cutter, 1998); community reinforcement procedures, which focus on contingency management in a community setting (Abbot, Weller, Delaney, & Moore, 1998); social skills training, which focuses on developing coping skills (Smith & McCrady, 1991); full-package cognitive behavioral therapy (CBT); 12-step interventions; and motivational enhancement therapy (Mack & Frances, 2003), which focuses on personal responsibility and stage of change

(Project MATCH Research Group, 1998). Despite their significant theoretical differences, these approaches all include social support, feedback on personal impairment, enhanced personal responsibility, enhanced commitment to change, drinking behavior viewed in a broader life context, therapeutic empathy, and enhanced coping skills and self-efficacy (Finney & Moos, 2002). Although many practitioners and consumers quickly think of Alcoholics Anonymous (AA) when considering treatment, AA has not been found "to be more effective than alternatives" (Finney & Moos, 2002, p. 160).

While efforts to match client characteristics to treatment approaches have been generally unsatisfactory, some findings have emerged. Clients with lower psychiatric severity demonstrate somewhat better outcomes with 12-step facilitations, clients with greater anger do better with motivational enhancement therapy, and clients lower in anger do substantially better with either CBT or 12-step facilitation (Finney & Moos, 2002). Further, clients with greater alcohol dependence do better when treated with 12-step facilitation, while clients with lower dependence demonstrate better outcomes with CBT.

Drug Use Disorders

Drug use disorders usually begin during adolescence or early adulthood and can be sustained for many years (APA, 2000). Both periods of excessive use and periods of abstinence are common, and drug use typically leads to many behavioral consequences in major life domains. For the clinical

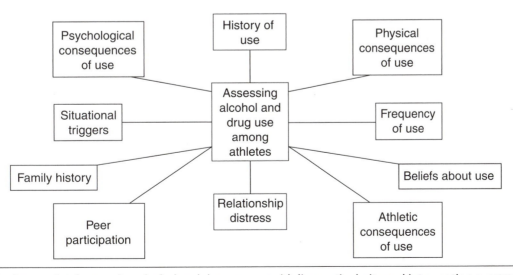

Figure 9.1 Appropriately assessing alcohol and drug use can aid diagnostic clarity and intervention success.

sport psychologist, drug use disorders may seem more common among a college population, but can certainly be seen among professional and elite athletes as well. Unfortunately, athletes typically do not report drug use for fear of repercussions from sport management, staff, coaches, and teammates, and needed treatment is often neglected. Symptoms may become clearer by creating a time line of the frequency and severity of consequences of drug use (this applies to alcohol use as well). For example, the practitioner can piece together that an athlete has received two DUIs (driving under the influence) over the past 2 y, was involved in a significant interpersonal dispute with a significant other within the past 6 mo (intensified by intoxication), has begun receiving poor grades, and has missed several practices during the current season due to stated tiredness or sickness despite no real illness. While these independent variables are not concerning in their own right, together they may indicate substance or alcohol abuse.

Characteristics

Substance abuse represents a serious legal and public health problem in the United States and has been consistently associated with crime and incarceration, neonatal complication, homelessness, and infectious disease (Antick & Goodale, 2003; Konkol & Olsen, 1996).

Drug use disorders are defined by a cluster of behavioral and physiological characteristics resulting from a pattern of ongoing use. As with alcohol use disorders, drug use disorders are often found in athletic populations and include drug use for recreation and performance enhancement (Carr & Murphy, 1995). A *DSM-IV-TR* diagnosis of substance abuse requires a pattern of use leading to significant distress or functional impairment as indicated by an athlete meeting at least one of the following criteria within 12 months (APA, 2000):

- Not fulfilling obligations in various life domains (through absences, poor work or athletic performance, suspensions, and so on) due to the use of substances
- Using substances in ways that can physically injure oneself or others
- Experiencing legal difficulties from the use of substances
- Continuing to use substances despite resultant difficulties in interpersonal relationships, social endeavors, or physical well-being

The criteria for substance abuse and alcohol abuse are similar, and the criteria for substance dependence are also nearly identical to the criteria for alcohol dependence. Indicators of drug abuse in an athlete population may include use in isolation, anger dysregulation including uncharacteristic violence, guilt over use that does not end the use, suicidal ideation, lying about use when confronted by others, increased tolerance, blackouts, and altered states of consciousness (Carr & Murphy, 1995).

The world of competitive athletics is by no means immune to drug abuse, whether it is for sensation seeking, emotionally self-medicating, pumping up, cooling down, relieving physical pain, or enhancing performance. With each of these reasons for use comes a list of processes and outcomes; cognitive, emotional, and behavioral consequences; beliefs about use; and addictive likelihoods. Compounding recreational drug use is the reality that the use of performance enhancing drugs is reinforced by the "win at any cost" mentality that typifies competitive sports. The clinical sport psychologist can expect to increasingly be called to intervene with athletes who use both recreational and performance enhancing drugs, and who have developed serious addictions.

Assessment

If the athlete does acknowledge drug abuse, the practitioner should fully assess several key elements:

- What the athlete has tried (if anything) to overcome or cut down on use
- The particular difficulties of past approaches
- What worked, and for how long
- How many stop–start cycles have occurred
- Changes in drug use activity or substance of choice
- New or additional life stressors that may be exacerbating the problem or that may interfere with treatment
- The athlete's readiness and motivation for change

In addition to understanding the patterns of drug use and related contingencies, screening tools and other measures may be particularly helpful in assessing drug use and abuse. Such inventories include the SCID-I (First et al., 1997), the Addiction Severity Index (McLellan et al., 1980), and the Drug Use Screening Inventory-Revised (DUSI-R) (Tarter & Hegedus, 1991).

When working with a singular drug use disorder or with a comorbid condition, it is critical to frequently reassess use patterns, as they quickly change and intensify. Also, practitioners must carefully assess for suicidal ideation, plans, and intent both during the initial intake and throughout treatment, with consistent follow-up in assessment. As with alcohol use disorders, a drug use problem requiring greater care than can be obtained on an outpatient basis (typical with alcohol and substance use disorders) should be referred to an inpatient or day treatment program.

Treatment

There are not, as of yet, any controlled trials comparing the relative efficacies of inpatient and outpatient interventions for substance use disorders. However, treatments such as relapse prevention (Maude-Griffin et al., 1998) and the community reinforcement approach (Budney & Higgins, 1998) have begun to accumulate empirical support and are currently categorized as probably efficacious treatments for substance abuse disorders according to the empirically supported treatment criteria (see chapter 5 for criteria).

The National Institute on Drug Abuse (1999) has identified the following principles of effective treatment for illicit drug abuse:

- No one treatment is appropriate for all clients with drug use disorders.

- Due to potential shifts in client needs, treatment plans should be assessed and updated regularly.

- Effective treatment should target psychological and life functioning beyond a simple focus on drug use.

- Staying in treatment for at least 3 mo appears to be critical for success.

- Individual and group behavioral treatments are essential for treatment effectiveness.

- Medications combined with counseling or behavioral interventions are necessary for many clients.

- When psychiatric disorders coexist with drug abuse, successful treatment should integrate both disorders into its focus.

- Physiological detoxification is a necessary first stage for many clients, but is insufficient to change long-term drug use patterns.

- Clients do not have to voluntarily enter treatment for it to be effective, and drug use during treatment must be carefully and regularly monitored.

- Comprehensive treatment includes testing for infectious diseases such as hepatitis B or C and HIV or AIDS along with counseling to modify risk-taking behaviors.

- Recovery from drug abuse is typically a long-term endeavor, and multiple attempts are likely.

The clinical sport psychologist should be aware of the evolving literature on drug treatment. Newer treatments utilizing motivational enhancement therapy (Miller & Rollnick, 1991) or mindfulness and acceptance techniques (Hayes et al., 1999; Segal et al., 2002) are appearing, offering new and potentially more effective treatments for this major problem area. In addition, practitioners are encouraged to compile a list of local resources that treat substance use disorders. Since treating such disorders is complex and time-consuming, referring athletes to local treatment facilities may best meet their needs.

Personality Disorders

The *DSM-IV-TR* defines personality disorders as clusters of personality traits (enduring behavioral characteristics) that are inflexible, are maladaptive, substantially deviate from cultural expectations, and cause significant subjective distress (and) or observable functional impairment in major life domains such as school, work, or family (APA, 2000). Prevalence rates suggest that 10 to 13% of the population experience these chronic disorders (Crits-Christoph & Barber, 2002). There is high comorbidity between personality disorders and mood disorders (36-65%), bulimia nervosa (39%), anxiety disorders (36-76%), and drug or alcohol abuse disorders (47-75%) (Crits-Christoph & Barber, 2002). Although personality disorders are not gender specific, antisocial personality disorder is more common in men, while borderline, dependent, and histrionic personality disorders are typically more common in women (APA, 2000). The features of the different personality disorders, typically apparent during adolescence or early adulthood, present as persistent ways of being in the world. As personality disorders are an inflexible, maladaptive, and *enduring* way of being, an individual is usually not diagnosed with a full personality disorder until age 18.

Characteristics

The *DSM-IV-TR* describes 10 specific personality disorders (referred to as Axis II disorders) grouped in three clusters (A, B, and C). The cluster groupings are based on disorder similarities (APA, 2000):

- **Cluster A,** the odd cluster, includes schizoid, paranoid, and schizotypal personality disorders and is characterized by odd and seemingly idiosyncratic interpersonal behaviors, styles of relating, and perceptions of the world.
- **Cluster B,** the dramatic cluster, includes histrionic, borderline, narcissistic, and antisocial personality disorders and is characterized by affective and behavioral dysregulation that often includes parasuicidal attempts and aggressive or violent behavior, unstable interpersonal relationships, lack of remorse, highly demonstrative and self-aggrandizing behavior, poor impulse control, and extreme emotional dysregulation.
- **Cluster C,** the anxious cluster, includes avoidant, obsessive-compulsive, and dependent personality disorders and is characterized by anxiety and avoidance of discomfort, responsibility, and independence.

Additionally, patients whose persistent patterns of behavior meet some but not all of the criteria for a specific personality disorder are categorized as personality disorder not otherwise specified (NOS).

There is no reason to believe that athletes are immune to these serious and unremitting disorders. These disorders are most readily noted through repetitive interpersonal difficulties with teammates and staff; difficulty accepting authority, structure, and rules; frequent disciplinary problems; aggressive violence; emotional dysregulation; and regular avoidance or disregard of personal responsibilities. These manifestations help explain the high comorbidity of personality disorders with drug and alcohol abuse, anger and violence, and depression.

Assessment

The assessment of personality disorders typically includes the use of semistructured or structured clinical interviews such as the Structured Clinical Interview for *DSM-IV*-Personality Disorders (SCID-

II) (First et al., 1995). Also helpful are psychometric measures such as the Young Schema Questionnaire, Long Form, Second Edition (YSQ) (Young, 1999) and the Millon Clinical Multiaxial Inventory-III (MCMI-III) (Millon et al., 1994). However, while many psychometric assessments for personality disorders have been developed, some have questioned their overall clinical utility (Koenigsberg, Woo-Ming, & Siever, 2002). Comorbid presentations may also be good indicators of personality disorders. For example, practitioners are encouraged to carefully evaluate for potential comorbid personality disorders in athletes presenting substance use or abuse.

Treatment

By thoroughly assessing and understanding the belief systems and behavioral strategies of individuals with personality disorders, the practitioner can target their specific treatment needs. Table 9.1 (Beck, Freeman, & Davis, 2004) highlights the differing beliefs and associated behaviors common among the various personality disorders. While empirical evidence via controlled studies for psychosocial treatment is limited, we can report some tentative findings.

There have been no controlled outcome studies of psychosocial treatments for Cluster A personality disorders (schizoid, paranoid, and schizotypal), although preliminary evidence suggests that antipsychotic medication can help alleviate some aspects of schizotypal personality disorder (Koenigsberg et al., 2002). Unfortunately, due to the state of research, no clear treatments can be recommended at this time (Crits-Christoph & Barber, 2002; Piper & Joyce, 2001).

The lack of controlled treatment outcome studies on Cluster B disorders hinders recommendations for evidence-based treatment of antisocial, narcissistic, and histrionic personality disorders. However, some evidence suggests that a structured form of cognitive-behavioral therapy may be the best available treatment for antisocial personality disorder (Piper & Joyce, 2001).

In treating borderline personality disorder (Cluster B), dialectical behavior therapy (Linehan et al., 2001) has demonstrated efficacy across several controlled outcome studies and at this time is considered probably efficacious according to the empirically supported treatment criteria (see chapter 5 for criteria) (Crits-Christoph & Barber, 2002). Dialectical behavior therapy (DBT) is a spe-

Table 9.1   Basic Beliefs and Strategies Associated with Traditional Personality Disorders

Personality disorder	Basic beliefs and attitudes	Strategy (overt behavior)
Dependent	"I am helpless."	Attachment
Avoidant	"I may get hurt."	Avoidant
Passive-aggressive	"I could be controlled."	Resistance
Paranoid	"People are dangerous."	Wariness
Narcissistic	"I am special."	Self-aggrandizement
Histrionic	"I need to impress."	Dramatics
Obsessive-compulsive	"I must not err."	Perfectionism
Antisocial	"Others are to be taken."	Attack
Schizoid	"I need plenty of space."	Isolation

Reprinted, by permission, from A.T. Beck, A. Freeman, and D.D. Davis, 2004, *Cognitive therapy of personality disorders,* 2nd ed. (New York: Guilford Press).

cialized cognitive-behavioral treatment designed specifically for borderline personality disorder, which according to Linehan "is primarily a dysfunction of the emotion regulation system" (p. 480) leading to consequences across various life domains. DBT treatment requires a full year of structured group and individual sessions focusing on psychoeducation, empathic validation, acceptance, and the development of distress tolerance and emotion regulation skills. There are four primary treatment stages (Linehan et al., 2001):

1. Attaining and maintaining a stable and functionally sound life pattern, indicated by reduced suicidality; enhanced emotional regulation, interpersonal communication, and self-management; and reduced behaviors interfering with therapy and overall life satisfaction

2. Reducing symptomatology and life patterns associated with posttraumatic stress

3. Achieving a better self-image, a functional level of happiness and enjoyment in life, and increased autonomy

4. Promoting self-awareness and sustained happiness and joy

In addition to DBT, a recent study has also demonstrated some success in treating borderline pathology using an 18-month partial hospitalization and a form of psychodynamic psychotherapy (Bateman & Fonagy, 1999). However, this treatment awaits replication across additional studies.

With respect to Cluster C disorders, there have been no published controlled outcome studies for dependent personality disorder. There is limited evidence, however, that a group-administered behavioral intervention consisting of graded exposure, standard social skills training, (and) or intimacy-focused social skills training can reduce its associated behaviors (Alden, 1989). In addition, some preliminary evidence suggests that supportive expressive dynamic psychotherapy (SE) altering core (repetitive) patterns of interpersonal conflict with short-term psychodynamic techniques may increase end-state functioning in clients with avoidant personality disorder (Barber, Morse, Krakauer, Chittams, & Crits-Christoph, 1997). This same treatment, focusing on core repetitive patterns of interpersonal behavior, may also help ameliorate obsessive-compulsive personality disorder (Barber et al., 1997). Similarly, long-term psychodynamic treatment appears somewhat promising for mixed (Cluster B and C) personality disorders (Crits-Christoph & Barber, 2002).

Controlled outcome data for the treatment of personality disorders are sparse. Additional promising treatments, such as schema-focused cognitive therapy (Young et al., 2003), have yet to be fully empirically tested in randomized controlled trials and therefore must be utilized carefully. Unfortunately, individuals demonstrating the behavioral and emotional dysregulation associated with these chronic disorders are typically in dire need of professional help to alleviate what is often extreme subjective distress and to enhance adaptive functioning in sport, work, school, and family domains.

In addition, although traditional cognitive therapy was originally developed to treat affective disorders, much has recently been written on applying it to personality disorders. At this time, however, this application still awaits controlled trials. In general, cognitive therapy for personality disorders (Beck et al., 2004) begins by collaborating with the client and formulating specific treatment goals; exploring the client's maladaptive processes, irrational beliefs, and relevant schemas; and exploring the client's reactions to the practitioner (transference) to further uncover thematic patterns. More specialized strategies depend on the particular pathology, require careful intervention timing, and fully integrate cognitive, behavioral, and experiential techniques. Cognitive techniques may include cognitive restructuring by identifying and countering automatic thoughts and irrational beliefs, validity testing and exploring alternative hypotheses for events and behaviors, enhancing responsibility for behaviors, and schema modification. Behavioral and experiential techniques can include client self-monitoring, mastery and pleasure activities, exposure, skill development via assertiveness training, modeling of the therapist, relaxation training, role playing, and behavioral rehearsal (Beck et al., 2004).

We previously discussed that many self-referred athletes seeking sport psychology services do not initially report intrapersonal or interpersonal difficulties, and suggested that practitioners not overlook their possible presence. In these cases, comprehensive assessment will be the best indicator of subclinical or clinical issues. On the other hand, athletes with personality disorders are typically referred by coaches and administration following discrete episodes or patterns of emotional and behavioral dysregulation. The presence of a personality disorder may be more quickly identifiable in these cases. It is critical for practitioners to recognize that athletes are

Although some level of aggressive behavior is acceptable in many sports, athletes with certain personality disorders may hold exaggerated beliefs about what is acceptable or lack empathy for other players.

Summary of Typical PI-II Issues

Common PI-II Difficulties

Extreme intrapersonal distress:

- Emotional rigidity or instability
- Restricted or demonstrative expressions of emotion
- Ego-syntonic view of the self

Resultant behavioral dysregulation:

- Challenged interpersonal relationships
- Drug and alcohol use
- Emotion-regulation deficits and excessive use of avoidance strategies
- Frequent altercations with others resulting in clear behavioral consequences

just as likely as the general population to have a personality disorder. In fact, we (FG and ZM) have both worked with a number of collegiate and professional athletes with identifiable personality disorders across the cluster spectrum. Regardless of the particular therapy, for the athlete, as for any other community member, personality disorders can be very debilitating. Although athletes with some personality disorders attain high levels of success and have only intermittent problems (referred to as functional personality disorders), others display pervasive difficulties. For most, interpersonal relationships in athletic, family, and social environments are usually chaotic and disruptive. The sport organization is likely to expend considerable time and energy helping the athlete, yet he may not seemingly appreciate the support or even acknowledge its need. Repetitive conflicts with coaches, teammates, and referees can be expected, as can overreaction to minute (perceived) insults. Athletes with personality disorders may also appear to have heightened self-importance and to lack empathy. These characteristics may be exacerbated by the celebrity status often accompanying high-level competitive athletics or by people who attempt to get close to athletes by aggrandizing and reinforcing all behavior (regardless if the behavior is good, bad, right, or wrong).

Final Thoughts

Although some have stated that clinical concerns are limited among athletes, athletes are just as likely as the general population to experience the disorders included in this chapter. These disorders may be missed entirely at subclinical or mild levels. This once again points to the need for careful assessment before intervention. A discussion of all possible disorders (such as schizophrenia, somatoform disorders, trichotillomania, and sexual dysfunction) is well beyond the scope of this chapter. However, we have reviewed the diagnostic categories most commonly experienced by athletes and have discussed assessing and treating such disorders using available empirical evidence and best-treatment guidelines. Certainly, restricting questioning to a nonclinical focus during the interview can result in a narrow view of the athlete that severely affects those in need of more clinical interventions. Although some practitioners may fear alienating their athletes by asking questions necessary to gain a full psychosocial picture, we suggest that in providing holistic psychological care, such a focus is necessary at least during the initial stages of the intervention process. This does *not* have to be done by asking rigid questions such as, "Do you frequently manipulate or harm others to meet your personal needs?" Obviously this type of question is inappropriate, and would not be asked in this way even with a clinical patient. As we have stated throughout the text, the practitioner can gain necessary information by having a collaborative conversation with the athlete, during which she weaves in and out of important topic areas in a flexible manner. The goal is not to ask a series of structured questions, but to collect a breadth and depth of client information during the session that can clarify the presenting issue and direct intervention. As stated previously, athletes are typically relieved by the opportunity to discuss difficulties that may be affecting more than the sport experience. Whether the athlete is simply experiencing mood fluctuations, competitive anxiety, brief interpersonal concerns, or more clinical issues, the clinical sport psychologist should consider all of these factors in order to provide the best care for the athlete.

To this point, we have discussed interventions to meet performance and developmental goals (chapter 6), to reduce psychological barriers affecting athletic performance and other life domains (chapter 7), and to address more clinical concerns (chapters 8 and 9). Chapter 10 discusses interventions to assist athletes who are transitioning out of the sport environment or experiencing a premature, unplanned termination from competitive athletics that is causing psychological distress.

CHAPTER 10

Performance Termination (PT)

In chapter 3, we briefly introduced performance termination (PT), the final MCS-SP categorization. Performance termination cases focus on problems relating to the timely or untimely end of an athletic career. The unfortunate reality in the sport domain is that all athletes must ultimately face the end of their career as competitive performers. In many respects, the athlete's career cycle resembles the career cycles of the rest of the population, although athletes experience a shorter, more defined period of involvement. Although some professional athletes continue their careers into their late 30s or early 40s, most athletes can expect a much earlier end. In fact, most collegiate athletes find their formal competitive careers ending as soon as the early 20s, and careers end even earlier in sports such as figure skating and gymnastics. The athlete must face and properly handle significant changes in identity and lifestyle along with a future requiring new areas of productivity in order to achieve optimal psychological well-being. Career termination is often viewed as the most significant experience in sport (Murphy, 1995) and, as such, consideration of this transitional period is essential for the clinical sport psychologist. In fact, termination issues can take on many forms depending on the developmental level of the athlete and the type of termination faced (such as timely versus untimely).

To review, the MCS-SP classification of PT-I refers to athletes whose termination from athletics is relatively predictable and possibly voluntary. This form of termination is typically due to natural aging and is often associated with the expected diminution of physical skills or graduation from high school or college. In contrast, PT-II refers to athletes facing unexpected and typically involuntary (and rapid) career termination due to injury or unacceptable performance leading to deselection (being cut). In both PT-I and PT-II, athletes often experience intense psychological reactions and must quickly face practical life issues. However, each classification is associated with very different issues and reactions, thus requiring different treatment foci and interventions.

Before considering the special intervention needs of athletes experiencing PT-I and PT-II and the subsequent intervention strategies, let's examine some fundamental aspects of athletic participation and the theory and research on athletic career transition.

Retirement from sport is a form of career termination that can be thought of as a life transition. For this reason, transitional models view termination from competitive sport as a "process" (Schlossberg, 1981). Schlossberg (1981) defined transition as "an event that results in a change of assumptions about oneself and the world and thus requires a corresponding change in one's behavior and relationships" (p. 5). Schlossberg and colleagues have also proposed a model of adaptation to transition in which three variables interact (Charner & Schlossberg, 1986, June; Schlossberg, 1981). These variables include the individual's personal characteristics (personality coping resources), the individual's perception of the transition (fair or unfair, in or out of control, and so on), and the characteristics of the pre- and posttransition environments (social and family supports, financial circumstance, and so on). A number of authors have adapted this transitional model to sport issues (Gordon, 1995; Pearson & Petitpas, 1990), and it has garnered some empirical support in sport career termination (Baillie & Danish, 1992; Parker, 1994; Sinclair & Orlick, 1994; Swain, 1991). But, others have argued that the transitional model lacks sufficient detail regarding the specific features related to the adjustment process (Taylor & Ogilvie, 1994; Taylor & Ogilvie, 1998). To explain and understand the transition process in greater detail, Taylor and Ogilvie (1998) proposed a model in which four components occur sequentially:

1. Cause of career termination (age, graduation, injury, deselection, free choice)
2. Developmental and intrapersonal variables (identity, perception of control, personality variables)
3. Personal resources (social support, financial considerations, coping skills)
4. Type of career transition (distressful or healthy)

Yet, how do athletes actually process and experience these issues? Many studies have researched the likelihood of athletes adequately adjusting, both emotionally and socially, to career termination. Lavallee and colleagues summarized the findings of 14 studies (n = 2653) conducted between 1982 and 1998 that evaluated psychological adjustment to career termination among athletes in amateur, collegiate, Olympic, and professional sports (Lavallee, Nesti, Borkoles, Cockerill, & Edge, 2000). The aggregate data from these 14 studies indicated that 20.1% (n = 535) of the athletes manifested psychological difficulties in response to athletic termination. This percentage strongly suggests the need for both preventative and remedial interventions.

Professionals counseling athletes for career termination issues should consider numerous factors, including retirement, the adaptation process (such as identity and cognitive schemas), and coping behaviors, that mediate the response to termination (Gordon, 1995; Taylor & Ogilvie, 1998). Let's discuss these three factors.

Retirement is a function of a variety of involuntary and voluntary variables. Some variables such as natural aging, high school or college graduation, and gradual skill diminution due to repeated injury are more predictable and allow for more social, financial, and psychological preparation. Career termination for these predictable reasons falls into the MCS-SP category of PT-I. Career-ending injuries and deselection (PT-II) are typically more traumatic and often allow little time to prepare for the reality of career cessation. Athletic termination from each of these causes and its associated interventions are discussed later in this chapter.

For the vast majority of competitive athletes, sport involvement plays a central role in the development and maintenance of personal identity. Being identified as an athlete has many positive consequences in society, and contemplating no longer being viewed as an athlete is often distressing for those considering the end of a competitive career. Issues of gender and ethnicity also impact termination, as in both collegiate and professional sports, fewer opportunities exist for females, African Americans, and Hispanics in coaching and sports administration (Murphy, 1995).

Previous research strongly suggests that sport participation is difficult to exit, as it has long provided the athlete with a sense of personal competence and mastery, social recognition, personal enjoyment, and numerous satisfying social relationships (Scanlan, Stein, & Ravizza, 1989; Taylor & Ogilvie, 2001). In addition, Pearson and Petitpas (1990) suggested that factors predicting difficulties transitioning out of sport include a strong and exclusive identity based on athletic performance, a large difference between athletic ability and athletic career expectations, behavioral deficits and emotional difficulties, and limited supportive social relationships. A great deal of empirical evidence supports the contention that overly identifying with the athlete role relates to poor social and emotional adjustment in response to career termination (Grove, Lavallee, & Gordon, 1997; Schmid & Schilling, 1997). Conversely, less exclusive athlete identity and alternative interests result in more adaptive transitional processes and better social and emotional adjustment upon termination (Lavallee, Gordon, & Grove, 1997; Schmid & Schilling, 1997; Sinclair & Orlick, 1993; Werthner & Orlick, 1986).

Drawing from our own experience in the collegiate and professional sport milieu, we have found that the loss of camaraderie with teammates, of social recognition, and of social relationships (often formed through the celebrity status of being an athlete) is particularly problematic. All three of these potential losses relate to an athlete's personal and professional identity. In this regard, athletes who remain fixed in their identity as a competitive performer and fail to adjust to their changing life realities may face significant challenges in the transition process. The term *situational foreclosure* describes situations in which an individual resists change in life circumstances due to lack of information and experience, but *does not* excessively identify with a particular role (Petitpas & Danish, 1995). With the accrual of information and the passage of time, situational foreclosure typically abates, and adequate adjustment naturally evolves. *Psychological foreclosure,* on the other hand, describes a process in which an individual's identity has become highly (and exclusively) connected with her role (i.e., athlete) (Petitpas & Danish, 1995). This rigid connection may be primarily due to a core belief system (schema). For example, an athlete who believes that social approval and thus personal adequacy can only come from that identity may be prone to psychological foreclosure. In keeping with the cognitive schemas presented in chapter 2, these individuals may be unwilling or unable to consider their changing realities and may not easily integrate new information or recognize new opportunities (Henry & Renaud, 1972; Perna et al., 1995).

Certainly, not all athletes experience significant distress when exiting the athletic environment and shifting identities and roles. Most athletes evolve through the life transition of career termination, and natural developmental processes allow them to move forward in their lives. However, many, especially those whose schemas result in psychological foreclosure, need professional assistance.

The remainder of this chapter carefully considers both PT-I and PT-II, discusses the psychological processes involved in each, and provides intervention options for working with this unique subset of the athletic population.

Performance Termination-I (PT-I)

PT-I refers to those cases in which an athlete's competitive career expectedly ends. This type of termination often results from free choice, the natural diminution of physical skills due to aging or the cumulative effects of injury, or to the expected end of competitive opportunity (such as high school or college graduation). As noted, the athletic life cycle is substantially shorter than that of other careers. Most people face the end of their careers later in life, and most often termination occurs by personal choice or is predictable based on life expectancy. As such, most individuals have substantial time to prepare for this eventuality and to develop social relationships, activities, and living arrangements that promote healthy adaptations.

Career termination is not always smooth and predictable, and the athletic career by its very nature involves a reduced likelihood of choice in when to terminate. Injury, the addition of new (and possibly better performing) athletes, the time-limited nature of high school and collegiate athletics, and normal aging (often resulting in

Although many athletes dream of athletic success, physical injury can quickly end an athletic career.

subtle yet increasingly obvious performance decrements) are typically unavoidable. Those few athletes who enjoy long and successful competitive careers nonetheless experience termination at an age that for nonathletes is associated with peak productivity, career development, and high energy. Since research indicates that athletes generally view themselves as happier and more competent in their athlete role compared to any other aspect of their lives (Griffin, Chassin, & Young, 1981), it can be understood that transitioning out of that role may leave the athlete particularly vulnerable and pessimistic.

As previously stated, the variables usually resulting in anticipated career termination are normal athletic aging, gradual skill diminution (possibly from significant but not immediately career-ending injury), and the additive effects of multiple injuries over time. Of course, depending on the sport, the aging process or the slow but steady effects of injury manifest at different ages. While the athlete's age and reasons for performance decline may vary, the athlete must effectively confront the impending transition for optimal well-being and personal satisfaction during the subsequent stages of life. The retiring athlete's pretransitional psychological makeup and available resources (social, financial, and educational) highly relate to the likelihood of positive adaptation.

To help the athlete optimally adjust, the clinical sport psychologist must understand the fundamental issues of career termination and the variety of its manifestations, and should maintain an ability to view the transition from the athlete's perspective. While studies evaluating the efficacy of interventions for career transitions have not been conducted and empirical evidence for any particular approach clearly lacks, the following sections outline a recommended intervention for promoting successful adaptation.

Empathic Joining and Emotional Support

In the first stage of intervention for the PT-I athlete, the clinical sport psychologist conveys a true understanding of not only the content of the athlete's concern, but also and most important, the affective tone of her experience. This understanding is successfully conveyed not through rote efforts at reflective listening, but rather through a reflection of feelings *demonstrated* but possibly not verbalized by the athlete. Frustration, anger, sadness, and anxiety, along with feelings of hopelessness and inadequacy, are often experienced but not always stated. The practitioner must be sensitive to the affective tone of the sessions and not focus exclusively on pragmatic issues (such as completing education and searching for future employment). These pragmatic concerns, while important, can only be addressed when the athlete is in a more adaptive psychological state, begins to accept his changing circumstance, and begins the long process of attaining a feeling of mastery and control. In this stage of the process, specific change is not the essential focus. Rather, a foundation is set that provides the athlete a place to be heard, understood, and supported. From this foundation of understanding and collaboration, often referred to as empathic joining (Rogers, 1959), the trust relationship that develops between the athlete and practitioner hopefully promotes a sense of safety and hope. These elements ultimately result in the athlete's readiness to hear and assimilate new information and to employ new behavioral (coping) strategies.

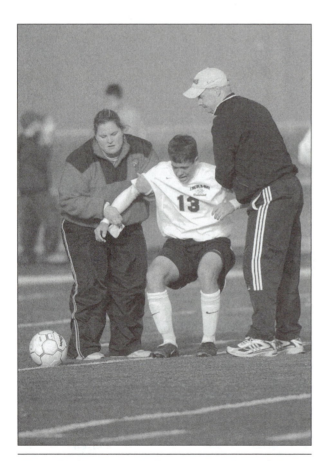

While all athletes eventually experience the end of their athletic careers, each athlete will respond with different concerns, fears, and expectations.

Behavioral Activation

Often in response to the transition out of sport, the athlete restricts involvement in usual (and enjoyable) activities, withdraws from available social supports, and generally alters how she engages in life. These changes typically do not serve new goals and valued life directions, and they often reduce the frequency and intensity of social reinforcement. Such changes and the resultant reduction of social and personal reinforcers can promote the belief that life has changed and is inevitably less satisfying. As a result, this behavioral deactivation (or inhibition) can result in dysphoric mood and a heightened sense of hopelessness. A fundamental intervention strategy that helps the athlete through behavioral planning and self-monitoring (to increase the frequency of enjoyable activities) is behavioral activation (Jacobson et al., 1996). Behavioral activation is commonly used when the client's disengagement from previously enjoyed social and personal activities results in sadness and hopelessness. This strategy has long been effectively utilized to reduce depression and enhance hopefulness (Jacobson et al., 1996). In addition to enhancing hopefulness, this strategy prepares the athlete for actively engaging in activities that promote a sense of control and increased hope, and challenge the athlete's belief that life is no longer satisfying.

Cognitive Restructuring

As noted several times, core belief systems about the self and others, referred to as cognitive sche-

mas, are the lenses by which we see and interpret the world (Young et al., 2003). Individuals who hold cognitive schemas of inadequacy or vulnerability may be more likely to respond negatively to losing an athletic identity (and its natural ego enhancement) and to view themselves as out of control. During career transitions, these athletes may be more prone to respond with psychological foreclosure and intense emotional reactivity. These athletes' core belief systems have associated rules that inevitably lead to conclusions that are extreme and emotionally charged. Some of the typical rule systems associated with inadequacy and vulnerability schemas are highlighted in figure 10.1. Further, the heightened affect associated with these rule systems, which the cognitive therapy literature also refers to as *intermediate beliefs* (Beck, 1976), typically results in compensatory behavior intended to regulate the negative affect. Such compensatory (escape) behaviors may include denial of the career termination, substance use or abuse, or other dysfunctional activities such as gambling, infidelity, or promiscuity. Although these forms of experiential avoidance are intended to reduce negative affect, they instead promote an increased focus on negative internal states and lead to further distress in major life domains.

As in treatments for depression and other psychological disorders (see chapter 8), interventions for expected career transition should first identify the thought processes activated by the triggering event (the impending career termination). Further intervention goals include restructuring the content of these thoughts to reflect reality and, where

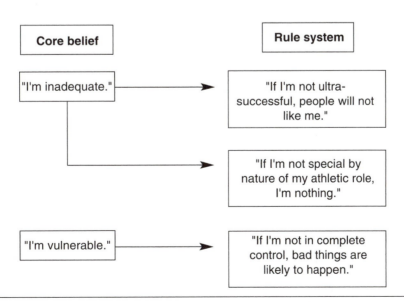

Figure 10.1   Common rule systems associated with inadequacy and vulnerability schemas.

possible, modifying the underlying core belief systems (Young et al., 2001).

Acceptance and Commitment

There are situations in which the opportunity to provide professional services is limited or where cognitive schemas are so strong that full modification is unrealistic. In such cases, an alternative approach known as acceptance and commitment therapy (ACT) (discussed in chapter 6) may help (Hayes et al., 1999). When using ACT with pre- and posttermination athletes, affective responses to the career termination are noted and experienced, as are the belief systems at their core. However, rather than reducing affect or changing cognitive content, ACT helps the client accept (experience) his emotions and thought processes. These internal experiences are not interpreted as good or bad, but as normal and expected aspects of life that need not be avoided or reduced. Particular emphasis is placed on maintaining an awareness of these internal experiences and viewing them as passing events that should be allowed to pass, rather than as absolute realities that should be modified. In essence, the athlete learns to be guided not by the desire to make uncomfortable thoughts and feelings go away, but by valued goals and life directions requiring action. Like other individuals experiencing intense negative affect, the athlete experiencing career termination may engage in avoidance or other behaviors in order to feel good in the moment (short-term emotion reduction). The ACT approach asserts that all avoidance must be replaced by a clear understanding of the client's goals and the actions needed to attain them. ACT places significant effort into helping the client appreciate the journey ahead rather than mourn the life left behind.

Career Planning

Once the athlete and practitioner have established a supportive relationship, the athlete has been reactivated, and cognitive-affective reactions have been addressed either by traditional change methods or by more recent acceptance approaches, the final stage of intervention for PT-I begins. This stage includes the pragmatics of actual career planning. Planning may be referred to professionals with special expertise or accomplished by clinical sport psychologists with education and training in career counseling.

The career planning process often involves identifying primary support systems, personal

> ## Summary of the General Treatment Protocol for PT-I
>
> - Empathic joining and emotional support
> - Behavioral activation
> - Cognitive restructuring
> - Acceptance and commitment to life goals
> - Career planning

strengths and weaknesses, and personal career needs; developing job skills; identifying job opportunities; and setting specific and realistic career goals (Murphy, 1995). Career planning has been described as a linear progression of self-exploration, career exploration, and, finally, career acquisition (Petitpas, Champagne, Chartrand, Danish, & Murphy, 1997). Of course, career exploration optimally occurs *during* the athlete's competitive career, and in fact, organizations such as the United States Olympic Committee have developed structured programs to promote planning for the inevitable career transition faced by all athletes. Yet for many if not most athletes, the exploration phase occurs in the midst of the transition and often requires the discussed therapeutic interventions as preliminary steps to initiating career planning.

This entire intervention protocol provides the PT-I athlete with a sense of personal control over her immediate situation and distal life efforts. The athlete moves from a pessimistic, past-oriented view in which the best part of life (athletic participation) is over to a more optimistic, future-oriented view in which the memories of the past live side by side with the challenges of new and meaningful life choices.

Performance Termination-II (PT-II)

PT-II refers to cases in which an athlete's competitive career comes to an unexpected (possibly traumatic) and involuntary end due to serious injury or certain types of deselection, typically leaving the athlete with few options for the future.

While PT-I career termination can be either voluntary or involuntary, it generally involves some degree of *expectation*. In contrast, PT-II refers to more rapid and often traumatic transitions in which *unanticipated* severe injury or deselection directly terminates an athletic career. Research suggests that adjustment to termination following injury is more difficult and that such athletes report lower ratings of life satisfaction than those whose careers ended less abruptly (Kleiber, Greendorfer, Blinde, & Samdahl, 1987; Werthner & Orlick, 1986). This same finding could be expected for athletes whose careers are terminated by a sudden and unanticipated deselection. The findings by Kleiber and colleagues (1987) highlight the necessity for the clinical sport psychologist to know the related literature and develop a skill set to assist such athletes, as many of these athletes clearly describe and exhibit psychological distress and emotional pain based on these fundamental life changes.

Understanding the transition for the severely injured athlete requires careful exploration of the psychological effects of injury leading to career termination. Suinn (1967) has suggested that athletes respond to injury-based termination the same way others respond to loss. Anecdotally, Suinn has connected the athlete's injury-based career loss with the well-known stages of grief proposed by Kubler-Ross (1969). The grief response model by Kubler-Ross follows a sequence of denial, anger, bargaining, depression, and acceptance. While only anecdotal evidence supports the contention that grief in athletes suffering from injury-based termination follows this model (Murphy, 1995), it is likely that preinjury personality variables play a major role in the psychological response to both the injury and its consequences. For example, a recent study by Gallagher and Gardner (2005) examined the relationship between cognitive vulnerabilities (early maladaptive schemas), coping strategy, and emotional response to injury. Results indicate that athletes who hold specific cognitive schemas related to abandonment and mistrust, and also manifest an avoidance-based coping style, are significantly more likely to experience high levels of negative affect to significant as well as minor injuries immediately upon injury. Further, athletes who hold vulnerability to harm and inadequacy schemas, and also manifest an avoidance-based coping style, are significantly more likely to experience heightened negative affect following full rehabilitation and immediately prior to competitive reengagement. In essence, athletes concerned with acceptance and social engagement (fitting in) experience greater distress when first injured (presumably due to fear of social isola-

tion). On the other hand, athletes who are more concerned with reinjury and competence are more likely to have difficulties after successful rehabilitation and before reengagement (possibly due to a form of fear of failure). This study was specifically conducted with injured athletes and, although not all of the injuries resulted in career termination, we can hypothesize from these data that individuals with specific early maladaptive schemas respond to traumatic injury-based career termination in a substantially more affect-laden, avoidant, and less adaptive manner. Future research is warranted to investigate the impact of premorbid cognitive schemas on career transition following severe injury. For the clinical sport psychologist, assessing and exploring the schemas noted in the Gallagher and Gardner study (2005) would likely not only provide a more in-depth understanding of cases, but may also enhance the practitioner's ability to reduce emotional reactivity and begin the process of smooth transition.

Additional research suggests that athletes with exaggerated athletic identities are more likely to poorly adjust to traumatic injury-based career termination, potentially with major depression and alcohol or drug abuse (Chartrand & Lent, 1987; Elkin, 1981; Hill & Lowe, 1974; Ogilvie & Howe, 1986). Once again, while still an open empirical question needing further exploration, athletes with exaggerated athletic identities experiencing traumatic disengagement from sport through unanticipated deselection may respond similarly.

We know that seriously injured athletes and those athletes transitioning away from the sport milieu frequently experience heightened emotional distress, often requiring assistance. As many sport practitioners do not consider *DSM* nosology when conceptualizing an athlete, an unfortunate number of athletes experiencing subclinical or clinical symptoms do not receive the focused treatment they require. We are specifically referring to athletes who, based on traumatic injury-based career termination, respond with subclinical or clinical forms of an acute stress disorder (ASD) (discussed in chapter 7) or posttraumatic stress disorder (PTSD) (discussed in chapter 8). According to the *DSM-IV-TR* (APA, 2000), acute stress disorder requires exposure to a traumatic event that involves serious injury, actual or threatened death, or threat to the physical integrity of self or others. Traumatic injury and unanticipated career-ending deselection meet the spirit of these criteria. In addition, an ASD diagnosis requires three or more of the following symptoms:

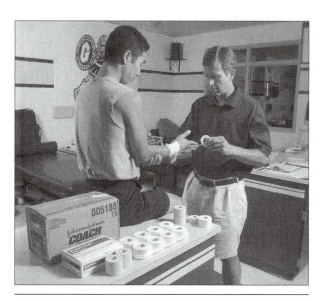

Some athletes will attempt to delay termination by minimizing the severity of injuries or pretending to be injured to overshadow growing skill decrements.

a) Detachment, numbness, or lack of emotion

b) Dazedness and incomplete awareness of the current surroundings

c) Derealization

d) Depersonalization

e) Poor recollection of the major details of the trauma

Further, individuals must persistently reexperience the trauma through recurrent thoughts, images, dreams, flashbacks, and so on. They must obviously avoid stimuli that may trigger recollections (including conversation about athletics) and must experience increased anger or anxiety. These symptoms must last for at least 2 d but no more than 4 wk. In addition, symptoms must begin within 4 wk of the traumatic event. Obviously, the symptoms must significantly distress or impair major areas of functioning, which can certainly be seen in many athletes undergoing traumatic termination.

When considering the seriousness of many athletic injuries and viewing the unanticipated end of an athletic career as a symbolic death, an athlete confronting serious injury meets the first and most fundamental criterion for either ASD or PTSD. In addition, as expected in PTSD, the response to a sudden termination of an athletic career has been reported to include such symptoms as reexperiencing injury (or reliving deselection) through recurring and intrusive thoughts or

images and distress when in contact with stimuli associated with athletics, including teammates and other reminders of the athletic career. Athletes may also demonstrate persistent avoidance and numbing, detachment, diminished or pessimistic future expectations, minimal interest and participation in previously enjoyed activities, and hyperarousal manifested by increased irritability and anger, difficulty sleeping, and altered concentration (Alfermann, 2000; Petitpas & Danish, 1995). Although practitioners not regularly working with clinical populations may think of ASD and PTSD as trauma-based disorders typically derived from sexual abuse, combat experiences, and car accidents, we encourage practitioners to remember that these short- and long-term disorders are in no way exclusively bound to traditional traumatic events. Remember that according to the *DSM-IV-TR* (APA, 2000), an individual does not even have to *personally* experience a traumatic event, but only must witness the event, before developing symptomatology. If this is true in clinical populations, athletes actually experiencing a traumatic event are obviously prone to developing ASD or PTSD.

In fact, according to a national (U.S.) probability sample, the prevalence rate for PTSD following *injury* is at least 9% of the general population (Resnick et al., 1993). For athletes, whose personal, social, and occupational identities center on athletic involvement, even higher PTSD prevalence rates following injury are certainly possible. Even if the rates stabilize at 9% (which is a high number), clearly the clinical sport psychologist must realize the likelihood of encountering PTSD and must become knowledgeable and skilled to intervene in such cases.

Let's highlight how an athlete's symptom picture can clearly meet PTSD criteria in order to understand how to organize the presenting data:

• **Event.** The athlete experienced a career-ending on-ice collision, which severely injured an already weakened knee. The athlete was unable to skate or walk off the ice and was removed by medical personnel while fans and teammates looked on.

• **Immediate emotional experience.** The athlete later reported that during the event, he felt intense fear that his career was over and immediately panicked that he was unable to walk.

• **Following the event.** The athlete reported that for months he thought constantly about the moment the injury occurred, almost as if he was still there reexperiencing it. His thoughts included images of being on the ice and being removed from the ice, recollections of the sounds of the crowd and his teammates' reactions, belief that there was something he could have done to prevent the injury, and replays of the event with alternate scenarios not leading to injury.

- He reported frequently and vividly dreaming about the experience, often awakening during these dreams with fear, sadness, anxiety, and feelings of hopelessness. Some changes in sleep patterns followed.

- When asked about substance and alcohol use, he stated that he subsequently began consuming a bit more alcohol, yet had to stop because even slight intoxication resulted in increased cognition and affect related to the event.

- He reported being hypersensitive to anything that could trigger memories of the event and injury. As such, he quickly became irritable with other people and events, refused to go to hockey games despite invitations, and would not watch hockey on television.

- He felt a looming sadness, which he attributed to the belief that he would now have no enjoyable future occupation.

- He experienced increased negative emotion whenever his knee even slightly ached.

Given this self-report information, the athlete in this case absolutely meets the full criteria for PTSD (APA, 2000). Yet, the athlete's initial and subsequent experiences of the event are not particularly odd or out of character to the situation or the new external realities. If his experience seems logical, we encourage readers to remain open to the possibility of encountering either ASD or PTSD when working with an athlete who has experienced a traumatic athletic termination. As this case demonstrates, a diagnosis of PTSD or ASD (which is by definition less intense than PTSD in a variety of ways) is a profound possibility for such athletes.

While it is difficult to predict who will experience the array of symptoms consistent with PTSD or ASD, recent research by Marx and Sloan (2002) suggests that experiential avoidance (excessive effort to avoid negative internal experiences such as thoughts, feelings, or bodily sensations) is a strong predictor of psychological disturbance following traumatic events. These data again suggest that premorbid behavioral characteristics, in this case using avoidance as a primary coping strategy, relate to the development of psychological difficulties in highly stressful and traumatic

circumstances. The implications of these findings for understanding and treating PT-II are clear. Interventions for the psychological and behavioral *responses* to unanticipated and traumatic career termination must consider (assess) premorbid behavioral characteristics and fully explore whether the symptom cluster resembles that of clinical disorders more typically associated with nonathletic trauma (namely ASD and PTSD). Practitioners working with these athlete issues should be very careful not to simply allow the athlete to vent her associated emotional pain. As suggested in chapter 7, critical incident stress debriefing (CISD) and interventions with similar methodology are contraindicated and potentially harmful. The practitioner should also resist focusing exclusively on career planning, financial planning, and role transition. Such exclusive or premature foci can have significant negative consequences.

While empirically supported protocols for PT-II are not yet available, there are empirically informed interventions for specific PT-II elements or subtypes. The model treatment protocol we present next is empirically informed and includes variations for athletes who experience deselection or injury-based termination.

Assessment of Trauma Symptoms

Given the traumatic quality of unexpected career termination, either through injury or deselection, symptom patterns consistent with ASD or PTSD must be carefully considered. As noted in chapter 8, self-report measures such as the PTSD Symptom Scale (Foa et al., 1993) or the ASD and PTSD modules from the SCID-I (First et al., 1997) can effectively accomplish this purpose. This assessment can readily be completed within the first meeting, and does not require the practitioner to take an overly clinical stance.

Emotional Support and Safety

As in the case of PT-I, establishing an emotionally supportive and caring therapeutic relationship is a priority and should be the primary focus of the first 1 or 2 sessions following interview. Note that avoidance of the difficult emotions associated with career termination is likely to manifest in multiple ways, including session lateness, absence, alcohol or substance use before sessions, lack of engagement and unwillingness to talk about troubling aspects of the transition, and efforts to prematurely end counseling. These behaviors are expected and need to be normalized and discussed openly and *early* in treatment to help promote a positive and safe therapeutic environment. Once again, as in the treatment of PT-I, it is imperative the clinical sport psychologist attend not only to the explicit message verbally communicated by the athlete, but also to the implicit affect conveyed as she presents her circumstance. Reflecting this affective tone is critical to conveying empathy, understanding, and safety.

Clients with vulnerability and safety schemas need to perceive the practitioner as accepting and nonjudgmental. However, individuals with these schemas often quickly perceive themselves as being judged or negatively viewed. The practitioner is encouraged to guard against rapidly offering direct suggestions for new behaviors, especially regarding career opportunities or strategies. The athlete may incorrectly assume that these suggestions emanate from a negative judgment about her and her current life situation or skill set. Certainly, this strategy may inadvertently trivialize the athlete's personal experience, her feelings and beliefs about herself, and her powerful emotions.

Self-Awareness Promotion

This next intervention phase elucidates the meaning of the athlete's career termination (including possibly the traumatic events directly leading to termination) and helps the athlete label and recognize his present emotions and thought processes, discover the connections among those thoughts and feelings, and develop awareness of the behaviors emitted in response to those thoughts and feelings. Promoting self-awareness is the first step in the corrective component of treatment, and it sets the stage for later cognitive restructuring, prolonged exposure exercises, and behavior change (including later career planning). During this phase the practitioner encourages the athlete to express his feelings and develops a sense of the athlete's possible cognitive distortions and core beliefs (schemas). This phase involves both in-session discussion and client homework. Homework exercises primarily consist of recording situations that trigger thoughts or emotions associated with deselection and injury-based termination. These homework assignments are often recorded on forms like the self-awareness log on the following page.

The completed homework is reviewed at the beginning of each meeting to explore and understand the relationships among triggering events, thoughts, feelings, and behaviors. In addition, the compilation of particular thought processes provides the practitioner with feedback on the athlete's notable schemas. For example, recorded thoughts that are essentially all negative statements about the self or negative predictions of the future (in terms of both career and relationships) implicate core beliefs about adequacy and vulnerability. Of course, these hypotheses ultimately guide intervention choices.

Prolonged Exposure and Cognitive Restructuring

Individuals frequently respond to a traumatic event with interpretations about the event ("This is the worst thing that could ever happen to me") and the subsequent loss ("My life is over"). These thoughts are typically accompanied by interpretations about oneself ("I'm a failure and I'll never be happy again") and the world ("People close to me will want to leave"). Considerable evidence suggests that these thought processes directly relate to the psychological difficulties the individual experiences following challenging life circumstances (Resick & Schnicke, 1993). Foa, Steketee, and Rothbaum (1989) have also suggested that psychological difficulties in response to significant negative life events occur due to the development of a fear network in the memory that results in avoidant (escape) behaviors. These fear structures include both external and internal factors associated with the difficult life event, such as the triggering stimuli, behavioral and affective responses, and personal meaning ascribed to the event. Later, external cues, thoughts, and feelings associated with the event may elicit the fear structure and trigger avoidance behaviors. These fear structures and the associated avoidance block the assimilation of new information. This may somewhat explain why athletes experiencing psychological foreclosure following career termination have difficulty integrating new information and adapting to new life circumstances.

These conceptualizations of the psychological response to significant negative events suggest that interventions need to provide repeated, prolonged, and systematic exposure to the traumatic situation. When done correctly, the exposure habituates the athlete to the emotional response and subsequently modifies the fear network. Exposure would also modify (restructure) the meaning elements (belief systems) associated with the

Self-Awareness Log

Name _____ **Week** _____

Situation or triggering event	Automatic thoughts	Emotional responses	Behaviors/actions	Consequences of behaviors/actions

event. Empirically supported interventions of prolonged exposure (PE) and cognitive therapy (CT) have been effectively utilized separately and in combination to alleviate psychological difficulties caused by traumatic events. In addition, PE and CT have been found to be more effective than no treatment or basic counseling (Resick & Schnicke, 1993).

Thus, the fourth phase in PT-II treatment involves prolonged exposure and cognitive restructuring. If the athlete does not manifest signs and symptoms of traumatic stress, prolonged exposure is unnecessary and cognitive restructuring of the meaning of career termination can be initiated by the self-monitoring homework utilized in the self-awareness promotion phase. However, evidence

of ASD or PTSD indicates the need for prolonged exposure and cognitive restructuring.

While a complete discussion of prolonged exposure (PE) is beyond the scope of this text (see Foa & Rothbaum, 1998), successful PE has some basic requirements. First, PE is *not* just a reexperiencing of the event, which is certainly cruel and undoubtedly retraumatizing. Just the opposite is true. PE requires clients to confront the traumatic situation (such as severe injury) by imagining themselves in the situation or by recalling it in detail for an extended time. During this, PE accesses the fear network so that the client can more fully experience and process its associated thoughts and emotions, breaking the previous (negatively reinforced) pattern of avoidance. PE protocols may use journal writing in which different elements of the traumatic memories are written in varying levels of detail (Resick & Calhoun, 2001). PE sessions can be as long as 90 min and may occur biweekly for some time. PE often includes relaxation training (Foa & Rothbaum, 1998) to promote a willingness to engage in its tasks. We encourage practitioners interested in PE to go well beyond this text to learn the appropriate use of this procedure. Although the appropriate use of prolonged exposure can produce incredible results, inadequate or incorrect use of this procedure can be extremely detrimental.

Cognitive restructuring is also necessary for effective treatment. Cognitive restructuring includes a detailed exploration of the interpretations, assumptions, and beliefs that existed *prior* to career termination. For some clients, prior belief systems may have been marginally pessimistic but did not hinder day-to-day activities. However, a significant life event (such as career termination) may increase the client's negative view of the self and the world. For others, pre-event belief systems may have been adaptive and functional, but may be substantially altered by the traumatic situation. An alteration of prior belief systems can occur when the trauma challenges the previously adaptive belief system. For example, following a significant negative life event, an individual who previously viewed the world as a safe place may suddenly feel vulnerable and view the world as threatening and hostile. Triggered or altered belief systems can be treated with a systematic intervention following Beck's basic cognitive therapy model (Beck, 1976; Beck et al. 1979; Beck, 1995). When the athlete experiences mild triggered or altered belief systems following unexpected termination but does not manifest a full traumatic response, the athlete can benefit from this approach prior to beginning career planning.

This phase of intervention constitutes the bulk of the therapeutic treatment for PT-II and generally requires 10 to 16 sessions. Yet, when the athlete seems unable or unwilling to modify her belief systems, an alternative approach with which you are now familiar, acceptance and commitment therapy, is available.

Acceptance and Commitment

As noted in the PT-I discussion, there are situations in which belief systems are held so strongly that modification becomes unrealistic and an alternative strategy becomes necessary. In the acceptance and commitment (ACT) model, affective responses to career termination are encouraged and experienced (as is done in PE). However, when applying ACT to PT-II, the clinical sport psychologist promotes the experiencing of internal states not to reduce affect, but to convey to the athlete that she can act toward distal goals while still feeling badly. Recalling traumatic events in order to fully experience the cognitive and affective responses to the memories is similar to prolonged exposure. However, the goal in ACT is not to change cognition, but rather to alter the idea that one has to feel better in order to act in line with goals and desires. Thus, internal experiences are not judged, but are seen as normal and expected aspects of the transitional process. The athlete hopefully develops the capacity to be guided by valued life directions instead of by the desire to eliminate uncomfortable thoughts and feelings. In this approach, the athlete learns to separate how she feels from how she acts, and thus can act to enhance her life while coexisting with the occasional pain that is often inextricably tied to the human condition. This process promotes accepting internal states and acting toward future life satisfaction. In the context of career termination, the athlete would engage with meaningful social supports, pursue activities that were satisfying before athletic disengagement, and begin to plan a future career.

Career Planning

As in PT-I treatment, the final phase of PT-II treatment involves career planning. At this point, the athlete no longer exhibits significant psychological or behavioral barriers, and is ready to move forward with the attainment of a new personal and professional identity. In the career-planning phase, the athlete identifies social supports, discusses his strengths and weaknesses, determines career needs and goals, develops new job skills, and identifies realistic job opportunities. Practitioners not trained to engage in this process should refer the athlete to another professional.

When seen as a whole, the PT-II intervention protocol builds on a sound and safe therapeutic relationship and aims to reduce behaviors that may interfere with moving toward a new and satisfying life circumstance. More traumatic PT-II cases require altering fear structures and traumatically triggered cognitive schemas in order to reduce avoidant behaviors that prevent successful career transition and that create psychological symptoms that reduce the athlete's quality of life. When traumatic symptoms are *not* present, intervention focuses on modifying the belief systems

Summary of the General Treatment Protocol for PT-II

- Assessment of trauma symptoms
- Emotional support and safety
- Self-awareness promotion
- Prolonged exposure and cognitive restructuring
- Acceptance and commitment to life goals
- Career planning

that interfere with the natural move forward in career and life planning. In all situations, the primary goal is functional improvement, that is, to increase behaviors that promote adjustment and future well-being (career planning, social engagement, and so on) and to reduce behaviors that maintain emotional dysregulation and impede the attainment of valued career and life goals.

Integrating Intervention Considerations

To fully understand the intervention considerations involved in PT, let's discuss the course of treatment for the PT cases presented in chapter 3. As you may recall, Kim was a 30-year-old competitive skier who faced the gradual and voluntary end of her competitive career. She was therefore classified as PT-I. Kim felt lost and feared that the relationships she developed through skiing would disintegrate after she completed her competitive career. When Kim sought consultation, the clinical sport psychologist first focused on establishing an empathic and supportive environment promoting the expression of affect and the open discussion of concerns and fears. This discussion evolved into cognitive restructuring and behavioral activation during which the practitioner encouraged Kim to actively engage in social activities with the particular people over whom she was concerned. She was encouraged to do this both to maintain involvement in previously enjoyed activities and to investigate her fears of losing her skiing relationships. As behavioral activation and cognitive restructuring were effectively completed and

maintained, Kim was able to begin active career exploration and planning and ultimately developed a successful and satisfying postathletic career in the fitness industry.

In the second PT example, Carlos was a 26-year-old minor league baseball player who suffered an unexpected, traumatic, and ultimately career-ending injury. Carlos experienced recurrent thoughts and images of his injury, withdrew from people or activities that reminded him of baseball and his playing career, and became increasingly despondent and angry. When his family referred him to a clinical sport psychologist, Carlos was clearly manifesting signs and symptoms of a traumatic stress disorder.

Treatment for Carlos began with building a supportive and empathic relationship in which he felt safe and willing to share his thoughts and feelings. After a number of missed appointments and late arrivals, Carlos slowly began to trust the practitioner and began to discuss his reactions to the termination of his athletic career. As this trust evolved to necessary levels (across 6 sessions spanning 10 wk), the practitioner overviewed the treatment process and explained to Carlos his symptomatology and the various phases of the intervention. The practitioner also discussed the common role of avoidance and explained that the urge to avoid treatment would likely be strong at times. Over the next 6 wk (2 sessions/wk), the practitioner employed a combination of prolonged exposure (PE) (aimed at the full and complete processing of traumatic memories and emotions) and cognitive restructuring (aimed at the modification of core beliefs and irrational thinking patterns). This was followed by 6 wk of 1/wk sessions utilizing the same techniques. At that point, Carlos demonstrated significantly fewer symptoms of traumatic stress and no longer met criteria for such a diagnosis. Once these symptoms abated and Carlos was engaged in behaviors more consistent with his pretrauma life, the practitioner began career planning and skill development, which took place over an additional 12 sessions in 4 mo. Following this phase of intervention, Carlos decided to complete his education and accepted a job as a pharmaceutical salesperson, which he found both interesting and lucrative.

Final Thoughts

All athletes face career termination at some point in their athletic pursuits. Those who are open to this eventuality and engage in ongoing consideration and planning typically handle this difficult life transition with a minimum of significant or long-term emotional difficulties. Others, especially those who experience an unexpected transition and those whose personal schemas keep them from considering athletic career termination, find the process taxing and can at times experience significant emotional distress. Without question, the clinical sport psychologist can help ameliorate such problems and promote ongoing career planning for all competitive athletes.

CHAPTER 11

Case Formulation in Clinical Sport Psychology

The professional practice of sport psychology involves a conceptually sound and evidence-based integration of assessment and intervention designed to provide high-level care to athletes. This chapter describes a systematic approach to case formulation in clinical sport psychology. Case formulation provides a working framework for understanding the athlete and the issues that she brings to the consulting room. Based upon a sound theoretical model (such as the IMAP) and a classification system (such as the MCS-SP), this method allows an idiographic intervention to be developed from nomothetic data, a process at the heart of the evidence-based practice of any sound profession. The formal discussion of case formulation has a long history in clinical psychology (Persons, 1989), yet it has been relatively overlooked in the sport psychology literature. We hope to spur interest in this critical topic.

Conceptualizing the Athlete

In the case formulation approach presented in this chapter, the practitioner's primary goal is to conceptualize the athlete's issues based on the information systematically collected during the assessment process. This conceptualization should include the following:

- A comprehensive evaluation of the presenting problem which allows for careful consideration of the environmental triggers, dispositional variables, problematic emotional and behavioral responses, and maintaining factors in the athlete's world (this leads to appropriate classification).

- A delineation of the psychological and behavioral processes that emanate from and are directly linked to the referral issue. Remember that we do *not* treat classifications or even end-point behaviors. Rather, our interventions target the processes that create or maintain the problematic behavior. The professional literature often refers to these processes as "mechanisms of action" (Barlow, Allen, & Choate, 2004).

- An empirically informed intervention strategy that is logically connected to the relevant psychological and behavioral processes and that will likely achieve the intervention goals set by the athlete and practitioner. See figure 11.1.

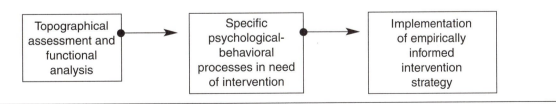

Figure 11.1 Goals of case formulation.

Assessing the Athlete

The practitioner begins case formulation by a comprehensive assessment (described in chapter 4) based primarily upon the IMAP theoretical model (chapter 2) and MCS-SP classification system (chapter 3). The answers to the following questions (posed in the assessment) guide the case conceptualization process, and subsequently aid in selecting the right interventions, as discussed in chapters 6 through 10:

- What are the presenting issues, how did these issues develop, and what factors trigger and maintain these issues?

- What are the situational and athletic demands of the athlete?

- What are the skill requirements of the athlete's sport and what is the athlete's development in the sport domain?

- What is the athlete's current skill level, how has she developed, and by what means has athletic skill development occurred (private coaching, self-development, organizational coaching)?

- What are the athlete's performance schemas (including attitudes and expectations about athletic performance and personal rules regarding effort, success, mistakes, failure, and so on)?

- What thoughts, emotions, and behavioral responses characterize varying aspects of athletic engagement?

- To what degree does the athlete focus on performance cues and contingencies and to what degree does she focus on self and performance ramifications during actual competition?

- How does the athlete respond to performance setbacks?

- To what degree (and when) does the athlete worry, procrastinate, or employ other forms of experiential avoidance?

- What athletic and personal performance learning experiences contribute to current issues?

- What are the current stressors and physical circumstances that contribute to the presenting issues?

- What is the athlete's cognitive and behavioral coping style in response to these issues, and how do the presenting issues affect her view of the self, others, and the future?

Many of the questions required for case formulation in clinical sport psychology are similar to those required for a clinically based functional analysis of behavior. All of these questions can be asked in the assessment process described in chapter 4 via semistructured interviews with the athlete. When appropriate, family members or coaches can provide additional information (with client consent).

The case formulation method presented in this text is systematic, comprehensive, and holistic. Both during and after assessment, the information gathered needs to be organized so that it provides an understanding of the larger picture of the athlete's presentation, leads to an appropriate MCS-SP classification, and culminates in correct intervention choices. Figure 11.2 presents the MCS-SP case formulation data form, which helps the practitioner organize data, formulate hypotheses, and subsequently determine interventions.

Next we discuss the eight specific elements of a comprehensive case formulation in clinical sport psychology and provide four examples of formulation, each representing a different MCS-SP classification.

Case Formulation Variables

In general, after eliciting the presenting problem or reason for referral, developing a useful case formulation requires a careful consideration of its first three elements: contextual performance demands, current athletic skill development, and relevant situational demands (including sport or nonsport events). These three separate but clearly interrelated elements must be carefully considered, whether the client is an individual athlete or an entire team. *Contextual performance demands* refer to the athlete's level of competitive activity and its inherent performance demands. It is crucial to assess the athlete's experience of the relevant performance demands, as the demands of professional sports greatly differ from the demands of a Division III collegiate program, which in turn differs from an elite youth travel team, and so on. In addition, each athlete will likely report a different personal experience than a teammate who is in the same environment and has the same performance demands. Practitioners who make quick assumptions about the likely experience of the athlete

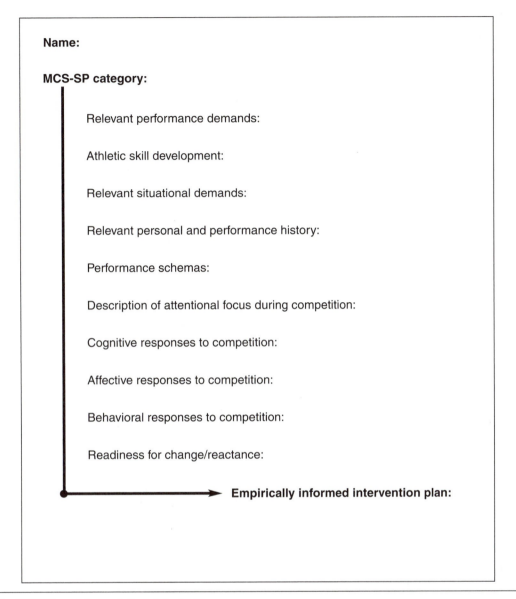

Name:

MCS-SP category:

Relevant performance demands:

Athletic skill development:

Relevant situational demands:

Relevant personal and performance history:

Performance schemas:

Description of attentional focus during competition:

Cognitive responses to competition:

Affective responses to competition:

Behavioral responses to competition:

Readiness for change/reactance:

Empirically informed intervention plan:

Figure 11.2 MCS-SP case formulation data form.

based on previous knowledge will inevitably misunderstand the athlete's experience.

Contextual performance demands intersect with the athlete's *skill level* to affect performance in a highly individualized way. Typically, the athlete's skills are developed to the point where the athlete can generally handle the contextual performance demands that arise. For instance, a Division II freshman point guard (with the typical skill of a Division II freshman) can perform at her expected level and, as such, experiences an appropriate intersection between contextual performance demands and athletic skill level. When adding *relevant situational demands,* the intersection takes an even more individualized

and unique shape. In the previous example, a situational demand would be thrusting the freshman point guard into a starting role due to a teammate's injury. The point guard then faces a set of performance demands very different from what she faces under normal circumstances. Additional situational demands may include playing for a team with a high preseason performance expectation, injuries to self or teammates resulting in a modified role, challenges to the athlete's interpersonal fit within the organization, a new coach, and so on.

The fourth element requiring consideration is the athlete's unique psychological characteristics, which also affect the intersection of these three variables. Personal psychological factors can include relevant performance schemas (such as a need to please others), current psychosocial stressors (such as a problematic romantic relationship, chronic family difficulties, or significant personal loss), or characteristic coping styles (such as a pattern of experiential avoidance).

At this point, the fifth element to be considered is the athlete's behavioral responses to competition, as it is ultimately the actual overt behavior that directs most athletes to consultation. Whether the goal is to further develop athletic performance, reduce responses to situational factors that are impeding athletic effort, or reduce worry and task avoidance, carefully reviewing referral questions in sport psychology leads to an unmistakable conclusion. Clients ultimately want to *function* (behave) more efficiently or effectively. For example, enhanced functioning could take the form of enhanced athletic performance or enhanced interpersonal relationships. Yet in every case, some form of enhanced behavioral functioning is at the center of the athlete's request for help. While *feeling better* is often thought to be required for enhanced functioning, the reality is that improved functioning can often occur in spite of feeling badly (which may secondarily improve affective states). The athlete who is angry with his coach or teammate or who is sad over the breakup of a significant relationship can nevertheless function by remaining focused on the cues and contingencies required for athletic competition. Of course, achieving this focus requires the capacity to de-center from (step back and self-observe) and accept internal states, and not to be guided by the need to feel better (immediate emotional relief). As such, defining the behavior in need of modification is the most rational means of understanding the athlete's current athletic (or personal) functioning and developing an intervention strategy that directly targets that functioning.

The clinical sport psychologist should carefully assess specific behavioral responses to practice, competition, and nonsport life domains to determine which of these behaviors needs modification. Athletic behaviors, especially in the context of better shooting percentages, speed times, golf scores, and so on, should be considered within the context of skill level before intervening. Considering the relative contributions of physical skills and behavioral responses allows for a deeper understanding of the athlete's needs. Only after the practitioner carefully considers the fit between performance goals and skill level (includ-

ing skill potential) can she truly understand the relevant contribution of psychological factors to performance issues. Accurately assessing skill level frequently requires discussion with coaches, trainers, and in some cases, parents (always with client consent).

As noted in chapter 2 and elucidated above, the integration of the athlete's performance history and psychological characteristics (particularly performance schemas) intersects with situational demands and actual skill level to set the stage for functional or dysfunctional competitive activity. For example, let's consider the athlete whose core performance schema involves personal competence and thus at times results in dysfunctional levels of perfectionism. If this athlete is required to play for a new demanding and frequently harsh coach, he will likely respond to performance demands quite differently than when he played for a more positive and supportive coach. The performance demands cannot be seen out of the context of the athlete's underlying psychological characteristics (relentless perfectionism) and the situational changes (punitive and harsh new coach). As every referral has a unique interaction between external demands and personal characteristics, the clinical sport psychologist should carefully examine this interaction before intervening. In the above case, if the practitioner is unaware of the dysfunctional perfectionism underlying the athlete's performance issue, the practitioner may quickly envision that self-talk strategies will help the athlete maintain focus and adjust to the

To meet the athlete's individualized needs, the sport psychologist considers numerous factors, including the athlete's dispositional characteristics, performance history and skill level, and external challenges.

new environment. However, the practitioner who recognizes the performance schema, and who is also aware of the professional literature, will know that under such circumstances, cognitive strategies will only exacerbate the problem.

Once the practitioner has determined the athlete's external demands and coexisting internal (psychological) and behavioral variables, he can move on and identify the sixth element in the case formulation approach, which is the athlete's relevant self-regulatory profile (highlighted in chapter 2). Most importantly, the practitioner should identify the direction of attentional focus (self versus task) during various points of athletic engagement. In addition, a thorough understanding of the problematic (or possibly most common) cognitive and affective responses that occur during performance is necessary. The practitioner should be able to answer the following questions:

- Are the athlete's thoughts self-referenced or task appropriate?
- Is the athlete engaged in the present moment of competition or is he concerned about the possibility of failure?
- Is the athlete worried about possible consequences or committed to the task ahead?
- Is the athlete experiencing anxiety, anger, dysphoria, or another emotion, and does he view the emotions as a problem to be overcome?

Understanding the cognitive-affective bonds triggered by various performance-related stimuli, the associated behavioral responses to these internal experiences, and the resultant behavioral consequences is a central component to the self-regulatory profile and is critical to an accurate and comprehensive case formulation.

The practitioner at this time would also benefit from considering the seventh and eighth elements in the case formulation method, which are the athlete's readiness for change and level of reactance. Both of these constructs have been related to intervention efficacy in the clinical psychology literature (Blatt, Shahal, & Zurhoff, 2002). Readiness for change is a central concept in the transtheoretical model (TTM) of human behavior change presented by Prochaska, DiClemente, and Norcross (1992). The TTM was initially developed for understanding and predicting change in health behaviors (Prochaska et al., 1992). The core of this model divides individuals into five subgroups, or stages, based on their change attitudes and behaviors. The first stage, *precontemplation,* includes individuals who deny the need to change and are not engaging in change behaviors. The second stage, *contemplation,* includes individuals who intend to change but are not yet actively involved in the change process. The third stage, *preparation,* is characterized by individuals preparing for a change in their behavior. People in the preparation stage are not actually changing, but are orienting themselves toward change (i.e., thinking about change, beginning active efforts to engage in new behaviors). The fourth stage, *action,* includes individuals who are actively engaged in serious change efforts. Individuals in the fifth and final stage, *maintenance,* are primarily concerned with retaining changes they have already made. Progression from action to maintenance has occurred when the behavior has been changed for 6 mo or more. According to TTM, success in intentional behavior change is hypothesized to result from sequential, although not necessarily linear, movement through each of these stages (Prochaska et al., 1992).

From the TTM perspective, different interventions and outcomes may be associated with individuals who differ qualitatively *or* quantitatively in their particular stage of change. An individual's stage of change, or readiness to change, reflects a number of interacting variables, including motivation, expectancy, efficacy, and openness to assistance (Burke et al., 2003). Considering an athlete's stage may help the practitioner determine the need for enhancing change readiness before beginning more active or structured interventions. Measures such as the Readiness for Change Questionnaire (RCQ) may help determine the athlete's stage of change (Forsberg, Halldin, & Wennberg, 2003).

Reactance has received research attention as a potential moderator that may selectively predict a client's response to different psychotherapy interventions. Reactance is a motivational state characterized by the client's tendency to restore or reassert her abilities and freedoms when she perceives that they are lost or being threatened by others (Beutler, Consoli, & Williams, 1995. The highly reactant individual has been described as "dominant," "individualistic," and "oppositional" (Dowd, Milne, & Wise, 1991; Dowd, Wallbrown, Sanders, & Yesenosky, 1994), and is likely to be reactive when faced with external influence (Beutler & Consoli, 1993). The characteristics noted in this definition can frequently be found in successful competitive athletes, and as such should be considered in case formulation. This information can be obtained during a semistructured interview and possible personality evaluation (as suggested in chapter 4).

Beutler, Consoli, and Williams (1995) and others (Dowd et al., 1994) have suggested that reactance is an important variable to consider when planning an intervention, as it is likely to predict client resistance to intervention efforts. The clinical sport psychologist should assess this variable, as evidence suggests that early intervention efforts should be *less* directive for clients high in reactance (Beutler et al., 1995) in order to prevent premature termination.

When all of the eight elements noted thus far are fully understood, a case formulation may be considered complete. Now, informed by the empirical findings pertinent to the specific details of the case formulation, the practitioner is ready to choose the most appropriate intervention for the athlete. In the following section we demonstrate the process of case formulation and identify particular issues that need to be addressed for the differing MCS-SP classifications. Let's begin by referring back to chapter 3 for a case example from each MCS-SP classification.

Case Formulation Example for PD

Bob, a 32-year-old professional golfer, consulted with a sport psychologist to improve his current level of performance and reach his full potential as a golfer. He recognized that mental factors play a significant role in success on the PGA tour and believed that he needed help in maintaining concentration and in recovering rapidly from mishaps and errors made during tournament play. His performance history indicated that he had been at the same level of play for several years and had not yet attained the level of golf performance expected of and predicted for him years earlier. He presented with no clinical symptoms and no significant interpersonal or intrapersonal difficulties. His overall life situation was stable and he functioned well in family, social, and recreational domains.

For this example, case formulation begins with a careful analysis of the behavioral outcomes associated with the presenting issue. We can infer several problematic outcomes to include in our formulation. Bob describes a stable level of performance, has not attained the level of performance that his skill might indicate, and reports losing attentional focus following performance errors. Interview data

indicate that Bob functions well as a teaching professional, but his competitive (golf tournament) performance varies from equivalent to his modal practice performance to several strokes poorer than his practice performance. As such, he has not progressed in tournament play, and his career remains stagnant. He is clearly not content. Interview data indicate that Bob spends an adequate amount of time practicing and effectively utilizes external coaching as needed.

Please note that these pieces of relevant information would come from a thorough interview, a careful analysis of actual performance, a comparison of practice performance to competitive performance, and an assessment of sport-related activities. Bob also describes getting angry at a poor shot or incorrect club selection during competition. He describes becoming "obsessed" with swing thoughts as a means of "getting back on track." He also becomes highly aware of his swing faults when faced with competitive pressure. Bob reports that he utilizes stimulus control techniques (i.e., precompetitive and preshot routines) to help control attention, yet he still experiences the reported cognitive and affective responses after less-than-stellar golf shots. In response, he finds himself distracted, even thinking about activities he has planned for that evening, or he engages in frantic efforts to concentrate by imagining the perfect swing and repeatedly telling himself to relax. Psychometric data was acquired from the Young Schema Questionnaire (YSQ) (Young et al., 2003), Penn State Worry Questionnaire (PSWQ) (Meyer et al., 1990), Readiness for Change Questionnaire (RCQ) (Forsberg et al., 2003), and Acceptance and Action Questionnaire-Revised (AAQ-R) (Hayes et al., 1999). Altogether, these measures only took approximately 20 min (total) to complete. The data suggest that Bob is a relatively well-functioning individual who does not experience clinical distress, engages in excessive but nonpathological worry, tries desperately to avoid negative emotions (experiential avoidance), and holds no particularly maladaptive performance schemas. From these data we can complete the case formulation data form:

- **Relevant performance demands:** Tournament competition
- **Athletic skill development:** Adequate for the desired activity; utilizes coaching appropriately
- **Relevant situational demands:** None of significance

- **Relevant personal and performance history:** Prolonged history of tournament play that has remained fairly constant and insufficient for his goals and skill level

- **Performance schemas:** None of clinical significance based on the Young Schema Questionnaire

- **Attentional focus during competition:** Tendency to engage in an excessive, self-judging, internal attentional focus and to lose metacognitive present-moment focus in favor of cognitive activity related to past and future

- **Cognitive responses to competition:** Frequent efforts to control or suppress self-referenced negative cognitive responses to poor play by using positive images and thought suppression or self-talk ("relax")

- **Affective responses to competition:** Heightened affect (i.e., anger, frustration, self-doubt) in response to poor play

- **Behavioral responses to competition:** Task disengagement (avoidance by thinking about postcompetitive activities) and efforts to reengage by exerting excessive cognitive self-control; actions do not lead to optimal performance, but are intended to help Bob feel better for the moment

- **Reactance and readiness for change:** Nonreactant, contemplation stage based on the Readiness for Change Questionnaire

Remember that the initial case formulation is a set of well-developed hypotheses that directs intervention planning, confirms or disconfirms initial hypotheses, and guides modification of the intervention as necessary. Case formulation also directs intervention outcome assessment, as it clearly describes triggering variables, mediating variables (mechanisms of change), and behavioral consequences.

Based on Bob's interview data, the case formulation, and his score of eight on the Performance Classification Questionnaire (PCQ) (Wolanin, 2005), it is clear that Bob meets a MCS-SP classification of performance development (specifically PD-II). As you will recall, an athlete is classified as PD when performance concerns are not primarily due to significant environmental, situational, intrapersonal, or interpersonal factors. Bob specifically falls into PD-II because he does not have subclinical or clinical concerns and he has already highly developed his athletic skills, yet he needs

more consistent performance to maximize those skills.

A sound case formulation of PD requires a thorough understanding of the athlete's self-regulatory profile described in chapter 2. After assessing Bob's relevant behavioral responses, including the consequences (positive and negative) of those responses, the clinical sport psychologist's first task is to describe the direction of Bob's attentional focus across a variety of performance demands and situations. In chapter 2, we described the importance of task-focused versus self-focused attention in the etiology of functional and dysfunctional performance. A clear understanding of the athlete's attentional focus is critical in determining appropriate PD interventions. The practitioner should understand what *circumstances* are associated with what *direction* of attentional focus. This leads to a rational understanding of the resultant cognitive, affective, and behavioral responses.

In this particular case, performance enhancement efforts should occur at several levels. Yet, since no clear empirically supported intervention has been established for athletic performance enhancement, the practitioner should determine the relevant empirically informed *process* that needs to be enhanced for performance to improve. According to case information, Bob appears to require help in developing the present-moment, nonjudging attentional focus theoretically and empirically related to optimal human performance. This can be achieved through the mindfulness exercises we described in chapter 6. In addition, Bob seems a good candidate for the mindfulness-acceptance-commitment (MAC) protocol, as he would likely benefit from the ability to notice and accept (as passing events) the negative thoughts and emotions he normally experiences immediately after mistakes. The MAC intervention would also help Bob focus on the functional requirements of tournament golf play, that is, the external cues and demands of the tournament as it happens. With such a focus, Bob could truly play golf one shot at a time. In keeping with the foundational philosophy of science informing practice, we must again note that the data on MAC presented in this text and elsewhere (Gardner & Moore, 2004a; Gardner et al., 2005; Wolanin, 2005) strongly suggest that MAC is most appropriate for athletes who are *not* experiencing psychological barriers. Given that Bob is a PD referral (not Pdy), the nomothetic data suggest that the MAC intervention is appropriate.

Case Formulation Example for Pdy

Joan, an 18-year-old female swimmer attending a NCAA Division I program, was referred to a clinical sport psychologist when her race times fell well below her personal best and she began repeatedly missing or showing up late for practice. Her performance history indicated that she was a state champion while in high school and had the potential to be a NCAA champion. She had no history of psychological problems before attending college. She reported feeling increasingly lethargic and unhappy, and while she was still functioning adequately in her social, academic, and recreational domains, she was becoming increasingly isolated and losing interest in friendship, schoolwork, and swimming. A recent physical examination was negative. Joan described being homesick and was spending extended periods away from home for the first time in her life. She was the youngest of four siblings and described herself as the baby of the family.

In this example, Joan's athletic performance, including engagement (practice) and competition (race times), began to deteriorate along with her academic motivation and social interaction. Upon interview, it became apparent that Joan was experiencing an intense psychological reaction to the separation from family inherent in being a college freshman and living away from home for the first time. While her relationship with her coach was described as "okay," Joan described the coach, a man in his late 20s, as "a young guy who doesn't really understand me." Conversely, she described her high school coach as a man in his 40s who spent time getting to know her. Her psychometric evaluation (completed within 15 min) suggested no gross psychopathology, but her score on the Beck Depression Inventory (Beck, 1976) indicated moderate depression. Although no significant performance or nonperformance schemas were noted on the Young Schema Questionnaire (Young, 1999), she is struggling with minor attachment issues now that she is away from home. Joan acknowledged that her commitment to swimming was at a minimum and indicated that she "didn't feel good enough to care or put out the effort necessary to compete." Although this was her chosen school, Joan reported that she was considering quitting the team and transferring to a school closer to her family home. From these data we can complete the following case formulation data form:

- **Relevant performance demands:** Division I college competition
- **Athletic skill development:** Adequate for the desired activity
- **Relevant situational demands:** College freshman, first time away from home
- **Relevant personal and performance history:** Youngest child, self-described as "the baby of the family"
- **Performance schemas:** No direct schemas, but clear attachment to the family was noted
- **Attentional focus during competition:** Attentional focus not on competitive demands; she appears to be focused on her internal experiences (thoughts and emotions) both before and during athletic engagement
- **Cognitive responses to competition:** Questions why she is involved, increasingly sees competition as less important, is considering changing schools and moving closer to home
- **Affective responses to competition:** Unmotivated, increasing sadness and despondency
- **Behavioral responses to competition:** Disengagement and avoidance
- **Reactance and readiness for change:** Nonreactant, contemplation stage based on the Readiness for Change Questionnaire

Joan is experiencing an intense psychological reaction to living on her own for the first time without the physical and emotional support from family to which she is accustomed. In addition, the relationship with her new coach does not offer the parent-like support she had grown accustomed to in high school. These changes in her external world (entering college and moving away from home) have led her to question her inability to do well so far from home. She experiences decreased interest and willingness to engage in athletic activities. She also demonstrates an attentional focus on her thoughts and feelings (internal experiences) rather than on the external requirements (cues and contingencies) of her athletic pursuits. In turn, she minimally engages in behaviors in the pursuit of valued goal attainment. The primary triggers leading to her current difficulties are the external transitional aspects of being away from home for the first time. Thus, the MCS-SP classification in this case is Pdy-I, which is supported by a score of 23 on the PCQ. As a reminder, an athlete is classified as Pdy-I when the presenting performance concerns are largely due to environmental, situational, transitional, or interpersonal factors. For Joan, exogenous life changes (being away from home) are resulting in interfering psychological reactions.

A sound case formulation of performance dysfunction requires a thorough understanding of the athlete's psychosocial functioning, including current life circumstances as well as relevant interpersonal and intrapersonal characteristics and a self-regulatory profile. After assessing the athlete's behavioral responses to the competitive environment, the primary task is to describe the interaction between current life circumstances and psychological strengths and weaknesses. The practitioner should conduct a functional analysis of behavior in order to understand

- what functional impairments or disruptions are affecting the athlete's life,
- how the deterioration of athletic performance directly connects to specific life events in the athlete's world, and
- how psychological characteristics may make the athlete particularly vulnerable to the external events she is confronting.

Given Joan's history of close family involvement and support (she reported being the baby of the family), she is more likely to respond strongly, with increased affect and disruptive behaviors, to being away from home support than the athlete without this history. The most appropriate empirically supported interventions for Joan are either cognitive therapy (CT) (Beck, 1976) or interpersonal psychotherapy (IPT) (Klerman & Weissman, 1993), both of which are well-established interventions based on the empirically supported treatment criteria. Both would focus on the issues of role change and conflict and on the dysfunctional cognitive processes and behavioral inhibitions inherent in her current psychological reaction. Over time, integrating the psychological skills of mindfulness and acceptance while particularly attending to valued goal clarification may prevent future episodes (Teasdale et al., 2000). However, on both theoretical and empirical grounds, mental

Untreated performance dysfunction can lead to decreased sport-confidence, interpersonal disruption and conflict, self-defeating thoughts and behaviors, and subclinical psychological reactions.

skills training is clearly not the appropriate *initial* intervention focus. Were traditional psychological skills training strategies initially instituted in this case, not only would it probably not improve performance, but it could also exacerbate Joan's despondency and result in negative long-term decisions (such as quitting the team and school).

The two case examples of Bob and Joan (PD-II and Pdy-I) demonstrate the case formulation method in clinical sport psychology and the interrelated connections among assessment, classification, case formulation, and intervention planning. The next two examples (PI and PT) are of the classic clinical variety, as PI cases decidedly involve diagnosable clinical concerns, and the adjustment to career termination (PT) can sometimes invoke clinical reactions as well (although this is certainly not always the case).

As such, the following case formulations take a slightly different focus and are more consistent with the usual psychotherapy case formulation seen in clinical psychology.

Case Formulation Example for PI

Caroline, a 23-year-old professional basketball player, was referred to a clinical sport psychologist after missing her third team practice in two weeks. Earlier in the season, Caroline behaved erratically on a road trip, missed a curfew check, and bought extravagant gifts on an extended shopping spree. She described times in which she felt "tremendous sadness and lack of energy" and other times in which she felt "wired," unable to relax, and as though her thoughts were racing. She felt unable to control these mood shifts and was afraid that she might be "going crazy."

In this example, Caroline was referred for behavior that was interfering with her ability to perform for her team. Upon interview it became apparent that Caroline was experiencing mood fluctuations characterized by periods of dysphoria and irritability. In addition, Caroline experienced periods of low and extremely high energy, racing thoughts, inability to concentrate, loss of interest in usual activities, and impulsive and self-destructive activities (buying sprees). While the impact on her ability to perform (function) in basketball was most obvious, the clinical picture and psychometric data present as bipolar I disorder, mixed episode, and thus Caroline's case fits into the MCS-SP classification of performance impairment. Caroline is specifically experiencing PI-I, as a clinical mood disorder is interfering with overall life functioning. In these situations, case formulation resembles what is seen in the traditional practice of clinical psychology. A comprehensive assessment would utilize interview formats such as the SCID-I (First et al., 1997), and could also include instruments such as the Minnesota Multiphasic Personality Inventory-II (MMPI-II) (Butcher et al., 1989), or the Millon Clinical Multiaxial Inventory-III (MCMI-III) (Millon et al., 1994) to clarify the diagnosis and determine additional relevant personality variables. The appropriately trained and licensed practitioner would develop a clinical case formulation based upon the overall clinical picture and would likely seek psychiatric consultation. The practitioner not trained or licensed to treat such cases would be expected to refer the athlete.

Although completing the case formulation data form is not as necessary in PI cases, since clinical needs can easily be conceptualized and treated according to sound clinical models, we nonetheless provide one for this example. Due to the clinical nature of the athlete's presenting difficulties, the data form does not illuminate the PI case as deeply as it does the PD and Pdy cases for which it was intended. Regardless, the case formulation data form can be completed as follows:

- **Relevant performance demands:** Professional competition
- **Athletic skill development:** Elite skill level
- **Relevant situational demands:** High level of performance expected, lifestyle demands of professional sports
- **Relevant personal and performance history:** Unknown family history of psychiatric difficulties, no previous significant performance problems
- **Performance schemas:** No direct performance schemas
- **Attentional focus during competition:** Attentional focus both on and off the court has become dysfunctional and erratic
- **Cognitive responses to competition:** No cognitive content specifically related to performance, overall cognitive content is often tangential and readily shifts from topic to topic
- **Affective responses to competition:** No affect specific to performance, overall affect generally fluctuates between dysphoria and mania
- **Behavioral responses to competition:** Behavioral dysregulation, disengaged from team
- **Reactance and readiness for change:** Non-reactant, contemplation stage based on the Readiness for Change Questionnaire

Following clinical case formulation, the practitioner would use existing empirical evidence to determine an appropriate intervention that has garnered some empirical support, which (as described in chapter 8) would likely be a combination of psychopharmacology and family focused therapy (Craighead et al., 2002). Only *following* these formal and crucial intervention efforts should the clinical sport psychologist reevaluate Caroline's psychosocial state to determine if an additional intervention (possibly including self-management skills training) would be of value to rebound from any performance decrements. At that point it would be appropriate to fully complete the case formulation data form again to clarify the nonclinical points of intervention. For example, it may be that following this episode, Caroline faces significant self-doubts and loses confidence and task-relevant focus. The case formulation would then identify these issues as the most relevant performance-related points of intervention, and a cognitive-behavioral intervention could help her reestablish her ideal performance state.

Case Formulation Example for PT

Carlos was a 26-year-old minor-league baseball player who had been a first-round draft choice and was previously viewed throughout professional baseball as a definite major-league pitching star. During the off-season two years earlier, Carlos suffered multiple injuries in a bar fight, including a serious tear of his rotator cuff. After surgery and a long period of rehabilitation, Carlos was once again approaching his presurgery level of performance, when during the first inning of a game he felt a pop in his pitching shoulder and left the game in pain. After medical testing, he was told that he had again torn his rotator cuff and that it was highly unlikely he would ever be able to pitch professionally. Carlos soon became angry, depressed, and socially withdrawn. He had recurrent flashbacks to the pitch that resulted in the tear and believed that he was useless and that his life was over. He had not completed college and saw no realistic possibility of future happiness. As Carlos became more despondent and angry, a family member referred him to a clinical sport psychologist.

In this example, Carlos experienced the end of a promising career in a single moment, and the termination of his athletic career came with a great deal of psychological reaction. This places Carlos in the PT category of the MCS-SP. Specifically, he falls into the PT-II category, as his career termination was based on a sudden and involuntary injury that left him with few immediate options. The pop in his shoulder and the resultant end of his career represented a symbolic death experience for Carlos, as the career that determined his sense of self died at the moment of reinjury. His flashbacks and intense affective response are

consistent with the symptom cluster seen in post-traumatic stress disorder (PTSD).

When interviewed, Carlos also spoke of significant self-recriminations over the original barroom fight, and he fluctuated between acceptance of his medical realities and a near total denial in which he confidently predicted a return to professional baseball. Psychometric assessment (all completed within 20 min) revealed an elevated score on the Beck Depression Inventory (BDI) (Beck, 1976) indicating moderate depression, an elevated score on the Acceptance and Action Questionnaire-Revised (AAQ-R) (Hayes et al., 1999) indicating avoidance of internal experiences and unwillingness to take necessary action, and an elevated score on the PTSD Symptom Scale (Foa et al., 1993) indicating PTSD symptoms and disruption of social and occupational functioning. Interview and psychometric evaluation indicated that Carlos was highly reactant and in a precontemplation stage of change based on the Readiness for Change Questionnaire (RCQ) (Forsberg et al., 2003). In addition, the Young Schema Questionnaire (YSQ) (Young et al., 2003) found four early maladaptive schemas, including a personal defectiveness schema (the belief that one is defective or inferior), a social alienation schema (the belief that one is isolated and different from others), an approval or recognition seeking schema (an excessive emphasis on gaining approval, attention, and acceptance from others), and a self-punishing schema (the belief that people should be harshly punished for their mistakes). Clearly, with these particular intrapersonal variables, Carlos is significantly less likely to make an adaptive adjustment to the sudden end of his high profile career without external psychological support.

As with PI cases, the case formulation data form is not as necessary in PT cases with distinct clinical features. Yet, the data form can still be a good tool for general case conceptualization. The data form for Carlos can be completed as follows:

- **Relevant performance demands:** Inability to compete due to severe injury
- **Athletic skill development:** Elite skill level prior to injury
- **Relevant situational demands:** No college degree, relationship strain
- **Relevant personal and performance history:** Barroom fight responsible for initial injury, former first-round draft choice

- **Performance schemas:** Relevant early maladaptive schemas relate to defectiveness, social alienation, approval seeking, and self-punishment
- **Attentional focus during competition:** Not applicable for sport, experiences flashbacks of injury
- **Cognitive responses to current situation:** "I will never be happy," "I have nothing to offer"
- **Affective responses to current situation:** Depression, anxiety, and anger
- **Behavioral responses to competition:** Disengaged, social isolation, and avoidance
- **Reactance and readiness for change:** Reactant, precontemplation stage based on the Readiness for Change Questionnaire

The intervention goals in this case are to ameliorate traumatic stress symptomatology and to help Carlos develop an appropriate acceptance of his life circumstance, develop a willingness to act in his best interest, and formulate a reasonably valued career plan. The well-established empirically supported interventions for posttraumatic

Overlooking subclinical or clinical issues, interpersonal concerns, or moderate to severe performance decrements places the athlete at increased risk for disruption in numerous life domains.

stress include variants of exposure and cognitive modification (the intervention for this case is presented in chapter 8). As Carlos was in the precontemplative stage of change and somewhat reactant, the clinical sport psychologist would need to take great care to establish a sound working relationship *before* beginning a directive treatment in order to maximize the likelihood of treatment adherence and minimize the likelihood of premature termination.

PI and severe PT are decidedly more similar to traditional clinical cases than PD or Pdy. Traditional clinical case formulations (which can be utilized for PI and PT cases) are beyond the scope of this text, but they can readily be found elsewhere (Eells, 1997). Although a more clinical case formulation is necessary, the practitioner would incorporate the sport context (including demands, expectations, and history) as a cultural factor just as she would incorporate sociocultural factors.

Final Thoughts

Whatever the MCS-SP classification, the practitioner collects all the information necessary for understanding the athlete's presenting problem in a complete psychosocial context. The goal is a full understanding of both the presenting problem and the vast array of individual client variables. In contrast to a rapid and excessive focus on athletic performance, the case formulation presented here allows for a holistic understanding of the athlete that can guide intervention selection and implementation. This approach requires a commitment to carefully collecting information and formulating this information into a sound working model for understanding the athlete. The clinical sport psychologist is strongly encouraged to guard against immediately focusing on performance concerns at the expense of the overall psychosocial consideration of the client. The result is a greater understanding of the athlete, a more efficacious intervention plan, and most important, an overall enhancement in all major life domains.

With the conclusion of part III, we hope that readers understand the differing needs of athletes, hold an appreciation for accurately assessing these needs, and have an initial understanding of the empirically informed interventions that can be applied to such needs. We now turn our attention to special considerations for practitioners and students interested in or currently practicing sport psychology.

PART IV

Special Considerations

So far, we have discussed how to understand, assess, and intervene with a wide variety of athlete needs, and have attempted to step out of the classroom and address the practitioners on the front line who need guidelines for assessment, classification, case conceptualization, and intervention planning and implementation. In Part IV of this text, we switch gears to consider special topics that often go unnoticed in sport psychology. Chapter 12 highlights the primary ethical issues that complicate sport psychology practice and provides a checklist to promote ethical self-awareness. Chapter 13 discusses the role of supervision in the training of sport psychologists and helpful supervision strategies that promote both technical skill refinement and self-efficacy among trainees. Finally, chapter 14 considers the future of the field and highlights several professional domains that can benefit from increased attention. Ultimately, we hope that by the conclusion of this text, readers will have developed a new perspective on the many possible roles of the sport psychologist and will be excited about *clinical sport psychology*.

CHAPTER 12

Ethics in Clinical Sport Psychology

Our ultimate goal as clinical sport psychologists is to enhance the athlete's well-being. The tasks that typically come to mind when we consider our role as sport psychologists include developing rapport with the athlete, collecting relevant personal data and formulating a sound case conceptualization, and providing the best possible intervention to meet the athlete's specific needs. However, we must remain cognizant that our goal is not just to do our jobs, but to do them competently and ethically. Regardless of population or setting, ethical issues naturally arise that require us to consider, consult, and potentially alter our services in order to ethically, legally, and competently meet the exceptional demands dictated by the professional setting (Moore, 2003a). Yet, the common ethical issues may markedly vary with population and setting. For the clinical sport psychologist, ethical challenges not only include those faced by traditional clinical and counseling psychologists, but also include dilemmas that arise from the particular service demands that accompany practice with such a unique clientele.

Typically for clinical and counseling psychologists, ethical challenges are addressed by the Ethical Principles of Psychologists and Code of Conduct of the American Psychological Association (2002). These guidelines and practice parameters help practitioners find "the ethical path that will assist them in resolving dilemmas in a manner that appropriately matches the psychologist's role responsibilities and the consumer's situation and needs" (Fisher & Younggren, 1997, p. 584). However, the APA Ethics Code most accurately reflects the needs of clients in common professional settings, which do not typically include sport psychology. This is also particularly problematic for psychologists practicing in rural settings (Catalano, 1997; Faulkner & Faulkner, 1997; Schank & Skovholt, 1997), military settings (Hines,

Ader, Chang, & Rundell, 1998; Johnson, 1995), and other nontraditional settings. Psychologists in these settings quickly discover that many of the ethical guidelines do not represent their common clientele, the particular setting demands, and the exceptional necessities accompanying their professional work and service delivery.

Since the development of sport psychology, sport psychologists have faced many of these ethical challenges, as their applied work necessitates some specific, nontraditional practice requirements. For example, in a rural environment, psychologists face challenges of confidentiality and potential dual-role relationships, as the small size of these communities increases contact between psychologists and clients. A rural psychologist may frequently encounter clients in stores, in restaurants, and at community events. Similarly, teams and sport organizations are small communities that are largely self-contained, and increased contact between athletes, management, and the clinical sport psychologist is inevitable. Whether during team travel or at the practice facility, the clinical sport psychologist is likely to pass athletes and staff in hotel halls, have back-to-back individual and group meetings with athletes and management, and provide quick consultation on the sidelines. We may not immediately consider these instances as ethically challenging, but they do allow potentially difficult and ethically compromised situations to develop.

Although many sport psychologists see athletes within a traditional private practice model of service delivery, our particular emphasis here is on practitioners who work with teams or are part of a sport organization. Although sport psychologists in private practice certainly face challenges to the APA Ethics Code, typical private practice does not specifically challenge adherence to or require alteration of the Ethics Code.

Particular challenges to the Ethics Code usually arise when the athlete is involved in a broader organizational system or when a third party hires the sport psychologist to provide psychological services to athletes and personnel. Like military and industrial/organizational settings, sport organizations wish to remain productive, and success is largely based on the abilities of all members to fulfill their specific tasks.

The clinical sport psychologist's role is to help the athlete optimally function in order to reach both personal and organizational goals. Thus, since the practitioner fundamentally serves the larger organizational goals, practice can become complicated for the clinical sport psychologist when the individual needs of the athlete conflict with the needs of the organization. For instance, an athlete experiencing a family crisis may need to spend time at home instead of play an important game. On the other hand, the team needs this athlete to fulfill his occupational role in order to meet the greater goals of the system. Another example may be the injured athlete who requires a specific rehabilitation regimen and time off from practice and competition. Yet, this athlete may be pressured to play an important game the following week (despite incomplete recovery) to help the team win. The athlete is clearly a part of the greater organizational system and thus is responsible for attaining the goals of the system. The clinical sport psychologist must learn to work effectively in such a setting.

The most common practice requirements for clinical sport psychologists include developing a working alliance with a clientele that often understates the need for psychological services and meeting the practical challenges of multilevel organizational demands, multiple relationships, confidentiality, service time and location, limits of competence, appropriate informed consent, and participation in indirectly therapeutic organizational activities. Several authors have discussed ethical considerations such as these in the sport psychology literature (Andersen, Van Raalte, & Brewer, 2001; Biddle, Bull, & Seheult, 1992; Gardner, 2001; Granito & Wenz, 1995; Linder, Pillow, & Reno, 1989; Lodato & Lodato, 1992; Meyers, 1995; Petrie & Diehl, 1995; Taylor, 1994; Whelan, Meyers, & Elkins, 2002; Zeigler, 1987), yet these ethical concerns have only recently been fully discussed as they pertain to the APA Ethics Code (2002) to which psychologists must adhere (Moore, 2003a). It certainly remains in the best interest of the client

for the clinical sport psychologist to follow APA's ethical parameters, and sport psychologists can also refer to the ethical principles defined by the Association for the Advancement of Applied Sport Psychology (AAASP). The AAASP standards are a helpful yet insufficient sport-specific adaptation of the APA Ethics Code. By thoroughly understanding the general Code established by APA and the additional suggestions provided by AAASP, clinical sport psychologists can more effectively engage in ethical practice. Yet even with these ethical guides, very few recommendations have been made in the professional literature to assist sport psychologists in developing and maintaining their own quality work standards in an atypical psychology field. In addition to discussing ethics in sport psychology, at the end of this chapter we provide a brief assessment tool that practitioners can utilize to determine if ethical difficulties are in sight within their own practices. This tool, the Ethical Self-Awareness Checklist for Sport Psychologists (Moore, 2003a), covers the primary ethical areas we review in our discussion. The remainder of this chapter considers confidentiality, informed consent, practicing within areas of competence, terminating the practitioner–client relationship, and balancing multiple roles, relationships, and organizational demands (see figure 12.1).

Confidentiality

"Confidentiality is the cornerstone of trust on which the therapeutic relationship is built," and as such, "clients must understand the limitations to their confidentiality if they are to make informed decisions about whether to enter into treatment and whether to disclose personal information during sessions" (Glosoff, Herlihy, Herlihy, & Spence, 1997, p. 573). When working with individual athletes and larger sport organizations, issues of confidentiality and privileged communication must be agreed upon by all involved parties at the *onset* of services, so that all individuals are aware of the limitations of confidentiality, and potential difficulties are minimized (Ethical Standards 4.01 and 4.02) (APA, 2002; Gardner, 2001; Moore, 2003a; Pope & Vasquez, 2001). Confidentiality is not typically challenged in private sport psychology practice, as practitioners can uphold confidentiality unless presented with certain issues, such as duty to warn. However, clinical sport psychologists hired by sport organizations cannot assume that typical confidentiality parameters apply

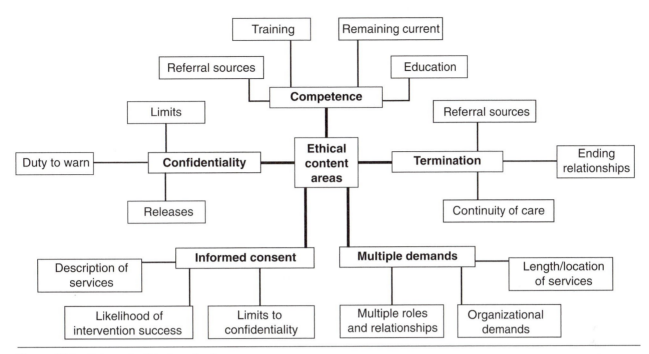

Figure 12.1 Relevant ethical content areas.

when working with athletes who are under the jurisdiction of the organization. The clinical sport psychologist cannot solely focus on the individual desiring services, but must place primary consideration on the organization's broader mission, intent, and goals. The APA Ethics Code (2002) Ethical Standards 3.07 and 3.11a require that psychologists serving a third party or organization (such as when working for a professional sport organization or college athletic department) must, at the onset of the consulting relationship with an individual member, present their professional roles and responsibilities, the recipients of any data or personal client information, and any and all limits of confidentiality that are part of their employment contract with the organization.

In some cases, the third party (sport organization) requesting consultation for its employees (athletes) may request employee information regardless of employee approval. Although the third party does not always request such information, the clinical sport psychologist and organizational staff must accurately inform athletes up front that information may be shared, with whom the information may be shared, and the specific uses of that information. The welfare of both the client and the greater organization must be fully respected, and service limitations must be clearly delineated early in the clinical sport psychologist's involvement. This helps ensure

Before athletes put their trust in a sport psychologist, the practitioner must discuss limits to confidentiality with both athletes and organizational staff.

continued prosperity within the organization while assisting the individual athlete in fulfilling her personal needs.

If releasing client information is necessary, clinical sport psychologists are encouraged to provide only the information particularly relevant to the purpose of the disclosure (Ethical Standard 4.04a) (APA, 2002). Just because a practitioner is asked for information, she does not have to give *every* piece of personal data she has learned from the athlete. The practitioner should ask herself, "What data are the organization asking for?", "What are the relevant data they need?", and "What data are not relevant?" Remember that "psychologists discuss confidential information obtained in their work only for appropriate scientific or professional purposes and only with persons clearly concerned with such matters" (Ethical Standard 4.04b) (APA, 2002). Although significant personal information may have been collected, such information may be withheld from the third party if it is not directly relevant to the particular request. Withholding nonrelevant personal information from third-party requests helps increase confidentiality, while fulfilling occupational responsibilities to both the client and the greater organization (Canter, Bennett, Jones, & Nagy, 1994).

As previously mentioned, clinical sport psychologists must carefully consider the mission and goals of the organization, as they have an obligation not only to the individual client receiving services, but also to the employing organization, whose effectiveness is based on the greater good of the system. Additionally, if the role of the clinical sport psychologist is to assess athletes, those athletes *must* be informed of the recipients of the (positive or negative) information. Under some circumstances, a clinical sport psychologist hired by a third party to provide counseling or psychotherapy to athletes may form a specific agreement with the hiring body to keep client information confidential from management or other personnel. Obviously, this is the optimal situation, but the clinical sport psychologist should not assume that this is the norm and reflexively expect this from the organization. Again, both the athlete and sport organization must be clearly aware of the arrangement prior to services, so that all parties are cognizant of any limitations (Canter et al., 1994). Sport organizations are typically realistic and understanding regarding confidentiality, but nevertheless, such issues need to be addressed openly and directly at the onset of any professional engagement in order to effectively meet everyone's needs.

Especially significant are confidentiality limits imposed by law, examples of which are mandated child and elder abuse laws, neglect laws, and duty to warn statutes. Practitioners must be aware of subtle signs of nontraditional forms of child abuse, such as parental pressures regarding weight, overtraining, competition loss, and return to play demands. These are most commonly reported by gymnasts, figure skaters, and wrestlers, but can be seen across a variety of sports. In addition,

psychologists are expected to keep and securely maintain appropriate records (Ethical Standard 6.01) (APA, 2002). This does not mean keeping records in a cabinet in the locker room or in a file in the coach's office where others can peruse them at will. It is the clinical sport psychologist's responsibility to care for records and ensure confidentiality of written material. The practitioner must also take reasonable steps to ensure that records remain available to maintain the client's best interest.

In addition to records of client contact and intervention data, these files must include appropriate documentation of informed consent. It remains necessary for sport psychology professionals to provide athletes with written and verbal informed consent prior to service delivery, as is discussed later in this chapter.

Case Example: Confidentiality

Jen is an 18-year-old collegiate lacrosse player receiving a full scholarship from her university. As such, she recently moved away from home to start college. Since the beginning of the first semester, she has not been meeting the athletic potential that the coaching staff had anticipated and that is expected of her. She has, however, seemingly been able to establish and maintain appropriate and fulfilling relationships with her teammates and the coaching staff. Due to her apparent athletic performance decrements, the coach recently referred her to a clinical sport psychologist for performance enhancement in order to maximize the athletic potential that the coach believes is possible. During the initial interview, Jen seemed closed about many areas of her life, both past and current, but was able to discuss performance concerns freely. Despite some holes in the information collected, it was clear that she could benefit from techniques to increase her ability to remain in the moment during practice and game situations and to better tolerate and move past the frustration that she has been feeling regarding disappointing performance outcomes. At the initial interview, Jen signed a release of information for the clinical sport psychologist to speak with the coach about her progress, because she believed it was the coach's right to know since he had given her the full scholarship and personally referred her for assistance.

After the first couple of sessions, however, Jen described additional concerns, such as transitional issues related to moving to college, academics, and mild anhedonia (the inability to experience pleasure). The clinical sport psychologist, appropriately trained to deal with such concerns, continued the weekly sessions with Jen, now for a variety of presenting complaints. Several weeks into treatment, the coach called to speak to the clinical sport psychologist about Jen's progress. Of course, the practitioner was allowed to speak to the coach, as Jen had signed a release of information at the onset of services. The coach began by asking questions about Jen's performance progress, and mentioned that he had noticed a slight improvement in her performance and ability to tolerate disappointing moments and outcomes. The coach then asked how she was handling the adjustment to school and being away from home, as he is always concerned about this transition and wants to help if possible. In addition to this inquiry, he mentioned that he occasionally senses that Jen's mood is low, and hoping that she is OK, asked if it was an issue.

The sport psychologist is now in an interesting and challenging situation (on a number of levels) that needs to be addressed appropriately and ethically. Let's discuss each of these individually for the sake of ease and clarity.

The practitioner *does* have a release to discuss treatment issues with the coach. Remember that unless the athlete has signed a release designating a break of confidentiality with the intended recipient of information, it is wholly unethical to have *any* conversation with anyone other than the client (barring appropriate case consultation and duty to warn). This standard even applies to speaking with a person who is calling to say he will be late picking the client up from a session. The clinical sport psychologist cannot even say, "OK, I'll tell her. Thanks." In this case, Jen has signed a release, but the question that remains is if the clinical sport psychologist should share *all* of the information for which the coach has asked.

At the time the release of information was signed, Jen had not shared all of her important issues with the clinical sport psychologist (including transitional issues and mood states) and was presenting only performance concerns. As stated in chapter 3, during initial presentation, athletes frequently minimize significant interpersonal, intrapersonal, or transitional/developmental concerns, yet such concerns often arise later during treatment. Although the coach is inquiring about such concerns, let's refer to our earlier discussion. Specifically, the clinical sport psychologist must provide only the information that particularly relates to the purpose of the disclosure (Ethical Standard 4.04a) (APA, 2002). *All* information unrelated to the referral question, including trivial information, must be withheld to protect the client. When Jen signed the information release, it should be assumed that she signed it based on the initial presenting performance complaints and not on issues that did not surface until several weeks later. Since Jen began treatment based on a performance referral from the coach, disclosing information to the coach about mood states (possibly depression), transitional issues, academic concerns, and so on is not warranted or acceptable.

Second is the issue of what to include in a release of information that may make a disclosure decision clearer for the practitioner. Instead of using a general release form that simply states that the clinical sport psychologist can speak to the coach about Jen's issues, the practitioner should use a release of information or consent for disclosure form that explicitly indicates the following:

• *With whom* the practitioner can speak. The specific persons should be listed. Refrain from simply stating "coaching staff," "athletic department," and so on unless truly indicated by the client.

• *What* information can be shared with the indicated party, as explicitly stated by the athlete. In the case of Jen, for example, the form may state, "Information to be released to the noted parties as necessary may specifically include discussion of performance frustrations due to game loss or poor performance by self or others, difficulties in motor performance and game execution, the use of techniques for performance enhancement, success and lack of success with such techniques, and on-field interpersonal concerns related to teammates." The list includes only what the client has specifically and explicitly stated as acceptable to be shared. Although Jen may face additional concerns, they are not listed for discussion because she did not consent to have them open for discussion. Information not listed on the release *cannot* be included in conversation with an outside party. Even though the coach requested seemingly harmless information, such as Jen's happiness with the decision to play for his school, Jen did not include this information on the list, so it *cannot* be discussed. Jen can, however, add to the list if she chooses, in which case a new release form must be constructed.

• *When* communication can occur. Can the practitioner provide information anytime, or only on specific occasions or under certain circumstances? If the latter, the form must explicitly state the occasions and circumstances and *how* to determine them.

In addressing a third important issue in Jen's case, the clinical sport psychologist may not have been in this situation at all (or may have an easier and more comfortable way out) by discussing the limits of confidentiality and disclosure when forming the professional relationship. This includes discussing with the coach the necessity to protect the athlete by sharing (with release, of course) only the information relevant to performance concerns and informing the coach ahead of time that questions regarding more personal concerns cannot be answered unless the athlete has *explicitly* consented to them in writing ahead of time. In addition, the practitioner should inform potential clients of these parameters (or lack thereof), so that they clearly understand their rights and the limits of confidentiality. This not only protects the client from undue harm, but also protects the practitioner from potential malpractice errors and allows athletes to more freely and openly engage in treatment.

Informed Consent

The clinical sport psychologist must develop and utilize appropriate informed consent not only because it is an ethical imperative, but also because it is critical to legal risk management. Informed consent must include all the information an athlete or organization needs to make an informed decision about the likely benefits and risks of engaging in the specific interventions and to develop a professional working relationship with the therapist/consultant. Informed consent must define the parameters of both the proposed intervention and the therapeutic relationship (Ethical Standards 9.03a and 10.01) (APA, 2002; Beahrs & Gutheil, 2001; Pope & Vasquez, 2001). Such parameters include service descriptions, detailed information on the likelihood of intervention success (i.e., empirically supported versus experimental interventions), financial issues, and limitations to confidentiality (Braaten & Handelsman, 1997; Canter et al., 1994).

In essence, the informed consent document is a contract that delineates the roles and responsibilities of both the practitioner and client and that defines what, why, how, when, and where services will be provided. Using informed consent is necessary when working with both individuals and organizations. This latter type of informed consent would be a contract with the organization. Failure to adequately develop appropriate informed consent clearly violates ethical principles (APA, 2002) and places the professional and the organization at significant risk for later legal action. Of course, it also threatens the integrity of the therapeutic relationship. Note that written informed consent does not sufficiently meet the spirit and letter of this ethical imperative. Ethical guidelines require that the practitioner explain the details of the written informed consent in language appropriate to the age, education, and cognitive ability of the client (Canter et al., 1994). This mandate exists even when the client is not of age to provide consent. The client's signature on the informed consent is not very valuable if the client does not understand the document. Discussing the issues in the informed consent assists the athlete's understanding and demystifies some of the unknown elements clients frequently confront regarding both the therapeutic relationship and the treatment itself.

There has been little formal discussion within the sport psychology literature on the use of informed consent, and as such, it may be possible that numerous sport psychologists do not offer verbal or written informed consents before providing services. As stated previously, it remains imperative that all clinical sport psychologists obtain informed consent, both for research and intervention purposes. For a more thorough description of informed consent and an adaptable sample form for private practice and organizational settings, refer to Zuckerman (1997).

Case Example: Informed Consent

Mark is a 29-year-old professional boxer who was referred by his agent to a clinical sport psychologist for a drop in positive performance and erratic behavior with others. Mark has been engaging in frequent arguments with his trainer, wife and children, and random individuals who provide frustration. The disrupted interpersonal relationships accompany a limited capacity to tolerate his recent athletic shortcomings. In addition, Mark has recently been more responsive to altercations with others, especially in bars, restaurants, and so on. In a recent altercation in a restaurant bar, the other individual threatened (but did not pursue) legal action. This was disconcerting not only to his trainer and wife, but also to Mark, who has been increasingly concerned about his behavioral responsiveness.

The clinical sport psychologist met with Mark for the initial assessment and interview and determined that Mark would benefit from a particular intervention. The practitioner therefore presented Mark with a basic informed consent indicating that they would meet weekly for an undetermined length of time and that treatment would "address the relevant issues" presented by Mark. It concluded that Mark was in agreement of the nature of the intended treatment and included Mark's signature.

Treatment began, but not without problems. Mark, unknowledgeable about the process of psychological treatment, anticipated quick symptom relief and was soon disheartened that he was not feeling or acting much better. Since significant others around him also did not notice change, they too insisted that Mark discuss the lack of progress with the practitioner. Mark decided to be proactive and brought up this issue with the clinical sport psychologist. The practitioner insisted that Mark would improve during the course of treatment and encouraged him to continue as planned. The problem was that Mark had no idea what was planned.

Should Mark understand and magically know what to expect during the treatment process? Of course not. His lack of knowledge was not helped by the informed consent to treatment, which was insufficient for a number of reasons. Before discussing the specifics of this case, let's review what an informed consent must include. Regardless of the intervention employed with an athlete, whether for performance enhancement or more clinical matters, informed consent to treatment must include (Braaten & Handelsman, 1997; Canter et al., 1994) four elements:

- **Description of services.** A thorough description of services will answer many questions that might otherwise later arise and potentially impair the therapeutic process or relationship. A sufficient description of services is not a single line such as "performance enhancement interventions" or "cognitive-behavioral interventions." What do those *really* mean? The clinical sport psychologist must be much more explicit, stating the specific intervention, goals, and basic strategies in terms that the client can understand. This section should also include the length of each intervention session (such as 45-50 min) and how long the intervention is likely to take (such as 16-20 sessions). This last point, while not exact, guides the client in his efforts to plan his life. For example, the clinical sport psychologist providing performance enhancement may state, "Over the next 12 to 16 weeks, we will meet twice a week for 45 minutes each session."

- **Likelihood of intervention success.** Since the movement for empirically supported treatments began, this component of informed consent has become increasingly important. Here, the clinical sport psychologist outlines the empirical research support for the intervention procedures. The practitioner should indicate if a strategy is solely based on correlational data, anecdotal accounts, or individual case studies and if so, it should be stated that the intervention is at that time experimental. Remember that a procedure that has accumulated support only from poorly designed experimental studies is not well supported. If, on the other hand, the intervention has accumulated support from a research base utilizing sound methodological standards (see chapter 5), the intervention should be described in these terms. Again, clinical sport psychologists have an ethical obligation to inform clients of these critical issues, as the client cannot fully consent to treatment if she does not clearly understand *what* will occur in treatment, *why* it is the chosen intervention, *how* the procedures will be employed, *when* treatment will occur, and *where* treatment will occur. Failure to state these parameters means that the client does not really know what she is getting involved in. As such, her signature on the informed consent is meaningless because it is not actually *informed*.

This section of the informed consent is also the place to describe the likely benefits and risks of the specific intervention to be used. The client already knows from the previous section what to expect in treatment, so now we describe how it is likely to help (or not help). Risks do not just imply psychological harm, but also imply false hope and ill-spent commitment, time, and money without successful outcome. Although no practitioner is going to include these possible risks in such terms, practitioners should certainly say that there is no guarantee of positive outcomes.

- **Expectations of the client.** Regardless of the intervention utilized, the client must fulfill certain expectations to truly benefit from treatment. Expectations may regard financial obligations, missed appointments, late arrivals, cancellations, practitioner availability, between-session homework assignments (when appropriate), and when, where, how, and why to contact the clinical sport psychologist.

- **Guidelines and limitations to confidentiality.** To review, confidentiality must be addressed so that the athlete is fully aware of its limitations and knows what to expect from the practitioner in this regard. This part of the informed consent discusses how the practitioner will use client information and how information will be protected (such as how progress notes and treatment plans are kept). Additionally, this section delineates who has access to files, to whom the clinical sport psychologist can or cannot disclose information and the reasons for such disclosure (based on any releases of information signed by the client), and under which circumstances confidentiality may be broken (such as duty to warn).

Now that we have discussed informed consent, let's examine how it relates to the case of Mark. Mark had begun to perform poorly, and his behaviors were challenging his interpersonal relationships. After receiving treatment for several weeks, Mark became concerned over his lack of progress and brought his concern to the practitioner, who responded less than optimally. The informed consent provided by the clinical sport psychologist was insufficient, providing only a rudimentary statement regarding session frequency (without proposing a time line) and stating that treatment would "address the relevant issues." In this case, a clearer and more comprehensive informed consent could have minimized, or even prevented, Mark's concerns.

Mark's informed consent was missing information from all four of the required domains. The description of services was very weak, inconclusive, and vague. Information regarding the likelihood of intervention success and limitations to confidentiality were completely excluded. The fact that there would be weekly sessions was the only mentioned expectation of the client.

Mark's primary concern was lack of treatment progress. Although many important components of the informed consent were clearly insufficient, let's determine how a complete informed consent could have specifically helped Mark's concern. The informed consent did not fully describe what Mark could expect during the treatment process. Thus, Mark had no way of knowing that quick change or rapid minimization of symptoms is not always typi-

cal, especially so soon after beginning treatment. Mark did not have a clear and realistic understanding of what he could gain during treatment and he also had no idea when he could expect benefits to occur. The "relevant issues" alluded to by the clinical sport psychologist did not indicate the interventions to be employed or whether the interventions were for Mark's performance concerns or behavioral dysregulation. Obviously, both foci are important and Mark is understandably eager for improvements in both performance and interpersonal domains. By providing an adequate informed consent, the practitioner would have fulfilled ethical responsibilities, avoided a violation of the APA Ethics Code (2002), and avoided or minimized the particular difficulty that arose for Mark.

Practicing Within Areas of Competence

Within sport psychology, practitioners are trained in a wide variety of disciplines, including clinical and counseling psychology and sport science arenas such as kinesiology and physical education. Although the intersection of these domains has likely added to the field, it raises an additional concern relating to practice competence. As a small discipline within professional psychology, sport psychology must be particularly sensitive to practicing outside general areas of competence (Taylor, 1994). While assessing and treating subclinical and clinical conditions (Pdy and PI, respectively) are clearly within the bounds of statutory certified practitioners of psychology and counseling, there are many opportunities for both mental and nonmental health practitioners to advertently or inadvertently practice outside of their areas of competence. Ethical Standard 2.01 stipulates that practitioners must "provide services, teach, and conduct research with populations and in areas only within the boundaries of their competence, based on their education, training, supervised experience, consultation, study, or professional experience" (APA, 2002). Thus, practicing clinical sport psychology is both inappropriate and unethical if services are based merely on an interest in a population or an intervention (Canter et al., 1994). The practitioner who fails to adhere to this standard risks charges of negligence (through unawareness or deceit) and malpractice, and significantly increases the risk for client and organizational harm.

A practitioner who works with an athlete for performance enhancement (a PD case) and recognizes a potential eating disorder (PI case) may be practicing outside of his competency area if he is not appropriately trained to treat such cases and does not refer the athlete to a qualified clinician. For those not sufficiently trained in assessment, the decision to utilize psychological assessments also requires great care. The unqualified use of assessment instruments may place the clinical sport psychologist outside of her area of competence and at risk for negligence, malpractice, and legal action. Of course, it could certainly jeopardize the well-being of the athlete and organization. Clinical sport psychologists must also carefully decide which instruments match the intervention purposes and their personal training and education (Ethical Standard 9.02) (APA, 2002). A less obvious example of practicing outside of areas of competence is the practitioner who is untrained to respond to an emerging, destructive parent–athlete or coach–athlete relationship that requires clinical attention. It is not enough for the practitioner to say, "I can handle it without a referral."

Further, psychologists can practice outside of their areas of competence by accepting positions or work involving sport psychology while having little or no education or training in this professional domain. There is an obvious distinction between the acceptable clinical and counseling relationship between a psychologist and a client who happens to be an athlete but does not desire performance enhancement and the unacceptable relationship in which a psychologist not trained in the sport domain is asked to provide performance enhancement services (outside of the clinical and counseling domain). It is clearly inappropriate, for example, for the untrained psychologist to attempt performance enhancement with a 13-year-old figure skater when unaware of the specific motor learning and development needs and expectations of a young skater. Although working with a skilled athlete may be interesting, enticing, and financially rewarding (Woody, 1997), a practitioner with excellence in sport psychology may be better able to meet the athlete's particular needs. Regardless, outside of referring to another professional, regular consultation with more experienced clinical sport psychologists is the best strategy for ensuring practice within competency areas.

Case Example: Practicing Within Areas of Competence

Will is a 31-year-old professional basketball player who has been demonstrating poor concentration,

lethargy, and low motivation during practices and games. As such, the coaching staff encouraged him to see the team's sport psychologist to get back on track. During their meeting, Will discusses his current performance-related difficulties and reports decreased relationship satisfaction and marital discord. Fluently trained in performance enhancement strategies, the practitioner determines that Will has not been fully focusing on his professional goals and has been increasingly self-critical, perhaps somewhat because of the relationship distress. Thus, the practitioner decides Will would benefit from an intervention package consisting of goal setting, cognitive self-regulation (self-talk) to decrease his negative thought content, and secondary counseling for the marital concerns.

Selective inattention is frequent in many professional settings. Selective inattention occurs when an individual trained in a certain area sees only those elements of the problem that are consistent with his training and minimizes other, perhaps more critical, elements that are inconsistent with his areas of competence. This is the case with Will's situation. The practitioner does recognize that there is marital discord. Yet, due to a belief (based on what the practitioner can provide) that it does not particularly need additional focus, assessment, or intervention, the discord (which is actually of primary importance) goes largely unattended. By quickly focusing on performance enhancement interventions to decrease negative self-talk and increase concentration and motivation, the sport psychologist limits himself to collecting this type of information. As a result, the practitioner completely misses that since the beginning of the severe marital discord (and potential relationship termination), Will has been having 3 to 4 panic attacks a week and meets the diagnostic criteria for panic disorder without agoraphobia (APA, 2000). By missing this critical information and beginning the proposed performance enhancement interventions, the practitioner may not be practicing outside of his competence area (he is doing what he has been trained to do), but he *is* engaging in unethical practice by overlooking critical elements and not referring Will to another professional trained to intervene in such cases.

If, on the other hand, the practitioner thoroughly investigates the presenting complaints and discovers the panic disorder, it should be obvious to him why Will experiences difficulty concentrating, lethargy, and low motivation when on the court. It would make little sense to the practitioner to engage in goal setting and self-talk procedures to increase focus on goal-directed activities and decrease self-critical cognitive content related to performance. With the full picture clarified, the practitioner is better able to make treatment decisions, engage in further assessment, or refer to another professional. If the practitioner had then decided that in addition to performance enhancement, he would treat Will for panic disorder, he would be practicing outside of his area of competence and engaging in an unethical practice that endangers the athlete.

In the above case example, what could the practitioner have done to avoid practicing outside of his area of competence or engaging in practice that was not appropriate for the client's needs? Several suggestions can be made. For example, the practitioner could have

- engaged in a thorough assessment, including semistructured interview, observation, and psychometric evaluation (see chapter 4);
- entered the therapeutic process with either few preconceived notions of the etiology of the problem or a clear awareness of his preconceived notions, in order to decrease the likelihood of professional bias and selective inattention;
- recognized the significant anxiety disorder following a thorough assessment and referred the athlete to another professional; and
- stated in his initial contract with the organization any limits to his professional training so that neither the organization nor the athlete held unrealistic expectations regarding his professional competencies.

By incorporating these suggestions into standard practice procedures, the clinical sport psychologist, regardless of educational background and training, can determine when he should refer to another professional, and when he can effectively and ethically assist athletes with their particular concerns.

Terminating the Practitioner–Client Relationship

When working with sport organizations, especially professional teams, a clinical sport psychologist's job can be as fleeting as a management position. Further, athletes come and go from team to team

and year to year, and often they do not have enough time to establish a therapeutic relationship with the sport psychologist. Regardless, practitioners have a fundamental responsibility to provide athletes (and clients in management as well) with a continuity of care, despite abrupt changes in organizational structure or personal employment. According to the APA Ethics Code (2002) Ethical Standard 3.12, "psychologists make reasonable efforts to plan for facilitating services in the event that psychological services are interrupted by factors such as the psychologist's illness, death, unavailability, relocation, or retirement or by the client's or patient's relocation or financial limitations." In addition, according to Ethical Standard 10.09:

> When entering into employment or contractual relationships, psychologists make reasonable efforts to provide for orderly and appropriate resolution of responsibility for client/patient care in the event that the employment or contractual relationship ends, with paramount consideration given to the welfare of the client or patient. (APA, 2002)

Termination issues must be discussed by all involved parties at the *onset* of service provision to prepare for termination in the event of abrupt change. It is unrealistic to assume that the clinical sport psychologist will always have a job with a given athlete or organization, have access to athletes once terminated from employment, or have access to athletes terminated from the team. In many cases, organizational demands make posttermination access to athletes difficult at best, especially in an environment where many do not believe such services are really necessary. Therefore, discussing this possibility and being prepared for the extant realities of the sport culture are crucial to ethically providing athletes with continuity of care. If organizational demands conflict with the ethical obligations regarding termination (Ethical Standard 1.03) (APA, 2002), it is the clinical sport psychologist's responsibility to fully assess the dilemma, express her professional obligation to the APA Ethics Code, and attempt to remediate the conflict. Nonetheless, conflict remediation must not compromise the practitioner's adherence to the APA Ethics Code.

If a clinical sport psychologist is abruptly terminated or has fulfilled contractual obligations, she cannot terminate the athlete without first securing other resources to further meet the athlete's needs (Canter et al., 1994). Regarding termination of the therapeutic relationship, the practitioner should discuss with the athlete his progress, further intervention needs, and options for continuity of care. The practitioner should also make referrals to ensure that the athlete has access to interventions. This is true even if the clinical sport psychologist deems that the client does not need further services. Referrals and contact information must be given in all circumstances. Although the practitioner cannot require the athlete to make necessary contacts for future care, she must make and thoroughly document reasonable efforts to provide continuity of care.

Case Example: Terminating the Practitioner–Client Relationship

Megan is a 24-year-old professional soccer player who is seeing the team's clinical sport psychologist weekly. Treatment began shortly after she was traded to the team, approximately one year earlier. Although Megan has been a productive team member and has met or exceeded both scouting and coaching expectations, she has been exceedingly unhappy. Since the trade, she has experienced the disruption of a romantic relationship that she mistakenly thought would continue following the trade, has had difficulty adjusting to her new surroundings, and has not formed relationships with her new teammates or coaches. In addition, her current playing time with this team is significantly less than the playing time she had grown accustomed to with the previous team and less than what she anticipated when traded.

Halfway through the season, the team's general manager was terminated from employment. With the new general manager came many changes that raised questions regarding the clinical sport psychologist's future with the organization. The practitioner recognized that her contract might not be renewed for the following season, yet continued to work with both Megan and the rest of team in an uninterrupted manner. After the season ended, the clinical sport psychologist waited to hear about the status of her employment for the following year. When her contract formally ended, team management had not yet had their postseason meeting, and thus had yet to decide on the practitioner's future with the team. Later, management indeed did not renew the contract, and since the contract had already ended, the clinical sport psychologist's work with Megan and others was considered complete. The

practitioner could play no further role with the organization without contractual obligations, and as such, Megan's treatment was over. This came as a surprise to Megan during a team meeting the following week, and since no new sport psychologist was hired, Megan was left with no clear options for continuing treatment. After termination, the clinical sport psychologist called Megan, but there was no answer. The psychologist also phoned another team member and left a brief message. Hearing this from the player, team management called the practitioner and stated that they expected her to stop contacting the athletes now that her contract was up and she no longer worked for the team.

Although this is a sticky situation, the clinical sport psychologist could have taken earlier action to minimize the current difficulties. As stated, it is the clinical sport psychologist's ethical responsibility to discuss, both with clients and team management, her ethical obligation to appropriately terminate athletes. If Megan's practitioner had done this, Megan would not have been left with minimal resources for continued treatment and insufficient closure to the treatment sequence and therapeutic relationship. The discussion that should have occurred would have emphasized the necessity for full closure and explained the required referral process for providing all clients (including Megan) with the best possible continued care. If this understanding had been in place at the onset of the clinical sport psychologist's employment (and included in the signed employment contract), team management likely would have allowed the practitioner to fulfill this obligation once terminated and probably would not have assumed that the clinical sport psychologist was attempting to continue work with the team without a contractual relationship. In addition, the best interests of the athletes would have been served. The practitioner could have discussed the possibility of termination, processed the termination with Megan and the others once it occurred, and provided the necessary resources and referrals for future treatment.

Although being prepared for possible termination is the best scenario, it did not happen in the case of Megan. Since the clinical sport psychologist did not adequately prepare for termination, what can she now do in remediation? Since her employment has been terminated with no previous agreement regarding the termination of intervention efforts with the athletes, she has only a few options. The best option is to contact the organization, present her ethical requirement to provide all clients with referrals for follow-up care and, if necessary, inform the organization of the APA ethical guidelines (2002) pertaining to the situation. Remember, however, that if the organization was unaware of which athletes were working with the practitioner, the practitioner cannot break confidentiality to the organization. The second suggestion is for the practitioner to send the athletes a letter providing only the necessary referral information so that the clients have access to continued care. Of course, it is critical that the clinical sport psychologist keep detailed contact records during this process.

Balancing Multiple Roles, Relationships, and Organizational Demands

When providing sport psychology services, concerns relating to multiple relationships may arise, such as competing organizational demands, practical issues like the length and location of services, and boundary issues. When facing these complicated issues, the clinical sport psychologist must carefully consider which plan of action will alleviate possible ethical dilemmas while she continues to effectively serve the individual athlete and the broader organizational system. Remediation of such concerns may require flexibility in adhering to the letter of the APA Ethics Code (2002), yet the practitioner must consistently strive to uphold the Code's spirit.

Multiple Relationships

A variety of multiple relationships can occur throughout psychological practice, often creating ethical dilemmas for involved parties. Since as humans we naturally interact with different people in different ways, we must define what exactly a multiple relationship is. Multiple relationships are "those situations in which the psychologist functions in more than one professional relationship, as well as those in which the psychologist functions in a professional role and another definitive and intended role" (Sonne, 1999, p. 227). According to Ethical Standard 3.05a, psychologists are encouraged to refrain "from entering into a multiple relationship" with clients (APA, 2002). In addition, the practitioner must be aware of the potential harm multiple relationships may cause the involved persons, such as causing the practitioner to lose

objectivity, damaging the therapeutic alliance and effectiveness of services, and possible exploitation of the client (Canter et al., 1994; Ebert, 1997; Kagle & Giebelhausen, 1994; Pope, 1991; Pope & Vasquez, 2001). The APA Ethics Code does *not* strictly prohibit practitioners from engaging in multiple relationships. However, it cautions practitioners of participating in a multiple relationship with an individual who depends on their services (Kagle & Giebelhausen, 1994; Pope, 1991). Why does the Code not strictly prohibit these relationships? A multiple relationship does not inherently and automatically create an ethical dilemma. Similarly, a multiple relationship does not inherently imply that the practitioner wishes to engage in ill intent or manipulate the client. In fact, "multiple relationships that would not reasonably be expected to cause impairment or risk exploitation or harm are not unethical" (Ethical Standard 3.05a) (APA, 2002). Difficulties typically arise when multiple roles conflict (Canter et al., 1994).

In military settings (Hines et al., 1998; Johnson, 1995), forensic settings (McGuire, 1997), rural settings (Catalano, 1997; Faulkner & Faulkner, 1997; Schank & Skovholt, 1997), and other small communities, multiple relationships are often unavoidable. For instance, a practitioner in a small community may encounter clients at the grocery store, post office, and local restaurant. The clinical sport psychologist may encounter clients at the practice facility, on road trips, or in many other situations. As for the rural psychologist, this will often be unavoidable, yet when conducted appropriately, this reality should not lead to difficulties. Care must be taken, and thoughtful consideration of this issue is a necessity.

Case Example: Multiple Relationships

Cassandra is a 19-year-old track athlete who has been working with a clinical sport psychologist for a couple of months at her university clinic. The practitioner has been working with Cassandra to improve her concentration, minimize task-irrelevant focus during competition, and enhance self-care associated with training (such as following a proper workout, nutrition, and sleep regime). At the same time, however, the practitioner is a bank customer at the local branch where Cassandra's mother and father are employed. He knows her parents from watching team practices, and Cassandra is aware of their occasional brief interactions at the bank. The practitioner typically sees her parents each time he enters the bank, frequently waves, and carries on with his business. Occasionally, one of her parents will say hello, with no intent other than remaining friendly. The practitioner seldom sees Cassandra at the bank, but he has seen her momentarily once or twice when she stopped by to see her parents. The practitioner is not uncomfortable with these brief interactions and sees no point in changing banks simply to minimize such contact outside of the professional domain.

In this case, as with any multiple relationship, the key to maintaining the original professional relationship is for the clinical sport psychologist to acknowledge the athlete's presence (and in this case also the presence of her parents), yet continue with his intended course of action. If the athlete insists on conversing, such conversation should remain brief and impersonal and should not focus on therapeutic material or events related to other team or staff members. Although an unexpected encounter may occasionally be uncomfortable, ignoring or pretending not to notice the individual can damage the interpersonal and professional relationship. It is advisable for the clinical sport psychologist and athlete (and any other known family) to agree at the onset of services how they will respond to each other in such circumstances. This alleviates discomfort with future interactions,

minimizes misinterpretation of the practitioner's responsiveness, minimizes dissolution of confidentiality, and maintains professional boundaries.

Multiple Organizational Demands

Although the challenges inherent in the clinical sport psychologist's work can markedly differ from those practicing clinical or counseling psychology, doing research, or employed as sport educators, we do share some concerns and difficulties with other professional psychology occupations. For example, when working with a sport organization, the practitioner has a role similar to a military psychologist's (Johnson, 1995), as both must carefully balance the needs of the larger organization with the needs of individual personnel. The clinical sport psychologist must balance specific psychological services to athletes, coaches, and organizational personnel with consultation to coaches and management. In order to do this effectively, the clinical sport psychologist must be able to critically evaluate the numerous organizational elements and how those elements interact with athlete variables. This critical balance is illustrated in figure 12.2.

This sport psychologist is describing his role and the services he can provide the athlete.

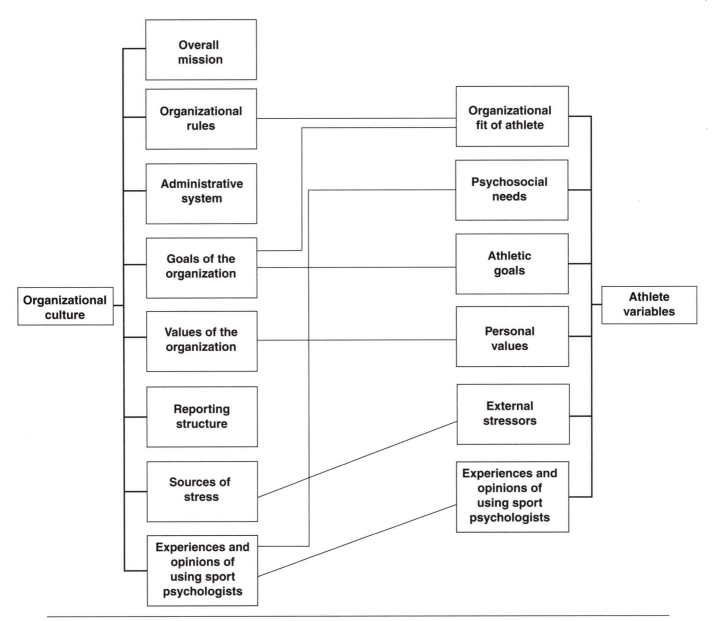

Figure 12.2   Understanding the balance between organizational culture and specific athlete variables.

In balancing the needs of the athlete with the needs of coaches, organizational personnel, and the greater organizational system, the practitioner who fails to establish his roles, limitations, and so on at the *onset* of services may run into a needs hierarchy. Such a hierarchy can complicate trust and rapport, which are necessary ingredients for effective psychological care and organizational acceptance. To minimize this possibility, the clinical sport psychologist should discuss at length with all involved parties issues such as reporting structure, athlete confidentiality, multiple relationship development, professional duties, scheduling criteria, accommodations, fee structure, client contact, limitations to services, and so on. Elucidating such issues early on helps the practitioner avoid many difficulties. If difficulties do arise, in order to both respect the dilemma and balance the differing needs of the involved parties, the clinical sport psychologist must ensure that confidentiality (as stated in the informed consent) is protected and that multiple roles do not conflict, endanger the well-being of the client or the greater organization, or alter the practitioner's objectivity to either party (Canter et al., 1994).

When working with a sport organization, the clinical sport psychologist may be asked to assist management in selecting players. Although assisting may be acceptable if it is the sole or limited role of the practitioner or if the players are not yet involved with the team (such as for selection), it could be unacceptable if it involves athletes with whom the practitioner has worked. In such cases, the clinical sport psychologist:

> *Has likely obtained insight into the personal and professional strengths and weaknesses of his or her clients and cannot objectively make such determinations without compromising his or her role with the [athlete] and misusing information that has been obtained in a confidential relationship, even when such information is not shared with others. (Canter et al., 1994, p. 48)*

Case Example: Multiple Organizational Demands

A clinical sport psychologist has been consulting for a professional basketball team for the past two years. Before his current employment, the practitioner worked for a different professional team within the league. During that time, he worked closely with several different players and gained substantial insight into their personalities, strengths, weaknesses, and overall life functioning. During the current season, the team contemplates a trade for one of the players that the clinical sport psychologist had closely worked with on the previous team. Naturally, the scouting staff and team management are very interested in the information the clinical sport psychologist previously gathered and in his overall opinion on acquiring the player. As such, they ask for a thoughtful recommendation. The practitioner's recommendation is not the sole factor in the decision, of course, but since none of the decision makers have a particular opinion about the player or have worked with him, they are especially curious about the clinical sport psychologist's thoughts.

Indeed, the practitioner has a specific opinion, as he had worked with the athlete on significant behavioral problems, interpersonal difficulties with teammates, and increasing alcohol consumption. Internally, the clinical sport psychologist has concerns about these issues. How does the practitioner ethically respond to the management's request for information?

The practitioner's foremost responsibility is to uphold the player's confidentiality. When the practitioner worked with the athlete on the previous team, he did not obtain an informed consent

stating that he could forever use the information provided in any way he deemed appropriate. One reason written informed consent is so important is that it protects the client's rights by defining the ways client information can be utilized, limiting the practitioner's use of the information to those ways it formally codifies. However, will the management staff understand the clinical sport psychologist's ethical parameters and back away from a source of information that not only exists, but is also remunerated for services? Indeed, team management may have a significant difficulty understanding if the practitioner states his ethical obligations only when they are particularly relevant. Since the management now expects the information, tensions are likely to run high if the information is withheld. This is especially true considering that as managers of a professional team, they will invest millions of dollars in this player if they go forward with the trade. If the clinical sport psychologist withholds information about the player's difficulties and their potential impact on both the interpersonal dynamics of the team and the team's success on the court, it would not be surprising if the practitioner quickly finds himself without a job.

In this case example, the practitioner has made a fundamental error. The error is not withholding client information, as in doing so the practitioner wholly abides by ethical standards and protects the client's right to privacy. The practitioner has not violated the Ethics Code. The error is in the *manner* in which the clinical sport psychologist communicated with team management. Team management may not have been pleased with his obligation to withhold information, but they would likely have respected his obligation if the practitioner had clearly explained limitations to confidentiality at the *onset* of employment with the team. Since ethical challenges inevitably arise during the practice of sport psychology, effective communication remains the key ingredient, as it *promotes* the capacity to remain ethical in challenging situations.

Discussing the ethical limitations of one's work before beginning services allows all involved parties to form realistic expectations of the practitioner's acceptable roles and professional abilities and limitations. This is especially critical considering that clinical sport psychologists often work *for* the team, but work *with* the athletes. Multiorganizational demands occur frequently in such professional arrangements and can pull at the practitioner from different angles. When demands conflict, the clinical sport psychologist, management, and individual athletes occasionally disagree with the limits the practitioner places on his roles. Again, effective and clear communication is warranted, and all parties in the organizational system with whom the clinical sport psychologist interacts must comprehend the ethical parameters inherent in sport psychology practice. If disagreements do arise, it is the practitioner's responsibility to respect and uphold the APA Ethics Code in the face of such challenges. Remaining within professional limits helps gain the respect of athletes and staff, maintain professional boundaries, and, most important, minimize potential harm to clientele.

Length and Location of Service

So far in this chapter, we have considered the important issues of confidentiality, informed consent, and multiple relationships. These are the issues that probably first come to mind when imagining ethical dilemmas. Yet, clinical sport psychologists must also recognize concerns regarding the location of services and the alteration of the traditional time constraints that are typically present for psychologists in private practice. These issues are not often considered potentially

detrimental to the athlete, the organization, or the professional relationship, but they do require thought and early planning.

Some clinical sport psychologists travel with teams during the athletic season and are required to be available throughout the trip to consult with or provide services to the athletic team or staff. Often, this includes providing consultation on buses and planes, at dinner, in the hotel, or over breakfast. This may not initially concern the reader, but it can interfere with providing effective services and place the client at risk. Given the scope of traditional clinical and counseling private practice, such locations could jeopardize the therapeutic relationship, appear inappropriate, and lead to a violation of the APA Ethics Code (Moore, 2001, March).

Case Example:
Length and Location of Service

During play-offs, the team's clinical sport psychologist was asked to meet with Philippe after a game. The next game was the following day, and winning was critical to progressing in the series. Philippe's success in this game was of utmost importance. The clinical sport psychologist met with Philippe, but did not abide by the session

Sport psychologists often see athletes in nontraditional settings, such as the locker room and clubhouse.

length typical to those practicing in other domains of psychology (45-50 min). Instead, the session lasted as long as the practitioner deemed necessary for preparing Philippe for the big game. Also, as the team was traveling, they could not meet in the practitioner's personal office. The practitioner had a few odd options for the session location, including the locker room, at dinner, in a hotel room with an open door, or on the bus. The clinical sport psychologist chose the hotel room with the open door and held a 1 hr and 45 min meeting with Philippe.

This case example does not seem as easily remedied as cases of confidentiality or informed consent. Although this type of practice may seem normal to the clinical sport psychologist, it possesses an inherent dilemma. On one hand, meeting with Philippe in a hotel room may be necessary to provide needed services. Although the practitioner in the example had a few location options, there may be times when acceptable locations are particularly limited. In the case of Philippe, the practitioner chose the hotel room with the open door—but could conducting such a meeting appear to others as a sexual or other malintended encounter? Possibly. Could the practitioner instead meet with Philippe in the hotel lobby? Probably not, because providing services in the lobby or other open area could easily violate client confidentiality. Such dichotomous professional difficulties are central to the practice of applied sport psychology and are often without clear and practical answers.

For a clinical or counseling psychologist in private practice, the mentioned arrangements may appear to violate confidentiality, breach boundary issues, or provide an opportunity for detrimental or exploitative multiple relationships (Anderson & Kitchener, 1999; Pope & Vasquez, 2001). However, such spontaneous and compromising decisions echo the demands faced by the clinical sport psychologist and therefore must be considered carefully (Petitpas, Brewer, Rivera, & Van Raalte, 1994). To help ameliorate this concern, the practitioner must clearly indicate to both athletes and organizational staff that in order to provide needed services under variable travel conditions and accommodations, compromised meeting schedules and settings will occasionally be necessary. If it has always been clear to Philippe, his teammates, and the team staff that a compromised arrangement may be necessary at times, it is more likely that all will be comfortable with the arrangements and respect these service demands.

Further, flexibility will be required of all parties to ensure the most adequate service possible. If the noise volume on the hotel floor gets too high, or too many people pass by the room, it may be necessary to relocate on the spur of the moment. Although relocating is not optimal, the understood need for flexibility will greatly enhance smooth transitions. Agreeing on understandings such as these minimizes potential difficulties.

Maintaining Boundaries

Issues such as multiple relationships, multiple organizational demands, location of services, and schedule flexibility inherently require clear and forthright professional boundaries. Although numerous ethical dilemmas may arise during service, the clinical sport psychologist should establish clear boundaries at the beginning of employment. This may alleviate concerns before they arise and sets a precedent for future decision making and boundary maintenance.

Sport psychology is an interesting and complicated field built on a sporting culture known for spontaneity and inconsistency. The job of the clinical sport psychologist is rarely without potential ethical complications, as the practitioner performs many roles, holds many relationships, and participates in numerous activities that do not typically mirror traditional practice. For example, the practitioner may be asked, or even obligated, to attend organizational events in order to maintain rapport with athletes and staff and further secure a position as an accepted, reliable, and trusted staff member. It may take considerable time for her to become fully accepted by both athletes and the larger organizational system, and rejecting such an invitation may damage even the most well-established therapeutic alliance. Thus, clinical sport psychologists must frequently decide the extent to which they will participate in such activities, to what degree such participation may violate boundaries and invite multiple relationships, and to what extent an invitational rejection may ultimately harm therapeutic relationships (Buceta, 1993; Moore, 2001, March).

It is certainly possible that these nontherapeutic, seemingly social interactions may lead to violations of the APA Ethics Code if conducted incorrectly or for the wrong reasons. On the other hand, if the clinical sport psychologist wants to be a part of the team personnel and wishes to be viewed as a trusted professional, it would be wise to participate in special team events. Being involved in some aspects of the team while withdrawing from special events may appear behaviorally incongruent. Behavioral inconsistency can potentially threaten the practitioner's job within the organization and her ability to effectively provide much-needed psychological services. For example, if the clinical sport psychologist consults with a team throughout the year, attends necessary practices and games, and facilitates relationship building, rejecting an invitation to a special team event in order to maintain boundaries and avoid real or perceived multiple relationships is not setting a positive and congruent example for those team members who accepted the practitioner into the organizational family and welcomed her services. It could certainly damage the therapeutic relationships already established with specific athletes, and those athletes who resisted services in the past may be less likely to ask for assistance in the future.

Maintaining boundaries is another area where the traditional psychologist's decision-making style does not neatly apply or direct the clinical sport psychologist. A clinical or counseling psychologist in private practice may invite multiple relationships by attending a client's party, which likely holds little therapeutic intent. However, the clinical sport psychologist may find it difficult to hold himself to such dichotomous standards when the additional activity outside of the therapeutic domain employs therapeutic intent as its foremost concern. Examples of this are attending organizational events, team meals, late-night staff meetings, and development meetings during training camp. The inherent goal of these meetings is not to socialize. Although the practitioner may not be performing his specific occupational duties, he nonetheless continues to represent himself professionally, and his particular role is understood to all involved parties. If the clinical sport psychologist does attend a more social organizational event, such as a championship dinner, it is imperative that he minimizes deep personal engagement with athletes and keeps conversations superficial (Canter et al., 1994). In this respect, the practitioner attends organizational events as part of his occupational duties, yet is social without actually socializing. This concept is critical, as the sporting culture naturally allows for downtime, and cutup behaviors run rampant. In essence, the clinical sport psychologist's obligation is not only to provide a multitude of services to the organization, but also to remain *professionally* involved in all aspects of the athletic environ-

ment that facilitate rapport and promote the use of services by the team and staff.

Case Example: Maintaining Boundaries

A clinical sport psychologist has been providing performance enhancement services to a local basketball team for a couple of years and has a strong rapport with the players. One night he went out with several friends to a restaurant and bar. Since there was a significant wait for a table, the group moved to the bar to wait, have a drink, and socialize. Around that time, several members of the basketball team entered and approached the crowded bar. Upon seeing the sport psychologist, the team members reacted positively, and insisted that the practitioner come over to say hello and chat. The practitioner moved to the bar and briefly conversed with the team members, trying to keep the conversation unrelated to work. A few moments later, one of the members asked the sport psychologist if he would like a drink, which the practitioner did not accept. After a few more moments, the practitioner said that he should return to his party, wished the group goodnight, and departed.

In this instance, the clinical sport psychologist made the right professional decisions. He could not be expected to restrict his entire social evening simply because members of the team happened to enter the same establishment. Yet, the way in which he maneuvered the situation was critical to maintaining appropriate boundaries. In this case, the athletes greeted the clinical sport psychologist and asked him to come say hello. This should not be surprising, since the athletes work with the practitioner, and they all participate in a common goal. Could the practitioner have ignored the athletes and pretended they were not there? Certainly not. Doing so would have damaged his professional relationship with these players. In addition, it wouldn't have been long before other members of the team and staff heard about the brush off. Any reasonable person (practitioner) would have said hello to the athletes and engaged in brief conversation. As the reader probably noticed, however, the sport psychologist did not allow the team member to buy him a drink, and he restricted the conversation to nonsport topics. Likewise, he found an appropriate time to break the conversation and return to his own party, leaving the athletes to enjoy their evening without insulting them by avoiding their contact.

What should the practitioner have done if the athlete had bought him a drink without his prior knowledge? We suggest that the practitioner simply thank the athlete for the thought, joke that "this isn't the typical session," and donate the drink back to the group. No harm would have been done, and the practitioner would have upheld all professional boundaries. Yet suppose that during the nonsport conversation, one of the team members jokingly stated, "Hey doc, you need to get into that new kid's head!" In this case, the clinical sport psychologist could reply, "Hey come on, are you out tonight to have a good time or to make me work hard?" By stating this, the practitioner has accomplished a few key tasks. He has informed the team members that he is not willing to disclose client information or discuss another team member, has protected the well-being of the athletes with whom he works, has not dissolved professional boundaries, and has potentially strengthened the confidence of these teammates by subtly informing them that he will uphold their privacy in similar circumstances. Although we could hypothesize numerous difficult examples and potential ways of resolving them, one point should be clear. The clinical sport psychologist must maintain professional boundaries at all times. Sometimes this requires thinking quickly during spontaneous challenges to boundary adherence. As seen in the above example, the practitioner does not have to be unfriendly, cold, or forceful. Purposeful humor often sends the best message, especially in the athletic domain, where humor is often considered an art among colleagues, teammates, and so on. As stated earlier, it is possible to be social without actually socializing. With this in mind, and with a clear understanding of the APA Ethics Code, clinical sport psychologists will be prepared to effectively uphold the ethical behavior necessary for professional success and client welfare.

Final Thoughts

We have provided numerous examples of ethical concerns that deserve careful consideration when working with athletes and sport organizations. There are many professional elements to think about, many of which require decision making that does not mimic the traditional psychology practice. So how can clinical sport psychologists combat ethical concerns, fulfill occupational needs, remain cognizant of best-practice guidelines, and respect the best interest of the client?

The clinical sport psychologist's ultimate role is to meet the needs of the client (whether working with PD, Pdy, PI, or PT cases), facilitate therapeutic utility, establish rapport, maintain pro-

fessional boundaries, and avoid ethical dilemmas (Moore, 2003a). The practitioner is responsible for providing (up front) a clear understanding of her professional roles within the athletic environment. Although the sport environment requires flexibility, spontaneity, and the ability to adapt to the changing needs of an entire organization of potential clients, the practitioner must adhere to the demands of both the team and the APA Ethics Code (APA, 2002; Nideffer, 1981).

Rules, standards, and limitations regarding confidentiality, informed consent, intervention, assessment, practitioner competence, and professional boundaries should be established and communicated to all involved parties at the onset of services to avoid potentially harmful ethical dilemmas, loss of objectivity, and exploitation of the client (Gardner, 1995). To do this, the clinical sport psychologist should know and professionally adopt the APA Ethics Code (2002). The Code helps practitioners "avoid ethical violations by sensitizing them to potential behaviors that can violate the rights and welfare of individuals with whom they work . . . [and] should help them avoid these pitfalls before an ethical problem develops" (Fisher & Younggren, 1997, p. 586). Although all of the Code's details do not directly mirror the specifics of the clinical sport psychologist's work, understanding the Code allows practitioners to adapt particular guidelines to better serve a unique population. In essence, adapting the letter of the APA Ethics Code allows the sport practitioner to fulfill the spirit of the Code's mission and intent. Once the practitioner understands and accepts these ethical responsibilities, she must strive to provide sound services and use professional judgment and collegial consultation as necessary (Gardner, 1995). Consultation is incredibly important for any professional. Thus, the clinical sport psychologist is encouraged to consult with colleagues when ethical issues arise (Ebert, 1997) and attempt to resolve such issues in a manner that is ethically bound; appropriate to the population, situation, and setting; and foremost concerned with the welfare of the athlete (Buceta, 1993; Ellickson & Brown, 1990). By establishing, communicating, and maintaining professional boundaries; practicing within areas of competence; recognizing and ameliorating inherent ethical difficulties that may arise; and maintaining competence and informed professionalism, the clinical sport psychologist can remain integrated in the athletic environment and provide the multifaceted services necessary to enhance sport participation.

Ethical Self-Awareness Checklist for Sport Psychologists

©2003 by Zella E. Moore

A guide for ethical and legal practice

	Yes	No	N/A
• Do I have the appropriate specialized education and training to offer and provide these services in this proficiency area of professional psychology?	___	___	___
• Is my role with the client or organization clearly defined and within defendable limits of competence as defined by my education and training?	___	___	___
• Am I describing and representing myself and my services honestly and accurately?	___	___	___
• Am I thoroughly aware of APA's Code of Ethics and how it pertains to my work?	___	___	___
• Do I integrate new research findings and professional developments within my field in order to remain up to date in my practice?	___	___	___
• Am I providing my clientele with written and verbal informed consent?	___	___	___
• Am I providing informed consent that is detailed and honest and appropriately describes the following:			
• Myself (the practitioner)	___	___	___
• The services I provide	___	___	___
• Expectations of the services	___	___	___
• Limitations of the services	___	___	___
• Empirical support (or lack thereof) for the services	___	___	___
• Issues of confidentiality	___	___	___
• Fees	___	___	___
• Other intervention options	___	___	___
• The extent to which these interventions are likely to be effective	___	___	___
• Have I exaggerated the likelihood of treatment success or promised the client an outcome that is unrealistic?	___	___	___
• Have I clearly defined confidentiality, limits of confidentiality, and how those limits are to be decided with clients, parents, coaches, organizational personnel, and so on?	___	___	___
• Am I receiving pressure from organizational staff to violate client confidentiality, blur boundaries, or engage in unnecessary or inappropriate interventions?	___	___	___
• If so, have I discussed these dilemmas with the appropriate individuals within the organization in an attempt to remediate the difficulties?	___	___	___
• Do I discuss clients and their relevant case material with other individuals outside of a consultative role?	___	___	___
• If I speak to other individuals about a client, have I obtained the necessary voluntary verbal and written consent from the client to do so?	___	___	___
• Prior to obtaining consent from the client to speak to other individuals about the case, have I made the client aware of the possible consequences and outcomes of sharing case information, so that the client can make an informed decision?	___	___	___

	Yes	No	N/A

- Have I recorded essential client information, evaluative information, progress notes, and so on in clients' records? ___ ___ ___
- Do I retain records and client data for the number of years mandatory in my state? ___ ___ ___
- Are these records kept in a safe and secure place? ___ ___ ___
- Are legal reporting requirements clearly presented and understood (i.e., child abuse, potential self-harm, potential harm to others)? ___ ___ ___
- Do I have any nonconsultative or nontherapeutic contacts with clients? ___ ___ ___
- If so, can I clearly defend the need for or unavoidable nature of these nonconsultative and nontherapeutic contacts with clients? ___ ___ ___
- If and when I attend organizational events, do I remain superficial in my contact with clients and avoid excessive socializing in order to limit the potential for loss of objectivity or the development of unnecessary dual-role relationships? ___ ___ ___
- Have I discussed with my clients the possibility of abrupt employment termination and made appropriate referrals ahead of time to provide continuity of care? ___ ___ ___
- Am I prolonging treatment past necessity and continuing in a therapeutic relationship with a client although my services are complete and intervention success has ensued? ___ ___ ___
- Have I developed an appropriate referral network so that issues out of my area of competence can be appropriately addressed and treated? ___ ___ ___
- Am I willing to refer clients to another professional if I can no longer be of assistance or if personal objectivity is compromised, the therapeutic relationship is damaged, or the client is not able to benefit from my services? ___ ___ ___
- Have I minimized the presence of more serious psychological concerns, and thus denied the need for referral, in order to continue working with a client? ___ ___ ___
- Have the services I provide become clouded by my own personal life circumstances and difficulties? ___ ___ ___
- Do I approach my client with a sense of negativity, feel anger or resentment toward my client, or have harmful or sexual feelings or fantasies about my client? ___ ___ ___
- If using psychological assessment instruments, do I have the necessary education and training to use them? ___ ___ ___
- Have I allowed a large debt for services to accumulate? ___ ___ ___
- If so, have I discussed this debt with the client, attempted to coordinate payment, and appropriately recorded any interactions between myself and the client regarding this issue? ___ ___ ___
- Do I have professional liability insurance? ___ ___ ___

When a concern or dilemma arises

	Yes	No	N/A

- Am I thoroughly aware of APA's Code of Ethics regarding this situation or dilemma? ___ ___ ___
- Have I read the Ethical Standard directly regarding this issue? ___ ___ ___

(continued)

219

(continued)

- Have I contemplated how the issue at hand may affect my clients?   ____   ____   ____
- Am I serving my needs and interests more than the needs and interests of my clients?   ____   ____   ____
- Have I consulted with a colleague or another professional in the field?   ____   ____   ____
- Have I contacted the APA Ethics Board for suggestion and guidance?   ____   ____   ____
- Have I read relevant literature within the field concerning similar issues and concerns?   ____   ____   ____
- Am I comfortable and confident that I could defend my decision or intervention in front of an ethics board or court of law if necessary?   ____   ____   ____
- If applicable, have I contacted my professional liability insurance provider?   ____   ____   ____
- If applicable, have I contacted a lawyer regarding this issue?   ____   ____   ____

CHAPTER 13

Professional Development and Supervision in Clinical Sport Psychology

Over the years, much has been written about the education, training, and certification of sport psychologists (Gardner, 1991; Silva, 1989) with hopes that researchers and practitioners will advance sport psychology by attaining competence in this dynamic and complex field. Yet much to the detriment of students, teachers, and practitioners, several critical professional and educational issues have received far less attention. To address this trend, this chapter promotes a new-found focus on developing a professional identity and benefiting from the profound potential of the supervisory relationship. Although these topics often fall by the wayside, they represent the core of the clinical sport psychologist. These issues are immeasurably important to both developing practitioners and to those supervising the next generation of sport psychologists.

In the initial segment of this chapter, we discuss professional development from the perspective of intervention *skill* development, borrowing from both the motor learning and self-regulatory literature. Following this discussion, we move on to the development of *personal characteristics* and related issues of effective practice and working alliances between clinical sport psychologists and athletes. Finally, we discuss supervision by integrating these factors and suggesting strategies to enhance self-awareness and skill proficiency among clinical sport psychology trainees.

Professional Development

An array of growth factors promotes the development of professional skills and competencies. In any area of elite performance, developing exper-

tise depends on combining knowledge (education) of the skill to be mastered with training (under supervision), personal abilities (characteristics), and numerous quality repetitions (practice). The development of expert performance has recently received significant attention among the professional psychology literature, and we believe that this development can be directly related to the development of superior practitioner skills.

Developing Expert Performance in Clinical Sport Psychology

Over the past two decades, research in cognitive science has significantly advanced our understanding of learning, particularly as it relates to developing expert performance (Starkes & Ericsson, 2003; Stoltenberg, McNeill, & Delworth, 1998). During this time, models of skill learning and development have emerged to describe the process by which high-level skill sets (including motor skills and other expert performance systems) can be explained (Ericsson, 2003; Fitts & Posner, 1967). Although these models are based on motor learning and self-regulatory principles, we have used them to better understand and help our clinical and sport psychology trainees as we assist them in their development as competent practitioners and scholars.

Three primary stages of skill development have generally been described to explain how people develop skills and expertise (Fischman & Oxendine, 1998). These stages are the cognitive stage, associative stage, and autonomous stage. Although these stages were not originally devised to describe the attainment of practitioner skills, they relate considerably to the educational training and skill development of clinical sport psychologists and have been similarly applied to the development of direct clinical skills (Stoltenberg et al., 1998). We have adapted these stages into an understanding of skill development that carefully considers how each stage affects the self-regulatory process of the clinical sport psychology trainee. We believe that this understanding can substantially impact both the supervisor's training philosophy and strategies and the trainee's experience during the progression from novice to skilled practitioner.

Cognitive Stage of Skill Development

The first stage of skill development is the *cognitive* stage (Fischman & Oxendine, 1998; Stoltenberg et al., 1998). The cognitive (novice) stage is the period in which verbal rules and mental representations are learned and guide the actions of the individual. In this stage, case conceptualization skills develop and become ingrained as a guide for professional decision making. Here, the novice trainee utilizes the previously (didactically) learned knowledge base of the presently needed skills, yet applies this knowledge in its most structured form. Therefore, at times the knowledge and skill sets appear overly programmed, as it takes great concentration to utilize these fundamental skills. From this perspective, the novice clinical sport psychologist engages in rule-governed behavior. When utilizing rule-governed behavior, the novice professional attempts to apply fundamental rules and strategies to his work and to form an internal representation of skill which contains a set of personal instructions to guide his activity. This *conscious attention* (Fischman & Oxendine, 1998) leads trainees to respond poorly to the cues and contingencies in their environments (such as the words and actions of the athlete). During this period, the novice trainee is not connected or responsive to the overt needs of the athlete and typically behaves in a mechanistic, controlled, and nonresponsive manner.

The cognitive stage is so named because cognitive activity predominates, with an emphasis on technical detail and self-focused attention. We know from chapter 2 that cognitive activity associated with self-focused attention does not lead to optimal human performance. In addition, as predicted by earlier accounts of the self-regulatory process, self-focused attention corresponds to increases in negative affect and a restricted range of behavior. Yet, this stage may seem remarkably familiar to any professional recalling her early professional development (likely with a sigh of relief that it is over). Educators are likely smiling, thinking of their most recent students in this anxiety-provoking state that typically results in few displays of technical competence. During this phase of skill development, autonomous professional activity is minimal and the trainee highly depends on supervisors, repeatedly asking, "What do I do when . . . ?" In short, the trainee is dominated by self-evaluation, predetermined scripts and rules, and high arousal, with minimal focus on the athlete's needs and feelings. Coupled with the inherent increase in arousal and inflexibility associated with rule-governed behavior, it should not be surprising that the trainee's behavior does not promote an effective therapeutic alliance, as the athlete and practitioner are disconnected. The following transcript between a clinical sport psychology trainee (T) and his supervisor (S) reflects the cognitive stage of professional development:

T: I really need help here. I was totally lost during the session. Every time Mary said something and I thought of something to say, she said something else and I lost my place.

S: Where were you most confused?

T: Mary mentioned that when she gets up to the plate, she looks into the stands, and if she sees her father, she just loses it and can't focus on the ball. I didn't know what to say. I mean, I know what's going on with her, but I can't put it into words.

S: Based on what happened in the session, what do you think is going on with her?

T: Her focus of attention is on her father and the meaning that he has to her, and she has self-focused attention instead of the task-focused attention necessary to perform optimally.

S: OK. You gave me a good example of that a minute ago from what she stated during the session with you.

T: Right. But I couldn't go anywhere with it. It was like the perfect moment, and I just sat there and let it pass by both of us.

S: OK. Let's say that statement truly reflects the problem. If you were in the session now, where would you go from there, and what would you do with her now to help her connect the moment with the goal?

T: Well, when she says something that tells me she's disconnected from the task, that's the

One goal of supervision is to help the trainee respond fluidly with the athlete based on the nuances of the session.

moment I'd encourage her to use a brief mindfulness of the breath exercise to disrupt the irrelevant thought process and get refocused. We could practice that in the session, and then she could transfer it onto the field.

The goal of the supervisor during the cognitive stage is to help trainees move from rule-governed behavior to contingency-shaped behavior so that they use their knowledge to respond to the contingencies in the session and fulfill the session requirements based on the case formulation. The trainee's goal in this stage is to move away from a rigid focus on a preconceived rule of what she *should* say or do and learn to let athlete responses be the stimulus for therapeutic behavioral choices. This stage is typically short and is complete when the trainee can execute the necessary therapeutic skills in their basic forms.

Associative Stage of Skill Development

The second stage of skill development is the *associative* stage (Fischman & Oxendine, 1998; Stoltenberg et al., 1998). During the associative (intermediate) stage, the learner assimilates and accommodates feedback and corrects errors accordingly. Additionally, the trainee begins to respond to accurate conceptualizations of in-the-moment athlete behavior rather than exclusively through rule-governed

behavior. As such, the trainee experiences greater connection to the athlete and responds to the cues and contingencies inherent in a consulting relationship more appropriately and with greater flexibility. The trainee begins to see issues more abstractly and recognizes patterns in the athlete's behavior. In turn, the trainee's therapeutic behaviors (words and actions) become more appropriate to the moment-to-moment words and actions of the client. For these reasons, the trainee forms a more effective therapeutic relationship with the athlete.

The self-focused attention that predominated the cognitive stage decreases and is replaced with increases in task-focused attention. This shift in attention is accompanied by lowered levels of arousal and more effective overall performance. Professional autonomy also increases during this time as self-efficacy is enhanced. Reflecting their growing competence, trainees are typically relieved that they no longer have to beg the supervisor, "What do I do now?" Supervisors are pleased that their students can integrate more meaningful client data and respond more spontaneously to the natural interpersonal connection with the athlete. Of course, when responding to novel professional situations, the trainee may revert to the rule-governed behavior of the earlier cognitive stage. This back-and-forth between the associative and cognitive stage is expected, and can occur for a prolonged period as the trainee accumulates numerous practice trials across an increasing number of professional situations and with corresponding complexity. The associative stage is reflected in the following transcript between a clinical sport psychology trainee (T) and her supervisor (S):

T: I had a really weird session with Steve today. He was really angry toward me for some reason—I was going to continue the values identification phase, and he starting acting really sarcastic and hostile with me.

S: How did you respond to that?

T: Well, I was aware of the hostility, and I was torn between following up on it and knowing that I needed to finish the values identification aspect of the protocol.

S: What did you decide to do?

T: I spent a little bit of time trying to investigate the source of his anger, and when I couldn't determine it quickly, I decided to just move on and continue to work on values identification.

S: How did he respond to that?

T: He seemed to get more frustrated and angry.

S: Has he been that way before with you?

T: No.

S: What did you do last week?

T: We began to discuss the concept of values and I gave a between-session assignment to complete a values identification questionnaire.

S: Did he complete the questionnaire?

T: No.

S: What do you think the possibility is that his response to you was directly related to the topic that you brought up last week and the assignment?

In this vignette, the trainee battled with the common elements of the associative stage. The trainee was generally aware of the in-the-moment process between herself and the athlete and understood the need to respond to the athlete's anger. However, she still responded with rule-governed behavior related to the need to complete the procedural task. Although she recognized the athlete's affective state, she didn't consider that the assigned task was possibly the stimulus for the athlete's hostility. Clearly, understanding the behavioral avoidance and affect related to the task would aid in its successful completion. It also highlights the importance of the assignment. As such, the supervisor's role was to continue the development of the trainee's capacity to view in-session behavior as a reflection of important issues that need to be dealt with and that directly relate to directive therapeutic strategies. Generally in this stage, the supervisor reinforces the trainee's in-session contingency-based behavior and promotes the trainee's flexibility in responding to in-the-moment demands. Unlike the cognitive stage, the associative stage can take numerous years to complete. As such, the professional typically remains in the associative stage for several years after graduate training. The stage is considered complete when the trainee demonstrates therapeutic skills consistently, commits fewer technical and relationship errors, and utilizes a more diverse set of skills in a flexible, consistent manner.

Autonomous Stage of Skill Development

The third stage of skill development is the *autonomous* stage (Fischman & Oxendine, 1998; Stoltenberg et al., 1998). In the autonomous (advanced) stage, the individual has evolved from trainee to supervised expert, or supervisee (we refer to the individual as a supervisee to denote a professional status beyond that of a trainee). The supervisee proficiently uses professional skills, and her responses are rapid and automatic. Increasingly automated expert performance evolves as focus on skill execution is replaced with mindful attention to the moment-to-moment interchange with the athlete. At this stage, the supervisee rapidly perceives and interprets client words and actions and effortlessly accesses potential responses from memory (Ericsson, 2003). The supervisee, now achieving an expert skill level, remains connected to the athlete and her professional behavior feels automatic and effortless. Autonomy is at its peak, as the supervisee believes in her capacity to respond to both familiar and novel professional situations. Arousal and heightened negative affect no longer overwhelm the supervisee, and she is therefore significantly more able to attend to the athlete's needs. The following transcript between a supervised clinical sport psychologist (P) and her supervisor (S) reflects the autonomous stage:

P: We began a discussion of Jane's performance issues, but her posture and tone of voice suggested that there was something else going on.

S: How were you feeling in response and then where did you go with that?

P: I was feeling put off by her. I decided to leave the performance issue and told her that her lack of eye contact and low voice indicated some other emotions. She then told me that she has been feeling increasingly sad. She said she has been withdrawn and that she thinks that nobody cares.

S: What was your response?

P: I tried to reinforce her opening up to me and empathized with being sad and having no one seeming aware. We then discussed that withdrawing and the nonexpression of feelings can be misinterpreted. We then discussed how others might interpret her behavior.

S: Where did she go with that?

P: We established a behavior activities schedule that included sharing her sadness with some close friends. We also agreed to put aside the performance issues temporarily and to focus on her mood state and interpersonal behavior for a while.

During this stage, the supervised clinical sport psychologist has a sound understanding of therapeutic skills and how to effectively utilize them. This professional spends little time actually thinking of the details of the skills she is utilizing. The supervisee in the autonomous stage no longer concentrates on specific procedures, but instead concentrates on the many variables present in the setting (including relational factors). Although the supervisee in this stage is a proficient clinical sport psychologist, attaining this stage does not suggest that there is no room for professional growth. Thus, in this stage the role of the supervisor is to help the professional maintain her skill level and to motivate her to further improve.

Conceptualizing experiential learning through self-regulation theory and the cognitive, associative, and autonomous stages of skill development can be useful to both the professional-in-training and the supervisor as a means of clarifying expectations, normalizing experiences, and providing ongoing feedback for minute skill refinement. Figure 13.1 summarizes the three stages of skill development.

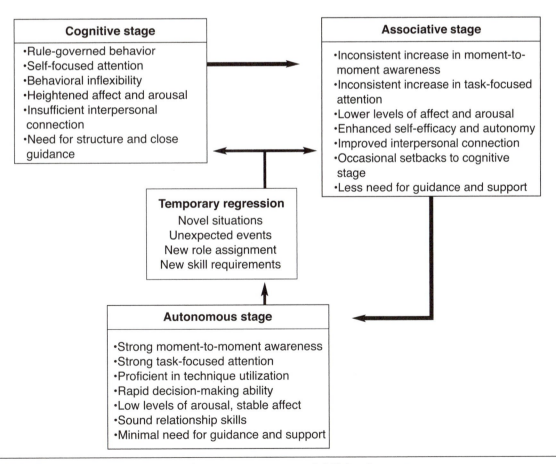

Figure 13.1 The cognitive, associative, and autonomous stages of skill development.

Assessment of Skill Development

The first step in effective supervision is correctly assessing the trainee's stage of skill development. To aid this assessment and to measure changes over time, we developed the Skill Development Stage Questionnaire (see sidebar below) to use with both clinical and clinical sport psychology trainees. This scale assesses the various components of the stages of skill development with a simple, brief series of questions in a Likert format. An overall score between 21 and 27 indicates the cognitive stage, between 11 and 20 indicates the associative stage, and 10 or less indicates the autonomous stage. These numbers are intended to be a guide and are by no means absolute. The scores, however, are theoretically consistent with the components of the stages of skill development and can be used to differentiate trainees at various levels of development who therefore have different supervisory needs and require different supervisory strategies. The supervisor must remember that when adopting this model, his goal is essentially to move the trainee into the next developmental stage. For example, the goals of supervising the trainee in the cognitive stage include increasing task-focus and responsiveness to in-the-moment client behavior, reducing cognitive and affective activity, increasing autonomy, and enhancing overall treatment effectiveness. In the associative stage, the supervisor's goals include improving the same dimensions, but automatic, effective, athlete-focused interventions should occur more frequently and consistently. Again, in the final, autonomous stage, the supervisory goals are maintaining skills and promoting continued professional growth.

Developing a Professional Identity

All professional psychologists know that a strong knowledge base and well-practiced clinical skills are necessary but not sufficient for effective practice. As uniquely interpersonal endeavors, all disciplines of professional psychology, including clinical sport psychology, involve personal factors that affect the psychologist and his capacity to relate to clients and to deliver services. These factors include empathy, genuineness, personal motives, self-awareness, life experiences, and cultural sensitivity (Striker, 2003).

Skill Development Stage Questionnaire

Copyright 2003 by Frank L. Gardner

Please rate trainee on each of these questions on the following scale:

1 (minimally)-------------2 (occasionally)--------------3 (frequently)-----------4 (often)

1. _____ Applies intervention in a mechanical (possibly inflexible) manner

2. _____ Appears self-focused and disconnected from client words and actions

3. _____ Responds to client with well-rehearsed (preset) strategies and procedures and does not deliver techniques in response to client behavior

4. _____ Requires close guidance and support (needs to know, "What do I do when . . .")

5. _____ Has difficulty rapidly assimilating in-session client behavior (into case conceptualization) and responding accordingly

6. _____ Appears to experience and display high levels of anxiety during clinical activities

7. _____ Demonstrates marginal overall clinical effectiveness

Total score: _____

Skill Development Stage Guide

Cognitive Stage = 21-27   Associative Stage = 11-20   Autonomous Stage = 1-10

Supervision Process Goals

- Enhance practitioner's task-focused attention
- Enhance practitioner's responsiveness to in-the-moment client behavior
- Reduce in-session practitioner affect
- Enhance practitioner's autonomy and promote effective clinical decision making

To effectively provide psychological services, an individual must possess a genuine concern for enhancing the well-being of others. The ability to communicate real concern and sensitivity for the feelings, perceptions, and stressors of others is referred to as empathy (Walker, 2001), and this ability is often viewed as a significant contributor to effective psychological services. The capacity to empathically engage a client, to combine knowledge with sensitivity, and to integrate therapeutic techniques with the client's present-moment needs are also essential for optimal performance as a psychologist. In addition, the ability to objectively observe client behavior is critical for work in human service professions. There are, however, factors particularly poignant in sport psychology that can interfere with these positive characteristics and significantly hinder the clinical sport psychologist's effectiveness (see chapter 12 for a discussion of ethical considerations).

First, it is natural for trainees (and even seasoned professionals) in sport psychology to be fascinated and even drawn to the excitement and celebrity aspect of sport involvement, particularly if they have been lifelong participants or observers of sports. However, the fascination can become problematic if the psychologist identifies too closely with the team or players and therefore loses focus on his purpose. Working in the sport domain provides an opportunity to achieve a status (real or imagined) that many people desire. It is of utmost importance that the psychologist maintains a fully grounded sense of his work and role.

Second, the clinical sport psychologist should be careful to not use her role in sport psychology to fulfill personal unmet sport-related goals. This is of particular concern when the sport psychologist is working at an elite level such as with Olympic, Division I collegiate, or professional athletes and

if the sport psychologist's own youthful athletic dreams did not come to fruition. The clinical sport psychologist should guard against the role of starstruck fan and be aware of her own athletic fantasies if she is to maintain an objective third-person perspective and uphold expected professional boundaries.

The general theme in these two scenarios is that clinical sport psychologists must recognize that their personal thoughts, feelings, and desires can influence judgment, assessment, and intervention decisions. To provide professional, ethical, and effective services, clinical sport psychologists must understand the responses in themselves (cognitive, affective, and behavioral) that are triggered by the athletic environment and those who hold celebrity status. This self-awareness is critical. That fan-like reactions may be triggered is not in and of itself problematic. It is the reluctance to recognize these reactions or the incapacity to respond in accordance with professional responsibilities that separates the fan masquerading as a professional from the true professional. In essence, what we advocate is a reflective self-awareness wherein the clinical sport psychologist develops a sound professional identity and personal style of ethical practice. With a sound professional identity based on self-reflection and acute self-awareness, the clinical sport psychologist can understand his tendencies (both helpful and unhelpful) and can not only recognize when they occur, but can also predict their triggers and respond appropriately.

These reactions may also include personal feelings toward individual athletes. Physical attraction is a part of life and feeling attracted to an athlete is not at all beyond the realm of possibility. Again, the attraction in and of itself is not problematic. The problem is acting on the attraction as opposed to acting in a manner consistent with ethical guidelines and valued professional goals. Similarly, negative, angry, or hostile reactions may occur. Openly and honestly discussing negative feelings with a supervisor or colleague is likely to lead to acceptable outcomes (working effectively with the athlete or referring the athlete to another provider). Problematic outcomes from naturally occurring feelings are more probable if these discussions and collegial guidance do not occur. Understandably, these are not easy topics for most trainees to bring up. Supervisors should strongly encourage trainees to bring up such matters if and when they arise and to not shy away from them for fear of negative evaluation. Naturally, the trainee typically takes the lead from the supervisor on these matters. If the supervisor does not seem open to such discussions, the trainee is unlikely to take the risk, and both the trainee and the athlete are likely to suffer as a result.

Personal life experiences and sensitivity to cultural diversity and individual differences also directly relate to the clinical sport psychologist's ability to provide ethical and effective services. Certainly, the athletic experiences of the practitioner are relevant, but they can have positive *or* negative consequences on the therapeutic relationship and intervention success. Positively, the practitioner's athletic experiences can enhance understanding and appreciation of the athletic milieu. However, his experiences can be problematic if he overidentifies with the sport, athletes, or team that he is employed to help or if he assumes that an athlete's responses and experiences are similar to the ones he once had. Such an assumption is a form of insensitivity—not cultural insensitivity, but experiential insensitivity that results from the practitioner's narrow frame of reference, poor self-awareness, or unwillingness to incorporate new and different information.

Supervision in Clinical Sport Psychology

Supervision is the staple of training in all subdisciplines of professional psychology (Stoltenberg et al., 1998), as it facilitates the integrated development of the professional skills and the professional and personal characteristics necessary for effective service delivery. Not unlike coaching in sports, supervision in professional psychology allows for new learning to occur and skill development to prosper. Supervision promotes self-examination, a greater understanding of the impact of personal styles on professional relationships, and the development of technical skills relating to assessment, case conceptualization, and intervention. While there is an obvious focus on developing ethical and competent practitioners, ultimately, the goal of supervision in clinical sport psychology is the same as in traditional psychology domains: to monitor and ensure that quality care is consistently provided.

There have been several relatively recent discussions in the professional literature on supervision in sport psychology (Andersen, 1994; Andersen & Williams-Rice, 1996; Van Raalte & Andersen, 1993, 2000). The average clinical and counseling psychologist receives 1,000 to 2,000 h

of supervised externship, 1,500 to 2,000 h of supervised doctoral internship, and at least 1,500 h of postdoctoral supervised experience (for a total of 4,000-5,500 h) before licensure. Sport psychology has required substantially less of its practitioners. A recent article by Andersen and colleagues stated that the average graduate student preparing for professional sport psychology work receives less than 400 h of supervised experience (Andersen, Williams, Aldridge, & Taylor, 1997). The Association for the Advancement of Applied Sport Psychology (AAASP) requires only 400 h of supervised experience to qualify for certified consultant status (Van Raalte & Andersen, 2000). Australian standards are better but still lacking, requiring 1000 h of supervised experience in both general and specialty settings (Van Raalte & Andersen, 2000).

When compared to the 4,000 to 5,500 supervised h required for clinical and counseling psychologists, the standards for supervised training in sport psychology bring into question sport practitioner competence and readiness for practice (at least among new practitioners). In an exciting development, the American Psychological Association (APA) recently passed the APA proficiency (APA, 2003) in sport psychology, which recommends 500 h of supervised experience in sport psychology *incorporated into* or *in addition to* the 4,000 to 5,500 h required for licensure as a psychologist. This is a major step in promoting the supervised experience necessary for competent practice as a clinical sport psychologist. However, since this only applies to those receiving a doctorate in psychology, it is important for training programs in the sport sciences to make similar changes to adequately prepare these students in a similar manner. On the other hand, although the accumulation of supervised hours is a necessary and vital training component, there is more to supervision than racking up hours. In fact, many factors figure into effective supervision.

Personality Variables Affecting Supervision

Before discussing the supervision of the clinical sport psychology trainee in detail, let's consider some of the personality variables that often interfere with supervision and overall professional development.

Supervisor Personality Variables

The supervisor's intra- and interpersonal characteristics can significantly affect the supervisory process. A study by Cook and Helms (1988) found that the supervisor's liking and interest in the trainee accounted for 69% of the variance in trainee satisfaction with supervision. This finding clearly demonstrates the power of the supervisory relationship. Other than situation-specific differences and conflicts between the trainee and the supervisor, which are always possible in this interpersonal activity, the single most toxic quality in a supervisor is a power-seeking motive. The nature of the supervisory relationship is that the trainee seeks the help, advice, support, and professionalism of the supervisor (not unlike the therapeutic relationship). This relationship has a natural power differential, as the supervisor has superior knowledge and skills and ultimately is professionally and legally responsible for the athlete's care. The supervisor influences the trainee's professional behavior in a variety of ways, and thus the control exercised by the supervisor is a significant variable.

Supervisor behaviors are expected to enhance the trainee's skills and ultimately the trainee's capacity to function independently and competently. The supervisor is a catalyst in that she promotes change and development in the trainee with little expectation of personal gain (apart from professional satisfaction). However, when supervisor behavior serves to enhance the supervisor's sense of power or serves some other self-interest, the supervisory relationship is unhelpful at best and unethical and harmful at worst. It is most often the situations in which the supervisor uses the supervisory relationship to demonstrate control, special competence, or superiority that create dysfunctional relationships with the trainee. These situations may occur with novice, inexperienced supervisors, insecure supervisors, and supervisors who have not yet reached the autonomous stage of professional development. They may also occur with experienced, skilled supervisors whose personal characteristics impair their ability to appropriately supervise trainees.

Power struggles are also detrimental to supervision. Power struggles typically occur when the trainee resists the appropriate efforts of the supervisor or when the supervisor utilizes his role to needlessly exert control over the trainee. It is often difficult to differentiate these two situations. The supervisor must carefully consider the purpose for using a particular supervisory strategy and must maintain appropriate self-awareness, understand the trainee's developmental stage, and focus on the ultimate goal of trainee autonomy and skill

development. Some control over a trainee is clearly necessary when a trainee resists working toward established goals or demonstrates problematic behavior. In these instances, the word *control* is not intended to hold negative connotations, but to reflect how the supervisor must set professional limits, establish structure, call for professional respect, and limit disrespectful, harmful, or malintended behaviors toward himself or the client. However, in other unfortunate situations, supervisory strategies are clearly based on the psychological needs of the supervisor rather than on the needs of the trainee. In this case, both the trainee and client ultimately suffer.

Of course, all psychologists have relational strengths and weaknesses, regardless of their current professional role (including trainee supervision). These individual strengths and weaknesses affect the extent to which the supervisor uses her role for the good of the trainee or for her own personal or professional benefit. This is especially true when supervisors have little training in supervisory techniques and theory. Most supervisors are not well-trained in this area, as becoming a supervisor often is not based on training and expertise, but on academic demands and limited personnel for the job. We recommend that untrained supervisors develop familiarity with theoretical concepts and empirical research in this area and participate in conference presentations, workshops, and other related didactic instruction. Our best recommendation is for supervisors to consult with other professional colleagues, as supervisors often need to be supervised on their *own* supervision.

Trainee Personality Variables

The trainee's intra- and interpersonal characteristics can also profoundly affect the supervisory process. As many trainees experience difficulty moving from the didactic learning style of classroom activities to the more experiential style found in supervision, they often become stuck in the cognitive stage of skill development. This occurs largely because they have difficulty moving from the robotic implementation of rules, techniques, and strategies to the interpersonally oriented, well-timed application of techniques based on the moment-to-moment therapeutic context. While all trainees experience this challenge to some degree, some trainees, due to personal characteristics related to fear of evaluation or failure, find this transition particularly difficult. It is our experience that this transition most often occurs when anxiety (often associated with the identification of weaknesses and the resultant exposure of personal vulnerability to the supervisor) predominates. As noted earlier, affect (particularly anxiety) is typically heightened during the cognitive stage. For some trainees, heightened anxiety can disrupt the self-regulatory process in a manner similar to its dysfunctional impact on athletic performance. Often, heightened anxiety is related to the anticipation of failure when trying new techniques while being evaluated by a supervisor that she may admire, respect, or even fear. As such, the trainee engages in excessive self-discrepancy evaluation (comparing herself to an expected norm, possibly even the supervisor) and, as predicted from self-regulatory processes in human performance, becomes overly self-focused, with associated increases in anxiety and avoidance.

Students training to be sport psychologists are often hypersensitive to (real or imagined) criticism and evaluation from their supervisors. Supervisor comments can easily shake the confidence of the most skilled trainee. It is also common for trainees (often highly motivated, hard-working individuals accustomed to success) to establish unrealistic standards for their performances, predisposing a maladaptive response to the demands of the supervisory relationship. As such, it is imperative that the supervisor and trainee establish personal and professional goals appropriate to the trainee's developmental stage. Both parties should openly discuss these goals so that all supervisory expectations are clear. Occasionally updating and modifying personal and professional goals may keep the trainee's professional development on track.

In other cases, the trainee's interpersonal characteristics may interfere with his ability to hear feedback and respond appropriately. Some trainees experience difficulty tolerating the structure, feedback, and natural power differential inherent in the supervisory relationship and may experience transferential reactions (both negative and positive) not unlike those seen in psychotherapy. In addition, a trainee's seeming overconfidence can result in premature independence, under-reliance on supervision, or overt rejection of supervisor feedback. Once again, direct feedback and clear goals are essential to minimizing such behavior. In these circumstances, specific interpersonal characteristics are in operation and are likely to result in difficult supervisor–trainee relations. The supervisor's challenge is to promote the trainee's necessary self-awareness and personal

development without becoming overly therapeutic with the trainee. While the distinction is often a fine line, the supervisor must be aware of the supervisory contract and maintain the appropriate professional boundary when working with the trainee. If the supervisor deems that psychological counseling is necessary for the trainee, she should sensitively and appropriately make that recommendation, but she should never conduct the counseling herself. Overall, there are many ways the supervisory relationship can become problematic. The supervisor should balance the development of the trainee's practitioner skills with the development of sound interpersonal skills (with colleagues, supervisors, and clients). Again, consultation with professional colleagues will allow the supervisor to maintain objectivity, uphold professional boundaries, and promote the skill development of trainees. Supervisors themselves often need supervision (of their supervision) and should consult with professional peers when facing technical and interpersonal struggles in the supervisory relationship.

Supervisory Techniques

While supervision involves a number of potential challenges, it remains the most critical vehicle for developing sport psychologists. In the remainder of this chapter, we discuss supervisory strategies that are widely used throughout training in psychology and that we have found effective in our work with trainees in both clinical psychology and clinical sport psychology.

In addition to standard case discussion, specific supervisory techniques can greatly add to the learning process during a supervision session. However, to optimize the utility of these techniques, the supervisor must ensure that the goal of the chosen supervisory technique is appropriate for the trainee's stage of skill development. Knowing the trainee's developmental stage is critical to successful supervision. In our experience, supervisors most commonly err by having unrealistic expectations of the trainee's autonomy and by overstating the trainee's capacity to deliver interventions effectively. This misalignment of actual and perceived trainee skill development helps create the overly self-focused attention related to performance dysfunction. Realistic expectations are most critical in the cognitive stage of professional development, when trainees have a number of specific needs and these needs compete for time and attention. In working with trainees in this early stage, the supervisor must know which techniques are likely to have a positive effect on trainee skill development and minimize any extreme interpersonal discomfort in the supervision room. In addition, the supervisor must understand the trainee's developmental need to receive close (structured) guidance and support and must be prepared to observe intervention implementation either directly or using a videotape or audiotape. One of the supervisor's main goals is to shape desired professional behavior by reinforcing successive approximations of the desired end product. The supervisor should recognize that unless the trainee in the cognitive stage of development has had the opportunity to observe (model) the correct intervention, she has little (other than prior readings and lecture) to guide her own intervention efforts.

In the associative stage of skill development, the supervisor must once again guard against unrealistic expectations of autonomy and skill development. In this stage, the trainee effectively responds to many day-to-day situations, often giving the impression of more advanced (and stable) skill development. In most cases, however, the trainee's experience lacks situational variety. As such, novel situations can create what may appear to be regressive behavior, requiring unexpected structure, support, and guidance. In fact, these seemingly backward steps should not only be anticipated, but should be supported as naturally occurring (and essential) components of this stage of professional development.

Also critical to successful supervision is establishing the correct supervisory context. One effective way to achieve this goal is to use a supervisory contract. The supervisory contract clearly defines the roles and responsibilities of the trainee and supervisor and also clarifies expectations and goals. The supervisory contract also facilitates an appropriate working alliance between the supervisor and trainee. This contract is similar to the informed consent required when working with clients (discussed in chapter 12). As previously noted, the supervisor must be keenly aware of the multiple elements of the supervisory relationship and sensitive to the impact of his own motives and behaviors on the supervisory process. This is best done by creating an open, honest, and safe relationship in which forthright discussions can occur. Since the trainee quality that effective supervisors most often value is honesty in discussing cases

(Farber, 2003), supervisors must recognize that such honesty can only occur in an atmosphere of safety and respect.

The following sections describe a variety of useful techniques and their uses across the various developmental stages. The first three techniques, didactic presentations, role-playing, and videotaped sessions, directly promote relevant knowledge and skill execution. The next two, personal response pattern demonstrations and mindfulness and acceptance training, aid in developing mindful awareness and attention to personal reactions and patterns (of the practitioner) and enhancing the trainee's capacity to respond to the athlete in the moment.

Didactic Presentations

There is a clear place for lecture and didactic presentation of basic knowledge in the supervisory process. Not all practitioners-in-training have mastered the foundational information necessary for effective interventions, indicating the judicious use of lecture and assigned readings. Didactic presentations are most likely to be effective in the cognitive stage of skill development. However, although they may be used cautiously in the associative stage, providing additional or very new information during this stage may promote temporary regression to the cognitive stage, as the trainee must accommodate this new information into a relatively new practice style. Regression based on new learning is particularly likely for trainees in the early phases of the associative stage. While this regression is both expected and relatively brief, the supervisor must accept and understand it and should increase support, encouragement, and guidance during the accommodation process. Failure to do so can cause the trainee to respond with excessive discrepancy adjustment, resulting once again in excessive self-focus, increased affect, and possible self-regulatory disruption. Didactic presentations are unlikely to have a regressive effect on trainees in the autonomous stage of skill development, as they have mastered the foundational knowledge and can easily assimilate and accommodate new information into their more developed practice styles.

Role-Playing

Role-playing is a commonly used technique in the armamentarium of the supervising clinical sport psychologist. Role-playing is similar in intent and

Supervision in small groups allows for role-play exercises, peer support, and generalized learning.

process to the simulation training of athletes (Hardy et al., 1996). Like simulation training, role-playing uses simulated situations to develop skills (through practice) by providing an opportunity for the trainee to shape her intervention behavior using immediate feedback from the supervisor. This procedure allows the trainee to practice her developing skills in a safe environment that (when correctly performed) mimics real-life situations (including the expected and unexpected). Role-playing provides the frequent repetition necessary for enhancing skill development (Ericsson, 2003). This technique can be general and relatively simple for the early trainee or more complex for the later trainee who needs to expand the situation specificity of her developing skills.

From a self-regulatory perspective, the trainee in the cognitive stage of development often becomes anxious and self-focused during role-playing exercises and tends to be hypersensitive to supervisor evaluations. The supervisor should thus remember the basic tenets of discriminative learning and should shape the desired behavior by reinforcing accurate demonstrations of the desired skill. The supervisor should provide immediate feedback, should positively reinforce (through acknowledgment) successful aspects of skill execution, and should provide corrective feedback on

less well-refined skill execution. Sometimes it may be best to tape the role-play exercise and provide feedback only at the end to more closely simulate an actual intervention. At other times, particularly in early development, it may be more helpful to provide immediate feedback by interrupting and then restarting the exercise.

Although we have described role-playing as an excellent strategy for enhancing technical skills, this exercise has additional benefits. It allows trainees to either habituate to or accept the anxiety related to their professional role through prolonged and repeated exposure to the simulated session. This increase in affect tolerance helps focus the trainee's attention outward (externally), thus allowing the trainee to develop mindful attention and greater contact with the athlete.

Taped Sessions

Although audiotapes and videotapes have a long history in professional psychology (Stoltenberg et al., 1998), there has been much less discussion of their use in sport psychology supervision. The primary purpose of taping is for the supervisor to directly observe in-session interactions between the trainee and the athlete. This procedure, particularly videotape review, allows the supervisor to see and hear the actual interaction between the athlete and the practitioner-in-training and to provide direct feedback on strategy, technique, and relational elements in the session. While taping is clearly valuable, it is not without shortcomings. For many trainees, particularly those in the cognitive or early associative stages, taping can be highly threatening and can raise anxiety levels that are already typically heightened. In addition, for some trainees it creates an artificial stimulus in the consultation room that would not otherwise be present. When taping occurs during a session, some trainees report that they think less clearly and respond differently to the client. Thus, for these individuals, taped sessions may not elicit the same intervention behaviors that occur during nontaped sessions.

We have found a couple of factors that help minimize the increased anxiety and behavioral changes noted by trainees under these circumstances. First, we suggest not beginning tape reviews until the trainee has already engaged in role-play exercises and has had the opportunity to get used to the supervisor's personal style and expectations. Second, the supervisor should incorporate taping *only* when the trainee has demonstrated adequate skill in simulated (role-playing) exercises. If taping is begun too quickly (before adequate skill development), the trainee may engage in excessive self-focus and self-evaluation, which may disrupt learning. Additionally, the trainee is likely to overemphasize performance outcomes rather than emphasize the performance process. However, if taping and review are done in the suggested sequence, tapes are less threatening and can be a highly useful supervisory technique. In addition, recording a number of tapes before actually reviewing any particular one habituates the trainee to the taping process. Trainees have reported that they like being consistently taped for several sessions before review, as they become used to being taped and may even forget that they are being recorded. This obviously reduces the trainee's anxiety, and the taping is unlikely to seriously inhibit behavioral functioning. It is therefore more likely that the interaction on tape will reasonably represent the trainee's skill level. When session tapes accurately reflect the trainee's level and functioning, taping can be incredibly helpful. So, what does the supervisor look for and comment on when viewing a taped session with a trainee? Generally, the supervisor will want to determine if the following are true:

- The techniques and procedures the trainee delivers are appropriate to the case formulation.
- The techniques and procedures the trainee executes are in fact those that the trainee says he is executing. Trainees often mistakenly report using specific techniques or procedures.
- The timing of the execution is appropriate for the context of the session. The trainee responds to the moment-to-moment interaction between herself and the client instead of mechanically responding without considering the requirements of the specific session.
- The trainee connects to and engages with the client in a collaborative professional relationship.

We encourage the supervisor to avoid focusing on the trainee's level of affect during the session. It is expected that the trainee will experience significant affect during skill development. Such affect, however, will decrease over time as the trainee gains skill and develops self-efficacy. Thus, unless the trainee asks for specific feedback on affect regulation or the trainee's affect significantly harms the athlete or the therapeutic relationship, the supervisor should only focus on the listed aspects of taping. Overemphasizing the trainee's affect can exacerbate both its presence and meaning for the trainee and can disrupt skill development.

Tape review is most helpful when supervising trainees in the associative stage of skill development. The trainee has developed a working knowledge of techniques, can effectively conceptualize cases, can interpersonally engage with the athlete, and can be reasonably proficient in delivering the appropriate interventions. The primary value of tape review in these cases is to enhance the moment-to-moment relational aspects of the consulting experience. Supervision focuses on the trainee's style and on the interaction between athlete needs and trainee responses. In essence, when taping the intermediate or advanced trainee, the primary focus is developing awareness and sensitivity to the athlete–trainee interchange. This supervisory focus enhances intervention timing and recognizes the role of the consulting relationship in the effective delivery of psychological or consulting services. Of course, enhancement can occur only when the trainee has reasonably mastered the basics of intervention, has moved beyond self-focus and affect-driven processes, and can focus on in-the-moment connections with the athlete.

Personal Response Pattern Demonstrations

A personal response pattern demonstration helps trainees develop an awareness of their response tendencies and the stimulus functions in their clients that elicit such tendencies (Gardner, 2003, August; Gardner & Moore, 2005c). Stimulus functions are the aspects of the client that are closely associated with the trainee's previous experience and learning history. A personal response pattern demonstration develops personal self-awareness and enhances the understanding of relationship factors in clinical sport psychology. While the contribution of relationship factors to successful psychological service has been accepted and empirically demonstrated (Norcross, 2002), the discussion and integration of these variables into the sport psychology literature has been minimal, with a few exceptions (Andersen, 2000a, 2000b; Barney & Andersen, 2000). Despite the literature's neglect of these important variables, the supervisor should carefully attend to them during the trainee's skill development. We often tell our students that intervention techniques are the ammunition of the professional, while relationships are the delivery system. Without attending to the relationship, the practitioner has a limited means to deliver even the most potent techniques. Conversely, a consulting relationship unaccompanied by appropriate evidence-based techniques is hollow, unlikely to create positive change, and similar to a caring friend. Being a friend is not the role of the clinical sport psychologist. A sound therapeutic relationship is necessary but not sufficient for sustained client change. On the other hand, although sound interventions can be effective *without* the development of a warm and engaging therapeutic relationship, the lack of a sound therapeutic relationship often leads to premature termination. Obviously, even the best practitioner is ineffective when the client does not show up for the session. The practitioner must therefore integrate these two critical variables for sustained client change to occur.

A central component in developing and maintaining an appropriate professional relationship is the practitioner's awareness of her responses to the athlete, including her thoughts, feelings, and behaviors. The first author (FG) developed the per-

sonal response pattern demonstration technique to enhance self-awareness in trainees from all the stages of skill development. However, we have found that this technique is particularly important in the associative through autonomous stages. It is most helpful during these stages because the more the practitioner focuses on the moment-to-moment interaction between herself and the athlete, the more responsibility she has in maintaining self-awareness of her own interpersonal patterns and social learning.

The personal response pattern demonstration begins by asking the trainee (or trainees, as this strategy is often employed in a group format) to list six people in his life (past or present) that he is or was strongly repelled by (strongly disliked). Then, the trainee lists six individuals who he is or was strongly drawn to (strongly liked). The supervisor then asks the trainee to study the list and find the common *characteristics* (physical, behavioral, intellectual, and so on) among the individuals on each list. This activity begins an active process of identifying the athlete characteristics that are most likely to trigger in-session trainee responses that could compromise the consulting relationship and intervention delivery. The trainee reflects on the common characteristics from each list and discusses any similarities with athletes he is currently seeing. Then the trainee lists his typical *affective* responses (i.e., internal reactions) to the people on his lists. Responses such as attraction, anger, and frustration as well as the desire to protect and take care of the athlete can be triggered by the stimulus functions of the athlete.

Next the trainee records the specific *behaviors* that characterize his relationships with, or responses to, these individuals. This significantly promotes self-awareness, allows the trainee to become aware of behavioral responses that may occur during sessions with similar athletes, and limits countertransference reactions that can hinder the effectiveness of services.

Personal response pattern demonstrations provide information that the trainee can easily see but has not necessarily considered before the exercise. The trainee can complete this exercise without informing the supervisor of the lists' contents. The supervisor does not need this information unless there have been previous breaches in trainee–client boundaries. Although this exercise can uncover uncomfortable realities for trainees (which obviously need to be in their realms of self-awareness), they typically feel comfortable engaging in it due to its confidential nature. The

Mindfulness exercises, which can be practiced alone, can help anxious trainees remain in the moment with the athlete.

primary purpose of the personal response pattern demonstration is the personal and professional development of the trainee through enhanced self-awareness. According to the most recent APA Ethics Code (2002), the supervisor must clearly state any personal information that may be required as part of the supervisory process before beginning supervision. Additionally, the supervisory contract agreed upon by both the trainee and supervisor must clearly state any required personal information. Thus, a secondary benefit of this exercise is the confidential nature of the material.

Mindfulness Exercises

As discussed in chapter 6, mindfulness training enhances our awareness of the present moment and helps us attend to the cues and stimuli that surround us at any given time (Segal et al., 2002). The advantages of mindfulness training are not restricted to our clients. It is our experience that regularly using mindfulness techniques as part of the supervisory process develops and enhances the fundamental skills in the armamentarium of the clinical sport psychologist. As we suggested earlier, these techniques can enhance competitive performance when used with athletes without clinical or subclinical presentations. Similarly, these

techniques can benefit the clinical sport psychology trainee in a number of ways. First, regularly using these techniques allows trainees to develop proficiency in their own use of mindfulness and to understand the difficulties and personal experiences that may arise when using mindfulness exercises with clients. Second, mindfulness can enhance the trainee's capacity to remain in the moment and connect to the needs and reactions of the athlete. Third, it allows the trainee to enhance her awareness of personal thoughts and feelings when working with athletes. This promotes greater self-awareness and helps prevent the trainee from engaging in interventions guided by personal reactions (countertransference) rather than by the needs and desires of the client.

Using mindfulness in supervision begins with exercises such as mindfulness of breath or body-scan mindfulness (Kabat-Zinn, 1994). These exercises should most often occur at the start of a supervision meeting as a way of bringing the trainee into the moment. Between supervision meetings, the trainee typically completes homework, which includes regularly practicing the mindfulness techniques and recording the personal reactions (positive, negative, and neutral) to using these techniques. Over time, as the skill becomes more automated, the trainee engages in mindful interaction with her client, in which she notes and responds to her moment-to-moment reactions and perceptions within the context of the particular intervention being utilized. See figure 13.2.

Working Alliances in Clinical Sport Psychology

Within the professional literature of clinical science, studies have suggested that the therapeutic alliance has a modest yet consistent relationship with outcome in psychotherapy (Horvath & Symonds, 1991). In a meta-analytic review of 68 studies, Martin, Garske, & Davis (2000) reported that the correlation between therapeutic alliance and intervention outcome was .22, suggesting that relationship factors account for approximately 5% of the variance in psychotherapy outcome. This effect was consistent across various forms of psychotherapy, source of ratings (patient, therapist, observer), point in treatment when the working alliance was assessed (early, middle, late, averaged across all sessions), and measures used to assess the alliance.

More specifically, studies have indicated that although the emergence of a productive therapeutic alliance by the end of the third session is generally associated with a positive treatment outcome, treatment outcome is generally poorer when clients demonstrate negativism, hostility,

and resistance (Strupp, 1993). Studies evaluating the interpersonal process in psychotherapy have indicated that conflictual interpersonal processes occur more often in cases that ultimately result in poorer outcomes (Gomes-Schwartz, Hadley, & Strupp, 1978; Henry, Schacht, & Strupp, 1986; Strupp, 1980a, 1980b, 1980c, 1980d).

Despite these important findings, the sport psychology literature has to date not fully examined the role of the working alliance in sport psychology practice. While this role is clearly an open empirical question requiring careful examination (beyond anecdotal report), the evidence to date suggests that the working alliance is likely to have a modest but consistent relationship with positive outcomes in athletic performance enhancement (as is the case in traditional psychotherapy). It would certainly behoove the sport psychology professional to develop and maintain an appropriate working alliance. Therefore, establishing an effective working alliance should be an important focus in the supervisory process during the professional and technical development of the clinical sport psychology trainee.

How can we monitor the working alliance between an athlete and a clinical sport psychology professional or trainee? The working alliance is often operationalized and assessed by the abbreviated version (Tracey & Kokotovic, 1989) of the patient report form of the Working Alliance Inventory (WAI) (Horvath & Greenberg, 1989). The WAI is one of the most commonly used and well-established measures of the working alliance. It is pantheoretical (cutting across theoretical models) and has been shown to predict treatment outcome in numerous studies (Horvath, 1994). The WAI conceptualizes the working alliance as consisting of three components:

1. Goals, reflecting client and practitioner agreement on the intervention goals
2. Tasks, reflecting client and practitioner agreement on how to achieve the goals
3. Bond, reflecting the affective quality of the client–practitioner relationship

The clinical sport psychologist attends to these three relational elements in the early stages of his work with athletes in order to maximize the effectiveness of the delivery of empirically informed techniques.

As we stated earlier, we conceptualize empirically informed interventions as the ammunition of

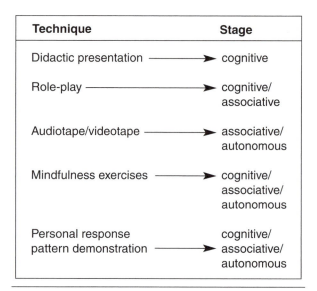

Technique	Stage
Didactic presentation	⟶ cognitive
Role-play	⟶ cognitive/ associative
Audiotape/videotape	⟶ associative/ autonomous
Mindfulness exercises	⟶ cognitive/ associative/ autonomous
Personal response pattern demonstration	⟶ cognitive/ associative/ autonomous

Figure 13.2 Relationship between development stage and supervisory techniques.

the practitioner and the working alliance (therapeutic relationship) as the delivery system for the ammunition. One component without the other is substantially less likely to meet the athlete's goals. As such, clinical sport psychology training should carefully attend to these variables both separately and together. It has long been suggested that one of the most powerful determinants of therapeutic success is the extent to which client and therapist goals match (Beck et al., 2004). The extent to which trainee and supervisor goals match should therefore enhance supervisory success as well. The role of the supervisor in helping the trainee develop an appropriate working alliance is to carefully analyze the interpersonal interchanges between the trainee and the athlete during the session. Obviously, undertaking this task requires carefully reviewing videotaped sessions, because trainees typically cannot accurately and objectively provide full and detailed information on the nuances of the interpersonal exchange after the session. Audiotapes are insufficient, as they do not demonstrate nonverbal behaviors, mannerisms, eye contact, and other data that are critical to the interpersonal dynamics between the athlete and trainee. Thus, in addition to the other benefits of taping covered earlier in the chapter, supervisory feedback on videotaped sessions is the best way to help the trainee develop the skills essential to creating good working alliances.

Final Thoughts

This chapter suggests that supervision in clinical sport psychology should be more than presenting intervention techniques and discussing details of particular cases. Rather, the goal of supervision is to carefully monitor athlete care as well as to systematically enhance the professional skills and personal development of the clinical sport psychology trainee. Based on skill development in other domains (Fischman & Oxendine, 1998; Stoltenberg et al., 1998), we presented a model of the stages of professional skill development and discussed their impact on the trainee's self-regulatory process. In addition, we discussed the use of particular supervisory strategies, which should be based on the trainee's skill level rather than on the preferences or idiosyncrasies of the supervisor. We hope this material provides the trainee with a clearer idea of what to expect from supervision and of the overall process of professional development as a clinical sport psychologist. We also hope it assists the supervisor by providing a deeper understanding of the trainee's needs and challenges during professional development and by providing clear suggestions to aid in this development. Finally, we hope this discussion sparks interest in generating a more careful practice and systematic study of the supervisory process in clinical sport psychology.

CHAPTER 14

Future Directions

In this text, we have described an approach to sport psychology that integrates clinical psychology and sport science into a holistic and comprehensive model for working with a range of athletes.

We have presented a model of practice that stresses the importance of considering the natural interrelatedness of dispositional and intrapersonal variables, self-regulation, situational and developmental variables, and physical skill in a comprehensive understanding of competitive athletics. In addition, this model requires the clinical sport psychologist to commit to an evidence-based or evidence-informed practice of psychology and to allow scientific data to guide her professional decisions instead of whim, fancy, or media popularity. It also requires the clinical sport psychologist to remain aware of the complex needs and desires of her athletes and to avoid the artificial dichotomous categorization of clinical versus performance issues.

The reality of clinical sport psychology practice is that athletes come to us for a variety of reasons, needs, and problems. While most athletes openly state a desire to enhance their competitive performance, the evidence strongly suggests that automatically utilizing techniques traditionally thought to enhance self-regulation may not be as effective as the professional literature has presented (Moore, 2003b, Moore & Gardner, 2002, August; Moore & Gardner, 2005). This is particularly true for athletes whose subclinical or clinical psychological issues interfere with performance (Gardner et al., 2003, October; Gardner et al., 2005; Wolanin, 2005).

As we have frequently stated, many athletes present with subclinical levels of both intrapersonal and interpersonal psychological difficulties. These psychological barriers usually require more than the traditional self-regulatory psychological skills training most commonly utilized in sport psychology. We hope this text spurs clinical sport psychologists to develop new interventions based on contemporary theoretical constructs and carefully scrutinized empirical findings in clinical and sport science. In addition, we hope that the practicing clinical sport psychologist will engage in a more thoughtful practice in which empirically informed intervention decisions are based on the specific needs of our athletes.

We have noted the empirical limitations of traditional approaches to applied sport psychology and presented an alternative way of classifying and conceptualizing athlete issues. This alternative approach presents an opportunity for a profession still in its relative infancy to grow and develop. While sport psychology has made many strides over the past 20 years, the empirical evidence suggests that we have been recently stagnant in both research and practice, maintaining a single practice model (psychological skills training) as the dominant intervention. However, psychological skills training (PST) was developed over 30 years ago, and although long ago supplanted through natural scientific evolution in clinical and counseling psychology domains, PST's theoretical and technical assumptions about mechanisms of change in performance enhancement have dominated both our research and practice models. The time has come for a paradigm shift in sport psychology in which we consider newer, theoretically sound, and empirically informed alternatives to traditional PST models. We must also reconsider the binary and artificial categorization of issues as either performance related or clinical. Further, we must recognize that we cannot simply rename subclinical (subsyndromal) issues and begin calling them "personal issues" in order to reflect psychological concerns not serious enough for *DSM* classification in order to justify practicing outside our areas of competence.

The growth and development of clinical sport psychology may receive added impetus by the American Psychological Association's recent acceptance of sport psychology as a formal proficiency (APA, 2003). This acceptance places sport psychology squarely within the domain of professional psychology and is likely to result in greater training opportunities and a greater openness within the major psychology journals to manuscripts on sport psychology research and practice. This proficiency will have an effect on the practitioners of clinical sport psychology, as they will be expected to more carefully follow the accepted scientific and professional standards which dominate the more well-established psychology domains. Issues of competence and legal rights to title, long discussed at sport psychology conferences and on Internet listservs, are likely to be carefully scrutinized by both state regulatory agencies and psychology ethics boards.

Times are changing. The acceptance of sport psychology as a formal practice emphasis raises the bar for the practitioner, requiring greater accountability while at the same time offering greater research and practice opportunities. The American Board of Behavioral Psychology, a specialty board of the American Board of Professional Psychology (ABPP), has long allowed practitioners to become board certified in behavioral psychology with a practice emphasis in sport psychology (American Board of Professional Psychology, 2004). We hope that an increasing number of clinical sport psychologists take advantage of this opportunity to achieve formal ABPP board certification. Board certification by the American Board of Professional Psychology is the field of psychology's equivalent to board certification in the medical community. We encourage sport practitioners to beware of overnight "board certification" groups in sport psychology, as these money-generating groups are not regulated by larger psychology boards and do not indicate expertise in the field. In fact, board certification by the American Board of Professional Psychology is the only psychology board formally recognized by the American Psychological Association (APA), and this certification represents the highest professional recognition available in the mental health professions.

Based on the practice model presented in this text, a number of research and practice opportu-nities appear to be on the horizon. The following sections detail some of these potential areas in clinical sport psychology.

Subclinical Barriers

As discussed in chapter 7, there are often psychological issues, referred to here as psychological barriers, that take the form of subclinical (subsyndromal) concerns. These concerns can be intrapersonal, such as perfectionism, worry, or other performance schema difficulties, or can be interpersonal, such as repetitive relational problems with authority figures, teammates, and significant others. Recent evidence suggests that these issues do not respond well to direct efforts at performance enhancement and that they require a focused intervention to both reduce the subjective discomfort that they cause the individual and to ameliorate the performance barrier that they pose (Gardner et al., 2003, October). As this is a new area for research and practice in sport psychology, there is tremendous opportunity for studying the impact of subclinical concerns on performance and the impact that interventions directly targeting these barriers may have on performance achievement. In addition, focused (and methodologically sound) study is warranted to develop possibly novel interventions targeting athletes experiencing subclinical difficulties. Cutting-edge cognitive-behavioral interventions, such as worry exposure and schema-focused methods, will likely be effective with this population when integrated into newer protocols, such as the MAC intervention. Such integration is under way in our clinical research laboratory, and we hope this text spurs similar research programs elsewhere.

Focused research with subclinical athlete presentations requires the integration of clinical and sport science and will result in a truly collaborative effort to develop the discipline of clinical sport psychology. As this particular problem area falls squarely between performance and clinical issues, many practitioners may have previously been unclear of how to recognize these phenomena. With the use of the Multilevel Classification System for Sport Psychology (MCS-SP), identification of subclinical concerns should now be much easier, clinical sport psychologists should be able to more effectively intervene with this subgroup of the athlete population, and practitioners can develop a practice niche above and beyond simple performance enhancement. Further, sport psychology should consider that its minimal acceptance and utilization at elite levels of sport may not be due to a lack of knowledge or advertising, but to a very real perception of limited intervention efficacy (for traditional measures) and of inconsistent service provision. This leads to the next area of consideration.

Uses of Assessment

With only a few exceptions (Nideffer & Sagal, 2001), perusing the professional literature on assessment in sport psychology suggests a primary focus on research with a minimal emphasis on practical application (Duda, 1998). When utilizing the MCS-SP, which requires formal assessment, the process of assessment takes a central role in the intervention planning necessary for proper athlete care. In the evidence-based approach to clinical sport psychology, the first step in enhancing athletic performance or ameliorating the psychological difficulties of clients is a thorough and comprehensive assessment. The semistructured interview for the MCS-SP presented in chapter 4 is an example of such an assessment approach (yet it is not an explicit psychometric tool). Assessment and intervention from this perspective are not separate, but are different stages of the same process. Assessment clarifies issues, focuses the clinician, and begins establishing the necessary therapeutic relationship and intervention contract. Theoretically sound interventions can then logically follow.

Despite its critics (Vealey & Garner-Holman, 1998), psychometric assessment is well-regarded and often used in professional sports as part of a rational and thorough selection process (Gardner, 1995, 2001). Utilizing the same methodologies long used in psychometric assessment in industrial/organizational psychology, clinical sport psychology can greatly benefit professional sports by utilizing well-designed, openly researched, reliable, and valid measurement tools for player selection. While assessment in player selection lures both proponents and critics, the reality is that if data collected over time from sport-specific or more dispositional measures are able to demonstrate predictive validity, assessment can and will be used in the same manner that business and military organizations all over the world utilize it in selecting sales personnel, executive personnel, officer candidates, and even security personnel. The critical variables are the reliability and validity of the measures under consideration, along with the empirical data collected over time utilizing clearly defined predictor variables. Since the number of sport psychologists working with professional teams is extremely low (such as approximately only 10 recently working in the NHL, including both authors), the *appropriate* use of assessment for athlete selection will enhance professional opportunities for clinical sport psychologists and open additional avenues for research and hypothesis generation.

State of Efficacy Research

The current status of efficacy research for performance enhancement in sport psychology requires significant attention if the discipline is to fully embrace evidence-based practice, comply with ethical guidelines to provide scientifically demonstrated services, and grow into a respected and utilized professional specialty. Despite the purported utility and professional popularity of performance enhancement interventions, most of the common procedures have accumulated little sophisticated support (Moore, 2003b; Moore & Gardner, 2005). When applying the standard criteria for empirical support utilized throughout allied areas of psychology (Chambless & Ollendick, 2001), the widely used traditional intervention strategies in sport psychology do not demonstrate efficacy in directly enhancing athletic performance (Moore, 2003b; Moore & Gardner, 2005). For decades, numerous sport psychologists have expressed concern about the equivocal support for the traditional performance enhancement interventions and have called for increased scientific accountability and more rigorous experimental standards in establishing intervention efficacy (Dishman, 1983; Greenspan & Feltz, 1989; Hill, 2001; Meyers et al., 1996; Smith, 1989; Strean & Roberts, 1992; Whelan et al., 1991). Unfortunately, empirical studies on goal setting, imagery, self-talk, arousal regulation, and multicomponent interventions have made little progress toward legitimately measuring and reporting intervention success. As a result, sport psychology has not wholly benefited from several decades of potential growth and has experienced marked setbacks in identifying effective intervention strategies.

Intervention research in sport psychology has also limited itself by using protocols that incorporate several techniques at one time to address a single problem (i.e., performance deficits). When a multicomponent psychological skills package is used in a study, multiple manipulations of variables would presumably (sooner or later) affect the cause of the performance difficulty and lead to performance improvement. Then what have we learned? Have we truly explained the mechanism of action for performance enhancement? Or have the multiple intervention packages precluded a more detailed understanding of relevant (and irrelevant) mechanisms? It is critical that studies be designed that will dismantle these packages so that we gain a better understanding of the relative contribution of intervention packages for the purpose of performance enhancement. Although multiple intervention packages may increase the likelihood of eventually gaining the appropriate outcome, interventions should be applied based upon a conceptually sound understanding of *why* and *how* they effect change. Randomly applying interventions and hoping for success is not in the best interest of the athlete, places the athlete at risk for further performance decrements, places the practitioner at risk for malpractice, and jeopardizes the consumer acceptance of the field.

For the client's well-being alone, it is crucial that interventions become more conceptually sound, theoretically grounded, empirically informed, and specific to targeted mechanisms of action. Similarly, more targeted interventions require assessment that clearly articulates intervention goals and parameters.

Considering the MCS-SP and the theoretical and methodological issues discussed in this text, we hope future efficacy studies reexamine traditional PST procedures as well as examine newer models for performance enhancement, such as the MAC protocol. We hope that researchers and practitioners recognize that athletes are a heterogeneous population and that athletes with subclinical issues may require different interventions than those who can benefit from performance enhancement strategies alone.

There is tremendous opportunity to reexamine the current knowledge base with new efficacy studies that are methodologically rigorous and based on cutting-edge theory. Efficacy studies modeled after randomized controlled trials in clinical psychology and psychopharmacology would help sport psychology become a truly scientific discipline. Case studies and single-subject designs, while useful in the theory building and protocol development stages of research, cannot supplant

The sport psychologist cannot ignore this athlete's difficult adjustment to a new school, even though the athlete may be more focused on improved performance.

well-designed randomized controlled trials that employ sound methodological standards. The recent well-intended article by Anderson, Miles, Mahoney, and Robinson (2002) stressed, as we do in this text, that the field of sport psychology must increase professional accountability by appropriately evaluating intervention effectiveness. We certainly agree with this position. However, Anderson and colleagues suggest that using randomized controlled trials is not feasible in sport psychology settings because "Standardized treatments associated with randomized control group and quasi-experimental designs are typically incompatible with a practice setting in which the practitioner aims to consider the individual needs of each athlete" (Anderson et al., 2002, p. 437). We (FG and ZM) suggest that the sport psychologist holding this view lacks an understanding of randomized controlled trials in professional psychology and is forgetting our true purpose, which is inherently to aid in the overall development and well-being of the individual person. The choice of measurement procedures and methodological design does not contaminate this ultimate goal.

Anderson et al. (2002) also stated that experimental research designs "create an artificial environment, which bears little resemblance to practice" (p. 437). We find this point especially interesting, in that very few randomized controlled trials in sport psychology are conducted in a laboratory setting or any other artificial environment. In fact, interventions that utilize RCT methodology can be conducted on the playing field, on the ice, in the ring, and on the court. Where the intervention is conducted has little to do with the measurement procedures used to interpret intervention data, thus making the "artificial environment" argument moot.

One particularly troubling fact is that sport psychology practitioners often forget that the athletes we work with are actually *human*, much the same way that clinical psychologists at times see disorders sitting in front of them instead of people. We (FG and ZM) stress that beneath all occupational roles, complex relationships, and symptom presentations, all people are just that . . . *people*. Thus, whether the person is obtaining a psychiatric evaluation in a hospital, working one-on-one with a teacher in school, or talking to a sport psychologist on the basketball court, the particular context is much less important than the *person* with whom we are working. As such, although we should respect the context in which the person functions, we must resist overvaluing

that context for danger of distorting the person. Although some people in every field suggest that the specific culture or context of their field places more profound challenges on those involved, the specific context in which we function is much less important than we think. As such, we (FG and ZM) suggest that although the sport culture does in fact place different demands on the athlete than she would have in another setting, the person beneath the specific role she carries is the same. This is the spirit of a truly person-centered approach to working with people. Despite fears of contaminating the context by creating an artificial environment, sport psychologists can ethically conduct appropriate randomized controlled trials and provide sound psychological services both within and apart from these trials.

While awaiting more of these studies, clinical sport psychologists should be very careful when presenting their interventions to athletes. As noted in chapter 5, traditional PST procedures including goal setting, imagery, self-talk, arousal regulation, and multicomponent interventions are considered experimental at this time. Even the newer MAC protocol, while promising, is still experimental, as it is currently in the development stage and undergoing its second significant phase of research. It is necessary that we discuss the present status of the interventions we use with our clients and obtain clear informed consent prior to beginning any intervention. This is especially important as PST procedures currently demonstrate limited success and newer procedures (such as the MAC protocol) have yet to accumulate enough support in well-designed trials. The current status of the procedures available for performance enhancement does not suggest that practitioners should not or could not use them. Rather than suggest a pessimistic view of traditional sport psychology procedures, the current data ratify the necessity for quality empirical research abiding by sound methodological principles, and the data also suggest that our use of traditional procedures should be cautious and idiographic. We strongly encourage clinical sport psychologists to fully describe the state of our knowledge to clients, discuss the options available, and present the likely benefits and costs (including money and time). This allows the clients to choose a course of action appropriate for their individualized needs.

Of course, the noted efficacy concerns strictly relate to the interventions utilized in sport psychology for performance enhancement. Standard interventions for subclinical or clinical concerns, such as performance dysfunction (Pdy) or performance impairment (PI) issues, are typically well-established and empirically supported. These interventions, which were covered in chapters 7, 8, and 9, have sufficient efficacy, and both clients and practitioners can be assured that these interventions will likely meet the athlete's needs (if the needs are appropriately identified and the practitioner is competent in providing the interventions).

Future Research

When considering Moore's finding (Moore, 2003b; Moore & Gardner, 2005) that the empirical support for traditional performance enhancement procedures is limited, several directions in research emerge that may have a profound effect on sport psychology. Specifically, although sound empirical studies can provide the valuable and reliable outcome data necessary to establish efficacy and develop the field of sport psychology, transgressions of rigorous scientific and methodological standards have consistently limited the number of methodologically sound studies available. Within the empirical literature, several research tendencies (discussed in the following sections) complicate the reliability and validity of outcome data.

Sample Characteristics

The criteria for determining empirical support (shown on page 68 in chapter 5) (Chambless & Ollendick, 2001) require studies to accurately and sufficiently report descriptive sample characteristics. Yet rarely have empirical studies in sport psychology properly described the specific characteristics of the athletes they utilized (Meyers et al., 1996; Vealey, 1994a). Rather, sport psychology researchers (and practitioners) often assume that most athletes are psychosocially well functioning, share essentially homogeneous personal characteristics and intervention needs, and can unanimously benefit from psychological skills training (Meyers et al., 1996; Vealey, 1994a). This assumption is rarely true. Researchers should therefore differentiate athlete issues and personal differences to ensure the optimal internal validity of their research programs and thus clarify intervention efficacy and the ecological validity (practical utility) of their research efforts. Our data on the MAC protocol's differing impact on athletes with and without psychological barriers (PD versus Pdy) (see chapter 6) support the proposition that some interventions inevitably work best for certain concerns. So, in order to enhance performance; intervene with transitional, developmental, interpersonal, or intrapersonal

While these athletes have all attained the same general level of sport expertise, each has different needs, dispositions, and sport expectations.

concerns; and successfully treat more serious clinical disorders, we must abandon any assumptions of athlete homogeneity.

Descriptive information necessary in future research includes age, gender, ethnicity, skill level, expectations of skill development, expectations of the success of intervention, specific intervention needs, history of use of performance enhancement procedures, and the potential presence of developmental issues or more serious clinical difficulties. Avoiding or restricting such participant information raises a serious concern both for researchers developing a nomothetic database and for practitioners attempting to idiographically apply the existing data.

Also, standard research in applied sport psychology typically assumes that all athletes can benefit equally from efforts to enhance performance (Meyers et al., 1996; Vealey, 1994a), further leading to insufficient reports of important sample characteristics within studies. Poor data collection and participant description obscure whether researchers have possibly understated or overstated the effectiveness of mental skills training by including athletes regardless of their personal needs. It is crucial that researchers accurately describe research participants in order to increase the internal validity of research studies and to allow applied professionals to generalize findings to their respective clientele (Meyers et al., 1996; Vealey, 1994a; Weinberg & Comar, 1994).

Intervention Description or Manualization

In addition to describing participants, in order to meet the empirically supported treatment criteria (shown on page 68 in chapter 5) (Chambless et al., 1998), efficacy studies must provide an intervention manual or succinctly and thoroughly explain the intervention in order to ensure procedural consistency within an intervention, maximize replicability, and help ensure that the intervention described is actually provided to the population. The intervention description or manual should clearly state the specific principles and procedures of the intervention. For example, an experimental study using imagery to enhance athletic performance could provide the actual imagery script (Murphy & Jowdy, 1992) so that readers can both evaluate the intervention and provide it to their respective clientele with reasonable assurance of similar results. Simply stating that an imagery script was utilized is insufficient for

generalization to the field and raises questions of treatment integrity and consistency across studies.

Some have criticized intervention descriptions and manuals as promoting inflexibility in the artful application of an intervention and restricting the practitioner's personal involvement in the intervention (Garfield, 1996; Henry, 1998). However, intervention descriptions and manuals provide the practitioner with considerable flexibility in the artful utilization of scientifically sound procedures (Chambless & Hollon, 1998; Chambless & Ollendick, 2001). Following general guidelines does not require blind allegiance to an impersonal procedure and does not restrict the practitioner from responding to the nuances of the therapeutic relationship or to the specific client–practitioner variables that inevitably emerge. In fact, applying clearly described or manual-based interventions requires considerable flexibility and adaptation to the specific needs of each client and setting. Sound intervention descriptions and manuals provide illustrative case examples, samples of client–practitioner interactions, and recommendations for overcoming obstacles that may arise during the intervention. Specifically within the sport psychology literature, descriptions may include imagery scripts and directions for use, thorough self-talk instructions and explanations, specific arousal and relaxation training procedures, and instructions and rationales for goal setting.

Intervention descriptions or manuals operationally define an intervention, which allows practitioners to determine the relevance of the procedure to their own practice and clientele (Chambless & Hollon, 1998; Chambless & Ollendick, 2001). Determining relevance is especially important, as many procedures may be included under the same general title, such as psychological skills training, cognitive-behavioral interventions, and performance enhancement. It is meaningless to say that an intervention works without accurately saying what the intervention entails. In fact, sport psychology professionals have long called for more thorough intervention descriptions among empirical studies (Murphy, 1990, 1994; Murphy & Jowdy, 1992), yet researchers have rarely adopted these suggestions.

Methodology

Sport psychology professionals have also noted methodological concerns that hinder the successful progression of the field, and these concerns largely support adopting the empirically supported intervention standards. Common concerns within empirical efficacy studies include lack of manipulation checks (Gould & Udry, 1994; Greenspan & Feltz, 1989; Murphy, 1994; Murphy & Jowdy, 1992; Vealey, 1994a), lack of attention to relationship and nonspecific factors (Meyers et al., 1996), little discussion of actual mechanisms of change (Gardner et al., 2003, October), lack of follow-up and maintenance of effects over time (Greenspan & Feltz, 1989; Meyers et al., 1996; Suinn, 1997), lack of generalizability of studies that utilize analogue populations and tasks (Meyers et al., 1996; Murphy & Jowdy, 1992), lack of consistent and appropriate controls, and poor replication of studies (Murphy, 1990, 1994; Murphy & Jowdy, 1992).

We hope that expanding awareness of these current difficulties can allow researchers to appropriately refine the methodological quality of the empirical studies conducted in sport psychology. Such refinement will increase the probability that interventions are evaluated according to rigorous scientific standards and thus promote clear efficacy and effectiveness findings. A more rigorous collection and analysis of empirical data will allow sport psychology practitioners to both legitimately analyze and utilize appropriate intervention strategies with athletic clientele and to accurately describe sport psychology services offered. As suggested by Weinberg and Comar (1994), "it is especially important, from an ethical standpoint, to ensure that consumers are not presented with exaggerated claims or unrealistic expectations regarding the efficacy of psychological techniques for enhancing performance" (p. 407).

Fortunately, sport psychology as an applied discipline has long professed (but not acted upon) its commitment to integrating science and practice (Dishman, 1983; Greenspan & Feltz, 1989; Hill, 2001; Meyers et al., 1996; Smith, 1989; Strean & Roberts, 1992; Whelan et al., 1991). Basic to an applied scientific discipline is its willingness to critically evaluate its theories and intervention strategies and its requirement that proponents of intervention strategies demonstrate the efficacy of their procedures (Lilienfeld et al., 2003). Although dismissing the need for sound scientific methodology may be easier than conducting rigorous empirical studies, responsible and ethical practice must utilize procedures that have demonstrated efficacy and effectiveness. Although adopting pseudoscientific ideals remains a personal choice, employing intervention strategies based on pseudoscience violates ethical guidelines, potentially places the athlete in danger, and endangers the credibility of the field (Dishman, 1983).

Sound research methodology and appropriate dissemination of findings will help sport psychologists remediate the above concerns, and will thus help the practitioner provide ethical, evidence-based professional services. As professionals in a human service field, sport psychologists are accountable for providing interventions that have been demonstrated to work (Dishman, 1983; Smith, 1989), and practitioners cannot ethically engage in interventions supported only by subjective, anecdotal, and correlational reports or methodologically weak empirical studies. Critical scientific scrutiny and the utilization of procedures validated by empirical research epitomize concern for the client's best interest. This is our fundamental obligation, as athletes expect sport psychologists to use best-practice procedures to meet their individual needs and goals.

Mechanisms of Change

As discussed in chapter 6, the field of sport psychology has long made major assumptions about the mechanisms of change underlying psychological skills training (PST) approaches to performance enhancement. Despite contradictory research, for many years researchers and practitioners in sport psychology assumed that reducing negative cognitive processes and negative internal states such as anxiety or that increasing confidence and positive thinking would enhance athletic performance (Hardy et al., 1996). However, the evidence suggests that while PST procedures do in fact reduce negative internal states, they do not significantly enhance performance. Conversely, our own recent studies suggest that performance can improve *without* corresponding changes in these previously assumed mechanisms of change (Gardner et al., 2005; Wolanin, 2005). The study of mechanisms of change in athletic performance enhancement is a potentially fruitful line of research. This line of study has become a mainstay of clinical research, but to date lacks recognition in the sport psychology literature. Developing effective and efficacious interventions requires understanding which elements of overt behavior to change in order to increase performance (for example, studies in our lab suggest that increasing concentration and aggressiveness increases performance when using the MAC protocol with psychologically healthy college athletes) and understanding the underlying mechanisms of performance enhancement (such as change versus acceptance of internal states). This understanding would guide practitioners as to what procedures to use for which clients and why. Understanding mechanisms of change would move the field even further toward becoming a viable, scientifically based profession.

Potential research areas include examining the mechanisms of change for minimizing subclinical difficulties (Pdy clients) and the effect these changes might have on both quality of life and athletic performance. These topics have not yet been studied in the sport context.

The understanding of mechanisms of change is of utmost importance for the clinical sport psychologist. The value of this concept cannot be overstated. Currently, due to the limited number of techniques discussed in the professional literature, most sport psychologists choose interventions from a short list of seemingly viable strategies and then aim these interventions at poorly defined and understood client difficulties. There is little discussion regarding the mechanisms by which most interventions (including PST procedures) work, therefore further threatening the effectiveness of the services provided to clients. Physicians do not provide medications because they are assumed to work. We expect them to have a viable working knowledge of *why* the medications work. This knowledge allows them to select the proper prescription and conversely to not choose a treatment with an underlying mechanism of action inappropriate to the problem at hand. Please note that good physicians do not prescribe medication after simply reviewing overt symptoms and patient wishes, but rather after soundly understanding the underlying elements of the pathology, which leads to rational treatment. This same process is typically found in clinical psychology, and this way of thinking should also be adopted by clinical sport psychologists.

Relationship and Common Factors

Unlike clinical and counseling psychology, which have a long history of considering the impact of common factors and relationship variables in effective psychotherapy (Norcross, 2002), the professional literature in sport psychology has rarely considered these issues and their impact on the success of interventions. As a result, practitioners often believe that whatever successes emerge from traditional PST procedures or athletic counseling result from the techniques in and of themselves. As discussed in chapter 13, we strongly believe that applied research in sport psychology should integrate treatment expectancies, therapeutic alliances, and other such concepts in order to enhance the scientific understanding of the complex processes faced by all humans, including athletes.

The relative contributions of technique and interpersonal factors to performance enhancement are important to understand, and we should not assume that the sport context differs from clinical and counseling psychology in these matters. We encourage clinical sport psychologists to utilize the data from clinical science to guide their thinking until relevant research on relationship factors, treatment expectancies, and common factors in sport psychology begins. The practitioner should consider the interpersonal context of the consulting experience, just as the psychotherapist must understand this context in clinical treatment. A collaborative working alliance and issues relating to practitioner responses to client and client responses to practitioner (transference and countertransference) are important aspects of intervention that can affect the efficacy of a particular procedure for a particular athlete. It is inaccurate to assume that the specific strategies involved in a given intervention are the only mechanisms needed to effect change and aid our clients. Likewise, the therapeutic relationship is a necessary yet insufficient tool, and thus it is equally inaccurate to assume that the practitioner–athlete relationship is the only critical mechanism of change.

Education, Training, and Supervision

With the culmination of this text, we should consider how clinical sport psychologists could and should be trained. In order for students and interested professionals to fully adopt and practice the model presented herein, the fundamental requirements of this model must be clearly defined.

For the graduate student in clinical or counseling psychology wishing to train as a clinical sport psychologist, the path is clear yet challenging. There are too few doctoral programs in clinical or counseling psychology that provide a structured educational experience in sport psychology that includes course work, externship, and research opportunity. The few that do exist demonstrate that such training is possible within a course concentration or track embedded in a comprehensive clinical or counseling program. We hope the recent APA proficiency for sport psychology fosters a professional environment that allows more psychology departments to offer *clinical* sport psychology as a concentration. Similarly, integrating doctoral programs in academic sport psychology with master's programs in professional counseling (hopefully with an evidence-based focus) may offer additional opportunities for comprehensive training.

Beyond the issue of program numbers, however, is the critical issue of substance. One of the tasks of this text has been to expand the professional definition of sport psychology to include a full range of evidence-based psychological services for athletes. We hope that this more comprehensive definition supplants the traditional view, which has largely restricted the practice of sport psychology to performance enhancement.

As discussed in chapter 13, the supervision of clinical sport psychologists needs to include a focus on the clinical and performance aspects of their work and skill development. The integrated balance of these domains will prepare the next generation of sport psychologists to both practice comprehensively and holistically and engage in a wide variety of professional roles, including those that focus on clinical difficulties, subclinical concerns, and performance requests. We sincerely believe that those professionals who identify with the clinical sport psychology model presented in this text will be best able to integrate the myriad of athlete information into a balanced, sound practice.

Role of the Clinical Sport Psychologist

Throughout this text, we have taken the position that clinical sport psychologists are behavioral health-care experts for athletic populations. We must therefore evolve away from the idea that our primary function is to provide performance enhancement. Instead, the clinical sport psychologist has the specialized knowledge and skill to fulfill a wonderful role—the role of behavioral expert in

the athletic domain. With this status, the job of the clinical sport psychologist could regularly involve selection, retention, organizational development, assessment, mental health care, and athletic performance enhancement. Whether developing performance or treating eating disorders, slumps, or perfectionism; responding to injury or responding to leaving home for the first time; or assessing a head injury or assessing a potential draft pick, the clinical sport psychologist would be the organizational and behavioral expert called upon to provide guidance and service. As is the case with a team physician, some circumstances would likely call for referral, but the clinical sport psychologist would be the expert engaging in behavioral triage and would add value to any athletic organization beyond the limited need for performance enhancement. This expanded scope of practice, discussed in chapter 1, would be a major change in the way sport psychologists frequently think about themselves and the services they provide. We hope that clinical and counseling psychologists entering this field will resist strict adherence to traditional sport psychology and will embrace clinical sport psychology as presented in this text. We also hope that the expanded scope and style of practice proposed in this text energizes current sport psychologists to take the field of sport psychology from a professional curiosity to an effective and useful professional necessity.

Final Thoughts

This text questions assumptions and models of intervention that have been presented in sport psychology for decades. We anticipate that the ideas and empirically informed material we presented will provoke anxiety and frustration for some and excite others. After reviewing the professional literature, we suggested alternative ways of conceptualizing our athletes and innovative strategies for performance enhancement. We discussed in detail interventions for nonclinical and subclinical clients whose psychological barriers must be effectively addressed. We presented current empirically supported or empirically informed interventions for the clinical disorders most often seen in our athletes, and we also presented a systematic approach to assessment and intervention planning (the MCS-SP). We illustrated the implications of the APA Code of Ethics (Moore, 2003a) that must be incorporated into sport psychologists' conceptual thinking, assessment, and intervention strategies in order to holistically and ethically serve our athletic clientele.

Finally, we presented a practice model that integrates the knowledge from both clinical and sport psychology and suggests a dynamic approach that expands the horizons of the field. We sincerely hope this text spurs discussion and debate and may be the impetus for future research and a more effective model of practice—*clinical sport psychology.*

References

References marked with an asterisk indicate studies included in the qualitative analysis described in chapter 5.

Abbot, P.J., Weller, S.B., Delaney, H.D., & Moore, B.A. (1998). Community reinforcement approach in the treatment of opiate addicts. *American Journal of Drug and Alcohol Abuse, 24* (1), 17-30.

Akiskal, H.S. (1996). The prevalent clinical spectrum of bipolar disorders: Beyond *DSM-IV. Journal of Clinical Psychopharmacology, 16* (Suppl. 1), 4-14.

Alden, L.E. (1989). Short-term structured treatment for avoidant personality disorder. *Journal of Consulting and Clinical Psychology, 57,* 756-764.

Alfermann, D. (2000). Causes and consequences of sport career termination. In D. Lavallee & P. Wylleman (Eds.), *Career transitions in sport: International perspectives* (pp. 49-58). Morgantown, WV: Fitness Information Technology.

Altman, E.G., Hedeker, D., Peterson, J.L., & Davis, J.M. (1997). The Altman self-rating mania scale. *Biological Psychiatry, 42* (10), 948-955.

Altman, E.G., Hedeker, D., Peterson, J.L., & Davis, J.M. (2001). A comparative evaluation of three self-rating scales for acute mania. *Biological Psychiatry, 50* (6), 468-471.

American Board of Professional Psychology. (2004). *The American Board of Behavioral Psychology.* Available: www.abpp.org [June 3, 2005].

American Psychiatric Association. (2000). *Diagnostic and statistical manual of mental disorders* (4th ed., Rev.). Washington, DC: Author.

American Psychological Association. (1992). Ethical principles of psychologists and code of conduct. *American Psychologist, 42,* 1597-1611.

American Psychological Association. (2002). Ethical principles of psychologists and code of conduct. *American Psychologist, 57* (12), 1060-1073.

American Psychological Association. (2003). *A proficiency in sport psychology.* American Psychological Association. Retrieved February, 2003, from the World Wide Web: www.psyc.unt.edu/apadiv47/about_divprojects.html [June 3, 2005].

Anastasi, A. (1996). *Psychological testing* (7th ed.). New York: Macmillan.

Andersen, M.B. (1994). Ethical considerations in the supervision of applied sport psychology graduate students. *Journal of Applied Sport Psychology, 6,* 152-167.

Andersen, M.B. (2000a). Beginnings: Intakes and the initiation of relationships. In M.B. Andersen (Ed.), *Doing sport psychology* (pp. 3-14). Champaign, IL: Human Kinetics.

Andersen, M.B. (Ed.). (2000b). *Doing sport psychology.* Champaign, IL: Human Kinetics.

Andersen, M.B. (2002a). Comprehensive sport psychology services. In J.L. Van Raalte & B.W. Brewer (Eds.), *Exploring sport and exercise psychology* (pp. 13-23). Washington, DC: American Psychological Association.

Andersen, M.B. (2002b). Helping college student-athletes in and out of sport. In J.L. Van Raalte & B.W. Brewer (Eds.), *Exploring sport and exercise psychology* (pp. 373-393). Washington, DC: American Psychological Association.

Andersen, M.B., Van Raalte, J.L., & Brewer, B.W. (2001). Sport psychology service delivery: Staying ethical while keeping loose. *Professional Psychology: Research and Practice, 32* (1), 12-18.

Andersen, M.B., Williams, J.M., Aldridge, T., & Taylor, J. (1997). Tracking graduates of advanced degree programs in sport psychology, 1989-1994. *The Sport Psychologist, 11,* 326-344.

Andersen, M.B., & Williams-Rice, B.T. (1996). Supervision in the education and training of sport psychology service providers. *The Sport Psychologist, 10,* 278-290.

Anderson, A.G., Miles, A., Mahoney, C., & Robinson, P. (2002). Evaluating the effectiveness of applied sport psychology practice: Making the case for a case study approach. *The Sport Psychologist, 16,* 432-453.

Anderson, S.K., & Kitchener, K.S. (1999). Nonromantic, nonsexual posttherapy relationships between psychologists and former clients: An exploratory study of critical incidents. In D.N. Bersoff (Ed.), *Ethical conflicts in psychology* (2nd ed., pp. 247-253). Washington, DC: American Psychological Association.

*Andre, J.C., & Means, J.R. (1986). Rate of imagery in mental practice: An experimental investigation. *Journal of Sport Psychology, 8,* 124-128.

*Annesi, J.J. (1998). Applications of the individual zones of optimal functioning model for the multimodal treatment of precompetitive anxiety. *The Sport Psychologist, 12* (3), 300-316.

Anshel, M.H. (1990). *Sport psychology: From theory to practice* (2nd ed.). Scottsdale, AZ: Gorsuch Scarisbrick Publishers.

Anshel, M.H. (1992). The case against certification of sport psychologists: In search of phantom experts. *The Sport Psychologist, 6* (3), 265-286.

Anshel, M.H. (2003). Exploring the dimensions of perfectionism in sport. *International Journal of Sport Psychology, 34* (3), 255-271.

Antick, J., & Goodale, K. (2003). Drug abuse. In M. Hersen & S.M. Turner (Eds.), *Diagnostic interviewing* (2nd ed., pp. 223-237). New York: Kluwer Academic/Plenum.

Antony, M.M., Orsillo, S.M., & Roemer, L. (2001). *Practitioner's guide to empirically based measures of anxiety.* New York: Kluwer Academic/Plenum.

Auweele, Y.V., Nys, K., Rzewnicki, R., & Van Mele, V. (2001). Personality and the athlete. In R.N. Singer, H.A. Hausenblas, & C.M. Janelle (Eds.), *Handbook of sport psychology* (2nd ed., pp. 239-268). New York: Wiley.

Babor, T., de la Fuente, J.R., Saunders, J., & Grant, M. (1992). *The alcohol use disorders identification test: Guidelines for use in primary health care.* Geneva: World Health Organization.

Bach, A.K., Brown, T.A., & Barlow, D.H. (1999). The effects of false negative feedback on efficacy expectancies and sexual arousal in sexually functional males. *Behavioral Therapy, 30,* 79-95.

Baillie, P.H.F, & Danish, S.J. (1992). Understanding the career transition of athletes. *The Sport Psychologist, 6,* 726-739.

Baillie, P.H.F., & Ogilvie, B.C. (2002). Working with elite athletes. In J.L. Van Raalte & B.W. Brewer (Eds.), *Exploring sport and exercise psychology* (2nd ed., pp. 395-415). Washington, DC: American Psychological Association.

Bandura, A. (1977). Self-efficacy: Towards a unifying theory of behavioral change. *Psychological Review, 84,* 192-215.

Barber, J.P., Morse, J.Q., Krakauer, I., Chittams, J., & Crits-Christoph, K. (1997). Change in obsessive-compulsive and avoidant personality disorders following time-limited supportive-expressive therapy. *Psychotherapy, 34,* 133-143.

Barkley, R.A. (1998). *Attention deficit hyperactivity disorder: A handbook for diagnosis and treatment* (2nd ed.). New York: Guilford Press.

*Barling, J., & Bresgi, I. (1982). Cognitive factors in athletic (swimming) performance: A re-examination. *Journal of General Psychology, 107,* 227-231.

Barlow, D.H. (1986). Causes of sexual dysfunction: The role of anxiety and cognitive interference. *Journal of Consulting and Clinical Psychology, 54,* 140-148.

Barlow, D.H. (Ed.). (2001). *Clinical handbook of psychological disorders* (3rd ed.). New York: Guilford Press.

Barlow, D.H. (2002). *Anxiety and its disorders: The nature and treatment of anxiety and panic* (2nd ed.). New York: Guilford Press.

Barlow, D.H., Allen, L.B., & Choate, M.L. (2004). Toward a unified treatment for emotional disorders. *Behavior Therapy, 35* (2), 205-230.

Barlow, D.H., Raffa, S.D., & Cohen, E.M. (2002). Psychosocial treatments for panic disorders, phobias, and generalized anxiety disorder. In P.E. Nathan & J.M. Gorman (Eds.), *A guide to treatments that work* (2nd ed., pp. 301-335). New York: Oxford University Press.

*Barnett, M.L., & Stanicek, J.A. (1979). Effects of goal setting on achievement in archery. *Research Quarterly, 50,* 328-332.

Barney, S.T., & Andersen, M.B. (2000). Looking for help, grieving love lost: The case of C. In M.B. Andersen (Ed.), *Doing sport psychology* (pp. 139-150). Champaign, IL: Human Kinetics.

Bateman, A., & Fonagy, P. (1999). Effectiveness of partial hospitalization in the treatment of borderline personality disorder: A randomized controlled trial. *Journal of Psychiatry, 156,* 1563-1569.

Bauman J. (2000, October). Toward consensus on professional training issues in sport psychology. In E. Dunlap (Chair), *Toward consensus on professional training issues in sport psychology.* Panel discussion presented at the conference for the Association for the Advancement of Applied Sport Psychology, Nashville.

Beach, S.R.H., Sandeen, E.E., & O'Leary, K.D. (1990). Depression in marriage: A model for etiology and treatment. New York: Guilford Press.

Beahrs, J.O., & Gutheil, T.G. (2001). Informed consent in psychotherapy. *American Journal of Psychiatry, 158* (1), 4-10.

*Beauchamp, P.H., Halliwell, W.R., Fournier, J.F., & Koestner, R. (1996). Effects of cognitive-behavioral psychological skills training on the motivation, preparation, and putting performance of novice golfers. *The Sport Psychologist, 10,* 157-170.

Beck, A.T. (1976). *Cognitive therapy and the emotional disorders.* New York: International Universities Press.

Beck, A.T., Freeman, A., & Davis, D.D. (2004). *Cognitive therapy of personality disorders* (2nd ed.). New York: Guilford Press.

Beck, A.T., Rush, A.J., Shaw, B.F., & Emery, G. (1979). *Cognitive therapy of depression.* New York: Guilford Press.

Beck, A.T., Steer, R.A., & Brown, G.K. (1996). *Manual for the Beck Depression Inventory* (2nd ed.). San Antonio: The Psychological Corporation.

Beck, J.S. (1995). *Cognitive therapy: Basics and beyond.* New York: Guilford Press.

Beidel, D.C., & Nay, W.T. (2003). Anxiety disorders. In M. Hersen & S.M. Turner (Eds.), *Diagnostic interviewing* (3rd ed., pp. 85-110). New York: Kluwer Academic/Plenum.

Bergman, R.L., & Craske, M.G. (1994, November). *Covert verbalization and imagery in worry activity.* Poster session presented at the 28th Annual Convention of the Association for Advancement of Behavior Therapy, San Diego.

Beutler, L.E., & Consoli, A.J. (1993). Matching the therapist's interpersonal stance to clients' characteristics: Contributions from systematic eclectic psychotherapy. *Psychotherapy: Theory, Research, Practice, Training, 30* (3), 417-422.

Beutler, L.E., Consoli, A.J., & Williams, R.E. (1995). Integrative and eclectic therapies in practice. In B.M. Bonger & L.E. Beutler (Eds.), *Comprehensive textbook of psychotherapy: Theory and practice* (pp. 274-292). London: Oxford University Press.

Beutler, L.E., & Malik, M.L. (Eds.). (2002). *Rethinking the DSM: A psychological perspective.* Washington, DC: American Psychological Association.

Biddle, S.J., Bull, S.J., & Seheult, C.L. (1992). Ethical and professional issues in contemporary British sport psychology. *The Sport Psychologist, 6* (1), 66-76.

Bisson, J.L., Jenkins, P.L., Alexander, J., & Bannister, C. (1997). A randomized controlled trial of psychological debriefing for victims of acute harm. *British Journal of Psychiatry, 171,* 78-81.

Blanchard, E.B., Jones-Alexander, J., Buckley, T.C., & Forneris, C.A. (1996). Psychometric properties of the PTSD Checklist (PCL). *Behaviour Research and Therapy, 34,* 669-673.

Blatt, S.J., & Blass, R.B. (1990). Attachment and separation: A dialectic model of the products and processes of development throughout the life cycle. *Psychoanalytic Study of the Child, 45,* 107-127.

Blatt, S.J., Shahal, G., & Zurhoff, D.C. (2002). Anaclitic/sociotropic and introjective/autonomous dimensions. In J.C. Norcross (Ed.), *Psychotherapy relationships that work* (pp. 315-334). New York: Oxford University Press.

Blatt, S.J., Zohar, A., Quinlan, D.M., Luthar, S., & Hart, B. (1996). Levels of relatedness within the dependency factor of the Depression Experiences Questionnaire for Adolescents. *Journal of Personality Assessment, 67* (1), 52-71.

Blatt, S.J., & Zuroff, D.C. (2002). Perfectionism in the therapeutic process. In G.L. Flett & P.L. Hewitt (Eds.), *Perfectionism: Theory, research, and treatment* (pp. 393-406). Washington, DC: USical Corporation.

Bond, F.W., & Bunce, D. (2000). Mediators of change in emotion-focused and problem-focused worksite stress management interventions. *Journal of Occupational Health Psychology, 5* (1), 156-163.

Bond, J.W. (2001). The provision of sport psychology services during competition tours. In G. Tenenbaum (Ed.), *The practice of sport psychology* (pp. 217-229). Morgantown, WV: Fitness Information Technology.

Borkovec, T.D. (1994). The nature, functions, and origins of worry. In G. Davey & F. Tallis (Eds.), *Worrying: Perspectives on theory, assessment, and treatment* (pp. 5-33). Sussex, England: Wiley.

Borkovec, T.D., Alcaine, O., & Behar, E. (2004). Avoidance theory of worry and generalized anxiety disorder. In R.G. Heimberg, C.L. Turk, & D.S. Mennin (Eds.), *Generalized anxiety disorder: Advances in research and practice* (pp. 77-108) New York: Guilford Press.

Borkovec, T. D., & Costello, E. (1993). Efficacy of applied relaxation and cognitive-behavioral therapy in the treatment of generalized anxiety disorder. *Journal of Consulting and Clinical Psychology, 61,* 611-619.

Borkovec, T.D., & Inz, J. (1990). The nature of worry in generalized anxiety disorder: A predominance of thought activity. *Behaviour Research and Therapy, 28* (2), 153-158.

Bowlby, J. (1982). *Attachment and loss: Vol. 1. Attachment* (2nd ed.). New York: Basic Books.

*Boyce, B.A. (1994). The effects of goal setting on performance and spontaneous goal setting behavior of experienced pistol shooters. *The Sport Psychologist, 8,* 87-93.

*Boyce, B.A., & Bingham, S.M. (1997). The effects of self-efficacy and goal setting on bowling performance. *Journal of Teaching in Physical Education, 16,* 312-323.

*Boyce, B.A., Wayda, V.K., Johnston, T., Bunker, L.K., & Eliot, J. (2001). The effects of three types of goal setting conditions on tennis performance: A field-based study. *Journal of Teaching in Physical Education, 20,* 188-200.

Braaten, E.B., & Handelsman, M.M. (1997). Client preferences for informed consent information. *Ethics and Behavior, 7* (4), 311-328.

Brewer, B.W., Van Raalte, J.L., & Linder, D.E. (1993). Athletic identity: Hercules' muscles or Achilles heel. *International Journal of Sport Psychology, 24,* 237-254.

Brown, T.A., DiNardo, P.A., & Barlow, D.H. (1994). *Anxiety disorders interview schedule for DSM-IV.* Albany, NY: Graywind Publications.

Brown, T.A., O'Leary, T.A., & Barlow, D.H. (2001). Generalized anxiety disorder. In D.H. Barlow (Ed.), *Clinical handbook of psychological disorders* (3rd ed., pp. 154-208). New York: Guilford Press.

Bryant, R.A., Sackville, T., Dang, S.T., Moulds, M., & Guthrie, R. (1999). Treating acute stress disorder: An evaluation of cognitive behavior therapy and supportive counseling techniques. *American Journal of Psychiatry, 156* (11), 1780-1786.

Buceta, J.M. (1993). The sport psychologist/athletic coach dual role: Advantages, difficulties, and ethical considerations. *Journal of Applied Sport Psychology, 5,* 64-77.

Budney, A.J., & Higgins, S.T. (1998). *National Institute on Drug Abuse therapy manuals for drug addiction: Manual 2. The community reinforcement plus vouchers approach* (NIH Publication No. 98-4308). Rockville, MD: National Institute on Drug Abuse.

*Burhans, R.S., Richman, C.L., & Bergey, D.B. (1988). Mental imagery training: Effects on running speed performance. *International Journal of Sport Psychology, 19,* 26-37.

Burke, B.L., Arkowitz, H., & Menchola, M. (2003). The efficacy of motivational interviewing: A meta-analysis of controlled clinical trials. *Journal of Consulting and Clinical Psychology, 71* (5), 843-861.

Burke, K.C., Burke, J.D., Regier, P.A., & Rae, P.S. (1990). Age at onset of selected mental disorders in five community populations. *Archives of General Psychiatry, 47,* 511-518.

Burney, R.C., Burdick, H., & Teevan, R.C. (1969). *Fear of failure.* New York: Van Nostrand Reinhold.

*Burton, D. (1989a). The impact of goal specificity and task complexity on basketball skill development. *The Sport Psychologist, 3* (1), 34-47.

*Burton, D. (1989b). Winning isn't everything: Examining the impact of performance goals on collegiate swimmers' cognitions and performance. *The Sport Psychologist, 3* (2), 105-132.

Burton, D., Naylor, S., & Holliday, B. (2001). Goal setting in sport: Investigating the goal effectiveness paradox. In R.N. Singer, H.A. Hausenblas, & C.M. Janelle (Eds.), *Handbook of sport psychology* (2nd ed., pp. 497-528). New York: Wiley.

Butcher, J.N., Dahlstrom, W.G., Graham, G.R., Tellegen, A., & Kaemmer, B. (1989). *Manual for administration and scoring: MMPI-2.* Minneapolis: University of Minnesota Press.

Butler, G., Fennell, M., Robson, P., & Gelder, M. (1991). Comparison of behavior therapy and cognitive behavior therapy in the treatment of generalized anxiety disorder. *Journal of Consulting and Clinical Psychology, 59,* 167-175.

Calabrese, J.R., Fatemi, S.H., Kujawa, M., & Woyshville, M.J. (1996). Predictors of response to mood stabilizers. *Journal of Clinical Psychopharmacology, 16* (Suppl. 1), 24-31.

Canter, M.B., Bennett, B.E., Jones, S.E., & Nagy, T.F. (1994). *Ethics for psychologists: A commentary on the APA Ethics Code.* Washington, DC: American Psychological Association.

Carr, C.M., Kennedy, S.R., & Dimick, K.M. (1990). Alcohol use and abuse among high school athletes: A comparison of alcohol use and intoxication in male and female high school athletes and non-athletes. *Journal of Alcohol and Drug Education, 36* (1), 39-45.

Carr, C.M., & Murphy, S.M. (1995). Alcohol and drugs in sport. In S.M. Murphy (Ed.), *Sport psychology interventions* (pp. 283-306). Champaign, IL: Human Kinetics.

Carter, W.R., Johnson, M.C., & Borkovec, T.D. (1986). Worry: An electrocortical analysis. *Advances in Behaviour Research and Therapy, 8,* 193-204.

Carver, C.S., & Scheier, M.F. (1988). A control perspective on anxiety. *Anxiety Research, 1,* 17-22.

Catalano, S. (1997). The challenges of clinical practice in small or rural communities: Case studies in managing dual relationships in and outside of therapy. *Journal of Contemporary Psychotherapy, 27* (1), 23-35.

*Caudill, D., Weinberg, R., & Jackson, A. (1983). Psyching-up and track athletes: A preliminary investigation. *Journal of Sport Psychology, 5,* 231-235.

Chambless, D.L., Baker, M.J., Baucom, D.H., Beutler, L.E., Calhoun, K.S., Crits-Christoph, P., Daiuto, A., DeRubeis, R., Detweiler, J., Haaga, D.A.F., Bennett Johnson, S., McCurry, S., Mueser, K.T., Pope, K.S., Sanderson, W.C., Shoham, V., Stickle, T., Williams, D.A., & Woody, S. (1998). Update on empirically validated therapies, II. *The Clinical Psychologist, 51* (1), 3-16.

Chambless, D.L., Caputo, G., Bright, P., & Gallagher, R. (1984). Assessment of fear in agoraphobics: The Body Sensations Questionnaire and the Agoraphobic Cognitions Questionnaire. *Journal of Consulting and Clinical Psychology, 52,* 1090-1097.

Chambless, D.L., & Hollon, S.D. (1998). Defining empirically supported therapies. *Journal of Consulting and Clinical Psychology, 66* (1), 7-18.

Chambless, D.L., & Ollendick, T.H. (2001). Empirically supported psychological interventions: Controversies and evidence. *Annual Review of Psychology, 52,* 685-716.

Chambless, D.L., Sanderson, W.C., Shoham, V., Bennett Johnson, S., Pope, K.S., Crits-Christoph, P., Baker, M., Johnson, B., Woody, S. R., Sue, S., Beutler, L., Williams, D.A., & McCurry, S. (1996). An update on empirically validated therapies. *The Clinical Psychologist, 49* (2), 5-18.

Charlton, B.G. (1996). The uses and abuses of meta-analysis. *Family Practice, 13* (4), 397-401.

Charner, I., & Schlossberg, N.K. (1986, June). Variations by theme: The life transitions of clerical workers. *The Vocational Guidance Quarterly, 33* (4), 212-224.

Chartrand, J.M., & Lent, R. (1987). Sports counseling: Enhancing the development of the student athlete. *Journal of Counseling and Development, 66,* 164-167.

Chorpita, B.F., & Barlow, D.H. (1998). The development of anxiety: The role of control in the early environment. *Psychological Bulletin, 124* (1), 3-21.

Clark, D.M., Ball, S., & Pape, K. (1991). An experimental investigation of thought suppression. *Behavior Research and Therapy, 31,* 207-210.

*Clark, L.V. (1960). Effect of mental practice on the development of a certain motor skill. *Research Quarterly, 31,* 560-569.

Cogan, K.D. (2000). The sadness in sport: Working with a depressed and suicidal athlete. In M.B. Andersen (Ed.), *Doing sport psychology* (pp. 107-119). Champaign, IL: Human Kinetics.

Cohen, A., Pargman, D., & Tenenbaum, G. (2003). Critical elaboration and empirical investigation of the cusp catastrophe model: A lesson for practitioners. *Journal of Applied Sport Psychology, 15* (2), 144-159.

Cook, D.A., & Helms, J.E. (1988). Visible racial/ethnic group supervisees' satisfaction with cross-cultural supervision as predicted by relationship characteristics. *Journal of Counseling Psychology, 35* (3), 268-274.

Conroy, D.E., & Meltzer, J.N. (2004). Patterns of self-talk associated with different forms of competitive anxiety. *Journal of Sport and Exercise, 26* (1), 69-89.

Conroy, D.E., Poczwardowski, A., & Henschen, K.P. (2001). Evaluative criteria and consequences associated with failure and success for elite athletes and performing artists. *Journal of Applied Sport Psychology, 13* (3), 300-322.

Conroy, D.E., Willow, J.P., & Meltzer, J.N. (2002). Multidimensional fear of failure: The Performance Failure Appraisal Inventory. *Journal of Applied Sport Psychology, 14* (2), 76-90.

*Corbin, C.B. (1967a). Effects of mental practice on skill development after controlled practice. *Research Quarterly, 38* (4), 534-538.

*Corbin, C.B. (1967b). The effects of covert rehearsal on the development of a complex motor skill. *Journal of General Psychology, 76* (2), 143-150.

Cordova, J.V., & Jacobson, N.S. (1993). Couple distress. In D.H. Barlow (Ed.), *Clinical handbook of psychological disorders: A step-by-step treatment manual* (2nd ed., pp. 481-512). New York: Plenum.

Cox, R.H. (1998). *Sport psychology: Concepts and applications* (4th ed.). Boston: McGraw-Hill.

Cox, R.H. (2002). *Sport psychology: Concepts and applications* (5th ed.). New York: McGraw-Hill.

Craft, L.L., Magyar, T.M., Becker, B.J., & Feltz, D.L. (2003). The relationship between the Competitive State Anxiety Inventory-2 and sport performance: a meta-analysis. *Journal of Sport and Exercise Psychology, 25* (1), 44-65.

Craighead, W.E., Hart, A.B., Craighead, L.W., & Ilardi, S.S. (2002). Psychosocial treatments for major depressive disorder. In P.E. Nathan & J.M. Gorman (Eds.), *A guide to treatments that work* (2nd ed., pp. 245-261). New York: Oxford University Press.

Craighead, W.E., Miklowitz, D.J., Frank, E., & Vajk, F.C. (2002). Psychosocial treatments for bipolar disorder. In P.E. Nathan & N.M. Gorman (Eds.), *A guide to treatments that work* (2nd ed., pp. 263-275). New York: Oxford University Press.

Cranston-Cuebas, M.A., & Barlow, D.H. (1995). *Attentional focus and the misattribution of male sexual arousal.* Unpublished manuscript.

Cranston-Cuebas, M.A., Barlow, D.H., Mitchell, W.B., & Athanasiou, R. (1993). Differential effects of a misattribution manipulation on sexually functional and dysfunctional males. *Journal of Abnormal Psychology, 102,* 525-533.

Craske, M.G. (1999). *Anxiety disorders: Psychological approaches to theory and treatment.* Boulder, CO: Westview Press.

Craske, M.G., & Barlow, D.H. (2001). Panic Disorder and Agoraphobia. In D.H. Barlow (Ed.), *Clinical handbook of psychological disorders* (3rd ed., pp. 1-59). New York: Guilford Press.

Crews, D.J., & Landers, D.M. (1993). Electroencephalographic measures of attentional patterns prior to the golf putt. *Medicine and Science in Sports and Exercise, 25,* 116-126.

Crews, D.J., Lochbaum, M.R., & Karoly, P. (2001). Self-regulation: Concepts, methods, and strategies in sport and exercise. In R.N. Singer, H.A. Hausenblas, & C.M. Janelle (Eds.), *Handbook of sport psychology* (2nd ed., pp. 566-581). New York: Wiley.

Crits-Christoph, P., & Barber, J.P. (2002). Psychological treatments for personality disorders. In P.E. Nathan & J.M. Gorman (Eds.), *A guide to treatments that work* (2nd ed., pp. 611-623). New York: Oxford University Press.

*Crocker, P.R.E., Alderman, R.B., & Smith, M.R. (1988). Cognitive-affective stress management training with high performance youth volleyball players: Effects on affect, cognition, and performance. *Journal of Sport and Exercise Psychology, 10* (4), 448-460.

Csikszentmihalyi, M. (1975). *Beyond boredom and anxiety.* San Francisco: Jossey-Bass.

Csikszentmihalyi, M. (1990). *Flow: The psychology of optimal experience.* New York: Harper & Row.

Danish, S.J., Petitpas, A., & Hale, B.D. (1995). Psychological interventions: A life development model. In S.M. Murphy (Ed.), *Sport psychology interventions* (pp. 19-38). Champagne, IL: Human Kinetics.

Davey, G.C.L., Hampton, J., Farrell, J., & Davidson, S. (1992). Some characteristics of worrying: Evidence for worrying and anxiety as separate constructs. *Personality and Individual Differences, 13,* 133-147.

*Davis, K. (1991). Performance enhancement program for a college tennis player. *International Journal of Sport Psychology, 22,* 140-164.

*Daw, J., & Burton, D. (1994). Evaluation of a comprehensive psychological skills training program for collegiate tennis players. *The Sport Psychologist, 8* (1), 37-57.

Derogatis, L.R. (1983). *SCL-90-R: Administration, Scoring and Procedures Manual.* Towson, MD: Clinical Psychometric Research.

*De Witt, D.J. (1980). Cognitive and biofeedback training for stress reduction with university athletes. *Journal of Sport Psychology, 2* (4), 288-294.

DiGiuseppe, R., McGowan, L., Sutton-Simon, K., & Gardner, F. (1990). Comparative outcome study of four cognitive therapies in the treatment of social anxiety. *Journal of Rational Emotive and Cognitive Behavior Therapy, 8* (3), 129-146.

DiGiuseppe, R., & Tafrate, R.C. (2003). Anger treatment for adults: A meta-analytic review. *Clinical Psychology: Science and Practice, 10* (1), 70-84.

DiGiuseppe, R., & Tafrate, R.C. (2004). *Anger Disorders Scale: Technical manual.* Minneapolis, MN: Multi-Health Systems.

DiNardo, P.A., Brown, T.A., & Barlow, D.H. (1994). *Anxiety Disorders Interview Schedule for DSM-IV: Lifetime Version (ADIS-IV-L).* San Antonio: Psychological Corporation.

Dishman, R.K. (1983). Identity crises in North American sport psychology: Academics in professional issues. *Journal of Sport Psychology, 5* (2), 123-134.

Dorfman, H.A. (1990). Reflections on providing personal performance enhancement consulting services in professional baseball. *The Sport Psychologist, 4,* 341-346.

Doss, B.D., Jones, J.T., & Christensen, A. (2002). Integrative behavioral couples therapy. In F.W. Kaslow (Ed.), *Comprehensive handbook of psychotherapy* (Vol. 4, pp. 387-410). New York: Wiley.

Dougher, M.S., & Hayes, S.C. (2000). Clinical behavior analysis. In M.J. Dougher (Ed.), *Clinical behavior analysis* (pp. 11-25). Reno, NV: Context Press.

Dowd, E.T., Milne, C.R., & Wise, S.L. (1991). The therapeutic reactance scale: A measure of psychological reactance. *Journal of Counseling and Development, 69* (6), 541-545.

Dowd, E.T., Wallbrown, F., Sanders, D., & Yesenosky, J.M. (1994). Psychological reactance and its relationship to normal personality variables. *Cognitive Therapy and Research, 18* (6), 601-612.

Duda, J.L. (Ed.). (1998). *Advances in sport and exercise psychology measurements.* Morgantown, WV: Fitness Information Technology.

Durham, R.C., Murphy, T., Allan, T., Richard, K., Treliving, L.R., & Fenton, G.W. (1994). Cognitive therapy, analytic psychotherapy and anxiety management training for generalized anxiety disorder. *British Journal of Psychiatry, 165,* 315-323.

D'Urso, V., Petrosso, A., & Robazza, C. (2002). Emotions, perceived qualities, and performance of rugby players. *The Sport Psychologist, 16* (2), 173-199.

Ebert, B.W. (1997). Dual-relationship prohibitions: A concept whose time never should have come. *Applied and Preventive Psychology, 6* (3), 137-156.

Eells, T.D. (Ed.). (1997). *Handbook of psychotherapy case formulation.* New York: Guilford Press.

Eisler, I., & Dare, C. (2000). Family therapy for adolescent anorexia nervosa: The results of a controlled comparison of two family interventions. *Journal of Child Psychology and Psychiatry, 41,* 727-736.

Elkin, D. (1981). *The hurried child.* Reading, MA: Addison-Wesley.

*Elko, K., & Ostrow, A.C. (1992). The effects of three mental preparation strategies on strength performance of young and older adults. *Journal of Sport Behavior, 15* (1), 34-41.

Ellickson, K.A., & Brown, D.R. (1990). Ethical considerations in dual relationships: The sport psychologist-coach. *Journal of Applied Sport Psychology, 2,* 186-190.

Ellis, A. (1962). *Reason and emotion in psychotherapy.* New York: Stuart.

Ellis, A., & Knaus, W. (1977). *Overcoming procrastination.* New York: Institute for Rational Living.

*Epstein, M.L. (1980). The relationship of mental imagery and mental practice to performance on a motor task. *Journal of Sport Psychology, 2,* 211-220.

Ericsson, K.A. (2003). Development of elite performance and deliberate practice: An update from the perspective of the expert performance approach. In J.L. Starkes & K.A. Ericsson (Eds.), *Expert performance in sports: Advances in research on sport expertise* (pp. 49-84). Champaign, IL: Human Kinetics.

Eyal, N. (2001). Reflections on sport psychology practice: A clinical perspective. In G. Tenenbaum (Ed.), *The practice of sport psychology* (pp. 169-196). Morgantown, WV: Fitness Information Technology.

Fairburn, C.G., & Beglin, S.J. (1994). Assessment of eating disorders: Interview or self-report questionnaire? *International Journal of Eating Disorders, 16,* 363-370.

Fairburn, C.G., & Cooper, P.J. (1993). The eating disorder examination. In C.G. Fairburn & G.T. Wilson (Eds.), *Binge eating: Nature, assessment, and treatment* (pp. 317-360). New York: Guilford Press.

Fairburn, C.G., Norman, P.A., Welch, S.L., O'Connor, M.E., Doll, H.A., & Peveler, R.C. (1995). A prospective study of outcome in bulimia nervosa and the long-term effects of three psychological treatments. *Archives of General Psychiatry, 52,* 304-312.

Farber, A. (2003). Self-disclosure in psychotherapy practice and supervision. *Journal of Clinical Psychology, 59* (5), 525-528.

Faulkner, K.K., & Faulkner, T.A. (1997). Managing multiple relationships in rural communities: Neutrality and boundary violations. *Clinical Psychology: Science and Practice, 4* (3), 225-234.

Feltz, D., & Landers, D. (1983). Effects of mental practice on motor skill learning and performance: A meta-analysis. *Journal of Sport Psychology, 5,* 25-57.

*Filby, W.C.D., Maynard, I.W., & Graydon, J.K. (1999). The effect of multiple-goal strategies on performance outcomes in training and competition. *Journal of Applied Sport Psychology, 11* (2), 230-246.

Finney, J.W., & Moos, R.H. (2002). Psychosocial treatments for alcohol use disorders. In P.E. Nathan & J.M. Gorman (Eds.), *A guide to treatments that work* (2nd ed., pp. 157-168). New York: Oxford University Press.

First, M.B., Spitzer, R.L., Gibbon, M., & Williams, J.B.W. (1995). The Structured Clinical Interview for *DSM-III-R* Personality Disorders (SCID-II): Part I. Description. *Journal of Personality Disorders, 9,* 83-91.

First, M.B., Spitzer, R.L., Gibbon, M., & Williams, J.B.W. (1997). *User's guide for the Structured Clinical Interview for DSM-IV Axis I Disorders—Clinician version (SCID-I).* New York: New York State Psychiatric Institute.

Fisher, C.B., & Younggren, J.N. (1997). The value and utility of the 1992 Ethics Code. *Professional Psychology: Research and Practice, 28* (6), 582-592.

Fishman, D.B., & Franks, C.M. (1997). The conceptual evolution of behavior therapy. In P.L. Wachtel & S.B. Messer (Eds.), *Theories of psychotherapy: Origins and evolution* (pp. 131-180). Washington, DC: American Psychological Association.

Fischman, M.G., & Oxendine, J.B. (1998). Motor skill learning for effective coaching and performance. In J.M. Williams (Ed.), *Applied sport psychology: Personal growth to peak performance* (3rd ed., pp. 13-27). Mountain View, CA: Mayfield.

Fitts, P., & Posner, M.I. (1967). *Human performance.* Belmont, CA: Brooks/Cole.

Foa, E.B., & Franklin, M.E. (2001). Obsessive-Compulsive Disorder. In D.H. Barlow (Ed.), *Clinical handbook of psychological disorders* (3rd ed., pp. 209-263). New York: Guilford Press.

Foa, E.B., Riggs, D.S., Dancu, C.V., & Rothbaum, B.O. (1993). Reliability and validity of a brief instrument for assessing post-traumatic stress disorder. *Journal of Traumatic Stress, 6,* 459-474.

Foa, E.B., & Rothbaum, B.O. (1998). *Treating the trauma of rape: Cognitive-behavioral therapy for PTSD.* New York: Guilford Press.

Foa, E.B., Steketee, G.S., & Rothbaum, B.O. (1989). Behavioral/cognitive conceptualizations of post-traumatic stress disorder. *Behavior Therapy, 20,* 155-176.

Follette, V.M., Ruzek, J.I., & Abueg, F.R. (Eds.). (1998). *Cognitive-behavioral therapies for trauma.* New York: Guilford Press.

Forsberg, L., Halldin, J., & Wennberg, P. (2003). Psychometric properties and factor structure of the Readiness for Change Questionnaire. *Alcohol and Alcoholism, 38* (3), 276-280.

Franklin, M.E., & Foa, E.B. (2002). Cognitive behavioral treatments for obsessive-compulsive disorder. In P.E. Nathan & J.M. Gorman, *A guide to treatments that work* (2nd ed., pp. 367-386). New York: Oxford University Press.

Freeston, M.H., Dugas, M.J., & Ladouceur, R. (1996). Thoughts, images, worry, and anxiety. *Cognitive Therapy and Research, 20* (3), 265-273.

Freund, B., Steketee, G.S., & Foa, E.B. (1987). Compulsive Activity Checklist (CAC): Psychometric analysis with obsessive-compulsive disorder. *Behavioral Assessment, 9,* 67-79.

Gallagher, B., & Gardner, F.L. (2005). *The relationship between early maladaptive schemas and affective and behavioral responses to injury in collegiate athletes.* Manuscript submitted for publication.

Gardner, F. (1980). Comparison of behavioral and cognitive-behavioral therapies for social anxiety. *Dissertation Abstracts, 40,* 1526.

Gardner, F.L. (1991). Professionalization of sport psychology: A reply to Silva. *The Sport Psychologist, 5* (1), 55-60.

Gardner, F.L. (1995). The coach and the team psychologist: An integrated organizational model. In S.M. Murphy (Ed.), *Sport psychology interventions* (pp. 147-175). Champaign, IL: Human Kinetics.

Gardner, F.L. (2001). Applied sport psychology in professional sports: The team psychologist. *Professional Psychology: Research and Practice, 32* (1), 34-39.

Gardner, F.L. (2003, August). Supervisory issues in externship training: Perspectives of a practicum supervisor. In F.L. Gardner (Chair), *Supervisor and supervisee perspectives on externship and internship training.* Symposium conducted at the meeting of the Annual Conference of the American Psychological Association, Toronto.

Gardner, F.L., & Moore, Z.E. (2001, October). *The Multi-level Classification System for Sport Psychology (MCS-SP): Toward a structured assessment and conceptualization of athlete-clients.* Workshop presented at the annual conference of the Association for the Advancement of Applied Sport Psychology, Orlando, FL.

Gardner, F.L., & Moore, Z.E. (2003, August). *Theoretical foundation for Mindfulness-Acceptance-Commitment (MAC) based performance enhancement.* Paper presented at the meeting of the Annual Conference of the American Psychological Association, Toronto.

Gardner, F.L., & Moore, Z.E. (2004a). A Mindfulness-Acceptance-Commitment (MAC) based approach to athletic performance enhancement: Theoretical considerations. *Behavior Therapy, 35,* 707-723.

Gardner, F.L., & Moore, Z.E. (2004b). The Multi-level Classification System for Sport Psychology (MCS-SP). *The Sport Psychologist, 18* (1), 89-109.

Gardner, F.L., & Moore, Z.E. (2005a). *Integrating clinical and sport science: The Integrative Model of Athletic Performance (IMAP).* Manuscript submitted for publication.

Gardner, F.L., & Moore, Z.E. (2005b). *New Developments in the Conceptualization and Treatment of Clinical Anger: Anger Regulation Therapy.* Manuscript submitted for publication.

Gardner, F.L., & Moore, Z.E. (2005c). *The role of professional development and supervision in the training of sport psychologists.* Manuscript submitted for publication.

Gardner, F.L., Moore, Z.E., & Wolanin, A. (2003, October). *Innovations in performance enhancement: The Mindfulness-Acceptance-Commitment based approach to enhancing competitive performance.* Symposium conducted at the meeting of the Annual Conference of the Association for the Advancement of Applied Sport Psychology, Philadelphia.

Gardner, F.L., Moore, Z.E., & Wolanin, A.T. (2004, July). *Efficacy and mechanisms of change in cognitive behavioral interventions for athletic performance enhancement: From change based to mindfulness and acceptance based strategies.* Symposium conducted at the meeting of the World Congress of Behavioral and Cognitive Therapies, Kobe, Japan.

Gardner, F.L., Taylor, J., Zinnser, N., & Ravizza, K. (2000, October). *Applied sport psychology interventions.* Symposium conducted at the meeting of the Annual Conference of the Association for the Advancement of Applied Sport Psychology, Nashville, TN.

Gardner, F.L., Wolanin, A.T., & Moore, Z.E. (2005). *Mindfulness-Acceptance-Commitment (MAC) based performance enhancement for Division I collegiate athletes: A preliminary investigation.* Manuscript submitted for publication.

Garfield, S.L. (1996). Some problems with "validated" forms of psychotherapy. *Clinical Psychology: Science and Practice, 3,* 218-229.

Garner, D.M. (1991). *Eating Disorders Inventory-2.* Odessa, FL: Psychological Assessment Resources.

Geller, N.L., & Proschan, M. (1996). Meta-analysis of clinical trials: A consumer's guide. *Journal of Biopharmaceutical Statistics, 6* (4), 377-394.

*Giannini, J.M., Weinberg, R.S., & Jackson, A.J. (1988). The effects of mastery, competitive, and cooperative goals on the performance of simple and complex basketball skills. *Journal of Sport and Exercise Psychology, 10* (4), 408-417.

Giges, B. (2000). Removing psychological barriers: Clearing the way. In M.B. Andersen (Ed.), *Doing sport psychology* (pp. 17-32). Champaign, IL: Human Kinetics.

Gillies, L.A. (2001). Interpersonal psychotherapy for depression and other disorders. In D.H. Barlow (Ed.), *Clinical handbook of psychological disorders* (3rd ed., 309-331). New York: Guilford Press.

Glosoff, H.L., Herlihy, S.B., Herlihy, B., & Spence, E.B. (1997). Privileged communication in the psychologist-client relationship. *Professional Psychology: Research and Practice, 28* (6), 573-581.

Gomes-Schwartz, B., Hadley, S.W., & Strupp, H.H. (1978). Individual psychotherapy and behavior therapy. *Annual Review of Psychology, 29,* 435-472.

Goodman, W.K., Price, L.H., Rasmussen, S.A., Mazure, C., Fleischmann, R.L., Hill, C.L., Heninger, G.R., & Charney, D.S. (1989). The Yale-Brown Obsessive-Compulsive Scale: I. Development, use, and reliability. *Archives of General Psychiatry, 46,* 1006-1011.

Goodman, W.K., Price, L.H., Rasmussen, S.A., Mazure, C., Delgado, P., Heninger, G.R., & Charney, D.S. (1989). The Yale-Brown Obsessive-Compulsive Scale: II. Validity. *Archives of General Psychiatry, 46,* 1012-1016.

Gordin, R.D., & Henschen, K.P. (1989). Preparing the USA women's artistic gymnastics team for the 1988 Olympics: A multi-modal approach. *The Sport Psychologist, 3,* 366-373.

Gordon, S. (1990). A mental skills training program for the Western Australian cricket team. *The Sport Psychologist, 4,* 386-399.

Gordon, S. (1995). Career transitions in competitive sport. In T. Morris & J. Summers (Eds.), *Sport psychology: Theory, applications and issues* (pp. 474-501). Brisbane, Australia: Jacaranda Wiley.

Gormally, J., Black, S., Daston, S., & Rardin, D. (1982). The assessment of binge-eating severity among obese persons. *Addictive Behaviors, 7,* 47-55.

Gould, D. (1998). Goal setting for peak performance. In J.M. Williams (Ed.), *Applied sport psychology: Personal growth to peak performance* (pp. 182-196). Mountain View, CA: Mayfield.

Gould, D., Damarjian, N., & Greenleaf, C. (2002). Imagery training for peak performance. In J.L. Van Raalte & B.W. Brewer (Eds.), *Exploring sport and exercise psychology* (2nd ed., pp. 49-74). Washington. DC: American Psychological Association.

Gould, D., Eklund, R.C., & Jackson, S.A. (1992). 1988 U.S. Olympic wrestling excellence: I. Mental preparation, precompetitive cognition, and affect. *The Sport Psychologist, 6,* 358-382.

Gould, D., & Krane, V. (1992). The arousal-athletic performance relationship: Current status and future directions. In T.S. Horn (Ed.), *Advances in sport psychology* (pp. 119-142). Champaign, IL: Human Kinetics.

Gould, R.A., Otto, M.W., & Pollack, M.H. (1995). A meta-analysis of treatment outcome for panic disorder. *Clinical Psychology Review, 15,* 819-844.

Gould, D., & Udry, E. (1994). Psychological skills for enhancing performance: Arousal regulation strate-gies. *Medicine and Science in Sport and Exercise, 26* (4), 478-485.

*Gould, D., Weinberg, R., & Jackson, A. (1980). Mental preparation strategies, cognitions, and strength performance. *Journal of Sport Psychology, 2* (4), 329-339.

Gould, D., Weiss, M., & Weinberg, R. (1981). Psychological characteristics of successful and nonsuccessful Big Ten wrestlers. *Journal of Sport Psychology, 3,* 69-81.

Granito, V.J., & Wenz, B.J. (1995). Reading list for professional issues in applied sport psychology. *The Sport Psychologist, 9* (1), 96-103.

*Gravel, R., Lemieux, G., & Ladouceur, R. (1980). Effectiveness of a cognitive behavioral treatment package for cross-country ski racers. *Cognitive Therapy and Research, 4* (1), 83-89.

Greenhill, L.L., & Ford, R.E. (2002). Childhood attention-deficit hyperactivity disorder: Pharmacological treatments. In P.E. Nathan & J.M. Gorman (Eds.), *A guide to treatments that work* (2nd ed., pp. 25-55). New York: Oxford University Press.

Greenspan, M.J., & Feltz, D.L. (1989). Psychological interventions with athletes in competitive situations: A review. *The Sport Psychologist, 3,* 219-236.

Griffin, N., Chassin, L., & Young, R.D. (1981). Measurement of global self-concept versus multiple role-specific self-concepts in adolescents. *Adolescence, 16,* 49-56.

Groth-Marnat, G. (1999). *Handbook of psychological assessment* (3rd ed.). New York: Wiley.

*Grouios, G. (1992). The effect of mental practice on diving performance. *International Journal of Sport Psychology, 23,* 60-69.

Grove, J.R., Lavallee, D., & Gordon, S. (1997). Coping with retirement from sport: The influence of athletic identity. *Journal of Applied Sport Psychology, 9,* 191-203.

Grove, W.M., Zald, D.H., Lebow, B.S., Snitz, B.E., & Nelson, C. (2000). Clinical versus mechanical prediction: A meta-analysis. *Psychological Assessment, 12* (1), 19-30.

Hall, C.R. (2001). Imagery in sport and exercise. In R.N. Singer, H.A. Hausenblaus, & C.M. Janelle (Eds.), *Handbook of sport psychology* (2nd ed., pp. 529-549). New York: Wiley.

*Hall, E.G., & Erffmeyer, E.S. (1983). The effect of visuomotor behavior research with videotaped modeling on free throw accuracy of intercollegiate female basketball players. *Journal of Sport Psychology, 5,* 343-346.

*Hall, H.K., Weinberg, R.S., & Jackson, A. (1987). Effects of goal specificity, goal difficulty, and information feedback on endurance performance. *Journal of Sport Psychology, 9,* 43-54.

Halliwell, W. (1990). Providing sport psychology consulting services in professional hockey. *The Sport Psychologist, 4* (4), 369-377.

Hanin, Y.L. (1980). A study of anxiety in sport. In W.F. Straub (Ed.), *Sport psychology: An analysis of athlete behavior* (pp. 236-249). Ithaca, NY: Movement Publications.

Hardy, L., Jones, G., & Gould, D. (1996). *Understanding psychological preparation for sport: Theory and practice of elite performers.* New York: Wiley.

Hatfield, B.D., Landers, D.M., & Ray, W.J. (1984). Cognitive processes during self-paced motor performance: An electroencephalographic profile of skilled marksmen. *Journal of Sport Psychology, 6,* 42-59.

*Hatzigeorgiadis, A., Theodorakis, Y., & Zourbanos, N. (2004). Self-talk in the swimming pool: The effects of self-talk on thought content and performance on water-polo tasks. *Journal of Applied Sport Psychology, 16,* 138-150.

Hayes, A.M., & Feldman, G. (2004). Clarifying the construct of mindfulness in the context of emotion regulation and the process of change in therapy. *Clinical Psychology: Science and Practice, 11* (3), 255-262.

Hayes, S.C., Jacobson, N.S., Follette, V.M., & Dougher, M.J. (Eds.). (1994). *Acceptance and change: Content and context in psychotherapy.* Reno, NV: Context Press.

Hayes, S.C., Masuda, A., & De May, H. (2003). Acceptance and Commitment Therapy and the third wave of behavior therapy (Acceptance and Commitment Therapy: een derde-generatie gedragstherapie). *Gedragstherapie (Dutch Journal of Behavior Therapy), 2,* 69-96.

Hayes, S.C., Strosahl, K., & Wilson, K.G. (1999). Acceptance and commitment therapy: An experiential approach to behavior change. New York: Guilford Press.

Hayes, S.C., Wilson, K.G., Gifford, E.V., Follette, V.M., & Strosahl, K. (1996). Experiential avoidance and behavioral disorders: A functional dimensional approach to diagnosis and treatment. *Journal of Consulting and Clinical Psychology, 64,* 1152-1168.

Hays, K.F. (2000). Breaking out: Doing sport psychology with performing artists. In M.B. Andersen (Ed.), *Doing sport psychology* (pp. 261-274). Champaign, IL: Human Kinetics.

Heimberg, R.G., Hope, D.A., Dodge, C.S., & Becker, R.E. (1990). *DSM-III-R* subtypes of social phobia: Comparison of generalized social phobics and public speaking phobics. *Journal of Nervous and Mental Disease, 178,* 172-179.

Heimberg, R.G., Liebowitz, M.R., Hope, D.A., Schneier, F.R., Holt, C.S., Welkowtiz, L.A., Juster, H.R., Campeas, R., Bruch, M.A., Cloitre, M., Fallon, B., & Klein, D.F. (1998). Cognitive behavioral group therapy vs. phenelzine therapy for social phobia: 12-week outcome. *Archives of General Psychiatry, 55,* 1133-1141.

Helzer, J.E., Robins, L.N., Croughan, J.L., & Welner, A. (1981). Renard Diagnostic Interview: Its reliability and procedural validity with physicians and lay interviewers. *Archives of General Psychiatry, 38,* 393-398.

Henry, M., & Renaud, H. (1972). Examined and unexamined lives. *Research Reporter, 7* (1), 5.

Henry, W.P. (1998). Science, politics, and the politics of science: The use and misuse of empirically validated treatments. *Psychotherapy Research, 8,* 126-140.

Henry, W.P., Schacht, T.E., & Strupp, H.H. (1986). Structural analysis of social behavior: Application to a study of interpersonal process in differential psychotherapeutic outcome. *Journal of Consulting and Clinical Psychology, 54,* 27-31.

Henschen, K.P. (1998). The issue behind the issue. In M.A. Thompson, R.A. Vernacchia, & W.E. Moore (Eds.), *Case studies in sport psychology: An educational approach* (pp. 27-34). Dubuque, IA: Kendall/Hunt.

Herjanic, B., & Campbell, W. (1977). Differentiating psychiatrically disturbed children on the basis of a structured interview. *Journal of Abnormal Child Psychology, 51,* 127-134.

Heyman, S.R., & Andersen, M.B. (1998). When to refer athletes for counseling or psychotherapy. In J.M. Williams (Ed.), *Applied sport psychology: Personal growth to peak performance* (pp. 359-371). Mountain View, CA: Mayfield.

Hill, K.L. (2001). *Frameworks for sport psychologists: Enhancing sport performance.* Champaign, IL: Human Kinetics.

Hill, P., & Lowe, B. (1974). The inevitable metathesis of the retiring athlete. *International Review of Sport Psychology, 9,* 5-29.

Hines, A.H., Ader, D.N., Chang, A.S., & Rundell, J.R. (1998). Dual agency, dual relationships, boundary crossings and associated boundary violations: A survey of military and civilian psychiatrists. *Military Medicine, 163* (12), 826-833.

Hinshaw, K. (1991). The effects of mental practice on motor skill performance: Critical evaluation and meta-analysis. *Imagination, Cognition, and Personality, 11,* 3-35.

Hinshaw, S.P., Klein, R.G., & Abikoff, H.B. (2002). Childhood attention-deficit hyperactivity disorder: Nonpharmacological treatments and their combination with medication. In P.E. Nathan & J.M. Gorman (Eds.), *A guide to treatments that work* (2nd ed., pp. 3-23). New York: Oxford University Press.

*Hird, J.S., Landers, D.M., Thomas, J.R., & Horan, J.J. (1991). Physical practice is superior to mental practice in enhancing cognitive and motor task performance. *Journal of Sport and Exercise Psychology, 13,* 281-293.

Hiss, H., Foa, E.B., & Kozak, M.J. (1994). A relapse prevention program for treatment of obsessive-compulsive disorder. *Journal of Consulting and Clinical Psychology, 62,* 801-818.

Hodgins, D.C., & Diskin, K.M. (2003). Alcohol problems. In M. Hersen & S.M. Turner (Eds.), *Diagnostic interviewing* (2nd ed., pp. 203-222). New York: Kluwer Academic/Plenum Publishers.

Hofmann, S.G., & Barlow, D.H. (2002). Social phobia (social anxiety disorder). In D.H. Barlow (Ed.), *Anxiety and its disorders: The nature and treatment of anxiety and panic* (2nd ed., pp. 454-476). New York: Guilford Press.

Hogan, R., Hogan, J., & Roberts, B.W. (1996). Personality measurement and employment decisions: Questions and answers. *American Psychologist, 51,* 469-477.

*Hollingsworth, B. (1975). Effects of performance goals and anxiety on learning a gross motor task. *Research Quarterly, 46,* 162-168.

*Holm, J.E., Beckwith, B.E., Ehde, D.M., & Tinius, T.P. (1996). Cognitive-behavioral interventions for improving performance in competitive athletes: A controlled treatment outcome study. *International Journal of Sport Psychology, 27* (4), 463-475.

Hopkins, H.S., & Gelenberg, A.J. (1994). Treatment of bipolar disorder—How far have we come? *Psychopharmacology Bulletin, 30,* 27-37.

Hopson, B., & Adams, J. (1977). Toward an understanding of termination: Defining some boundaries of termination. In J. Adams, J. Hayes, & B. Hopson (Eds.), *Transition: Understanding and managing personal change* (pp. 3-25). Montclair, NJ: Allanheld & Osmun.

Horvath, A.O. (1994). Research on the alliance. In A.O. Horvath & L.S. Greenberg (Eds.), *The working alliance: Theory, research, and practice* (pp. 259-286). Oxford, England: Wiley.

Horvath, A.O., & Greenberg, L.S. (1989). Development and validation of the Working Alliance Inventory. *Journal of Counseling Psychology, 36* (2), 223-233.

Horvath, A.O., & Symonds, B.D. (1991). Relation between working alliance and outcome in psychotherapy: A meta-analysis. *Journal of Counseling Psychology, 38,* 139-149.

*Howard, W.L., & Reardon, J.P. (1986). Changes in the self-concept and athletic performance of weight lifters through a cognitive-hypnotic approach: An empirical study. *American Journal of Clinical Hypnosis, 28* (4), 248-257.

Hsu, L.K.G. (1990). *Eating disorders.* New York: Guilford Press.

*Isaac, A.R. (1992). Mental practice—Does it work in the field? *The Sport Psychologist, 6* (2), 192-198.

Jacobson, N.S., Dobson, K.S., Fruzetti, A.E., Schmaling, K.B., & Salusky, S. (1991). Marital therapy as a treatment for depression. *Journal of Consulting and Clinical Psychology, 59,* 547-557.

Jacobson, N.S., Dobson, K.S., Truax, P.A., Addis, M.E., Koerner, K., Gollan, J.K., Gortner, E., & Prince, S.E. (1996). A component analysis of cognitive-behavioral treatment for depression. *Journal of Consulting and Clinical Psychology, 64,* 295-304.

Janelle, C.M., Hillman, C.H., Apparies, R.J., Murray, N.P., Meili, L., Fallon, E.A., & Hatfield, B.D. (2000). Expertise differences in cortical activation and gaze behavior during rifle shooting. *Journal of Sport and Exercise Psychology, 22,* 167-182.

Janelle, C.M., Hillman, C.H., & Hatfield, B.D. (2000). Concurrent measurement of electroencephalographic and ocular indices of attention during rifle shooting: An exploratory case study. *International Journal of Sport Vision, 6,* 21-29.

*Johnson, J.J.M., Hrycaiko, D.W., Johnson, G.V., & Halas, J.M. (2004). Self-talk and female youth soccer performance. *The Sport Psychologist, 18,* 44-59.

*Johnson, S.R., Ostrow, A.C., Perna, F.M., & Etzel, E.F. (1997). The effects of group versus individual goal setting on bowling performance. *The Sport Psychologist, 11* (2), 190-200.

Johnson, W.B. (1995). Perennial ethical quandaries in military psychology: Toward American Psychological Association-Department of Defense collaboration. *Professional Psychology: Research and Practice, 26* (3), 281-287.

Jones, G., Hanton, S., & Swain, A.B.J. (1994). Intensity and interpretation of anxiety symptoms in elite and non-elite sports performers. *Personality and Individual Differences, 17,* 657-663.

Jones, G., Swain, A.B.J., & Hardy, L. (1993). Intensity and direction dimensions of competitive state anxiety and relationships with performance. *Journal of Sport Sciences, 11,* 525-532.

Jones, J.C., Bruce, T.J., & Barlow, D.H. (1986, November). *The effects of four levels of "anxiety" on sexual arousal in sexually functional and dysfunctional men.* Poster session presented at the 20th Annual Convention of the Association for Advancement of Behavior Therapy, Chicago.

Jones, L., & Stuth, G. (1997). The uses of mental imagery in athletics: An overview. *Applied and Preventive Psychology, 6,* 101-115.

Kabat-Zinn, J., Massion, A.O., Kristeller, J., Peterson, L.G., Fletcher, K.E., Pbert, L., Lenderking, W.R., & Santorelli, S.F. (1992). Effectiveness of a meditation-based stress reduction program in the treatment of anxiety disorders. *American Journal of Psychiatry, 149,* 936-943.

Kabat-Zinn, J. (1994). *Wherever you go there you are.* New York: Hyperion.

Kagle, J.D., & Giebelhausen, P.N. (1994). Dual relationships and professional boundaries. *Social Work, 39* (2), 213-220.

Kanfer, F.H., & Schefft, B.K. (1988). *Guiding the process of therapeutic change.* Champaign, IL: Research Press.

Kassinove, H., & Sukhodolsky, D.G. (1995). Anger disorders: Basic science and practice issues. In H. Kassinove (Ed.), *Anger disorders: Definition, diagnosis, and treatment* (pp. 1-26). Washington, DC: Taylor & Francis.

Kassinove, H., & Tafrate, R.C. (2002). *Anger management: The complete treatment guidebook for practitioners.* Atascadero, CA: Impact Publishers.

Kazdin, A.E. (1998). *Research design in clinical psychology* (3rd ed.). Boston: Allyn & Bacon.

Kazdin, A.E. (2000). *Research design in clinical psychology* (4th ed.). New York: Allyn & Bacon.

Kazdin, A.E. (2001). *Behavior modification in applied settings* (6th ed.). Belmont, CA: Wadsworth.

Kendall, P.C., & Chambless, D.L. (Eds.). (1998). Empirically supported psychological therapies [Special issue]. *Journal of Consulting and Clinical Psychology, 66.*

*Kendall, G., Hrycaiko, D., Martin, G.L., & Kendall, T. (1990). The effects of an imagery rehearsal, relaxation, and self-talk package on basketball game performance. *Journal of Sport and Exercise Psychology, 12* (2), 157-166.

Kessler, R.C., McGonagle, K.A., Zhao, S., Nelson, C.B., Hughes, M., Eshelman, S., Wittchen, H.U., & Kendler, K.S. (1994). Lifetime and 12-month prevalence of *DSM-III-R* psychiatric disorders in the United States: Results from the National Comorbidity Survey. *Archives of General Psychiatry, 51,* 8-19.

Kessler, R., Sonnega, A., Bromet, E. Hughes, M., & Nelson, C. (1995). Post-traumatic stress disorder in the National Comorbidity Survey. *Archives of General Psychiatry, 52,* 1048-1060.

Kirk, A.B., & Madden, L.L. (2003). Trauma related critical incident debriefing for adolescents. *Child and Adolescent Social Work Journal, 20* (2), 123-134.

Kirkpatrick, D. (1982). Success conflict 65 years later: Contributions and confusions. *Canadian Journal of Psychiatry, 27,* 405-409.

*Kirschenbaum, D.S., Owens, D., O'Connor, E.A. (1998). Smart golf: Preliminary evaluation of a simple, yet comprehensive, approach to improving and scoring the mental game. *The Sport Psychologist, 12* (3), 271-282.

Kleiber, D.A., Greendorfer, S.L., Blinde, E., & Samdahl, D. (1987). Quality of exit from university sports and subsequent life satisfaction. *Sociology of Sport Journal, 4,* 28-36.

Kleinmuntz, B. (1990). Why we still use our heads instead of formulas: Toward an integrative approach. *Psychological Bulletin, 107,* 296-310.

Klerman, G.L., & Weissman, M.M. (1993). Interpersonal psychotherapy for depression: Background and concepts. In G.L. Klerman & M.M. Weissman (Eds.), *New applications of interpersonal psychotherapy* (pp. 3-26). Washington, DC: American Psychiatric Press.

Klinger, E., Barta, S.G., & Glas, R.A. (1981). Thought content and gap time in basketball. *Cognitive Therapy and Research, 5* (1), 109-114.

Koenigsberg, H.W., Woo-Ming, A.M., & Siever, L.J. (2002). Pharmacological treatments for personality disorders. In P.E. Nathan & J.M. Gorman (Eds.), *A guide to treatments that work* (2nd ed., pp. 625-641). New York: Oxford University Press.

Kohlenberg, R.J., & Tsai, M. (1995). Functional analytic psychotherapy: Behavioral approach to intensive treatment. In W.T. O'Donohue & L. Krasner (Eds.), *Theories of behavior therapy: Exploring behavior change* (pp. 637-658). Washington, DC: American Psychological Association.

Konkol, R.J., & Olsen, G.D. (Eds.). (1996). *Prenatal cocaine exposure.* Boca Raton, FL: CRC Press.

Kozak, M.J., Liebowitz, M.R., & Foa, E.B. (2000). Cognitive-behavior therapy and pharmacotherapy for OCD: The NIMH-sponsored collaborative study. In W. Goodman, M. Rudorfer, & J. Maser (Eds.), *Obsessive-compulsive disorder: Contemporary issues in treatment* (pp. 501-530). Mahwah, NJ: Erlbaum.

Kubler-Ross, E. (1969). *On death and dying.* New York: Macmillan.

Kyllo, L.B., & Landers, D.M. (1995). Goal setting in sport and exercise: A research synthesis to resolve the controversy. *Journal of Sport and Exercise Psychology, 17,* 117-137.

Lachmund, E., & DiGiuseppe, R. (1997, August). How clinicians assess anger: Do we need an anger diagnosis? In R. DiGuiseppe (Chair), *Advances in the diagnosis, assessment, and treatment of angry clients.* Symposium conducted at the 105th Annual Convention of the American Psychological Association, Chicago.

*Landin, D., & Hebert, E.P. (1999). The influence of self-talk on the performance of skilled female tennis players. *Journal of Applied Sport Psychology, 11* (2), 263-282.

*Lane, A., & Streeter, B. (2003). The effectiveness of goal setting as a strategy to improve basketball shooting performance. *International Journal of Sport Psychology, 34,* 138-150.

Lauterbach, D., & Vrana, S. (1996). Three studies on the reliability and validity of a self-report measure of posttraumatic stress disorder. *Assessment, 3,* 17-25.

Lavallee, D., Nesti, M., Borkoles, E., Cockerill, I., & Edge, A. (2000). Intervention strategies for athletes in transition. In D. Lavallee & P. Wylleman (Eds.), *Career transitions in sport: International perspectives* (pp. 111-130). Morgantown, MV: Fitness Information Technology.

Lavallee, D., Gordon, S., & Grove, J.R. (1997). Retirement from sport and the loss of athletic identity. *Journal of Personal and Interpersonal Loss, 2,* 129-147.

Leahy, T. (2001). Reflections of a feminist sport psychologist. In G. Tenenbaum (Ed.), *The practice of sport psychology* (pp. 37-47). Morgantown, WV: Fitness Information Technology.

*Lee, C. (1990). Psyching up for a muscular endurance task: Effects of image content on performance and mood state. *Journal of Sport and Exercise Psychology, 12,* 66-73.

*Lee, A.B., & Hewitt, J. (1987). Using visual imagery in a flotation tank to improve gymnastic performance and reduce physical symptoms. *International Journal of Sport Psychology, 18,* 223-230.

*Lerner, B.S., & Locke, E.A. (1995). The effects of goal setting, self-efficacy, competition, and personal traits on the performance of an endurance task. *Journal of Sport and Exercise Psychology, 17,* 138-152.

*Lerner, B.S., Ostrow, A.C., Yura, M.T., & Etzel, E.F. (1996). The effects of goal-setting and imagery training programs on the free-throw performance of female collegiate basketball players. *The Sport Psychologist, 10,* 382-397.

*Li-Wei, Z., Qi-Wei, M., Orlick, T., & Zitzelsberger, L. (1992). The effect of mental-imagery training on performance enhancement with 7-10-year old children. *The Sport Psychologist, 6* (3), 230-241.

Lilienfeld, S.O., Lynn, S.J., & Lohr, J.M. (2003). Science and pseudoscience in clinical psychology: Initial thoughts, reflections, and considerations. In S.O. Lilienfeld, S.J. Lynn, & J.M. Lohr (Eds.), *Science and pseudoscience in clinical psychology* (pp. 1-14). New York: Guilford Press.

Linder, D.E., Pillow, D.R., & Reno, R.R. (1989). Shrinking jocks: Derogation of athletes who consult a sport psychologist. *Journal of Sport and Exercise Psychology, 11* (3), 270-280.

Linehan, M.M., Cochran, B.N., & Kehrer, C.A. (2001). Dialectical behavior therapy for borderline personality disorder. In D.H. Barlow (Ed.), *Clinical handbook of psychological disorders* (3rd ed., pp. 470-522). New York: Guilford Press.

Little, L.M., & Simpson, T.L. (2000). An acceptance based performance enhancement intervention for collegiate athletes. In M.J. Dougher (Ed.), *Clinical behavior analysis* (pp. 231-244). Reno, NV: Context Press.

Litz, B.T., Gray, M.J., Bryant, R.A., & Adler, A.B. (2002). Early intervention for trauma: Current status and future directions. *Clinical Psychology: Science and Practice, 9*, 112-134.

Lodato, F.J., & Lodato, J.E. (1992). An ethical model for sport psychologists. *Revista Interamericana de Psicologia, 26* (1), 99-102.

*Lohr, B.A., & Scogin, F. (1998). Effects of self-administered visuo-motor behavioral rehearsal on sport performance of collegiate athletes. *Journal of Sport Behavior, 21* (2), 206-218.

Luborsky, L. (1984). *Principles of psychoanalytic psychotherapy: A manual for supportive-expressive treatment.* New York: Basic Books.

Mack, A.H., & Frances, R.J. (2003). Treatment of alcohol use disorders in adolescents. *Journal of Psychiatric Practice, 9* (3), 195-208.

*Madden, G., & McGown, C. (1988). The effect of hemisphericity, imagery, and relaxation on volleyball performance. *Journal of Human Movement Studies, 14*, 197-204.

Magee, W.J., Eaton, W.W., Wittchen, H.U., McGonagle, K.A., & Kessler, R.C. (1996). Agoraphobia, simple phobia, and social phobia in the National Comorbidity Survey. *Archives of General Psychiatry, 53*, 159-168.

Mahoney, M.J. (1974). *Cognition and behavior modification.* Cambridge, MA: Ballinger.

Martens, R. (1977). *Sport competition anxiety test.* Champaign, IL: Human Kinetics.

Martens, R. (1987). Science, knowledge, and sport psychology. *The Sport Psychologist, 1* (1), 29-55.

Martens, R., Burton, D., Vealey, R.S., Bump, L.A., & Smith, D.E. (1990). Development and validation of the Competitive State Anxiety Inventory-2. In R. Martens, R.S. Vealey, & D. Burtons (Eds.), *Competitive anxiety in sport* (pp. 117-190). Champaign, IL: Human Kinetics.

Martin, D.J., Garske, J.P., & Davis, M.K. (2000). Relation of the therapeutic alliance with outcome and other variables: A meta-analytic review. *Journal of Consulting and Clinical Psychology, 68*, 438-450.

Marx, B.P., & Sloan, D.M. (2002). The role of emotion in the psychological functioning of adult survivors of childhood sexual abuse. *Behavior Therapy, 33* (4), 563-577.

Mattick, R.P., & Clarke, J.C. (1998). Development and validation of measures of social phobia scrutiny fear and social interaction anxiety. *Behaviour Research and Therapy, 36*, 455-470.

Maude-Griffin, P.M., Hohenstein, J.M., Humfleet, G.L., Reilly, P.M., Tusel, D.J., & Hall, S.M. (1998). Superior efficacy of cognitive-behavioral therapy for urban crack cocaine abusers: Main and matching efforts. *Journal of Consulting and Clinical Psychology, 66*, 832-837.

*Maynard, I.W., Hemmings, B., & Warwick-Evans, L. (1995). The effects of a somatic intervention on competitive state anxiety and performance in semi-professional soccer players. *The Sport Psychologist, 9*, 51-64.

*Maynard, I.W., Smith, M.J., & Warwick-Evans, L. (1995). The effects of a cognitive intervention strategy on competitive state anxiety and performance in semi-professional soccer players. *Journal of Sport and Exercise Psychology, 17* (4), 428-446.

Mayou, R.A., Ehlers, A., & Hobbs, M. (2000). Psychological debriefing for road and traffic accident victims. *British Journal of Psychiatry, 176*, 589-593.

McCrady, B.S. (2001). Alcohol use disorders. In D.H. Barlow (Ed.), *Clinical handbook of psychological disorders* (3rd ed., pp. 376-433). New York: Guilford Press.

McCullough, J.P., Jr. (2000). *Treatment for chronic depression: Cognitive behavioral analysis system of psychotherapy (CBASP).* New York: Guilford Press.

McGuire, J. (1997). Ethical dilemmas in forensic clinical psychology. *Legal and Criminological Psychology, 2* (2), 177-192.

McLellan, A.T., Luborsky, L., O'Brien, C.P., & Woody, G.E. (1980). An improved diagnostic instrument for substance abuse patients: The Addiction Severity Index. *Journal of Nervous and Mental Disorders, 168*, 26-33.

McNair, D., Lorr, M., & Dropplemen, L. (1971). *Profile of mood states.* San Diego: Educational and Industrial Testing Services.

McNally, I.M. (2002). Contrasting concepts of competitive state-anxiety in sport: Multidimensional anxiety and catastrophe theories. *Athletic Insight, 4* (2). Retrieved August 23, 2004 from: http://www.athleticinsight.com/Vol4Iss2/Anxiety_Issue_2.htm [June 3, 2005].

Meehl, P.E. (1954). *Clinical versus statistical prediction: A theoretical analysis and a review of the evidence.* Minneapolis: University of Minnesota Press.

Meehl, P.E. (1965). Seer over sign: The first good example. *Journal of Experimental Research in Personality, 1,* 27-32.

Meichenbaum, D. (1977). *Cognitive behaviour modification: An integrative approach.* New York: Plenum Press.

Meyer, T.J., Miller, M.L., Metzger, R.L., & Borkovec, T.D. (1990). Development and validation of the Penn State Worry Questionnaire. *Behaviour Research and Therapy, 28,* 487-495.

Meyer, V. (1966). Modification of expectations in cases with obsessional rituals. *Behaviour Research and Therapy, 4,* 273-280.

Meyers, A.W. (1995). Ethical Principles of the Association for the Advancement of Applied Sport Psychology. *AAASP Newsletter, 10,* 15-21.

*Meyers, A.W., & Schleser, R. (1980). A cognitive behavioral intervention for improving basketball performance. *Journal of Sport Psychology, 2,* 69-73.

*Meyers, A.W., Schleser, R., & Okwumabua, T.M. (1982). A cognitive behavioral intervention for improving basketball performance. *Research Quarterly for Exercise and Sport, 53,* 344-347.

Meyers, A.W., Whelan, J.P., & Murphy, S.M. (1996). Cognitive behavioral strategies in athletic performance enhancement. In M. Hersen, R.M. Eisler, & P.M. Miller (Eds.), *Progress in behavior modification* (Vol. 30, pp. 137-164). Pacific Grove, CA: Brooks/Cole.

Miklowitz, D.J. (2001). Bipolar disorder. In D.H. Barlow (Ed.), *Clinical handbook of psychological disorders* (3rd ed., pp. 523-561). New York: Guilford Press.

Miklowitz, D.J., & Goldstein, M.J. (1997). *Bipolar disorder: A family-focused treatment approach.* New York: Guilford Press.

Miller, J.J., Fletcher, K., & Kabat-Zinn, J. (1995). Three-year follow-up and clinical implications of a mindfulness meditation-based stress reduction intervention in the treatment of anxiety disorders. *General Hospital Psychiatry, 17,* 192-200.

*Miller, J.T., & McAuley, E. (1987). Effects of a goal-setting training program on basketball free-throw self-efficacy and performance. *The Sport Psychologist, 1* (2), 103-113.

Miller, W.R., & Rollnick, S. (1991). *Motivational interviewing: Preparing people to change addictive behavior.* New York: Guilford Press.

Miller, W.R., Tonigan, J.S., & Longabaugh, R. (1995). *The Drinker Inventory of Consequences (DrInC).* Bethesda, MD: National Institute of Health.

Millon, T., Millon, C., & Davis, R.D. (1994). *Millon Clinical Multiaxial Inventory-III.* Minneapolis: National Computer Systems.

*Minas, S.C. (1978). Mental practice of a complex perceptual-motor skill. *Journal of Human Movement Studies, 4,* 102-107.

*Ming, S., & Martin, G.L. (1996). Single-subject evaluation of a self-talk package for improving figure skating performance. *The Sport Psychologist, 10,* 227-238.

Mischel, W., & Shoda, Y. (1995). A cognitive-affective system theory of personality: Reconceptualizing situations, dispositions, dynamics, and invariance in personality structure. *Psychological Review, 102,* 246-268.

Mitchell, W.B., Marten, P.A., Williams, D.M., & Barlow, D.H. (1990, November). *Control of sexual arousal in sexual dysfunctional males.* Paper presented at the meeting of the 24th Annual Convention of the Association for Advancement of Behavior Therapy, San Francisco.

Moore, Z.E. (2001, March). *Working with elite athletes of the opposite gender: Ethical and practical concerns.* Panel discussion presented at the meeting of the Third Annual Southwest Sport Psychology Conference, Phoenix.

Moore, Z.E., & Gardner, F.L. (2001, October). *Taking applied sport psychology from research to practice: Integrating empirically supported interventions into a self-regulatory model of athletic performance.* Workshop presented at the meeting of the Annual Conference of the Association for the Advancement of Applied Sport Psychology, Orlando, FL.

Moore, Z.E. (2003a). Ethical dilemmas in sport psychology: Discussion and recommendations for practice. *Professional Psychology: Research and Practice, 34* (6), 601-610.

Moore, Z.E. (2003b). Toward the development of an evidence based practice of sport psychology: A structured qualitative study of performance enhancement interventions (Doctoral dissertation, La Salle University, 2003). *Dissertation Abstracts International-B, 64* (10), 5227. (UMI No. 3108295)

Moore, Z.E., & Gardner, F.L. (2001, October). *Taking applied sport psychology from research to practice: Integrating empirically supported interventions into a self-regulatory model of athletic performance.* Workshop presented at the meeting of the Annual Conference of the Association for the Advancement of Applied Sport Psychology, Orlando, FL.

Moore, Z., & Gardner, F. (2002, August). *Psychological skills training for athletic performance enhancement: An evidence-based approach.* Symposium presented at the meeting of the Annual Conference of the American Psychological Association, Chicago.

Moore, Z.E., & Gardner, F.L. (2005). *Evaluating the efficacy of performance enhancement interventions.* Manuscript submitted for publication.

Morey, L.C. (2003). *Essentials of PAI assessment.* New York: Wiley.

MTA Cooperative Group. (1999a). Fourteen-month randomized controlled trial of treatment strategies for attention-deficit hyperactivity disorder. *Archives of General Psychiatry, 56,* 1073-1086.

MTA Cooperative Group. (1999b). Moderators and mediators of treatment response in children with attention-deficit/hyperactivity disorder: The MTA Study. *Archives of General Psychiatry, 56,* 1088-1096.

Mulig, J.C., Haggerty, M.E., Carballosa, A.B., Cinnick, W.J., & Madden, J.M. (1985). Relationships among fear of success, fear of failure, and androgyny. *Psychology of Women Quarterly, 9,* 284-287.

*Mumford, B., & Hall, C. (1985). The effects of internal and external imagery on performing figures in figure skating. *Canadian Journal of Applied Sport Sciences, 10,* 171-177.

Murphy, S., & Tammen, V. (1998). In search of psychological skills. In J.L. Duda (Ed.), *Advances in sport and exercise psychology measurement* (pp. 195-209). Morgantown, WV: Fitness Information Technology.

Murphy, S.M. (1990). Models of imagery in sport psychology: A review. *Journal of Mental Imagery, 14* (3-4), 153-172.

Murphy, S.M. (1994). Imagery interventions in sport. *Medicine and Science in Sport and Exercise, 26,* 486-494.

Murphy, S.M. (1995). *Sport psychology interventions.* Champaign, IL: Human Kinetics.

Murphy, S.M., & Jowdy, D.P. (1992). Imagery and mental practice. In T.S. Horn (Ed.), *Advances in sport psychology* (pp. 222-250). Champaign, IL: Human Kinetics.

*Murphy, S.M., & Woolfolk, R. (1987). The effects of cognitive interventions on competitive anxiety and performance on a fine motor skill accuracy task. *International Journal of Sport Psychology, 18,* (2), 152-166.

Murray, C.J.L., & Lopez, A.D. (1996). *The global burden of disease: A comprehensive assessment of mortality and disability from diseases, injuries, and risk factors in 1990 and projected to 2020.* Cambridge: Harvard University Press.

Nathan, P.E., & Gorman, J.M. (2002). *A guide to treatments that work* (2nd ed.). New York: Oxford University Press.

National Institute of Mental Health. (1999). *The numbers count* (NIH Publication No. NIH 994584). Retrieved June 15, 2004 from the World Wide Web: www.NIMH.NIH.gov/publicat/numbers.CFM [June 3, 2005].

National Institute on Drug Abuse. (1999). *Principles of addiction treatment: A research-based guide* (NIH Publication No. 99-4180). Rockville, MD: National Institute on Drug Abuse.

Naughton, T.J. (1987). A conceptual view of workaholism and implications for career counseling and research. *Career Development Quarterly, 35,* 180-187.

Nideffer, R.M. (1976). Test of attentional and interpersonal style. *Journal of Personality and Social Psychology, 34,* 394-404.

Nideffer, R.M. (1981). *The ethics and practice of applied sport psychology.* New York: Mouvement Publications.

Nideffer, R.M., & Sagal, M. (1998). Concentration and attention control training. In J.M. Williams (Ed.), *Applied sport psychology: Personal growth to peak performance* (pp. 296-315). Mountain View, CA: Mayfield.

Nideffer, R.M., & Sagal, M. (2001). *Assessment in sport psychology.* Morgantown, WV: Fitness Information Technology.

*Noel, R.C. (1980). The effect of visuo-motor behavior rehearsal on tennis performance. *Journal of Sport Psychology, 2,* 221-226.

Norcross, J.C. (Ed.). (2002). *Psychotherapy relationships that work.* New York: Oxford University Press.

Nostofsky, D.L., & Zaichkowsky, L.D. (2001). *Medical and psychological aspects of sport and exercise.* Morgantown, WV: Fitness Information Technology.

Novaco, R.W. (1976). Treatment of chronic anger through cognitive and relaxation controls. *Journal of Consulting and Clinical Psychology, 44,* 681.

O'Donohue, W., & Krasner, L. (1995). Theories in behavior therapy: Philosophical and historical contexts. In W. O'Donohue & L. Krasner (Eds.), *Theories of behavior therapy* (pp. 1-22). Washington, DC: American Psychological Association.

O'Farrell, T.J., Choquette, K.A., & Cutter, H.S.G. (1998). Couples relapse prevention sessions after behavioral marital therapy for male alcoholics: Outcomes during the three years after starting treatment. *Journal of Studies on Alcohol, 59,* 357-370.

Ogilvie, B.C., & Howe, M. (1986). The trauma of termination from athletics. In J.M. Williams (Ed.), *Applied sport psychology: Personal growth to peak performance* (pp. 365-382). Mountain View, CA: Mayfield.

Onestak, D.M. (1991). The effects of progressive muscle relaxation, mental practice, and hypnosis on athletic performance: A review. *Journal of Sport Behavior, 14* (4), 247-282.

Orlick, T. (1989). Reflections on sportpsych consulting with individual and team sport athletes at summer and winter Olympic games. *The Sport Psychologist, 3,* 358-365.

Orlick, T., & Partington, J. (1988). Mental links to excellence. *The Sport Psychologist, 2,* 105-130.

Orsillo, S.M., Roemer, L., & Barlow, D.H. (2003). Integrating acceptance and mindfulness into existing cognitive behavioral treatment for GAD: A case study. *Cognitive and Behavioral Practice, 10* (3), 222-230.

*Palmer, S.L. (1992). A comparison of mental practice techniques as applied to the developing competitive figure skater. *The Sport Psychologist, 6* (2), 148-155.

Pappo, M. (1983). Fear of success: The construction and validation of a measuring instrument. *Journal of Personality Assessment, 47,* 36-41.

Parker, K.B. (1994). "Has-beens" and "wanna-bes": Transition experiences of former major college football players. *The Sport Psychologist, 8,* 287-304.

*Pates, J., Cummings, A., & Maynard, I. (2002). The effects of hypnosis on flow states and three-point shooting performance in basketball performance. *The Sport Psychologist, 16,* 34-47.

*Patrick, T.D., & Hrycaiko, D.W. (1998). Effects of a mental training package on an endurance performance. *The Sport Psychologist, 12* (3), 283-299.

Pearson, R.E., & Petitpas, A.J. (1990). Transitions of athletes: Developmental and preventive perspectives. *Journal of Counseling and Development, 69,* 7-10.

*Perkos, S., Theodorakis, Y., & Chroni, S. (2002). Enhancing performance and skill acquisition in novice basketball players with instructional self-talk. *The Sport Psychologist, 16,* 368-383.

Perna, F., Neyer, M., Murphy, S.M., Ogilvie, B.C., & Murphy, A. (1995). Consultations with sport organizations: A cognitive-behavioral model. In S.M. Murphy (Ed.), *Sport psychology interventions* (pp. 235-252). Champaign, IL: Human Kinetics.

Persons, J.B. (1989). *Cognitive therapy in practice: A case formulation approach.* New York: Norton.

Petitpas, A.J., Brewer, B.W., Rivera, P.M., & Van Raalte, J.L. (1994). Ethical beliefs and behaviors in applied sport psychology: The AAASP ethics survey. *Journal of Applied Sport Psychology, 6,* 135-151.

Petitpas, A., Champagne, D., Chartrand, J., Danish, S., & Murphy, S. (1997). *Athlete's guide to career planning: Keys to success from the playing field to professional life.* Champaign, IL: Human Kinetics.

Petitpas, A., & Danish, S.J. (1995). Psychological care for injured athletes. In S.M. Murphy (Ed.), *Sport psychology interventions* (pp. 255-281). Champaign, IL: Human Kinetics.

Petrie, T.A., & Diehl, N.S. (1995). Sport psychology in the profession of psychology. *Professional Psychology: Research and Practice, 26,* 288-291.

Petrie, T.A., & Sherman, R.T. (2000). Counseling athletes with eating disorders: A case example. In M.B. Andersen (Ed.), *Doing sport psychology* (pp. 121-137). Champaign, IL: Human Kinetics.

*Peynircioglu, Z.F., Thompson, J.L., & Tanielian, T.B. (2000). Improvement strategies in free-throw shooting and grip-strength tasks. *Journal of General Psychology, 127* (2), 145-156.

Phillips, K.A., Hollander, E., Rasmussen, S.A., Aronowitz, B.R., de Caria, C., & Goodman, W.K. (1997). A severity rating scale for body dysmorphic disorder: Development of reliability and validity of a modified version of the Yale-Brown Obsessive-Compulsive Scale. *Psychopharmacology Bulletin, 33,* 17-22.

Philpott, R. (1975). Recent advances in the behavioral measurement of obsessional illness: Difficulties common to them and other instruments. *Scottish Medical Journal, 20,* 33-40.

Piper, W.E., & Joyce, A.S. (2001). Psychosocial treatment outcome. In W.J. Livesley (Ed.), *Handbook of personality disorders: Theory, research, and treatment* (pp. 323-343). New York: Guilford Press.

Pope, K.S. (1991). Dual relationships in psychotherapy. *Ethics and Behavior, 1* (1), 21-34.

Pope, K.S., & Vasquez, M.J.T. (2001). *Ethics in psychotherapy and counseling* (2nd ed.). San Francisco: Jossey-Bass.

*Powell, G.E. (1973). Negative and positive mental practice in motor skill acquisition. *Perceptual and Motor Skills, 37,* 312.

*Prapavessis, H., Grove, J.R., McNair, P.J., & Cable, N.T. (1992). Self-regulation training, state anxiety, and sport performance: A psychophysiological case study. *The Sport Psychologist, 6* (3), 213-229.

Prochaska, J.O., DiClemente, C.C., & Norcross, J.C. (1992). The transtheoretical approach. In J.C. Norcross & M.R. Goldfried (Eds.), *Handbook of psychotherapy integration* (pp. 300-334). New York: Basic Books.

Project MATCH Research Group. (1998). Matching alcoholism treatments to client heterogeneity: Project MATCH three-year drinking outcomes. *Alcoholism: Clinical and Experimental Research, 22,* 1300-1311.

Purdon, C. (1999). Thought suppression and psychopathology. *Behaviour Research and Therapy, 37,* 1029-1054.

Radloff, L.S. (1977). The CES-D Scale: A self-report depression scale for research in the general population. *Applied Psychological Measurement, 1,* 385-401.

Rank, M.G., & Gentry, J.E. (2003). Critical incident stress: Principles, practices, and protocols. In W.G. Emener, W.S. Hutchison, M.A. Richard (Eds.), *Employee assistance programs: Wellness/enhancement programming* (3rd ed., pp. 208-215). Springfield, IL: Charles C Thomas.

Rapee, R.M. (1993). The utilisation of working memory by worry. *Behaviour Research and Therapy, 31* (6), 617-620.

Rapee, R.M., Craske, M.G., & Barlow, D.H. (1995). Assessment instrument for panic disorder that includes fear of sensation-producing activities: The Albany Panic and Phobia Questionnaire. *Anxiety, 1,* 144-122.

Rapee, R.M., Craske, M.G., Brown, T.A., & Barlow, D.H. (1996). Measurement of perceived control over anxiety-related events. *Behavior Therapy, 27,* 279-293.

Rapee, R.M., & Lim, L. (1992). Discrepancy between self and observer ratings of performance in social phobics. *Journal of Abnormal Psychology, 101,* 728-731.

Ravizza, K. (1988). Gaining entry with athletic personnel for season-long consulting. *The Sport Psychologist, 2,* 243-254.

Ravizza, K. (1990). Sportpsych consultation issues in professional baseball. *The Sport Psychologist, 4* (4), 330-340.

Ravizza, K. (2001). Reflections and insights from the field on performance-enhancement consultation. In G. Tenenbaum (Ed.), *The practice of sport psychology* (pp. 197-215). Morgantown, WV: Fitness Information Technology.

*Rawlings, E.J., Rawlings, J.L., Chen, S.S., & Yilk, M.D. (1972). The facilitating effects of mental practice in the acquisition of rotary pursuit tracking. *Psychonomic Science, 26,* 71-73.

Resick, P.A., & Calhoun, K.S. (2001). Posttraumatic stress disorder. In D.H. Barlow (Ed.), *Clinical handbook of psychological disorders* (3rd ed., pp. 60-113). New York: Guilford Press.

Resick, P.A., & Schnicke, M.K. (1993). *Cognitive processing therapy for rape victims: A treatment manual.* Newbury Park, CA: Sage.

Resnick, H.S., Kilpatrick, D.G., Dansky, B.S., Saunders, B.E., & Best, C.L. (1993). Prevalence of civilian trauma and posttraumatic stress disorder in a representative national sample of women. *Journal of Consulting and Clinical Psychology, 61,* 984-991.

Rich, A.R., & Woolever, D.K. (1988). Expectancy and self-focused attention: Experimental support for the self-regulation model of test anxiety. *Journal of Social and Clinical Psychology, 7* (2-3), 246-259.

Robins, L.N., Cottler, L., Bucholz, K., & Compton, W. (1995). *Diagnostic Interview Schedule for DSM-IV.* St. Louis: Washington Press.

Robins, L.N., Helzer, J.E., Cottler, L.B., & Goldring, E. (1989). *NIMH Diagnostic Interview Schedule, Version III-Revised.* St. Louis: Washington University School of Medicine.

*Rodgers, W., Hall, C., & Buckolz, E. (1991). The effect of an imagery training program on imagery ability, imagery use, and figure skating performance. *Journal of Applied Sport Psychology, 3,* 109-125.

Roemer, L., & Orsillo, S.M. (2002). Expanding our conceptualization of and treatment for general anxiety disorder: Integrating mindfulness/acceptance-based approaches with existing cognitive-behavioral models. *Clinical Psychology: Science and Practice, 9* (1), 27-44.

Rogers, C.R. (1959). Client centered therapy. In S. Arieti (Ed.), *American handbook of psychiatry* (Vol. 3, pp. 183-200). New York: Basic Books.

Rogers, R. (1995). *Diagnostic and structured interviewing: A handbook for psychologists.* Odessa, FL: Psychological Assessment Resources.

*Rogerson, L.J., & Hrycaiko, D.W. (2002). Enhancing competitive performance of ice hockey goaltenders using centering and self-talk. *Journal of Applied Sport Psychology, 14* (1), 14-26.

Rotella, R.J. (1990). Providing sport psychology consulting services to professional athletes. *The Sport Psychologist, 4* (4), 409-417.

Roth, A., & Fonagy, P. (1996). *What works for whom?* New York: Guilford Press.

Rothbaum, B.O., & Foa, E.B. (1992). Exposure therapy for rape victims with post-traumatic stress disorder. *Behavior Therapist, 15,* 219-222.

Rothbaum, B.O., & Foa, E.B. (1993). Subtypes of post-traumatic stress disorder and duration of symptoms. In J.R.T. Davidson & E.B. Foa (Eds.), *Post-traumatic stress disorder: DSM-IV and beyond* (pp. 23-35). Washington, DC: American Psychiatric Press.

Rushall, B.S. (1984). The content of competition thinking. In W.F. Straub & J.M. Williams (Eds.), *Cognitive sport psychology* (pp. 51-62). Lansing, NY: Sport Science Associates.

Russell, G.F., Szmukler, G.I., Dare, C., & Eisler, I. (1987). An evaluation of family therapy in anorexia nervosa and bulimia nervosa. *Archives of General Psychiatry, 44,* 1047-1056.

Russell, M.T., & Karol, D.L. (1994). *The 16PF fifth edition administrator's manual.* Champaign, IL: Institute for Personality and Ability Testing.

*Ryan, E.D., & Simons, J. (1981). Cognitive demand, imagery, and frequency of mental rehearsal as factors influencing acquisition of motor skills. *Journal of Sport Psychology, 3* (1), 35-45.

Safran, J.D., & Segal, Z.V. (1990). *Interpersonal process in cognitive therapy.* Northvale, NJ: Jason Aronson.

Salazar, W., Landers, D.M., Petruzzello, S.J., & Han, M. (1990). Hemispheric asymmetry, cardiac response, and performance in elite archers. *Research Quarterly for Exercise and Sport, 61,* 351-359.

Santanello, A.P., Gardner, F.L., Moore, Z.E., & Turk, C. (2004, November). *Are there empirically supported treatments for anger?: Toward the development of a university based center for the treatment and study of anger.* Paper presented at the meeting of the Annual Conference of the Association for Advancement of Behavior Therapy, New Orleans, LA.

Santanello, A.P., Gardner, F.L., & Moore, Z.E. (2005). *Are there empirically supported treatments for anger? A qualitative review of the efficacy of interventions for anger in outpatient populations.* Manuscript submitted for publication.

*Savoy, C. (1993). A yearly mental training program for a college basketball player. *The Sport Psychologist, 7,* 173-190.

Sbrocco, T., & Barlow, D.H. (1996). Conceptualizing the cognitive component of sexual arousal: Implications for sexuality research and treatment. In P.M. Salkovskis (Ed.), *Frontiers of cognitive therapy* (pp. 419-449). New York: Guilford Press.

Scahill, L., Riddle, M.A., Mc Swiggen-Hardin, M., Ort, S.I., King, R.A., Goodman, W.K., Cicchetti, D., & Leckman, J.F. (1997). Children's Yale-Brown Obsessive-Compulsive Scale: Reliability and validity. *Journal of the American Academy of Child and Adolescent Psychiatry, 36,* 844-852.

Scanlan, T.K., Stein, D.L., & Ravizza, K. (1989). An in-depth study of former elite figure skaters: II. Sources of enjoyment. *Journal of Sport and Exercise Psychology, 11,* 65-83.

Schank, J.A., & Skovholt, T.M. (1997). Dual-relationship dilemmas of rural and small-community psychologists. *Professional Psychology: Research and Practice, 28* (1), 44-49.

Schlossberg, N.K. (1981). A model for analyzing human adaptation to transition. *The Counseling Psychologist, 9,* 2-18.

Schmid, J., & Schilling, G. (1997). Identity conflicts during and after retirement from top-level sports. In R. Lidor & M. Bar-Eli (Eds.), *Proceedings of the IX World Congress of Sport Psychology* (pp. 608-610). Netanya, Israel: International Society of Sport Psychology.

*Seabourne, T.G, Weinberg, R., Jackson, A., & Suinn, R.M. (1985). Effects of individualized, nonindividualized, and package intervention strategies on karate performance. *Journal of Sport Psychology, 7,* 40-50.

Segal, D. (1997). Structured interviewing and *DSM* classification. In S.M. Turner & M. Hersen (Eds.), *Adult psychopathology and diagnosis* (pp. 24-57). New York: Wiley.

Segal, Z.V., Williams, J.M.G., & Teasdale, J.D. (2002). *Mindfulness-based cognitive therapy for depression.* New York: Guilford Press.

Sherman, R.T., & Thompson, R.A. (2001). Athletes and disordered eating: Four major issues for the professional psychologist. *Professional Psychology: Research and Practice, 32* (1), 27-33.

*Shick, J. (1970). Effects of mental practice on selected volleyball skills for college women. *Research Quarterly, 41* (1), 88-94.

*Short, S.E., Bruggeman, J.M., Engel, S.G., Marback, T.L., Wang, L.J., Willadsen, A., Short, M.W. (2002). The effect of imagery function and imagery direction on self-efficacy and performance on a golf-putting task. *The Sport Psychologist, 16* (1), 48-67.

Silva, J. (1989). Toward the professionalization of sport psychology. *The Sport Psychologist, 3* (3), 265-273.

Sinclair, D.A., & Orlick, T. (1993). Positive transitions from high performance sport. *The Sport Psychologist, 7,* 138-150.

Sinclair, D.A., & Orlick, T. (1994). The effects of transition on high performance sport. In D. Hackfort (Ed.), *Psycho-social issues and interventions in elite sports* (pp. 29-55). Frankfurt, Germany: Lang.

Singer, R.N. (1996). Future of sport and exercise psychology. In J.L. Van Raalte & B.W. Brewer (Eds.), *Exploring sport and exercise psychology* (pp. 451-468). Washington, DC: American Psychological Association.

Singer, R.N., Hausenblas, H.A., & Janelle, C.M. (2001). *The handbook of sport psychology* (2nd ed.). New York: Wiley.

Skinner, B.F. (1953). *Science and human behavior.* New York: Macmillan.

Skinner, H.A., & Allen, B.A. (1982). Alcohol dependence syndrome: Measurement and validation. *Journal of Abnormal Psychology, 91,* 199-209.

Slavin, R.E. (1995). Best evidence synthesis: An intelligent alternative to meta-analysis. *Journal of Clinical Epidemiology, 48* (1), 9-18.

Smith, R.E. (1986). Toward a cognitive affective model of athletic burnout. *Journal of Sport Psychology, 8,* 36-50.

Smith, R.E. (1989). Applied sport psychology in an age of accountability. *Journal of Applied Sport Psychology, 1* (2), 166-180.

*Smith, M., & Lee, C. (1992). Goal setting and performance in a novel coordination task: Mediating mechanisms. *Journal of Sport and Exercise Psychology, 14* (2), 169-176.

Smith, D.E., & McCrady, B.S. (1991). Cognitive impairment among alcoholics: Impact on drink refusal skill acquisition and treatment outcome. *Addictive Behaviors, 16,* 265-274.

Smith, R.E., Smoll, F.L., & Schutz, R.W. (1990). Measurement and correlates of sport-specific cognitive and somatic trait anxiety: The Sport Anxiety Scale. *Anxiety Research, 2,* 263-280.

Sonne, J.L. (1999). Multiple relationships: Does the new ethics code answer the right questions? In D.N. Bersoff (Ed.), *Ethical conflicts in psychology* (2nd ed., pp. 227-230). Washington, DC: American Psychological Association.

Sotsky, S.M., Glass, D.R., Shea, M.T., Pilkonis, P.A., Collins, J.F., Elkin, I., Watkins, J.T., Imber, S.D., Leber, W.R., Moyer, J., & Oliveri, M.E. (1991). Patient predictors of response to psychotherapy and pharmacotherapy: Findings in the NIMH Treatment of Depression Collaborative Research Program. *American Journal of Psychiatry, 148,* 997-1008.

Spielberger, C.D. (1999). *Manual for the State-Trait Anxiety Inventory-2.* Odessa, FL: Psychological Assessment Resources.

Spielberger, C.D., Gorsuch, R.L., Luschene, R., Vagg, P.R., & Jacobs, G.A. (1983). *Manual for the State-Trait Anxiety Inventory.* Palo Alto, CA: Consulting Psychologists.

Spirito, A. (1999). Empirically supported treatments in pediatric psychology [Special issue]. *Journal of Pediatric Psychology, 24,* 87-174.

Starkes, J.L., & Ericsson, K. (2003). *Expert performance in sports: Advances in research on sport expertise.* Champaign, IL: Human Kinetics.

Starkes, J.L., Helsen, W., & Jack, R. (2001). Expert performance in sport and dance. In R.N. Singer, H.A. Hausenblas, & C.M. Janelle (Eds.), *Handbook of sport psychology* (2nd ed., pp. 174-201). New York: Wiley.

*Start, K.B., & Richardson, A. (1964). Imagery and mental practice. *British Journal of Educational Psychology, 34,* 28-284.

Stein, R.J., Goodrick, G.K., Poston, W.S.C., & Foreyt, J.P. (2003). Eating disorders. In M. Hersen & S.M. Turner (Eds.), *Diagnostic interviewing* (3rd ed., pp. 279-299). New York: Kluwer Academic/Plenum.

Stoltenberg, C.D., McNeill, B., & Delworth, U. (1998). *IDM Supervision: An integrated developmental model for supervising counselors and therapists.* San Francisco: Jossey-Bass.

*Straub, W.F. (1989). The effect of three difference methods of mental training on dart throwing performance. *The Sport Psychologist, 3* (2), 133-141.

Strean, W.B., & Roberts, G.C. (1992). Future directions in applied sport psychology research. *The Sport Psychologist, 6* (1), 55-65.

Striker, G. (2003). The many faces of self-disclosure. *Journal of Clinical Psychology, 59* (5), 623-630.

Strupp, H.H. (1980a). Success and failure in Time-Limited Psychotherapy: A systematic comparison of two cases (Comparison 1). *Archives of General Psychiatry, 37,* 595-603.

Strupp, H.H. (1980b). Success and failure in Time-Limited Psychotherapy: A systematic comparison of two cases (Comparison 2). *Archives of General Psychiatry, 37*, 708-716.

Strupp, H.H. (1980c). Success and failure in Time-Limited Psychotherapy: With special reference to the performance of a lay counselor (Comparison 3). *Archives of General Psychiatry, 37*, 831-841.

Strupp, H.H. (1980d). Success and failure in Time-Limited Psychotherapy: Further evidence (Comparison 4). *Archives of General Psychiatry, 37*, 947-954.

Strupp, H.H. (1993). The Vanderbilt psychotherapy studies: Synopsis. *Journal of Consulting and Clinical Psychology, 61*, 431-433.

Suinn, R.M. (1967). Psychological reactions to physical disability. *Journal of the Association for Physical and Mental Rehabilitation, 21*, 13-15.

Suinn, R.M. (1985). Imagery rehearsal applications to performance enhancement. *The Behavior Therapist, 8* (8), 155-159.

Suinn, R.M. (1997). Mental practice in sport psychology: Where have we been, where do we go? *Clinical Psychology: Science and Practice, 4* (3), 189-207.

Swain, D.A. (1991). Withdrawal from sport and Schlossberg's model of transitions. *Sociology of Sport Journal, 8*, 152-160.

*Swain, A.B.J., & Jones, G. (1995). Goal attainment scaling: Effects of goal setting interventions on selected subcomponents on basketball performance. *Research Quarterly for Exercise and Sport, 66*, 51-63.

Swain, A.B.J., & Jones, G. (1996). Explaining performance variance: The relative contribution of intensity and direction dimensions of competitive state anxiety. *Anxiety, Stress, and Coping: An International Journal, 9*, 1-18.

Swoap, R.A., & Murphy, S.M. (1995). Eating disorders and weight management in athletes. In S.M. Murphy (Ed.), *Sport psychology interventions* (pp. 307-329). Champaign, IL: Human Kinetics.

Tarter, R.E., & Hegedus, A.M. (1991). The Drug Use Screening Inventory. *Alcohol Health and Research World, 15*, 65-76.

Taylor, J. (1994). Examining the boundaries of sport science and psychology trained practitioners in applied sport psychology: Title usage and area of competence. *Journal of Applied Sport Psychology, 6* (2), 185-195.

Taylor, J., & Ogilvie, B.C. (1994). A conceptual model of adaptation to retirement among athletes. *Journal of Applied Sport Psychology, 6*, 1-20.

Taylor, J., & Ogilvie, B.C. (1998). Career transition among elite athletes: Is there life after sports? In J.M. Williams (Ed.), *Applied sport psychology: Personal growth to peak performance* (3rd ed., pp. 429-444). Mountain View, CA: Mayfield.

Taylor, J., & Ogilvie, B.C. (2001). Career termination among athletes. In R.N. Singer, H.A. Hausenblas, & C.M. Janelle (Eds.), *Handbook of sport psychology* (2nd ed., pp. 672-694). New York: Wiley.

Taylor, J., & Schneider, B.A. (1992). The Sport-Clinical Intake Protocol: A comprehensive interview instrument for applied sport psychology. *Professional Psychology: Research and Practice, 23* (4), 318-325.

Taylor, J., & Wilson, G. S. (2002). Intensity regulation and sport performance. In J.L. Van Raalte & B.W. Britton (Eds.), *Exploring sport and exercise psychology* (2nd ed., pp. 99-130). Washington, DC: American Psychological Association.

Teachman, B.A., & Woody, S.R. (2004). Staying tuned to research in implicit cognition: Relevance for clinical practice with anxiety disorders. *Cognitive and Behavioral Practice, 11* (2), 149-159.

Teasdale, J.D., Segal, Z., & Williams, J.M. (1995). How does cognitive therapy prevent depressive relapse and why should attentional control (mindfulness) training help? *Behavior Research and Therapy, 33*, 25-39.

Teasdale, J.D., Segal, Z.V., Williams, J.M.G., Ridgeway, V.A., Soulsby, J.M., & Lau, M.A. (2000). Prevention of relapse/recurrence in major depression by mindfulness based cognitive therapy. *Journal of Consulting and Clinical Psychology, 68* (4), 615-623.

Tenenbaum, G. (2001). An introduction to the book: From personal reflections to the practice of sport psychology. In G. Tenenbaum (Ed.), *The practice of sport psychology* (pp. 1-15). Morgantown, WV: Fitness Information Technology.

*Thelwell, R.C., & Greenlees, I.A. (2001). The effects of a mental skills training package on gymnasium triathlon performance. *The Sport Psychologist, 15* (2), 127-141.

*Thelwell, R.C., & Greenlees, I.A. (2003). Developing competitive endurance performance using mental skills training. *The Sport Psychologist, 17*, 318-337.

*Thelwell, R.C., & Maynard, I.W. (2003). The effects of a mental skills package on "repeatable good performance" in cricketers. *Psychology of Sport and Exercise, 4*, 377-396.

*Theodorakis, Y. (1995). Effects of self-efficacy, satisfaction, and personal goals on swimming performance. *The Sport Psychologist, 9*, 245-253.

*Theodorakis, Y., Chroni, S., Laparidis, K., Bebetsos, V., & Douma, I. (2001). Self-talk in a basketball-shooting task. *Perceptual and Motor Skills, 92*, 309-315.

Thomas, P. (1990). *An overview of the performance enhancement process in applied psychology.* Colorado Springs: United States Olympic Center.

Tice, D.M., Bratslavsky, E., & Baumeister, R.F. (2001). Emotional distress regulation takes precedence over impulse control: If it feels good do it! *Journal of Personality and Social Psychology, 80* (1), 53-67.

Tracey, T.J., & Kokotovic, A.M. (1989). Factor structure of the Working Alliance Inventory. *Psychological Assessment, 1* (3), 207-210.

Tresemer, D. (1976). Do women fear success? *Signs, 1*, 863-874.

Truax, P., & Selthon, L. (2003). Mood disorders. In M. Hersen & S.M. Turner (Eds.), *Diagnostic interviewing*

(3rd ed., pp. 111-147). New York: Kluwer Academic/ Plenum.

Turk, C.L., Heimberg, R.G., & Hope, D.A. (2001). Social anxiety disorder. In D.H. Barlow (Ed.), *Clinical handbook of psychological disorders* (3rd ed., pp. 114-153). New York: Guilford Press.

Turk, D.C., Meichenbaum, D., & Genest, M. (1983). *Pain and behavioral medicine.* New York: Guilford Press.

Turner, S.M., Beidel, D.C, Dancu, C.V., & Stanley, M.A. (1989). An empirically derived inventory to measure social fears and anxiety: The Social Phobia and Anxiety Inventory. *Psychological Assessment, 1,* 35-40.

United States Olympic Committee. (1983). U. S. Olympic Committee establishes guidelines for sport psychology services. *Journal of Sport Psychology, 5,* 4-7.

*Van Gyn, G.H., Wenger, H.A., & Gaul, C.A. (1990). Imagery as a method of enhancing transfer from training to performance. *Journal of Sport and Exercise Psychology, 12,* 366-375.

Van Raalte, J.L., & Andersen, M.B. (1993). Special problems in sport psychology: Supervising the trainee. In S. Serpa, J. Alves, V. Ferreira, & A. Paulo-Brito (Eds.), *Proceedings of the VII World Congress of Sport Psychology* (pp. 773-776). Lisbon: International Society of Sport Psychology.

Van Raalte, J.L., & Andersen, M.B. (2000). Supervision I: From models to doing. In M.B. Andersen (Ed.), *Doing sport psychology* (pp. 153-166). Champaign, IL: Human Kinetics.

Van Raalte, J.L., & Brewer, B.W. (Eds.). (1996). *Exploring sport and exercise psychology.* Washington, DC: American Psychological Association.

Van Raalte, J.L., & Brewer, B.W. (Eds.). (2002). *Exploring sport and exercise psychology* (2nd ed.). Washington, DC: American Psychological Association.

Van Raalte, J.L., Brewer, B.W., Brewer, D.D., & Linder, D.E. (1992). NCAA Division II college football players' perceptions of an athlete who consults a sport psychologist. *Journal of Sport and Exercise Psychology, 14,* 273-282.

*Van Raalte, J.L., Brewer, B.W., Lewis, B.P., Linder, D.E., Wildman, G., & Kozimor, J. (1995). Cork! The effects of positive and negative self-talk on dart throwing performance. *Journal of Sport Behavior, 18* (1), 50-57.

Vealey, R.S. (1986). Conceptualization of sport confidence and competitive orientation: Preliminary investigation and instrument development. *Journal of Sport Psychology, 8,* 221-246.

Vealey, R.S. (1990). Advancements in competitive anxiety research: Use of the Sport Competition Anxiety Test and the Competitive State Anxiety Inventory-2. *Anxiety Research, 2,* 243-261.

Vealey, R. (1994a). Current status and prominent issues in sport psychology interventions. *Medicine and Science in Sport and Exercise, 26* (4), 495-502.

Vealey, R. (1994b). Knowledge development and implementation in sport psychology: A review of *The Sport Psychologist,* 1987-1992. *The Sport Psychologist, 8,* 331-348.

Vealey, R.S., & Garner-Holman, M. (1998). Applied sport psychology: Measurement issues. In J.L. Duda (Ed.), *Advances in sport and exercise psychology measurements* (pp. 433-446). Morgantown, WV: Fitness Information Technology.

Wagner, A., & Gardner, F.L. (2005). *Is experiential avoidance a mediator in the relationship between maladaptive perfectionism and worry?* Manuscript in preparation.

Waldman, I.D., & Lilienfeld, S.O. (1995). Diagnosis and classification. In M. Hersen & R.T. Ammerman (Eds.), *Advanced abnormal child psychology* (pp. 21-36). Hillsdale, NJ: Erlbaum.

Walker, M.T. (2001). Practical applications of the Rogerian perspective in post-modern psychotherapy. *Journal of Systemic Therapies, 20* (2), 41-57.

*Wanlin, C.M., Hrycaiko, D.W., Martin, G.L., & Mahon, M. (1997). The effects of a goal-setting package on the performance of speed skaters. *Journal of Applied Sport Psychology, 9* (2), 212-228.

*Ward, P., & Carnes, M. (2002). Effects of positive self-set goals on collegiate football players' skill execution during practice and games. *Journal of Applied Behavior Analysis, 35* (1), 1-12.

Watson, D., & Friend, R. (1969). Measurement of social-evaluative anxiety. *Journal of Consulting and Clinical Psychology, 33,* 448-457.

Watson, J.B., & Rayner, R. (1920). Conditioned emotional reactions. *Journal of Experimental Psychology, 3,* 1-14.

Weathers, F.W., Litz, B.T., Herman, D.S., Huska, J.A., & Keane, T.M. (1993, October). *The PTSD Checklist: Reliability, validity and diagnostic utility.* Paper presented at the meeting of the Annual Meeting of the International Society for Traumatic Stress Studies, San Antonio.

Wegner, D.M., Ansfield, M., & Pilloff, D. (1998). The putt and the pendulum: Ironic effects of the mental control of action. *Psychological Science, 9,* 196-199.

Wegner, D.M., Shortt, J.W., Blake, A.W., & Page, M.S. (1990). The suppression of exciting thoughts. *Journal of Personality and Social Psychology, 58,* 409-418.

Wegner, D.M., & Zanakos, S. (1994). Chronic thought suppression. *Journal of Personality, 62,* 615-640.

Weinberg, R.S. (1982). The relationship between mental preparation strategies and motor performance: A review and critique. *Quest, 33* (2), 195-213.

Weinberg, R.S. (1994). Goal setting and performance in sport and exercise settings: A synthesis and critique. *Medicine and Science in Sport and Exercise, 26* (4), 469-477.

Weinberg, R.S. (2002). Goal setting in sport and exercise: Research to practice. In J.L. Van Raalte & B.W. Brewer (Eds.), *Exploring sport and exercise psychology* (2nd ed., pp. 25-48). Washington DC: American Psychological Association.

*Weinberg, R.S., Bruya, L.D., Garland, H., & Jackson, A. (1990). Effects of goal difficulty and positive reinforcement on endurance performance. *Journal of Sport and Exercise Psychology, 12* (2), 144-156.

*Weinberg, R.S., Bruya, L.D., & Jackson, A. (1985). The effects of goal proximity and goal specificity on endurance performance. *Journal of Sport Psychology, 7* (3), 296-305.

*Weinberg, R., Bruya, L., Jackson, A. (1990). Goal setting and competition: A reaction to Hall and Byrne. *Journal of Sport and Exercise Psychology, 12* (1), 92-97.

*Weinberg, R.S., Bruya, L.D., Jackson, A., & Garland, H. (1987). Goal difficulty and endurance performance: A challenge to the goal attainability assumption. *Journal of Sport Behavior, 10,* 82-92.

Weinberg, R.S., & Comar, W. (1994). The effectiveness of psychological interventions in competitive sport. *Sports Medicine Journal, 18,* 406-418.

*Weinberg, R.S., Gould, D., & Jackson, A. (1981). Relationship between duration of the psych-up interval and strength performance. *Journal of Sport Psychology, 3* (2), 166-170.

*Weinberg, R.S., Jackson, A., & Seabourne, T.G. (1985). The effect of specific versus nonspecific mental preparation strategies on strength and endurance performance. *Journal of Sport Behavior, 8,* 175-180.

*Weinberg, R.S., Seabourne, T.G., & Jackson, A. (1981). Effects of visuo-motor behavior rehearsal, relaxation, and imagery on karate performance. *Journal of Sport Psychology, 3,* 228-238.

*Weinberg, R.S., Seabourne, T.G., & Jackson, A. (1982). Effects of visuo-motor behavior rehearsal on state-trait anxiety and performance: Is practice important? *Journal of Sport Behavior, 5,* 209-219.

*Weinberg, R., Seabourne, T., & Jackson, A. (1987). Arousal and relaxation instructions prior to the use of imagery. *International Journal of Sport Psychology, 18,* 205-214.

*Weinberg, R.S., Smith, J., Jackson, A., & Gould, D. (1984). Effect of association, dissociation and positive self-talk on endurance performance. *Canadian Journal of Applied Sport Sciences, 9,* 25-32.

*Weinberg, R.S., Stitcher, T., & Richardson, P. (1994). Effects of seasonal goal setting on lacrosse performance. *The Sport Psychologist, 8,* 166-175.

Weinberg, R.S., & Williams, J.M. (1998). Integrating and implementing a psychological skills training program. In J.M. Williams (Ed.), *Applied sport psychology: Personal growth to peak performance* (pp. 329-358). Mountain View, CA: Mayfield.

Wells, A. (2000). *Emotional disorders and metacognition: Innovative cognitive therapy.* New York: Wiley.

Wenzlaff, R.M., Wegner, D.M., & Klein, S.B. (1991). The role of thought suppression in the bonding of thought and mood. *Journal of Personality and Social Psychology, 60,* 500-508.

Werthner, P., & Orlick, T. (1986). Retirement experiences of successful Olympic athletes. *International Journal of Sport Psychology, 17,* 337-363.

Wheeler, J.G., Christensen, A., & Jacobson, N.S. (2001). Couple distress. In D.H. Barlow (Ed.), *Clinical*

handbook of psychological disorders: A step-by-step treatment manual (3rd ed., pp. 609-630). New York: Guilford Press.

*Whelan, J.P., Epkins, C., & Meyers, A.W. (1990). Arousal interventions for athletic performance: Influence of mental preparation and competitive experience. *Anxiety Research, 2,* 293-307.

Whelan, J., Mahoney, M., & Meyers, A. (1991). Performance enhancement in sport: A cognitive-behavioral domain. *Behavior Therapy, 22,* 307-327.

Whelan, J.P., Meyers, A.W., & Elkins, T.D. (2002). Ethics in sport and exercise psychology. In J.L. Van Raalte & B.W. Brewer (Eds.), *Exploring sport and exercise psychology* (2nd ed., pp. 503-523). Washington, DC: USical Association.

*White, K.D., Ashton, R., & Lewis, S. (1979). Learning a complex skill: Effects of mental practice, physical practice, and imagery ability. *International Journal of Sport Psychology, 10* (2), 71-78.

Wiggins, D.K. (1984). The history of sport psychology in North America. In J. Silva & R. Weinberg (Eds.), *Psychological foundations of sport* (pp. 9-22). Champaign, IL: Human Kinetics.

*Wilkes, R.L., & Summers, J.J. (1984). Cognitions, mediating variables, and strength performance. *Journal of Sport Psychology, 6,* 351-359.

Williams, J.M. (Ed.). (1998). *Applied sport psychology: Personal growth to peak performance* (3rd ed.). Mountain View, CA: Mayfield.

Williams, J.M., & Leffingwell, T.R. (2002). Cognitive strategies in sport and exercise psychology. In J.L. Van Raalte & B.W. Brewer (Eds.), *Exploring sport and exercise psychology* (2nd ed., pp. 75-98). Washington, DC: American Psychological Association.

Williams, J.M., & Straub, W.F. (1998). Sport psychology: Past, present, future. In J.M. Williams (Ed.), *Applied sport psychology: Personal growth to peak performance* (3rd ed., pp. 1-12). Mountain View, CA: Mayfield.

Wilson, G.T., & Fairburn, C.G. (2002). Treatments for eating disorders. In P.E. Nathan and J.M. Gorman (Ed.), *A guide to treatments that work* (2nd ed., pp. 559-592). New York: Oxford University Press.

Wilson, G.T., & Pike, L.M. (2001). Eating disorders. In D.H. Barlow (Ed.), *Clinical handbook of psychological disorders* (3rd ed., pp. 332-375). New York: Guilford Press.

Wolanin, A.T. (2005). Mindfulness-acceptance-commitment (MAC) based performance enhancement for Division I collegiate athletes: A preliminary investigation (Doctoral dissertation, La Salle University, 2003). *Dissertation Abstracts International-B, 65* (7), p. 3735-3794.

Woodman, T., & Hardy, L. (2001). Stress and anxiety. In R.N. Singer, H.A. Hausenblas, & C.M. Janelle (Eds.), *Handbook of sport psychology* (2nd ed., pp. 290-318). New York: Wiley.

Woody, R.H. (1997). Dubious and bogus credentials in mental health practice. *Ethics and Behavior, 7* (4), 337-345.

*Woolfolk, R.L., Murphy, S.M., Gottesfeld, D., & Aitken, D. (1985). The effects of mental practice of task and mental depiction of task outcome on motor performance. *Journal of Sport Psychology, 7,* 191-197.

World Health Organization. (1992). *International Classification of Diseases* (9th ed.). Geneva: Author.

*Wraith, S.C., & Biddle, S.J.H. (1989). Goal-setting in children's sport: An exploratory analysis of goal participation, ability and effort instructions, and post-event cognitions. *International Journal of Sport Psychology, 20* (2), 79-92.

Wrisberg, C.A. (2001). Levels of performance skill: From beginners to experts. In R.N. Singer, H.A. Hausenblas, & C.M. Janelle (Eds.), *Handbook of sport psychology* (2nd ed., pp. 3-19). New York: Wiley.

*Wrisberg, C.A., & Anshel, M.H. (1989). The effects of cognitive strategies on the free throw shooting performance of young athletes. *The Sport Psychologist, 3,* 95-104.

Young, J.E. (1999). *Cognitive therapy for personality disorders: A schema-focused approach* (3rd ed.). Sarasota, FL: Professional Resource Press.

Young, J.E., Klosko, J.S., & Weishaar, M.E. (2003). *Schema therapy: A practitioner's guide.* New York: Guilford Press.

Young, J.E., Weinberger, A.D., & Beck, A.T. (2001). Cognitive therapy for depression. In D.H. Barlow (Ed.), *Clinical handbook of psychological disorders* (3rd ed., pp. 264-308). New York: Guilford Press.

Yusuf, S. (1997). Meta-analysis of randomized trials: Looking back and looking ahead. *Controlled Clinical Trials, 18* (6), 594-601.

Zaichkowsky, L.D., & Baltzell, A. (2001). Arousal and performance. In R.N. Singer, H.A. Hausenblas, & C.M. Janelle (Eds.), *Handbook of sport psychology* (2nd ed., pp. 319-339). New York: Wiley.

Zaichkowsky, L.D., & Perna, L.D. (1992). Certification of consultants in sport psychology: A rebuttal to Anshell. *The Sport Psychologist, 6* (3), 287-296.

Zeigler, E.F. (1987). Rationale and suggested dimensions for a code of ethics for sport psychologists. *The Sport Psychologist, 1* (2), 138-150.

Zinsser, N., Bunker, L., & Williams, J.M. (1998). Cognitive techniques for building confidence and enhancing performance. In J.M. Williams (Ed.), *Applied sport psychology: Personal growth to peak performance* (pp. 270-295). Mountain View, CA: Mayfield.

Zuckerman, E.L. (1997). *The paper office: Forms, guidelines, and resources* (2nd ed.). New York: Guilford Press.

Index

Note: The italicized *f* and *t* following page numbers refer to figures and tables, respectively.

About the Authors

Photo courtesy of Shawn Avery

Frank L. Gardner, PhD, ABPP, is an associate professor and director of the PsyD program in clinical psychology at La Salle University in Philadelphia, Pennsylvania. He received his PhD in clinical sport psychology from Hofstra University. Gardner is board certified in clinical psychology by the American Board of Professional Psychology, a distinction that fewer than 5% of licensed psychologists attain. Gardner has 24 years of experience as a practicing clinical psychologist, graduate educator and supervisor, and sport psychologist. He has worked with youth, collegiate, Olympic, and professional athletes. For 19 years he has been highly involved as a sport psychologist at the professional level, working extensively for multiple teams within the National Hockey League, the National Basketball Association, and Major League Baseball.

A member of the American Psychological Association (APA), Gardner was one of the first psychologists to receive the Certified Consultant designation by the Association for the Advancement of Applied Sport Psychology. He was one of the primary developers of the APA Proficiency in Sport Psychology and has developed the curriculum for the training of sport psychologists for two sport psychology training programs.

Zella E. Moore, PsyD, is an assistant professor of psychology at Manhattan College in New York City. She is also associate director of research and development for the Center for the Treatment and Study of Anger and Violence at La Salle University in Philadelphia, Pennsylvania. Moore received her PsyD in clinical psychology from La Salle University in 2003, and has been a sport psychology consultant for teams in the National Hockey League, the National Basketball Association, and the World Indoor Soccer League. She is a member of APA and the Association for Behavioral and Cognitive Therapies. She is responsible for teaching and supervising both undergraduate psychology students and clinical and clinical sport psychology doctoral students.